The
HOME OF HEROES

FIFTY YEARS OF RACING AT UTICA-ROME SPEEDWAY

BY BONES BOURCIER

Limited Edition Printing

COASTAL 181
PUBLISHER

CREDITS

Book Design *Tammy Sneddon*
Composition and Photo Work *Tammy Sneddon, Jamie Griffin, Bill Rosner, Drew Sneddon*
Cover Design *Joyce Cosentino Wells*
Editing *Cary Stratton*

Front Cover
Aerial photo *Photos by Fine*
Lazzaro #4 *John Grady Photo*
Richie Evans #61 *John Grady Photo*
Stewart Friesen #1 *Images by DC*

Front Cover Flap
Bones Bourcier *Cary Stratton Photo*

Back Cover
Charland #3 *John Grady Photo*
Cook #38 *John Grady Photo*
Planck #77 *John Clifford Photo*
Modified lineup, 2002 *PostTime Photo*

Every reasonable effort was made to locate and credit the original copyright holders and photographers of the photos included in this book. If your photo appears in this book and you are not properly credited, please contact the publisher.

ISBN 10: 0-9789261-9-6
ISBN 13: 978-0-9789261-9-9

For additional information or copies of this book, contact:

Utica-Rome Speedway LLC
PO Box 499
Vernon, NY 13476
315-829-4557
www.uticaromespeedway.com

© Copyright 2011 by Utica Rome Speedway LLC. All rights reserved.

No part of this book may be reproduced in any form, or by any means, without permission in writing from the copyright holder.

The author, publisher and copyright holder shall not be held liable for any incidental or consequential damages that might result from the content of this book.

First printing July 2011

Published by Coastal 181, Newburyport, MA
www.coastal181.com, 877-907-8181

Printed in the United States of America

Table of Contents

vii   Acknowledgements

1   1960: Joe and Rene: The Odd Couple
5   1961: The Start of Something Big
11   1962: New Lights, New Challengers, Same Old Charland
17   1963: Big Plans, Big Races, and Big Lou
23   1964: Steady Eddie, Fast Eddie
29   1965: Kotary, Kotary, and Cook
35   EYEWITNESS, 1961–1965: DICK WATERMAN

39   1966: All Roads Led to Vernon
45   1967: Calm Faces in Exciting Times
51   1968: The Mayor of Vernon Center
57   1969: Distant Tragedy, Local Sorrow, and Healing
63   1970: Heroes, Anti-Heroes, and Underdogs
69   EYEWITNESS, 1966–1970: JUNIOR BIANCO

73   1971: Stories, Stories, Everywhere
79   1972: The Reformation of Richie Evans
85   1973: Richie and Jerry, Part I
89   1974: Richie and Jerry, Part II … Soggy Fridays … and Geoff Bodine
95   1975–1976: It Looked Good on Paper
99   EYEWITNESS, 1971–1975: JERRY COOK

103   1977: New Faces, Same Old Sinking Feeling
107   1978: Black Days for the Blacktop
113   COLOR PHOTOS: 1961–1978: *The Pavement Era*
121   THE STRAIGHT AND NARROW… AND THE FUN! *Fast, Loud Times at the Utica-Rome Dragway*
129   IN THE MARGINS: *Airplanes, Open-Wheelers, Wild Animals, Demo Derbies, Vampires, Hippies, and Other Utica-Rome Oddities*
137   1979: Saturday Night Jive
141   1980: All The News Was Bad
145   EYEWITNESS, 1976–1980: ANDY ROMANO

149   1981: Fresh Start: The Brothers Compani, and DIRT
153   1982: The Tide Never Turned
         1983: Closed
         1984: Closed

continued

157	1985: A New Venture
163	EYEWITNESS, 1981–1985: DAVE LAPE
167	1986: A Good Year for All, Especially Brett Hearn
173	1987–1988: Tremont Shines; New Venture Fades
177	1989: Bub Saves the Day
181	1990: Who Wants to Win?
187	EYEWITNESS, 1986–1990: RON MOSHIER
191	1991: Kinsella Comes Alive
197	1992: Jensen's Career Year?
203	1993: Jensen, Pauch Star; So What Else Is New?
207	1994: A Star Is Born
211	1995: Planck Repeats in a Year of Change
215	EYEWITNESS, 1991–1995: PAUL JENSEN
219	1996: Alex, Here and Gone
225	COLOR PHOTOS: 1979–2001: *Utica-Rome's Turbulent Middle Age*
233	1997: Dale the Dominant
239	1998: An(other) Irregular Season
243	1999: Lemonade, Anyone?
247	2000: Hot Shoe, Indeed
253	EYEWITNESS, 1996–2000: DALE PLANCK
257	2001: Todd's Turn
263	2002: New Management, New Champion, Sentimental Winners
269	2003: Planck
275	2004: Friesen Ignites; Jessica Delights
281	2005: Willy Boy Is Here
285	EYEWITNESS, 2001–2005: GENE COLE
289	2006: Hometown Hero, Take Two
295	2007: Two Great Names Return: The New Yorker and Friesen
301	2008: Veteran's Day
307	2009: Laid-Back Pat, and Throttle Control
311	2010: Stewart's Big Dance
317	EYEWITNESS, 2006–2010: Stewart Friesen
321	COLOR PHOTOS: 2002–2010: *Stable and Strong*
329	Race Records and Statistics
387	Index

Acknowledgements

This book could never have been produced without the support and active participation of literally hundreds of people: Utica-Rome Speedway staff; current and former drivers, team owners, and mechanics; photographers and journalists; and countless friends and fans. Some opened their homes, others opened their race shops, and all opened their memory banks.

In particular, we would like to tip our hats to Doug Zupan for his tireless research, his phenomenal grasp of history, and, perhaps most important, his endless patience as we dug through the hundreds of photographs and thousands of details involved in publishing a book of this breadth and depth. Doug is a young fellow with an old racing soul.

We also owe a special thanks to Rod Nacewicz for sharing his photo collection as well as his priceless stories; and to photographer John Grady, sentimental keeper of the flame when it comes to short-track racing in New York.

Above all, it's important to recognize track owner Gene Cole for his desire to capture, for the record, the first 50 years of a place he clearly loves. This book becomes just one more piece of Gene's Utica-Rome legacy.

Additionally, we are grateful to the following for their invaluable contributions:

Joseph Achzet, Jeff Ackerman, Joe Alexander, Shane Andrews, *Area Auto Racing News*, Dick Berggren, Junior Bianco, Ed & Betty Biittig, Alex and Helen Bruce, Ted Bundy, Fred Burrows, Barb Clark, John Clifford, Fran Connelly, Jerry Cook, Derak Covey, Ken Dippel, Don Edds, Doug Elkins, Jay Fish, C.J. Flay, Stewart Friesen, Fultonhistory.com, Andy Fusco, *Gater Racing Photo News*, Otto Graham, Ken Gypson, Ron Hedger, Craig Henry, Mary Ellen Higley, Bob Hunter, Ron Ingraham, Paul Jensen, Earl Krause, Chip Lanz, Dave and Jackie Lape, Tom Loughlin, Clancy Miller, Bill Moore, Lynn Morton, Ron Moshier, Pete and Ginny Neff, New York State Stock Car Association, Danny Ody, *Oneida Daily Dispatch*, Oneida Public Library, Joe Patrick, Dale Planck, Connie Plows, Rich Post, John Rock, Andy Romano, Len Sammons, Saratoga Auto Museum, Rita Seamon, Willy Seamon, Frank Simek, Tom Skibinski, Carl and Dianne Smith, Mark Southcott, Brian Spaid, Gary Spaid, Gary Spangler, Marie Tallini, Kerry Thieme, Jo Towns, *Utica Observer Dispatch*, Dick Waterman, Alan Weaver, and Bill Wimble.

Finally, we thank the talented graphic designers and photo specialists who worked so hard to bring all this material together and onto the printed page.

If we have left anyone out, we apologize in advance. Please know that it was not intentional, and that your help was appreciated.

Bones Bourcier
Coastal 181

July 2011

1960

Joe and Rene: The Odd Couple

In the beginning there was Joe Lesik, and there was Rene Charland. The story of the Utica-Rome Speedway starts with them. A race driver is nothing without a place to compete, so he needs the track owner. The track owner knows that no one will buy a ticket to see him, or to stare at his silent, empty speedway, so he needs heroes, personalities. He needs race drivers. So Lesik, who built the track, and Charland, who arguably became its first big star, were a team. If Lesik fathered the Utica-Rome Speedway, it's fair to say Charland served as midwife, taking an active role in ensuring that the birth was successful.

Lesik hailed from western Massachusetts, near Springfield. Few in the Northeastern racing community knew much about him when he started scratching out the speedway, and fewer can tell you anything about him today. Veteran photographer John Grady, who across the last 50 years seems to have befriended every driver, mechanic, and promoter in New York, including the man who built Utica-Rome, says, "What do I know about Joe Lesik? Very little. And nobody else knows a hell of a lot, either."

Hall-of-fame race car builder Fred Rosner, who came from the same neck of the woods as Lesik, says, "He kept his cards very close to the vest. He never *told* you anything; you had to find it out for yourself. He was very secretive, let very little out."

Rosner recalls Lesik operating a service station in Springfield with one or more of his brothers, John and Stanley. An odd sideline connected the brothers to auto racing: With Joe in charge, they constructed "rest-back" seats designed to make bleacher-type grandstands more comfortable, and rented them to fans at the Riverside Park Speedway in Agawam, Massachusetts. At that time, Riverside was one of the region's most successful short tracks, running two nights a week.

Rene Charland, who lived in Agawam, had been a Riverside Park crowd-pleaser throughout the 1950s before joining NASCAR and hitting the road as the '60s dawned. Fred Rosner was his chief mechanic, so both he and Charland were aware of—though clearly not close to—that fellow who had the rest-back concession.

"I guess Joe must have made a few bucks with those seats," says Rosner, "because the next thing we knew, he had bought some property in New York and was building Utica-Rome."

The man with the plan: Joe Lesik, track owner and visionary. (John Grady Photo, Mary Ellen Higley Collection)

Lesik and his brothers broke ground in late 1960, a mile or so east of the town of Vernon, on what had previously been the Yaddow family farm. Records show that the purchase price for the land was $21,000. Joe Lesik told local newspapers he planned on staging "stock car and midget races," and that he would install "bleachers seating about 5,000" people. Some thought that sounded a bit optimistic; many track operators would have been thrilled with crowds half that size.

But Vernon had some history as a racing town. Its fairgrounds had been home to a half-mile dirt track that hosted everything from local jalopies to the NASCAR Grand National (now Sprint Cup) series. And it's important to remember that if this man Joe Lesik knew anything about racing, it was seating. He also seemed to understand that nothing made the fans leap from those seats like colorful drivers. Personalities. Heroes. Stars.

~

The track Lesik envisioned and built was a quarter-mile asphalt oval, with its corners more tilted (at just three degrees) than truly banked. There would be no outer walls or guardrails, other than, of course, a barrier protecting the grandstands along the front straightaway.

In the autumn of 1960, the *Utica Observer-Dispatch* reported that "the quarter-mile hardtop track will be a sunken affair, making it easier for the spectators to see the events." Half a century later that sentence is still confusing, but it sure sounded good. "Lights are to be installed in the spring," the paper declared, "and it is expected races will be staged Friday or Saturday night of each week." That proved wrong two counts: The lights did not go in until June of 1962, and Sunday was race day in Vernon in the beginning and has been, except for rare deviations, ever since. But, hey, those were small details.

"The promoters hope to become affiliated with NASCAR, the national stock car racing organization," the newspaper said.

~

Work plodded along through the fall months, until frost and snow set in and put things on hold. But by that point, Joe Lesik—without really trying—had found his first big star. Or maybe it's more accurate to say that his star found him. According to Dick Waterman, who purchased the track in 1964 and heard tales of its construction from Lesik himself, Rene Charland had become something of a Utica-Rome Speedway regular even before there *was* a Utica-Rome Speedway.

"Joe told me that while the track was being built, Rene would occasionally come by," says Waterman.

This was tangible proof of the theory that opposites attract. Joe Lesik, as we have heard, was quiet, modest,

Even before Utica-Rome, Rene Charland was a star. Here he is after a Riverside Park win. (Shany Lorenzet Photo, Dick Berggren Collection)

reticent. Charland was none of those things. Flashy, often profane, always out for a laugh, he was going to be the center of attention, one way or another. Somehow, a relationship developed; calling it a bond might be stretching things a bit, but there certainly seemed to be attachment of sorts.

Of course, a relationship with Charland carried its risks.

"While they were building the track," Waterman says, "Joe and his brothers would sleep right there in a little trailer on the grounds. And Joe told me it got to the point where it wasn't a matter of *if* one of Rene's cherry bombs was going to explode beneath the trailer, but *when* it was going to explode. They'd all be trying to sleep, and at the same time they just know that at some point that cherry bomb is going to go off!"

And then there was the afternoon when Joe and Stanley Lesik were hustling to finish up the roof on the announcer's tower just as Charland stopped in for a visit.

"He saw Joe and his brother Stanley up there, working on that roof," Waterman says, recounting Lesik's tale. "So what does Rene do? He takes the ladder down and lays it on the ground. Then he gets back in his car, and he drives away.

"Now, he didn't just drive off for a few minutes. No, Rene drove home to Massachusetts! Those guys were up there for hours until somebody just happened to pull in to take a look around. They saw Joe and Stanley waving, and put that ladder back up."

Charland's new Sunday home was taking shape. So was Joe Lesik's race track.

~

Before long, there would be other stars showing interest. Some of the biggest names of the era were raising their eyebrows at all this talk about the new asphalt track being built over in …

Where, exactly?

John Grady recalls, "I said to Joe Lesik one day,

'The track is in Vernon. Why did you name it Utica-Rome?' He said he wanted people to identify it with the nearby cities. The little town of Vernon might not be on their maps. But if they could find Utica and Rome, they'd be close."

You can picture it: It's the spring of 1961, and folks are talking racing, and someone mentions this new speedway. "What's it called? Utica-Rome?" And, just like that, on garage workbenches and kitchen tables, highway atlases are opened and laid flat, and there begins a lesson on central New York geography.

Out west, in Buffalo and Niagara Falls, some of the hottest racing names in the state were looking into Utica-Rome. In Massachusetts and Connecticut, where Charland had done some talking, similar investigations were underway. And it's a safe bet that all the serious local racers—from the hard-living veteran Chuck Mahoney to the quiet, determined Lou Lazzaro, just 25 years old—cruised by to check the place out.

Ah, yes. The Utica-Rome Speedway was on its way.

1961
The Start of Something Big

Rome wasn't built in a day, and neither was Utica-Rome. Joe Lesik's construction project saw delay after delay, leading to an untidy sequence of missed "opening days." Some of this may have been weather-related; central New York's heavy snows and late thaws do not make for ideal working conditions in March and April. And maybe Lesik's optimism was partly to blame. After all, the man had never built a speedway before.

A May item in the local press whetted everyone's appetite: "The new Utica Auto Speedway [sic] is expected to be open in time this month for the traditional Memorial Day races." That report proved as daffy as its odd use of the word "traditional." Next came

What a glorious day! Coupes on the track, fans in the stands for Utica-Rome's grand opening. (Rod Nacewicz Collection)

Rene Charland, like many drivers, found the track surface a tad tricky on opening day. (Rod Nacewicz Collection)

false alarms about a grand opening on Aug. 6, a practice day on Aug. 27, and a full slate of racing on Aug. 20.

"The track just wasn't ready," says photographer John Grady.

One thing, however, had worked out: Lesik was indeed able to secure the NASCAR sanction he had sought. Ralph Ouderkirk, a familiar face at many New York tracks, would serve as chief steward. Eventually, they put together a realistic timetable. The abbreviated 1961 season would consist of three Sunday programs—Sept. 10, Sept. 17, Sept. 24—for NASCAR Sportsman cars. The first two would be highlighted by 30-lap features; the finale would go 50.

~

The opening day crowd was a fine one. Admission was $1.50, just 75 cents for kids. Not only was there was no competition from televised racing, there was little television, period. Curiosity, mixed with a little boredom, brought 3,500 souls to Utica-Rome. The $1,600 purse wasn't going to be an issue.

But there was an issue with the track surface. Perhaps the fresh asphalt hadn't fully cured, or the late-summer sun had drawn out its oils and made the place slippery. According to mechanic Fred Rosner, attending to his man Rene Charland, "They could barely get around the track at first. Oh, they had a hell of a time. Rene spun a couple times, I remember that."

Somehow, everyone adapted. Bill Wimble, NASCAR's 1960 national Sportsman champion, won the first heat. Jack Sleicher, in from Troy, took the second. The 30-lap main was an entertaining affair, with the leaders weaving through lapped traffic. Out front when the checkers waved was Sleicher's #8, nicknamed "Untouchable" in deference to the popular TV series starring Robert Stack as crime-buster Eliot Ness. Trailing Sleicher at the finish were Billy Rafter, Charland, and a hot young kid from Utica, Lou Lazzaro. The fans roared their approval, and promoter Lesik surely allowed himself a sigh of relief, if not a smile.

Not so fast, Joe.

Over in the pits, there was a buzz around the winning car. NASCAR officials were going over Sleicher's ride, a nifty Chevy coupe. Something about its Dodge engine apparently ran contrary to the NASCAR rulebook. After a brief debate, Sleicher was stripped of the victory. It went instead to Rafter, who had hauled nearly 200 miles from his home in Niagara Falls.

Though it was not exactly a storybook ending for the track's first race, there was an upside: While many speedway openings are forgotten over time, trivia buffs have kept fresh the memory of that Sunday.

Q: Who won the first Sportsman feature ever held at Utica-Rome Speedway?

A: The guy who finished second.

Just having Rafter on the grounds added to the luster of the day. The man was a racing giant in the Empire State. He had fiddled with Midgets a bit, cracking some ribs in his teenaged debut in Caledonia, New York. But once he found stock cars, the trophies piled up. In 1949, at age 19, he won his first feature at Buffalo's Civic Stadium, a place he would soon dominate. In the next two decades, he cut a wide and winning swath across the western portion of the state, and dipped successfully into Canada.

Dirt, asphalt, it didn't matter to Rafter. On one amazing weekend in the '50s, he took a 100-lapper at the

~

Right: Jack Sleicher's #8 coupe seemed to win the first feature win at Utica-Rome ... until it flunked tech inspection! (Rod Nacewicz Collection)

Bottom: Bill Rafter is in the history books forever as Utica-Rome's first official NASCAR Sportsman winner. (John Grady Photo)

The Start of Something Big

NASCAR points brought Bill Wimble to Utica-Rome in 1961, and he never really left. (John Grady Photo)

Monroe County Fairgrounds on Friday night; won a pair of 100-lappers on Saturday, first Syracuse and then Civic Stadium; and pulled off another double on Sunday, grabbing an afternoon feature at Ontario's Merrittville Speedway before dashing back over the border to top a night show at Waterloo. Three days, five victories.

Rafter's record includes the 1959 NASCAR New York state championship, four wins on the Syracuse mile, and track titles at Civic Stadium, Merrittville, and Lancaster. Yes, Billy Rafter was stud material.

Jack Sleicher's life was different, but no less heroic. A gung-ho student, he had designed the Troy High School emblem, the Trojan Winged Horse. Upon graduating he joined the Navy, serving as a radio operator on the destroyer U.S.S. Dale, active in the Pacific during World War II. Like so many ex-military men, Sleicher found stock cars the perfect antidote for sedate postwar life. He supported his racing, not to mention a wife and seven children, working at the Troy city garage.

After 82 years filled with noise and color, Jack Sleicher passed away quietly in 2008.

~

As the sun sank late in the afternoon of Sept. 17, Bill Wimble stood in victory lane at Utica-Rome. It was the last place he had figured he'd be when his season opened.

Winning the previous year's national Sportsman title had worn him out. From his home in Lisbon, New York, up on the St. Lawrence River, every trip was a hassle. But in 1960, "chasing points all over the damn place," he pushed things to extremes. Aboard Dave McCredy's #33 and a number of pickup rides, Wimble raced from Daytona to Montreal, with stops in Tennessee, Virginia, North Carolina, and across the Northeast.

"After 1960," he says, "I swore I'd never do that again."

Then Wimble had himself such a crackerjack spring and summer of '61 that, come the end of August, he checked the NASCAR standings and realized he had "a mathematical chance" of catching the leader, Dick Nephew. Just like that, Wimble says, "I was back chasing those almighty points." That required Sunday stops in Vernon, where in week number two Wimble took the checkers ahead of Howard "Jeep" Herbert.

One of the region's premier dirt-track drivers, Herbert was especially good at the quirky Fonda Speedway, where he'd already won 24 features. But he could also get it done on pavement; though he never won a feature at Utica-Rome, Jeep scored five top-three finishes there between 1961 and '63.

A footnote on Sept. 17: For years, Rene Charland has been cited as that day's winner, though the reason for that is a mystery. The next day's newspapers from Oneida, Rome, and Utica all credited Wimble. Perhaps Charland's name accidentally got typed into a retrospective account, and it was then passed along often enough that Rene became the accepted winner.

Wimble has no recollection of the day—ah, the "curse" of having been so successful that the great days all blend together—but he takes a practical view: "The local papers couldn't have *all* gotten it wrong."

Mr. Charland would soon find his own glory at Utica-Rome.

~

The Sept. 24 rundown showed just how wide a net was being cast by Utica-Rome's NASCAR programs. Ed Ortiz got the 50-lap win, ahead of Ernie Gahan, Pete Corey, and Herbert.

Ortiz hailed from Ransomville, New York, 200 miles to the west. Gahan lived on the New Hampshire coast, 350 miles in the other direction. The New York State Thruway was relatively new, having been completed in the second half of the 1950s, and Ortiz and Gahan—having towed down their share of country roads—were happy to help I-90 rubber in.

Ernie and Ed were the geographic bookends in a great cast of drivers, car owners, and mechanics pulling into Vernon. Here they came, from Amsterdam and Auburn, Fort Plain and Fulton, Rotterdam and Rochester. And what a scene they set—hulking cars, squealing tires, daring moves—for thousands of folks looking to spice up their Sundays.

Up in the bleachers was a Rome kid named Ted Puchyr, who later worked on pit crews and would one day oversee the motorsports programs of Rite Aid and Auto Palace. Puchyr was just 16 in that 1961 season, but he had racing in his blood. His father had once co-owned a stock car, an Olds Rocket 88 driven at the Vernon Speedway by Bernie Ingersoll, whose name we will encounter again.

"I started going to Utica-Rome when the track was brand new," Puchyr says. "That was a big, big deal for kids from around here, going to the race track."

~

Though shut out of the winner's circle, Rene Charland placed well enough in those three features to be crowned Utica-Rome's first track champion. By just two points he edged Sleicher, who would have won easily but for his opening-day disqualification. Third came Lazzaro, who was clearly the area's up-and-comer, having already won on the dirt at Fonda and Duanesburg's Victoria Speedway.

In hindsight, having Charland as champion was a lucky break for Utica-Rome. He had built a high profile in 1961, barnstorming up and down the Atlantic coast. In the company of some New England cohorts—most notably Ed Flemke, who would soon play a starring role at Utica-Rome himself—Rene made weekly stops at the Fort Dix Speedway in New Jersey, the Southside Speedway in Richmond, and the Old Dominion Speedway in Manassas, Virginia. The troupe, which also included Connecticut drivers Dennis Zimmerman and Red Foote, was labeled the Eastern Bandits, and they brought attention to every speedway they visited.

The Dixie promoters offered fat purses and deal money, but what really made those trips pay was the fact that, in addition to being terrific drivers, the Bandits all hailed from New England, where pavement racing was predominant. Their flyweight coupes—Flemke, the group's chassis guru, was notorious for his skeletal cars—totally outclassed the tank-like Southern machinery, built to withstand the rigors of dirt-track racing. Charland found the same advantage at Utica-Rome.

"Let's face it," says Fred Rosner, "most of the guys there had big, heavy dirt cars."

Still, it had to be a gas to hear over the Utica-Rome loudspeaker that the fellow charging through the field had won earlier that weekend in *Virginia*, rather than at Fonda or Monroe County.

Wimble says, "Rene quickly became a fixture at Utica-Rome, and he ended up winning his share there."

The two men, both great racers, had a lukewarm

relationship. "Rene and I were not bosom buddies," Wimble says. "We were never enemies; we got along. But we were very different kinds of people."

Incidentally, Wimble just did manage to catch Nephew in that chase for the national Sportsman title. They finished in a controversial tie, the only co-champions in NASCAR history. And over the winter, Charland decided he wanted some of that action in 1962.

A smile and a cigar were the calling cards of Utica-Rome's first NASCAR Sportsman champion, Rene Charland. (Bob Hunter Photo, Dick Berggren Collection)

1962

New Lights, New Challengers, Same Old Charland

Satisfied with the dress rehearsal that was 1961, Lesik laid out his plans for '62. First he shuffled his roster of officials. Rome's Chuck Mahoney, an ex-driver and a regional character whose path would intersect with Utica-Rome for the next 20 years, was named NASCAR chief steward, replacing Ralph Ouderkirk. (Ralph would be back before long.) Up on the flagstand went Utica's Jim Camino, who had, according to the announcement, "picked up years of racing knowledge in Midget and Sprint Car racing." And lights went up, with starting times shifting from afternoons to evenings in mid-June, once Sunday was no longer a "school night." The schedule called for 17 NASCAR Sportsman races, though one was lost to rain.

Come autumn, Rene Charland had himself another track championship. As always, Rene was both consistent and quick, with four wins—one each in May, June, July, and August—and an equal number of second-place finishes.

Rounding turn four and mashing the throttle, the Sportsman stars mix it up. (Rod Nacewicz Collection)

In this same season, he mounted what turned out to be a successful challenge for the NASCAR National Sportsman crown, and it remained atop his head through the end of 1965. Those four straight titles gave Charland the nickname he wore like a badge, proudly and forever: "The Champ."

His success, his wisecracks, and his constant hijinks made Charland a polarizing figure at any number of short-track outposts, and Utica-Rome was no different. Every Sunday, his appearance drew a loud and mixed reaction.

"The way I figure it, they know I'm around," Rene told the *Utica Observer-Dispatch*. "So if they cheer, that's fine. And if they boo, that's all right too."

~

Of course, every champion needs a foil, someone to knock him down occasionally. Enter Ed Ortiz, who won the final Utica-Rome feature of 1961 and came back in '62 to win on opening day. Ortiz fought Charland from one end of the season to the other, and ended up second in the standings.

Like Charland, Ortiz won four times: the May 20 opener, regular shows on June 17—the first night race—and July 8, and a Labor Day weekend 100 in which he held off Charland despite a flat left-front tire. "When Ortiz was right," says Junior Nimey, part of Lou Lazzaro's team, "he blew everybody away."

Ortiz remembers the Vernon oval being tight, saying, "If you started somewhere near the front, you had a *much* better chance of finishing up front." The downside for him—but not for the paying customers—was the weekly handicapping system, which started the best

Right: Chuck Mahoney, once a hotshot stock car shoe himself, took a job as Utica-Rome's NASCAR chief steward in '62. (John Grady Photo)

Bottom: Smooth Ed Ortiz won four Sportsman features in 1962, including the track's first-ever night race. (John Grady Photo, Rod Nacewicz Collection)

Here's how Rene Charland and his mechanic, Fred Rosner, chased (and won) the 1962 NASCAR national championship! (John Grady Photo)

cars deep in the field. To get to the front, Ortiz and Charland had to maneuver past their top rivals, plus the usual Tail-End Charlies.

"Rene and I had a lot of good races," Ortiz says.

To both men, Utica-Rome was neutral ground. Just as Charland had cut his teeth a few hours to the east, Ortiz made his bones "out west," as the locals say, meaning in the Buffalo area. And just like Charland, Ed Ortiz didn't much care what a track was like; dirt, pavement, bullring or big 1/2-miler, he was going to be fine. In the course of his colorful career, he was a track champ at Lancaster Speedway, the Merrittville Speedway "across the bridge" in Ontario, and his hometown track, Ransomville Speedway, which he actually helped build in 1957-58.

In the early '60s, Ortiz was in peak form, strutting his stuff at home and venturing east to run at Victoria Speedway near Schenectady, and at Fonda, where he won twice in 1962. Looking to fill a Sunday hole in his schedule, and buoyed by his win the previous September, Ortiz settled on Utica-Rome. Though his ride—John Burlingame's #0, with John Clement spinning the wrenches—was built for dirt, it also got around Utica-Rome in fine style. Every Sunday morning, Ortiz recalls, he and Clement would "stiffen up the suspension a little, change the tires, and go run the asphalt."

All this running around was tough on Ortiz, who had obligations back home. "We always had five to seven cows around, and I had to milk 'em in the morning," Ed chuckles. "They didn't necessarily get milked *on time*, but I always got the job done."

~

Hectic though it was, the schedule Ortiz chose was a picnic next to Charland's. Rene was still doing his thing with the Eastern Bandits, heading south each weekend, but Utica-Rome—specifically, the NASCAR Sportsman points to be found there—changed things up a bit. He continued to hit Fort Dix on Thursdays and Richmond on Fridays, but from there he'd split away from his fellow travelers and head back north.

The other Bandits didn't place much value on the NASCAR standings. "You can't eat points," muttered Ed Flemke, who was more interested in the fat purses and deal money he'd found down South. But Charland, no dummy himself when it came to racing economics, didn't plan to simply *chase* the Sportsman championship. He planned to *win* it. Between the NASCAR point fund and perks from various sponsors, the national title paid fairly well. Maybe a guy couldn't eat points, Charland concluded, but that championship could put some groceries on the table.

En route to Utica-Rome, Charland and Freddy Rosner often made Saturday-night detours to Long Island's claustrophobic, 1/5-mile Islip Speedway. "We'd get out of Islip late, run up the highway, and get close to Utica-Rome around sun-up," Rosner recalls. "Then we'd get a motel room and sleep until it was time to get up and go to the race track."

That's a 300-mile overnight haul, and on some weekends—when, for example, another NASCAR track offered double points—their pull was even longer. Rosner remembers "towing to Utica-Rome straight from Manassas, Virginia." Don't bother looking it up: it's about 420 miles.

Laughing, Rosner adds, "The guys on some of these tours today complain about running three or four races a month. We did four, five, six nights a week! I loved it, and I guess Rene felt the same way."

The Champ ate well in 1962, and those Sunday points sure helped.

~

Defending the local honor against such trespassers was not easy, but Rome's Tom Kotary won three Utica-Rome features in the heart of the summer.

Just one of a family of racers—older brother Cliff was a Northeast icon, first as a driver and later as an official, and kid brother Robbie also won big—Tom was no choirboy. Folks called him Tiger Tom and Terrible Tom, and claimed he was as quick with his fists as he was on the speedway. But former driver Otto Graham, whose Internet remembrances have helped fuel the nostalgia movement in New York stock car racing, has suggested that Kotary was simply a hard-driving product of a hard-driving era.

"Tom was a decent guy," wrote Otto. "Took a nip or two, or three, sometimes was ornery and combative … [But] if you respected him for his no-back-down attitude, and didn't let him intimidate you, you were OK."

In August, Robbie Kotary got a Utica-Rome victory the hard way, outrunning Charland and Ortiz in a 25-lapper.

"They were good guys to race against, those Kotarys," says Ortiz, who should know.

Also winning Sportsman features in '62 were Bill Wimble, Ken Meahl, and Cam Gagliardi. Meahl and Gagliardi, both from the western part of the state, hung

Rome's Tom Kotary gave the local fans something to crow about in '62, driving to three victories in Vernon. (John Grady Photo)

around Utica-Rome for a few more seasons, and each made a bit of noise. And Wimble? Well, bespectacled Bill—"the Flying Dairy Farmer," the press called him—would become one of Vernon's fastest and most popular visitors, Sunday after Sunday, year upon year.

~

New in '62 was a Late Model class, which in the early months played a support role on Sundays and later headlined a budget-minded Thursday program. Stock enough to attract novice racers, yet with enough ambiguity in the rulebook to entice every backyard mechanic who saw himself as the next Smokey Yunick, the Late Models were an instant hit.

"They had so many of those jalopies out there together," chuckles Ortiz, "that it seemed like the guy starting last was about to get lapped before the race even began."

The division's first champion was Clarence "Speedy" Williamson, out of Westernville. He edged out Norm House, Clayton "Sonney" Seamon, Ernie Vandewalker, and another Westernville racer, one Richie Evans. Interestingly, Williamson helped launch the oval-track career of this Evans kid, a hot-rodding ex-farm boy who had picked up the nickname Oil Can, as well as a growing reputation at the area's drag strips. First, Chuck Mahoney told Evans that circle-track racing was the way to go, preaching, "You gotta stop racing just for trophies. Build a stock car." Next, with technical help from Williamson, Evans prepped a 1954 Ford in a gas station owned by his friend Joe Jones. The number on the door was 109, after the torpedo boat PT-109 commanded in World War II by America's dashing young president, John F. Kennedy.

Top: Ken Meahl rode in from the West (western New York, that is) and parked his coupe in the winner's circle. (John Grady Photo)

Left: Speedy Williamson won the track's first Late Model crown, while mentoring a Westernville rookie by the name of Richie Evans. (John Grady Photo)

At the outset, Evans and Jones were partners, but that arrangement was brief. "The first time I totaled the car," Richie later reminisced to writer Pete Zanardi, "Joe turned the whole operation over to me."

~

The season ended with two Sportsman specials—a 100-lapper on Sept. 2, and a 150 the following Sunday—and an ARDC Midget event on Sept. 16. The Midget race, won by New Jersey ace Tony Romit, was a promotional risk, so Lesik added a demolition derby. Local boy and Late Model shoe Sonney Seamon out-smashed all comers, pleasing the crowd.

The Sportsman 100 went to Ortiz and his crafty mechanic, John Clement, aided by four secret weapons. "A guy in Oswego had some tires he said were the best things going," Ed recalls. "We drove up and bought a set. It took John's paycheck and my paycheck, but we had to have those tires."

A very young, very green Richie Evans after what is believed to be a Late Model heat race victory. (Billy Nacewicz Collection)

Vernon Center's own Sonney Seamon, looking every bit the rough-and-tumble stock car racer. (Rita Seamon Collection)

The 150-lapper went to Lazzaro, who sure picked a big week to grab his first Utica-Rome trophy. Already a star on the dirt at Fonda and Victoria, he was clearly getting asphalt racing figured out. "The difference in racing on dirt and on asphalt is like night and day," Louie had told the *Utica Observer-Dispatch* at mid-season. "But we've been working on it, and we'll have it right before long."

Mission accomplished.

~

Throughout 1962, a positive vibe had built along Route 5. The crowds were great; despite seats added in August that boosted capacity to 6,000, "hundreds of fans were turned away" from September's 100-lapper, according to the *Utica Daily Press*.

And down in the pits, things were about as communal as could be expected. There were smiling men sitting on trailers and leaning on colorful coupes which, less than 24 hours earlier, had been scattered across the Northeast. Junior Bianco, Lazzaro's right-hand man, recalls, "Before the races started, we'd all talk about who won and who was fast wherever we'd been the night before. Then it came time to race, and everybody would get busy."

1963

Big Plans, Big Races, and Big Lou

Central New York, with its brutal winters, is a great place to hibernate from November through March. But the deep freeze of 1962-63 only made Joe Lesik restless. Once again he was percolating with ideas for Utica-Rome. A February item in the *Utica Observer-Dispatch* trumpeted "a new 1/3-mile track around the existing 1/4-mile oval," a boost in seating "to almost 7,000," and a drag strip. Why, Lesik even alluded to hosting NASCAR's Grand National tour. That event would be scheduled "probably in August."

With spring came reality. Lesik did revamp the oval, kicking out and banking the turns, and seating increased. But the drag strip did not come online until 1965, and, no, NASCAR never brought its top series to Vernon.

But Joe's Grand National dream was not as far-fetched as "newbie" fans might imagine. In the '60s, short tracks—from Martinsville to dirt bowls like North Carolina's Dog Track Speedway—made up the bulk of the GN season. Heck, NASCAR's finest made repeat stops at Fonda, and at Long Island's Islip Speedway. And in 1970-71, Richard Petty won twice at the Albany-Saratoga Speedway, a 1/3-mile paved oval built by … *Joe Lesik*.

The "enhanced" Utica-Rome made its debut in June, with five weeks of racing already in the books. The first three winners were Tom Kotary, Jim Luke, and Lou Lazzaro. Then Rene Charland grabbed two in a row.

Funny story: In the build-up to the "new" track's debut, one scribe insisted the reconfiguration would trip up "the Flashy Frenchman," as Charland was dubbed. The Vernon track would now be "as new to him as it is to the rest of the field. With the bank of the turns increased from three degrees to 11, it is estimated the new course will add 15 miles an hour to the average speed of a Sportsman car." That jump, the writer opined, "will work against the Frenchman," whose prior success was chalked up to familiarity with the old layout. "This advantage was buried along with portions of the old quarter-mile oval when the [new] asphalt was poured."

So what happened? Rene won again, passing Bill Wimble for the lead with two laps to go.

Top: At the tail end of this New Yorker 400 conga line is Massachusetts invader Jack Malone (79), following Lou Lazzaro. (Waterman Collection)

Right: Connecticut's Bill Slater was among the New Yorker 400 favorites, but broke down just after taking the lead. (John Grady Photo)

~

Missing out on the Grand Nationals did not mean Utica-Rome lacked a major event in 1963. Lesik penciled in a homegrown substitute called the New Yorker 400, on the Sunday of Labor Day weekend. He posted a record purse for NASCAR Sportsman cars, some $6,800.

Pre-race gab centered on who might show up, the marathon length—a couple of 400-lappers had been tried at the Norwood Arena, outside Boston—and the confusion it might produce. And the New Yorker delivered on all counts. Oh, what a spectacle it was.

There were big-name Canadians (Jean-Paul Cabana, Andre Manny, Jean-Guy Chartrand), big-name New Englanders (Gene Bergin, Fats Caruso, Bill Slater), big-name shoes from even further afield (New Jersey's Bob Rossell, Long Island's Fred Harbach), plus the regular Utica-Rome rowdies. In all, 36 cars rolled out for time trials.

Rossell, who could haul the freight on both dirt and asphalt, set fast time at 15.23 seconds. From the pole, he led the first 20 laps. Then Bergin, the 1962 Riverside Park champ, took the long way around Rossell and spent the next 100 laps out front. But as Bergin lapped Chartrand, they bumped wheels, and Bergin's car bit the concrete. That gave the lead to Slater, a maestro who seemed to win at will at Norwood and at Connecticut's Waterford Speedbowl. But Slater's sharp coupe, black with a yellow V-8 on its door, broke down almost immediately, putting Rossell back in front.

Rossell pulled steadily away, until his closest pursuer, Lazzaro, was two laps back. The top prize was $1,500, and Rossell looked sure to take home every penny. Then his engine fluttered, sputtered, and quit. On lap 398, he was out of gas. Since mileage calculations in 1963 amounted to guesswork, many competitors had opted to pit and top off. Rossell had not.

He was rolling silently, dead-stick, when he felt a nudge from behind. It was Rene Charland's bumper. Said the *Oneida Daily Dispatch*, "The crowd of 5,200 had trouble believing their eyes when they saw Charland, the NASCAR champion, come to the rescue of Rossell."

For all his pranks and barbs, Charland was often quick to help a racer in trouble, and Rossell was sure in trouble now. So Rene, running a distant sixth, pushed Rossell for two full laps, and beneath the checkered flag.

But wait! Many tracks had procedural rules about cars finishing under their own power, though such rules were vague. What if the leader ran dry on the last lap, exiting turn four, but crossed the line first? Hadn't that happened, and hadn't that guy always gotten the trophy? Besides, who was to say that Rossell hadn't re-fired his car and run the final 50 yards on fumes, after that two-lap push from Charland?

Everyone had an opinion—particularly Lazzaro, who felt he deserved the win—but no one in power wanted to make a decision. So while the remainder of the field was paid for their finishes—third through fifth were Ernie Gahan, Wimble and Cabana—Lazzaro and Rossell each pocketed second-place money, $1,000, with the winner's balance of $500 withheld pending a final decision. Then track officials got in touch with the NASCAR brass, saying, in essence, "Daytona, we have a problem."

The process took more than six weeks. Ultimately, NASCAR decided a two-lap push was too big an assist to be considered legit. Lazzaro entered the books as winner of the inaugural New Yorker 400, with Rossell second.

"We had a big fight about that one," recalls Junior Bianco, Lazzaro's sidekick. "We felt like it wasn't right for [Rossell] to win that way, and in the end NASCAR agreed with us."

~

It was quite a year for Louie. He not only won that crazy 400, he also cemented his first Utica-Rome title. Charland topped the win list with five, but skipped two September events to run some points-rich Southern races on his way to another NASCAR championship. Lazzaro, meanwhile, was solid as a rock. He won a 25-lapper in May and another in September, and always hovered near the top five. Said Fred Rosner, Charland's wrench, "Lazzaro's cars were never anything special to look at, but they always handled. And Lou was obviously a very good driver."

Charland's win on May 19 heated things up. He had tangled early with Robbie Kotary, and the papers reported that Kotary "attempted to mix it up with the Frenchman" in victory lane, forcing officials to "restrain the disgruntled Roman." That might have been an interesting scrap. Robbie was not afraid of much—no Kotary ever was—but Rene, an ex-Marine, was no creampuff himself.

Lots of folks saw glory in '63. Lanky Jim Luke won for a second time, and Wimble also doubled up. Single victories went to Gahan, Ken Meahl, Bill Torrisi, and a startling rookie named Jerry Cook. Just 18 and mentored by Cam Gagliardi, Jerry had fielded winning coupes for a while, most notably with Meahl driving. He was studying mechanical engineering at Erie County Technical Institute. A newspaper profile said,

1963 was the season in which Lou Lazzaro established himself as a Utica-Rome hero. (John Grady Photo, Rod Nacewicz Collection)

Top: Teenaged Jerry Cook shook up the NASCAR Sportsman establishment with a Utica-Rome victory. More would follow! (John Grady Photo, Rod Nacewicz Collection)

Right: William "Lucky" Sutton, out of Rome, was the 1963 champion in the Flathead division. (John Grady Photo, Rod Nacewicz Collection)

"Cook expects to make as much money this summer as any other college student with a vacation job."

Across the next 20 seasons, Jerry Cook won six NASCAR Modified championships and more fame than that crew-cut college kid ever imagined.

~

For 1963, track officials divided the Late Model division, by engine type, into two classes: Overheads and Flatheads. Munnsville's Lou Smith, former scourge of the area's karting scene, dominated the Overheads with a dozen victories, but advanced to the Sportsman class before the Late Model season concluded. Playing catch-up, Rome's Willie Herrig was able to tie Smith in the standings, and they shared the Overhead title. (Meanwhile, Smith notched a pair of top-five finishes against Utica-Rome's best Sportsman pilots. This kid was a comer, no doubt about that.)

The Flathead king was William "Lucky" Sutton, another Roman. Though his *nomme de guerre* sounded like something coined by a Hollywood screenwriter, Sutton's multiple victories proved he was for real.

~

One of the Late Model division's finest hours occurred on an offbeat August night, when Joe Lesik partnered with Connecticut's Harvey Tattersall Jr. on a 200-lapper for the traveling Grand American series.

Tattersall was a carny-style promoter who once ruled several tracks in New England and New York. But as the '50s waned, so did his sphere of influence. Harvey's bread-and-butter joint was Riverside Park, and surely that was where he met Lesik, making his own pretty penny on those rest-back seats. Now Tattersall was back on the hustle, with an interesting road show; his Grand American series featured what were billed as "new cars." If you squinted just a bit, they resembled NASCAR's popular Grand Nationals.

A crowd of 5,000 came to Utica-Rome to see the Grand Americans, but the show had two serious drawbacks.

Drawback #1: Tattersall's stars got little respect. After Roy Hallquist won a thrilling battle with Dick Dixon, the *Utica Observer-Dispatch* butchered Hallquist's last name and referred to Dixon as, humorously enough, "Dick Nixon." Bear in mind, Dixon was already a Modified hero with three Riverside 500 victories, and Hallquist was also top-drawer talent, having made a couple of NASCAR Grand National starts.

Drawback #2: Only nine Grand American cars towed to Vernon, prompting Lesik to beg his Late Model regulars—on hand as the undercard—to fill out the field. "They told us that on top of the prize money for wherever we finished, we'd each get 50 bucks," remembers Dave Kotary, nephew to Tom and Robbie, and in 1963 a rising star in his own right.

Though seriously short on horsepower, Kotary joined fellow homers Herrig and Smith in rocketing toward the front, cheered by the partisan crowd. "Those [Grand American] guys would slide up in the corners," says Kotary, "and that gave me all the room I needed." Though Kotary was eliminated by a crash, Herrig and Smith finished third and fourth.

Dave still grins as he recalls the visiting hot dogs wandering past his pit stall, shaking their heads as they checked out one of the low-dollar cars that had just blown them into the weeds.

"They couldn't believe it."

~

Dave Kotary, on the rise, was among the track's top Late Model shoes in the early '60s. (John Grady Photo, Rod Nacewicz Collection)

Big Plans, Big Races, and Big Lou

And then, of course, there was Ed Flemke. Though still regularly raiding the Virginia and North Carolina tracks, Flemke stopped by Utica-Rome to check out the Sportsman scene and set the place alight. Dig this: The man had three top-five finishes in 1963, all of them victories! He and his #21X took 25-lappers in June and September, and, before 7,000 spectators, topped his Bandit pals Charland and Denny Zimmerman in a July 100-lapper. That last score paid Flemke $1,000.

Eddie mentioned that he might be around more often in 1964.

NASCAR chief steward Ralph Ouderkirk (right) hands a 1963 trophy to the track's newest sensation, Ed Flemke. (John Grady Photo)

1964

Steady Eddie, Fast Eddie

No one ever seemed to understand what made Joe Lesik tick, save for perhaps his brothers, Stanley and John, and they weren't telling. So it's no great surprise to learn when Lesik sold his Utica-Rome Speedway in the spring of 1964, not even Dick Waterman, one of the four purchasing partners—and the one who came to best know Lesik—could fully grasp the reasoning behind the sale.

"I think Joe liked the idea of *building* speedways more than he liked the idea of *running* speedways," Waterman shrugs. "He didn't seem interested in the day-to-day side of things." (That theory is backed up by the fact that Lesik immediately constructed another track, the Albany-Saratoga Speedway, only to unload it soon after its opening in 1965.)

Joe Lesik (left) and Dick Waterman. In 1964, Lesik sold the speedway to Waterman and three partners. (John Grady Photo)

Of the Utica-Rome deal, the bare essentials are these: The track was purchased by an entity called Ro-Cam Inc., the top officers of which were two Rome businessmen: Bernie Ingersoll, an ex-racer who owned a moving company, and Waterman, who operated an upholstery shop. The other partners were Chuck LeRicheux and Lou Brando, friends of Waterman's. The sale price was $150,000. Incredibly, the deal was finalized less than a week before the April 26 season opener.

Over a period of years, Waterman became the track's sole owner. His first-person account of the Lesik transaction, and of his early days at the helm of Utica-Rome, can be found elsewhere in this book. But let us be clear on the following: Dick Waterman played a vital role in the speedway's history, steering the place to great heights in the rollicking 1960s and '70s.

~

Eddie Flemke was a paradox. There's just no getting around that. A small, quiet man, he is frequently described in the biggest, loudest superlatives: the best *this*, the smartest *that*. "If we're talking about short-track racing, I always felt Eddie was the king," proclaims Elton Hill, a Flemke protégé from whom we'll hear again. The king! Now *there's* a superlative!

And there's no doubt that the superlative season of Utica-Rome's pavement era was the one Flemke authored in 1964. How about 11 feature wins, eight more than his nearest rival? How about five straight at season's end, including both halves of the New Yorker 400, run for the first time as a "split" event? How about doing all this against Charland, Lazzaro, Ortiz, Wimble, Gahan, the Kotary brothers, young Cook, and all the other scrappers we've met thus far?

Here's how tough Flemke was at Utica-Rome in 1964: He finished second just once, and never finished third. Translation: If he got anywhere close to the front, he didn't fool around. He closed the deal.

Eddie was also a pragmatist. From 1961-63 he had regularly loaded up his coupe and headed toward the Mason-Dixon line, forsaking several tracks within a few hours of his Connecticut home, because the money was better in the South. His success in Dixie made Flemke perhaps the best-known Modified racer of the era. But just as he preached to Charland and others that "you can't eat points," Flemke also knew that headlines weren't nutritious; good payoffs bought the groceries. And according to John Stygar, Flemke's mechanic and sometime car owner, it was the rising purses at tracks like Utica-Rome and Norwood Arena that ended Steady Eddie's glorious Eastern Bandits road show.

"There was a pretty good NASCAR circuit coming together in the Northeast," Stygar says. "Eddie was always a guy who looked at the dollars, so it just made more sense to stay closer to home. Fewer expenses."

Flemke not only looked at Utica-Rome's dollars in 1964, he took most of them home. He turned the New Yorker 400 into a $2,000 heist. The new format called for a straight-up start for the first 200 laps, then a half-time break, followed by a complete inversion of the running order for the second 200. The overall winner would be the fellow with the best average finish. Flemke left no room for error. He set quick time and led every lap of the first 200-lap segment, beating Fred Harbach and Mario "Fats" Caruso. Then he started the nightcap 23rd, took 118 laps to motor to the front, and led Robbie Kotary and Charland beneath the checkers.

"Eddie was a great driver, just a master at going through traffic," says Waterman. "And he was smart."

~

Flemke's 11 wins weren't enough to give him the Utica-Rome Sportsman crown. He finished only third in the standings. Instead the track championship went again to Mr. Charland, over Jerry Cook. It was Rene's third track title in four seasons. Charland won three times

Steady Eddie Flemke came with the "dollar sign" and left with the dollars, winning 11 features. (John Grady Photo)

Ever cunning, Rene Charland won three features and sewed up his third Utica-Rome championship. (John Grady Photo)

in '64, one on opening night and two, including a 150-lapper, in the heavy August heat.

It didn't hurt Charland's cause when better purses—what else?—lured Flemke elsewhere on a couple of Sundays. But take nothing away from Rene, who placed second seven times, third five times, fourth twice, and fifth once. He wasn't called The Champ for nothing.

Though they had raced together, traveled together, and followed each other up and down a hundred highways, Flemke and Charland couldn't have been more different.

Flemke seemed to make friends instantly. "Eddie was so pleasant to talk to," Junior Bianco recalls. He was also a promoter's dream, a showman. When fast enough to win by half a lap, Flemke, watching his mirrors, would win by a few car-lengths instead. Then, for the crowd and the papers, he'd say something like, "I was sweating Wimble all the way."

Charland was more of an acquired taste. He kept a fat cigar jammed in his teeth, boasted constantly, and harassed friends, foes, and total strangers. "You just never knew what Rene was going to do next," says a grinning Waterman. "But he made things interesting." Some loved The Champ; others were more ambivalent. Predictably, things sometimes went awry.

"One night, Rene and Lou Lazzaro had a squabble," Fred Rosner says. "Well, Lou always had his dog with him, a great big German Shepherd. He got that dog after Rene, and Rene scrambled up on top of the truck to get away."

From his safe perch atop the truck, Charland recovered quickly. Playing to onlookers, he taunted the dog and its owner. But Lazzaro had the last laugh.

"Lou left that dog there," Rosner chuckles. "And there was no way the dog was going to let Rene come down. He was up on that truck for a long time. Oh, it was great!"

But why wouldn't Rosner, Charland's mechanic and presumed lieutenant, rush to his driver's aid in such a circumstance? Well, Freddy knew Rene better than anyone. He had seen Charland's whole catalog of gags, from rubber snakes to a putrid-smelling "cologne" he'd ask an innocent victim to sniff before splashing some on the poor fellow's clothing.

Jerry Humiston, a champion at Riverside Park in Massachusetts, also had a winning touch at Utica-Rome. (John Grady Photo, Rod Nacewicz Collection)

"Rene pulled stuff on everybody," says Rosner. "But this time, Lou pulled something on him. I loved it."

~

The successes of Charland from 1961-63 and of Flemke in '63 sparked an outbreak of Utica-Rome fever in New England. Right from the start of the '64 season, there were a few more Sportsman cars being hauled across the Berkshires, which sure made things tough on the home-state heroes. Not until May 31, when Boonville's versatile Bob Zeigler grabbed a 30-lapper, did a New York driver reach victory lane.

Week in and week out, the top of the order was dotted with drivers from Connecticut, Massachusetts, and New Hampshire. Gahan won a 30-lapper on May 10. Gene Bergin, Bill Slater, and the ever-thrilling Caruso each notched multiple top-five finishes.

Then there was Jerry Humiston, from Springfield. A year earlier he'd been unknown to most Utica-Rome fans, but top-five finishes in the final three races of 1963 had swung some heads his way. He came out of the blocks strong in 1964, with a pair of thirds and a fourth

Lou Lazzaro with his dog, Blackie, who one night sent Charland scrambling for safety! (John Grady Photo)

in Utica-Rome's first four weeks, then drove to a 30-lap Sportsman victory on June 21.

As tight as Utica-Rome was, it must have seemed downright spacious to Humiston. He'd made his bones on the flat 1/5-mile Riverside Park Speedway, the same tough finishing school that had polished Flemke and Charland. Before he'd ever turned a wheel at Utica-Rome, Jerry won three track championships (1954, '69, '61) at the Park.

Among others winning Sportsman features in 1964: Lazzaro, Wimble, and Kenny Meahl, with one apiece.

~

Having decimated the Friday-night Late Model competition in '63, Lou Smith was now a Sunday-night full-timer in the coupes. His transition was seamless. In April, just getting warmed up, he'd scooted into Massachusetts and won at Riverside, a venue rarely kind to outsiders. And at Utica-Rome, Smith was outstanding. He won Sportsman features on May 31, June 28 and Aug. 9. Each time, the youngster earned his pay; the respective runners-up on those nights were past Utica-Rome winners Ed Ortiz and Wimble, and the hard-charging Bergin. No one-trick pony, Smith also excelled on dirt, winning 1964's top rookie honors down the Thruway at Fonda.

No, it wasn't all smooth sailing. Smith's June victory had Charland absolutely outraged. Rene had attempted a pass with two laps to go, but his car shot off the outer lip of the track in turn three after he and Smith banged wheels. Charland filed an official protest with NASCAR officials, leveling a "rough driving" charge at the rookie.

But the protest went nowhere, and the whole thing only served to boost Lou Smith's soaring popularity. Imagine, a local boy—Smith's home in Munnsville was maybe a dozen miles from the track—getting picked on by a two-time NASCAR champion!

Munnsville's Lou Smith copped three Sportsman features in 1964, and seemed destined for great heights. (Rod Nacewicz Collection)

Steady Eddie, Fast Eddie

The Grand American "new cars" visited for the second straight summer, again going 200 laps, but this time the show had less sparkle. The crowd, though respectable at 4,000, was off 20 percent from 1963 despite the addition of the traveling Hurricane Hell Drivers thrill show.

On the bright side, this time the local papers got winner Dick Dixon's name right, and Dixon definitely deserved that much. He swapped the lead 18 times with runner-up Roy Hallquist, the last exchange occurring on lap 196. Unfortunately, the sportswriters and editors again muffed "Hallquist."

Chick Stockwell, a Grand American champion better known as one of the all-time Modified greats at Connecticut's Danbury Fair Racearena, came home third.

~

Sonney Seamon, the 1964 Overhead champ, hailed from Vernon Center, but his ties to Utica-Rome went beyond mere residence. In 1961 he had done some welding work for Joe Lesik, helping build the steel wall on the frontstretch!

In the Flatheads, Lucky Sutton was lucky again, winning his second straight title. Both divisions featured drivers who would soon become familiar to Utica-Rome fans; there was another Kotary in victory lane after Dave grabbed an Overhead victory, and names like Dick Fowler, Bernie Miller, Richie Evans, Frank Mathalia, Ken Platt, Ralph Holmes, and Buddy Thurston appeared in the two Late Model classes. They were seeds just beginning to sprout.

All is in order, but not for long! The Late Models prepare to take the green flag. (Rod Nacewicz Collection)

(L-R) Ed Flemke, Lucky Sutton, Dave Kotary, and Lou Lazzaro, four of the track's 1964 crowd-pleasers. (John Grady Photo)

Hoisting the checkers is Late Model shoe Ralph Holmes, flanked by race starter Cliff Kotary. (Rod Nacewicz Collection)

1965

Kotary, Kotary, and Cook

And now, a round of applause for Rome's Kotary clan, right up there on anyone's ballot for the unofficial First Family of Utica-Rome. The family tree is more like a tangled vine, thick with brothers, sons, nephews, and cousins, many of them racers, most of them winners.

But 1965 was a family milestone. Tom Kotary, part of the three-brother act that kept the surname in headlines throughout the first half of the 1960s, won Utica-Rome's Sportsman championship with a run of top-five finishes highlighted by a July 11 victory. And just a week before Tom's win, on Independence Day, his nephew Dave rolled out a new Falcon-bodied Sportsman and outran the world, winning his heat race and the 30-lap main.

Tom Kotary was a study in consistency en route to his 1963 Utica-Rome Sportsman championship. (John Grady Photo)

Fourteen times in 1965, one Kotary or another was among the top three Sportsman finishers. The family was simply woven into the fabric of those noisy Sunday evenings along Route 5.

Cliff Kotary, born in 1919, was the trailblazer, his legacy built on multiple victories at the Syracuse mile. He never won at Utica-Rome, but only because the track wasn't built sooner. He did score a top-five finish there in 1962, but, as his rival Ed Ortiz respectfully jokes, "Cliff was an old-timer by then." Later, both Joe Lesik and Dick Waterman were wise enough to make Cliff an official, and he did some time on the Utica-Rome flagstand. Waterman recalls a drivers meeting at which Cliff warned, "Guys, don't try to pull any baloney out there. Remember, I've done it all." He sure had.

Tom, the middle brother, and Robbie, youngest of the three, had won at Utica-Rome before. So it wasn't surprising that Tom was up front again in '65; what shocked folks was that, atypically, he *stayed* up front.

"Tiger Tom could be a bit wild," says Waterman. "At one point our insurance company wanted me to put a guardrail all the way around the track, and I said that if I did that, one particular driver would never finish a race. I was talking about Tom Kotary. I can't tell you how many times I watched him slide off the backstretch."

But in '65, Tom was as steady as a Swiss watch. In one six-race stretch, he finished third, first, second, second, third, and second.

Meanwhile, young Dave—son of Albert Kotary, a mechanical whiz who was a brother to Cliff, Tom, and Robbie—hit the Sportsman class like a jolt of electricity. Tipped for big things at Utica-Rome right from his Late Model days, it was at Brewerton Speedway that he really laid down his marker. In 1963, on the way to his second straight title there, he won 17 of the 20 main events. He was only 20 years old.

"I did a lot of racing before I got into the Modified/Sportsman cars, and it came easy," says Dave. "Of course, as you move up it gets a little harder."

Father Al built that Sportsman car in a rush after Dave's Late Model was demolished in the spring. He just missed getting it done for the June 27 program, but it sure leapt out of the box on July 4.

Top winner in the NASCAR Sportsman class was crewcut Jerry Cook, who saw six checkered flags. (John Grady Photo)

Lou Smith won the 1965 Sportsman opener. Three weeks later, he lost his life in a crash on the Fonda dirt. (John Grady Photo)

Dave Kotary and his Falcon ran the final ten Sundays of the season. In addition to that debut victory, he scored two seconds and three thirds.

~

For large chunks of the previous few Utica-Rome seasons, Rene Charland and Ed Flemke had looked all but unbeatable. In 1965, Jerry Cook measured up to them both, literally. Charland won four times—May 9, May 30, Aug. 15 and Sept. 12—while Flemke took two June features, one a 100-lapper. But Cook's total of six victories equaled their combined Sunday-night win production.

The memory still brings a smile. "Eddie and Rene had been the guys to beat there," Jerry says. "I really paid attention to them."

History remembers Cook as methodical, conservative, from his tech-school background to the way he later produced NASCAR titles as reliably as a stamping press. He wasn't the first Northeasterner who raced for a living, but he exhibited a structured discipline lacking in many of the professional racers—Charland, Lou Lazzaro, Ernie Gahan—who came before him. Ted Puchyr, still early in his journey from bleacher kid to crewman to sponsor liaison, saw Cook right from his earliest outings at Utica-Rome. "Even back then," Puchyr says, "you could almost picture Jerry thinking, 'OK, I've got to buy a new refrigerator on Monday,' then going out and earning the money."

But this image of Cook as a thinking man's racer blurs the fact that he could also stand on the gas. The lasting echo of that glorious '65 season is of Utica-Rome announcer Jack Burgess, one of New York racing's great voices, calling home Cook's #38 as it swept beneath the checkered flag.

Two of his half-dozen wins, 30-lappers in May and June, came with a tired coupe he had run for a couple of years. The other four came in a Falcon he unveiled, coincidentally, on the same night Dave Kotary so dramatically unveiled his own Falcon. Cook's version won on July 18, its third outing, and on the next two Sundays, including a 150-lapper on Aug. 1.

It took God and Uncle Sam to halt Cook's streak. Rain fell on Aug. 8, after which Jerry left to fulfill a two-week obligation—here again, that structure and discipline—with the U.S. Army reserves. When he returned to Utica-Rome on Aug. 29, he parked his Falcon right back in victory lane.

~

Just thinking about the '65 Utica-Rome season brings a tinge of sadness to longtime fans, for that was the year they lost Lou Smith and all the promise his career had offered.

Young Lou had lit up the Vernon oval in 1964, with those three Sportsman victories and his refusal to back down against the formidable Charland. When he won the 1965 opener over Kenny Meahl and Cook on April 25, he stopped cold any talk of a sophomore slump.

Like Cook—as well as Wimble, Lazzaro, and Charland himself—Smith was still running the dirt. On May 15, just three weeks after that Utica-Rome victory, Lou climbed into the storied #62 coupe of Frank Trinkhaus and strapped himself in for a Fonda feature. As he battled with the great Kenny Shoemaker, Smith's car clipped the fence out of turn four and tumbled violently. The popular kid from Munnsville was hauled away with serious head injuries, his prospects grim.

It rained on Sunday, and the Utica-Rome program was called off. Just as well. It's doubtful anyone felt like racing.

Lou Smith, just 24, was dead within days.

~

The "two races, one overall winner" concept behind the New Yorker 400 was truly tested for the first time in 1965 when Charland, having finished second in both 200-lap segments, was crowned the victor.

Bill Wimble, crafty as ever, was running a nice, steady third with three quarters of the first 200-lapper in the bank. Up ahead, rookies Frank Mathalia and Dave Kotary were running one-two, each doing a nice job. Suddenly, two back-markers collided. In trying to avoid that mess, Mathalia and Kotary collided, too. From there, Wimble cruised home, holding Charland and Cook at bay.

The nightcap 200 was a rumble, with the lead in dispute all the way. In the end, Long Island's Fred Harbach held off Charland, Jerry Humiston, Wimble, and Dick Dixon. It was the only Utica-Rome triumph of Harbach's splendid career.

With a first and a fourth, Wimble barely missed the overall win. His effort aboard the Dave McCredy #33, built to run dirt, had been tremendous, but he was swimming against a tide of purpose-built asphalt machinery. Car owner McCredy had seen enough. He contracted Fred Rosner, who had split with Charland, to build Wimble a pavement #33 for 1966.

~

After finishing second in both 200-lap segments, Rene Charland was crowned overall winner in the New Yorker 400. (John Grady Photo)

Bob Zeigler, out of Boonville, cruised to a Sportsman victory in June of '65. (John Grady Photo, Rod Nacewicz Collection)

Flemke had a quiet year on the track, by his standards, but he was quite active behind the scenes. There were even more cars from Connecticut in the pits at Utica-Rome, as well as at Airborne Park in Plattsburgh and the new Albany-Saratoga Speedway in Malta. Drivers like Elton Hill, Don Moon, and Billy Harman were stretching their legs a bit, and Flemke had something to do with it.

"Eddie talked to the promoters up there," says Hill, who had finished second to Flemke in Utica-Rome's '64 finale. "I guess he told them he could bring up four or five coupes from this area."

The promoters played ball. Hill and his car owner, Darrell McClelland, loved the arrangement. "We got our [highway] tolls paid," says Elton, "and a little extra money on the side."

On May 2, in the second race of the '65 season, Hill beat Flemke and Fats Caruso to win a 30-lapper. Moon and Harman were also on the gas; on June 13, they finished second and third, respectively, behind Flemke.

~

Hoping to capitalize on a craze popular at Riverside Park and Islip, the Utica-Rome management carved out a Figure 8 track, paving an "X" through the center of the oval. Response proved lukewarm. Dick Fowler, who over time would race and win in every class the Vernon track offered, was the class champion.

Buddy Thurston, from nearby Sherrill, topped the former Late Models, now consolidated into one division and rechristened Hobby cars.

~

Those dozen wins gathered up by Cook, Charland, and Flemke left precious few table scraps for the other Sportsman shoes. For the second straight year, Bob Zeigler visited victory lane, topping a June 30-lapper. And on Sept. 19, the season's final night, a dark-haired 24-year-old from Westernville who had moved to neighboring Rome—and who, in concert with Cook, would one day put that city on the national motorsports map—quietly picked up the first win of what became a brilliant career.

In his first few oval-track seasons, Richie Evans hadn't done much to mark himself as anything special. His Late Model outings were spotty. But Evans, never short on grit, kept at it. When he jumped up to the Sportsman division in 1965, the extra power and speed seemed to suit him. "He didn't know yet how to make a car go around in circles, mechanically," says Wilbur Jones, an Evans crewman. "But he picked it up, and picked it up…"

In the final Sportsman feature of the 1965 season, young Richie Evans won his first NASCAR feature. (John Grady Photo)

On July 11, Evans mounted what the papers called "a late charge," finishing a close second to Tom Kotary. Just over two months later, on Sept. 19, there stood Richie, checkered flag in hand, having held off fellow Late Model grads Sonney Seamon and Bernie Miller.

The occasion did not trigger alarm bells. The local press paid more attention to the evening's 100-lapper for the Late Models (won by Thurston) than to this first-time Sportsman winner. But those close to Evans correctly figured that Sept. 19, 1965 was just the start.

"Just from his attitude alone," says Jones, "I thought Richie would make it."

EYEWITNESS

1961–1965: DICK WATERMAN

*"The first race I ever saw there,
I watched as one of the owners!"*

NOTE: Across much of its history, Utica-Rome tended to chew up and spit out promoters and management teams. But Dick Waterman was the owner of the track—or, in his earliest days, the part-owner—for 15 years, the bulk of its heyday as a magnet for NASCAR's Modified and Sportsman coupes. Strangely enough, his long tenure began by accident, when a series of events cast him in what first appeared to be a supporting role in the four-way partnership that purchased the track from its builder, Joe Lesik. But Waterman soon emerged as top man at the Vernon oval, and stayed there as promoter and sometime landlord through 1978. Armed with a sharp memory and a hearty laugh, Waterman is a repository of tales from one of Utica-Rome's finest eras. In 2009, he was inducted into the New York State Stock Car Association Hall of Fame.

Utica-Rome had been around a couple of years before I got involved with it. That's a story in itself. In February of 1964, I was going to Daytona for the 500. I had asked my friend Bernie Ingersoll—who had been involved in racing for years—if he wanted to ride to Florida with my wife, Dorothy, and me, but he said he wasn't going. Then, just a few days before I was ready to leave, he said he and his wife, Marge, would ride down with us after all. I said that was no problem, and the four of us took off for Daytona.

It turned out the main reason Bernie went down there was because he was involved in trying to buy Utica-Rome from Joe Lesik, and Joe was going to be at Daytona. They discussed this deal, day by day, at the track.

Now, I was not involved at all; Bernie had another man who was apparently going to be his partner. But it rained all week, so they ended up holding their business meetings in my car in the infield, which meant that I sat through most of

Rene Charland could be a promoter's delight, or a prank-filled thorn in a promoter's side, as Waterman was to learn. (John Grady Photo)

these meetings simply because it was my car and there was no place else to go to get out of the rain!

They got pretty close to a deal before we came home. But somewhere along the way, Bernie's partner backed out. So Bernie said, "Dick, do you want to take half of this thing?" I didn't know if I could handle half, because I had a lot going on; just like today, I had my business, Camden Upholstery. But I told Bernie that maybe I could get a couple of friends together and get involved. And that's what happened. Eventually, four of us—Bernie, myself, Chuck LeRicheux and Lou Brando—bought the place.

Now, I was already a race fan—I had been to Daytona, of course, and I used to go to Oswego quite often—but I had never even seen an event at Utica-Rome Speedway to that point. So the very first race I ever saw there, I watched as one of the owners.

Over time, through a series of things, I became the sole owner. After two years, Bernie wanted out, so the other three partners bought his share. A couple years after that, Chuck had a heart attack at the front gate and died. Two years after *that*, I bought out Lou. For about the last nine years I was there, I had the place by myself.

All along, I was lucky in that I was able to get advice from Joe Lesik, and I thank the Lord that I was usually smart enough to listen to him. He'd say, "Well, Dick, it's not my track anymore. But if it was, here's what I'd do …" Joe was one of the smartest men I ever knew. I'd put him right up there with Bill France Sr. when it came to foresight. Joe and Big Bill were great influences on me, as was Ed Otto, who worked with NASCAR for years and promoted races from Canada to Florida. I only wish I had asked those three men more questions, because every time I did, I learned something.

I had a great relationship with NASCAR. From the standpoint of any race driver, particularly in those days, NASCAR was the greatest thing they had going for them. If you raced at a NASCAR-sanctioned track, you knew you were insured, and you knew you were going to get paid, which wasn't necessarily the case everywhere. You also got more recognition. Bill Wimble and I have discussed this; he once told me he wasn't sure how important NASCAR really was. I said, "Well, where would you have gotten if you just ran little dirt tracks in upstate New York, up along the Canadian border? Who would have ever heard of Bill Wimble?" People knew him because he was a NASCAR champion. And from the standpoint of a promoter—even though they did things I wasn't always in favor of—I knew they were thinking about the good of the sport.

Utica-Rome was a very tough place. We had the best drivers in the business, every Sunday. Even in the mid-'60s, we had Wimble, Eddie Flemke, Rene Charland, Ernie Gahan. Lou Lazzaro. By that time, Jerry Cook had moved to Rome, and he was coming on strong. Later on, Richie Evans came along, and we'd get Fred DeSarro and Bugsy Stevens from over in New England. Ray Hendrick came up from Virginia for some of the bigger races. It was absolutely a Who's Who of Modified racing.

Back then, we had so many colorful characters in the sport. Charland, as everyone knows, was certainly one of the *most* colorful. One year, NASCAR had a promotion in which they gave away the Daytona pace car—it was, as I remember it, a souped-up Dodge convertible—to whoever could sell the most NASCAR memberships. Well, Rene really hustled, and he won that contest. One day I was at my upholstery shop, and here comes Rene, driving that convertible. There were three young men in the store with me, my son and a couple of neighbor boys. I said, "Rene, why don't you give the kids a ride in the pace car? That would be a real thrill for them, especially with the national champion driving them."

So Rene gets these three boys in the car, with the top down, and off they go. Well, before you know it, they're on the road out of town and Rene has got that thing flying. There's a set of railroad tracks out there, and apparently he went up over the top of those tracks at over 100 miles per hour. Oh, he wrung that car out. Later on, the father of one of those boys came to see me, madder than hell. His son had gone home, and naturally he couldn't wait to tell his dad about this ride they'd been on. All I could do was apologize to the man, and assure him that if I'd known Rene was going to do that, *my* son wouldn't have been in that car, either. He gave those boys a ride, all right. But, you know, that was Rene, completely unpredictable.

Speaking about Rene reminds me of another story. At one point very early in my involvement with the track, when Bernie Ingersoll was still a partner, I had a fan walk right up and knock me out cold. There was no argument, no nothing, just a sucker punch. It was a situation in which the fellow had been drinking, and he had apparently made a five-dollar bet with his

Steady Eddie Flemke, just one star in Utica-Rome's bright 1960s galaxy. (Rod Nacewicz Collection)

Top: Every track needs local heroes, and the ascendance of Richie Evans gave Utica-Rome another one. (Alan Weaver Collection)

Right: Waterman, at left, with current track owner Gene Cole. That's a lot of speedway history in one photo! (Images by DC)

buddy over which one of 'em would take a swing at the promoter. So they went off looking for either me or Bernie, and, just my luck, they found me first! I had just been talking with two plainclothes police officers, but they'd walked away a moment earlier. They heard a commotion, and when they turned back around I was laid out on the ground.

They grabbed the guy who hit me, and of course he was arrested. But when he went to court to face charges, this man started telling the judge about how he'd been injured in the fight, too. He said he'd suffered a cut lip. I said, "Cut lip? Fight? I never even had a chance to raise my hands!"

The fellow replied, "No, but the guy who was *with* you hit me!"

Well, the guy with me had been Rene Charland. I didn't know it at the time, but I guess as soon as that fellow hit me, Rene popped him. So we had a discussion about all this in the courtroom, and I was asked about the man who'd been walking with me. I said I didn't know who it was. I figured, Why get Rene involved? But I always appreciated that Rene had come to my defense that way.

And, you know, that was a very unusual occurrence. Most of the fans were wonderful people, and they just loved their racing. I came to feel as if I knew many of them, because I'd see them so often. In fact, one night we got an emergency phone call for this one particular man; his son had been killed. Terrible thing. So, obviously, we had to locate this fellow. The person who'd taken the call asked if we should have the man paged over the loudspeaker. I said, "We don't have to do that. I know where to find him." See, he was at the track every week, and he always sat in the same area, if not the very same seat. Now, there might have been 5,000 people there that night, but I knew where he'd be. It was a sad thing, of course, but it shows how familiar I had become with that man, and it was like that with many, many fans.

I had 15 great years at Utica-Rome. I truly enjoyed it. It takes, I believe, a certain type of personality to run a track. I probably wasn't the greatest at it, but, with the help of a lot of good people, I think we did OK.

You know, Joe Lesik and I remained friends, and sometimes when we'd talk about the track he'd say to me, "Can you imagine how many lives we have changed?" I think about that today, and he was absolutely right.

1966

All Roads Led to Vernon

The off-season had been a busy one. First came Bernie Ingersoll's resignation as president of Utica-Rome's operating corporation. Dick Waterman filled the role and also bought his friend's stake in the track, paring ownership to himself, Chuck LeRicheux and Lou Brando. They immediately renewed Utica-Rome's relationship with NASCAR, and this story had a nice twist: Joe Lesik's Albany-Saratoga oval, ruled in its maiden '65 season by Harvey Tattersall's United Stock Car outfit, was joining the NASCAR fold. The two tracks, just over 100 miles apart, signed five-year sanctions, forming a nice Friday-Sunday circuit.

And as spring arrived, the speedway announced that its weekly programs would be headlined by both Sportsman cars and Modifieds, running together. The two classes were virtually indistinguishable; the Modifieds were heavier, but had bigger engines and

Ernie Gahan traveled to all points on the compass on the way to his 1966 NASCAR national Modified title. (John Grady Photo, Rod Nacewicz Collection)

more liberal induction systems, including fuel injection. At fast tracks like the 5/8-mile Thompson Speedway in Connecticut, the Modifieds usually held the advantage; at tight places like Norwood and Islip, the lighter Sportsman cars often won out. A handful of drivers raced Modifieds at some tracks, Sportsman cars at others.

In 1966, the best guys in both divisions spent their Sundays in Vernon.

~

Come autumn, handshakes and backslaps were due Ed Flemke and Bill Wimble after they'd wrapped up Utica-Rome's Modified and Sportsman titles, respectively. Wimble, aboard Dave McCredy's new pavement car, took four features and an overall win in the New Yorker 400. Flemke scored twice and placed in the top-three on seven other occasions. It was the first Utica-Rome track championship for either man.

But Flemke and Wimble are overshadowed in tales of that Utica-Rome campaign by a pair of *national* champs. In 1966, both Ernie Gahan and Don MacTavish made frequent stops there en route to clinching the biggest titles of their storied careers.

Now, as we've seen, Utica-Rome's crowds were no strangers to NASCAR royalty. Rene Charland, the national Sportsman king four years running, was a Sunday constant, and even in its first abbreviated season the track had hosted Wimble as both reigning champion and contender. But adding Modifieds made Utica-Rome a major player in two NASCAR divisions. And so it was that Gahan and MacTavish rumbled into town whenever possible. Often they arrived late, nerves jangled from violating every speed limit on I-90, having raced that very afternoon at Thompson, 250 miles to the east.

Gahan won a pair of Utica-Rome 30-lappers, one each in June and July, on his way to the NASCAR Modified title. MacTavish, the Sportsman champ, also won twice: a 100-lapper on June 5, and the second of the twin 200s that comprised September's New Yorker 400.

The first-ever Utica-Rome Modified championship went to Ed Flemke, here with starter John Tallini. (John Grady Photo, Rod Nacewicz Collection)

Two huge Utica-Rome wins helped boost charismatic Don MacTavish toward the NASCAR national Sportsman crown. (John Grady Photo)

Both men lived in Dover—though Gahan's hometown was in New Hampshire, MacTavish's in Massachusetts—and both loved to race. In every other way, they were opposites. Though he turned 24 just that summer, Mac had the respect of veteran pitsiders. "He was phenomenal," recalled Junior Bianco. "A smart kid, a nice kid." Already it was whispered that his speed and natural charm might soon elevate dashing Don beyond the coupes, toward superspeedway fame. Gahan, too, had a certain charm, but his was a backwoods variety. He might be a great racer and a fun guy, went the thinking of the sport's image-conscious higher-ups, but it would take some polish to make Ernie ready for the big-time.

Years later, reminiscing with writer Lew Boyd, Gahan recalled clinching his Modified crown at Atlanta. "Doesn't [NASCAR founder] Bill France come right up to me and say, 'Now, Ernie, we're gonna have to send you off to that Dale Carnegie School of Speech.' I said, 'Bill, I am a damn race driver, not a speaker. My thing is winning races.'"

It sure was. Gahan's career victory total ran well into triple digits.

~

Two of Utica-Rome's top names made big news elsewhere in 1966. First, Charland was badly burned in an Albany-Saratoga crash. With his feet apparently trapped by the pedals, he'd been wrenched from the flames by Flemke, his great rival and friend, who jumped from his own car and dove into Charland's. Photographer John Grady called it "the bravest thing I've seen in my whole life." After healing for a few

Painful burns suffered in an Albany-Saratoga fire could not keep Rene Charland out of the Utica-Rome win column. (John Grady Photo)

weeks, The Champ proved the burns hadn't slowed him down, setting fast time and leading an entire Utica-Rome 100 on July 3.

And Jerry Cook, the previous year's six-time winner in Vernon, was held to only two in '66, but still had a banner year. He took four victories in the Saturday-night NASCAR dirt show over at Fonda. Interestingly, Cook says he never had a great dirt-track technique, choosing instead to run Fonda as if it was blacktop. "I mostly kept the car straight," he says. This not only paid off if Fonda became hard and slick, it also saved Jerry some Sunday labor. There was no need to throw a Utica-Rome setup at the car, because he'd been using his Utica-Rome setup all along! "The only difference I remember," he says, laughing, "was whether I ran slicks or *grooved* slicks."

~

On the opposite end of the spectrum from luminaries such as those above stood weekend warriors like Elton Hill. Upon losing his aircraft-industry job in Connecticut, Elton had decided to chuck the 9-to-5 life and take a stab at racing for a living. Taking Flemke's advice, he set his eyes on New York, where the pavement scene was in full bloom.

Hill loved the bullrings, having won at his local track, Plainville Stadium, and at Riverside Park. Utica-Rome, he says, "felt like home to me." And it was there that on July 10, 1966, Elton and the McClelland #74X outgunned Utica-Rome's version of Murderers Row. In a tense 30-lapper, he beat Flemke, Wimble, Charland and Cook.

Fondly remembered by his contemporaries—Grady describes him as "a journeyman who never had the big numbers of a Charland or a Flemke, but alwaysgot the job done"—Hill spent less than four full seasons at Utica-Rome. But he personified the track's allure to racers from throughout the Northeast. It wasn't only the point-chasers and regional heroes to whom Utica-Rome meant something. The place was a magnet.

Elton Hill turned a lot of heads, beating the best NASCAR coupe shoes in the business at Utica-Rome. (John Grady Photo)

"You'd look around the pits," says Hill, "and just be amazed at all the great racers who were there."

Elton modestly classifies himself as having been "a so-so driver." He's wrong about that. So-so drivers didn't cut the mustard at Utica-Rome.

~

Burly Kenny Shoemaker, best known for wrestling oversized coupes on the dirt, could also finesse a good pavement car. Proving that in 1966, he bagged three Utica-Rome features aboard the white #24 of Cliff Wright and the Zautner brothers, Donnie and Bobby. Also finding victory lane were Gene Bergin and Lou Lazzaro, the latter on July 17, when 7,000 fans jammed the place for a regular weekly show augmented by a celebrity demolition derby won by a Utica broadcaster.

Bergin was an interesting case. A constant threat in New England, he seldom roamed on a steady basis, and May 8 marked his only Utica-Rome score. But whenever Gene showed up, he made it count. He notched five runner-up finishes between July '63 and August '64.

All this, from the wanderings of Gahan and MacTavish to the solo wins of Hill and Bergin, was prelude to the fourth annual New Yorker 400.

Rains over Labor Day weekend postponed the big show, but 5,000 spectators turned out on Sept. 11. No one was surprised when Wimble, smooth as silk, won the first 200-lapper over Shoemaker, Charland, Sonney Seamon, and Cook. Novice fans, however, may have been shocked when MacTavish outran Robbie Kotary and a surging Wimble in the second leg. To the unknowing, Mac's dinged and dented Circle J looked like a candidate for the scrapyard. But in carrying MacTavish to his national title, the black coupe ran upwards of 100 features, with 11 victories among its 80 top-five finishes. The Circle J had earned its scars.

Gene Bergin was never a Utica-Rome regular, but he made his visits count. In May of '66, he copped a feature win. (John Grady Photo)

"MacTavish drove some real iron," laughs Ted Puchyr, by then a helper in the Richie Evans camp. "But he was every bit as good as anybody in those days."

Wimble, first and third, now wore the New Yorker 400 crown he'd nearly earned in '65.

~

Every speedway has that racer who just can't do enough. At Utica-Rome, it was Frank Mathalia. Always quick to lend a part to a local foe or shop space to a traveling team, Mathalia helped ease the lives of many competitors.

"What a guy Frankie was!" Elton Hill declares. "Any problem you had, he'd open up his garage and help you get straightened out so you could race. He didn't stop and say, 'Hey, this guy might beat me tonight.' He'd give you anything you needed."

While doing his quiet good-guy thing, Mathalia had himself a terrific Utica-Rome season. Seven times, he finished in the top five, including a terrific third behind Charland and Flemke in that July 100-lapper. When the dust settled, Frank Mathalia was second in the track's Modified standings, and the whole pit area was happy for him.

~

Three times in 1967, Kenny Shoemaker hustled the Wright-Zautner #24 to victory in Vernon. (John Grady Photo)

All Roads Led to Vernon

Top: Ken Platt topped the Hobby division points chase, a sign of more good results to come. (Rod Nacewicz Collection)

Left: Frankie Mathalia, everybody's pal, placed second in the track's Modified standings. (Rod Nacewicz Collection)

The Hobby guys had their usual rock-'em, sock-'em time, with Ken Platt earning the division championship. Like so many folks in the support class, Kenny had his heart set on climbing into a Modified ride and chasing the big prize in Utica-Rome's headline division. Unlike most, he had the talent and dedication to get there. For now, though, he was paying his dues, rubbing fenders and piling up seat time—and posing seven times holding the winner's trophy—with his trusty Late Model.

Dick Delaney, from Lee Center to the north, was the Figure 8 champ.

~

One last thought on 1966: Utica-Rome's weekly top-five was always studded with legends, but was there ever a Modified/Sportsman feature anywhere with a finishing order as emblematic of its times as the one held there on June 12?

When the checkers waved after 30 laps, the top five were Shoemaker, Evans, Pete Hamilton, Flemke, and Wimble. In Shoemaker and Wimble you had two of the last great crossover artists, proficient on both dirt and asphalt, in the fading light of an era when such versatility was commonplace. In Flemke you had the road-dog spirit of the '60s, when mom-'n'-pop motels and cheap gas beckoned every restless Modified guy with a sturdy hauler and a high degree of wanderlust. In Evans, just hitting his stride, you had the work-hard, play-hard ethos of the good-time racer, a role Richie would eventually make his own. And in Hamilton you saw ambition, and the idea that a hungry, talented kid could still steer a coupe from nowhere right to the very top. Less than four years after that third-place run, Pete Hamilton won the 1970 Daytona 500.

All that talent, all those personalities—some fully formed, some still evolving—and all that history, rumbling out of turn four at Utica-Rome. Wow.

1967
Calm Faces in Exciting Times

There has never been a Modified/Sportsman hero quite like Bill Wimble. Maybe it was those glasses, that easy smile. Dressed up, he could have passed for a high school math teacher. Dressed down, in work clothes, he looked like the dairy farmer his childhood prepared him to be. Either way, he seemed made for the peace and quiet. He became instead one of the titanic short-track racers of his time and place.

Long after his own brilliant career had ended, Pete Hamilton marveled about the natural gifts only the best drivers seemed to possess. Hamilton said, "When you take a good race car—a beautiful, perfect, shiny race car that goes like stink—and you [add] a driver who's really good, *magic* happens." And Bill Wimble, added Pete, "did things that I never thought were possible."

He looked like a math teacher, or maybe a farmer. Instead, Bill Wimble was a stock car champion. (Bob Hunter Photo, Gater Racing News *Archive)*

Though Wimble preferred dirt tracks—blacktop, he said, made for "tip-toe racing"—he sure had Utica-Rome figured out. In '67, steering the same Rosner car his McCredy team had unveiled the previous year, Wimble grabbed a Modified track championship to go with the Utica-Rome Sportsman title he'd earned in '66. He won two 30-lap features, one on Memorial Day weekend and the other on July 30.

But his real trick in 1967 was also winning championships at Albany-Saratoga, his Friday track, and Fonda, his Saturday home.

"Think about what he accomplished," says former Utica-Rome owner Dick Waterman, Wimble's friend of nearly 50 years. "One of those tracks, Fonda, was dirt. The other two were asphalt, but they each had different configurations. Yet he won all three championships, over some great drivers.

"Bill could drive anything, anywhere. If he ran a place long enough, sooner or later he'd be the track champ."

Wimble himself, ever modest, says of 1967, "It was always a goal of mine to win three [titles] in one season. That year the stars were properly aligned, and it happened. And now it's a nice memory for me."

~

Yes, there was only one Bill Wimble. But Utica-Rome, as if trying to produce a matched set of anachronistic champions, served up smiling Bernie Miller as its Sportsman titlist. Miller was already a veteran, having started at old Vernon Downs, and over a long career his sunny disposition graced pit areas up and down the East Coast. But Utica-Rome, just up the road from his place in Canastota, was home. He had played around in the Late Models, but by 1965 he was tooling around in a nifty Sportsman coupe. And in '67, that trusty coupe, bearing the #41 that would amount to a Miller trademark, was constantly floating around the top half of the Utica-Rome finishing order.

His best finishes were a pair of thirds and a couple of fourths, but Bernie's secret was that he always got to the checkered flag. Sixth, ninth, seventh, sixth again, he'd be just out of the spotlight but piling up the points.

Today on the north side of 80 years old, Miller cherishes one bit of 1967 trivia. "They ran the Modifieds and the Sportsman cars together, and of course Bill Wimble was the Modified champion. But, you know, I actually had more points than Bill did. I was pretty proud of that."

His memory is as sharp as his driving was: Miller finished with 764 points, Wimble 734.

"That," says Bernie, "was a great year."

~

Left: No one scored more points in Utica-Rome's 1967 season than the track's Sportsman kingpin, friendly Bernie Miller. (Bob Hunter Photo)

Bottom: Quiet, ambitious, and gifted. Those three words sum up NASCAR's 1967 national Sportsman champion, Pete Hamilton. (John Grady Photo, Alan Weaver Collection)

Fran Kitchen won twice at Utica-Rome in 1967. At the top of his game, Kitchen showed he could beat the best. (Rod Nacewicz Collection)

Speaking of great Sportsman years, let's get back to Pete Hamilton. It was in 1967 that he won NASCAR's national Sportsman title, which led indirectly to a Grand National (now Sprint Cup) ride in 1968. Another Flemke acolyte, Hamilton made a handful of Utica-Rome appearances in '67. In his strongest run, he was lying third in an August 100-lapper, with the white flag waving, when his engine blew.

Unlike Don MacTavish and Ernie Gahan the previous year, Hamilton ran Utica-Rome only "if we were really pressing things." Leading the standings all season, his team usually called it a Sunday after Thompson's afternoon program. And that was fine with Pete, who liked Utica-Rome but says, "Those Thompson-to-Utica runs were just insane."

Hamilton's mentor, meanwhile, didn't seem to mind a weekly dose of crazy. Though never a points-chaser, Ed Flemke simply loved to race. In 1967, he and the owner of his Modified ride, Bob Judkins, wore their own grooves in the Massachusetts Turnpike and the New York Thruway, pulling off the Sunday double so often that Flemke finished the season in the top 10 at both tracks. "They'd hold up the consolation race at Utica-Rome if they knew we were coming," Judkins recalls.

Once again, Flemke was the track's top winner. He and the Judkins #2X, one of pavement Modified racing's great combinations, grabbed 100-lappers in June, July, and August, and stole a regular show in June when a lapped car forced leader Gahan wide on lap 27 of 30.

~

The season's biggest shock came early. On opening day, a veteran named Fran Kitchen, known for his scattered dirt-track successes, hauled his brand-new Modified to Utica-Rome, thinking it might make a fine pavement car. Kitchen, from Clinton, New York, was right on the money. At day's end he was posing for the winner's photo, having beaten Kenny Shoemaker, Miller, Ray Sitterly, and Frank Mathalia.

The area diehards knew Kitchen, but he was hardly a tip-of-your-tongue name with the blacktop set. More than a few folks were stunned. Well, darned if Fran

Calm Faces in Exciting Times

In 1967, Sonney Seamon took the first two victories of his Utica-Rome Modified/Sportsman career. (Alan Weaver Collection)

Kitchen didn't do it again. Though he ran Utica-Rome only sporadically, on July 16 he was back in victory lane after topping Don Wayman, popular Dick Clark, Andy Romano, and Cook.

Sonney Seamon also scored twice, the first Modified/Sportsman wins of a career that was quickly picking up speed. Sonney's initial checkered came on June 18, over Flemke and Lou Lazzaro. He won again on Sept. 10, topping Dick Fowler, another guy on the rise.

Other weekly-show winners included Lazzaro, Gahan, and Rene Charland, plus a lovable rogue from Chepachet, Rhode Island, named George Pendergast.

Every bit the charmer, Pendergast could talk his way into a free meal or a car owner's wallet. But wave a green flag, and he got serious. On June 18 he'd had second place sewn up before being taken out by a lapped car on the final corner. One week later, on June 25, George beat Richie Evans, the great Pete Corey, and his own best friend among his fellow drivers, Billy Harman.

~

Lost to the filing gods are several 1967 support-division results, as well as the champions for the Late Model and Figure 8 classes. What is known is that Late Model wins went to Don O'Neil, Ron Newman, Ron Fazio, and three-timer Buddy Thurston.

Figure 8 winners included Glenn Forward, Ralph Holmes, and Jim Bechy, the latter a future Utica-Rome promoter.

~

Best remembered as the coupe era's smiling clown prince, George Pendergast could also mash the gas. (Alan Weaver Collection)

The 1967 New Yorker 400 marked the second edition in which the overall victor did not win one of the 200-lap segments. Instead the big trophy went to Canadian hero Jean-Paul Cabana, third in the first segment (behind Dave Kotary and Flemke) and fifth in the second (behind MacTavish, Bugs Stevens, Wimble, and Cook). Though best remembered as a Late Model star, Cabana was an outstanding Modified/Sportsman driver, shining in coupe events throughout Vermont and Quebec.

That runner-up finish in the nightcap marked the first top-five run for Stevens at Utica-Rome. Born Carl Berghman in Massachusetts but afraid of being caught racing while AWOL from Lackland Air Force Base in Texas, he mated his schoolyard nickname to the surname of a pal. Forever more, he drove as Bugs Stevens. What lured him to Utica-Rome was the same thing that lured Charland, Gahan, MacTavish, and Hamilton: NASCAR points. Bugsy was sailing toward the first of three straight national Modified titles.

The segment winners, MacTavish and Kotary, were very different young men. The fiery Kotary had won at Utica-Rome in 1965, but his best result since had been a second to Flemke in June of '67. By September he was a tightly coiled spring. His wife, Betty, says, "He was so competitive. He had to win, or else."

Sometimes, even that wasn't enough. As he recalls that '67 New Yorker 400, there is tension in Dave's voice. "I set fast time, started on the pole, and won the first 200," he says. "So I started in the rear for the second race. Got up to third or fourth, and had a right-rear tire go flat."

Still disgusted, he mutters, "The ones that got away…"

In contrast, MacTavish, that '66 Sportsman title behind him, had throttled back a bit. With his services now in demand, he jumped into a variety of cars before landing in Len Bosley's L&R Speed Shop coupe. A strong summer lifted Mac toward an eventual runner-up finish in the 1967 national Modified standings. His fight to establish himself had been won. These may have been the most carefree days of his life.

On Sept. 23, Utica-Rome's season ended with a rare Saturday-night event, a 150-lap NASCAR special. Don MacTavish won that, too.

~

Top: Dave Kotary, wired for speed, might have swept both New Yorker segments if not for a flat tire in the second half. (Rod Nacewicz Collection)

The 1967 season ended with a 150-lap special event, topped by freewheeling Don MacTavish. (John Grady Photo)

MacTavish also starred in what became a lasting memory for a young driver just beginning to make a name for himself. It happened right there at Utica-Rome, and the lad's name was Dave Lape.

Still a teenager from Canajoharie honing the dirt-track skills that would make him famous, Lape had begun to dabble in pavement racing. Almost immediately, he poked his nose into Utica-Rome's star-studded top five. In May of '67 he finished fourth twice, and on July 30 he was a terrific second, just behind Wimble.

One night, for reasons long forgotten, he showed up without a ride. MacTavish was wheeling the L&R in the evening's 100-lapper, but had brought along his Circle J coupe.

"I stopped to talk with him," Lape recalls, "and he said, 'Hey, you want to drive this car?' So I did. What I remember most is that the seat was falling out of the damn thing! I'd go into the corner and the seat would tip up on its side, then settle back down on the straightaway. I don't know how I made it the whole race like that, but I finished 10th."

Grinning broadly, Lape says, "I thought I did pretty good, and I remember thinking, 'Wow, maybe I'll get paid something!' Nope. Mac was like, 'Thanks, kid. See ya later.'

"But what a great night, and what a great thing for me to remember. I mean, I can say I ran the Circle J."

~

Fantastic times! So thrilling were those Utica-Rome nights that the inevitable adrenaline crash could leave you spent, drained. Elton Hill and his car owner, Darrell McClelland, often found themselves unable to complete their 240-mile ride home to Connecticut.

"I can't tell you how many times I slept on park benches along the New York Thruway," says Hill. "Our truck had a bench seat, but Darrell and I couldn't both sleep there. So I'd just climb out and lay down on those benches."

1968
The Mayor of Vernon Center

After 1967, NASCAR decided that it made little sense to have two divisions race together—with cars identical except to the mechanically trained eye—and killed off the Sportsman coupe. It was a logical move. Few tracks had run Modifieds only, or Sportsman cars only; most had chosen instead to combine them, as did Utica-Rome in 1966 and '67. But this could get a bit confusing, especially for casual fans. How, they must have wondered, could the fellow who had just finished fourth have actually "won" anything? And what was this business about two different sets of points?

A combo platter of chassis knowledge and driving talent, Sonney Seamon was a hero to area fans and racers. (John Grady Photo, Rod Nacewicz Collection)

From 1968 onward, the open-wheeled NASCAR stock cars once known as Modified/Sportsman cars were now simply called Modifieds, with one set of rules. No longer would tracks in the Northeast go through the strange ritual of crowning two separate but equal champions.

So when the engines went silent to close the 1968 Utica-Rome season, there was only one man of the hour. And, oh, what a happy hour that was.

~

Clayton "Sonney" Seamon wore a frown when serious and a wide smile when having fun. Whichever way he happened to be leaning, he gave it his all. In 1968, his all was good enough for a Utica-Rome championship.

In '67, Seamon won twice in placing second to Bernie Miller in the track's Sportsman standings. Though he failed to win a single feature in '68, he was as predictable as a rooster. Counting the twin 200-lappers that made up the New Yorker 400, Utica-Rome hosted 16 Modified features in 1968; Sonney finished in the top five in 10 of them. And he was on the gas, not cruising for points: On May 26, he ran second in both ends of a double-feature program. That 0 in his win column could easily have been a 2.

By finishing fourth and second in those two New Yorker segments, he clinched the title by four points over Lou Lazzaro. He was a popular champ. Even Junior Bianco, Louie's wrench, says, "Everybody loved Sonney."

He lived up to his nickname: The Mayor of Vernon Center.

Though his Modified career was still young, two things about Seamon had made a quick impression. One was his innate mechanical skill; already he was welding together cars that could run with those built by some of the Northeast's brightest minds. "Sonney was a lot like an Eddie Flemke," says former driver Andy Romano, paying Seamon a high Modified compliment. "He came up with a lot of his own ideas, and they worked."

And then there was Sonney's driving. The man was fearless.

"One of the gutsiest drivers I ever saw," says Dick Waterman. "Nothing scared him. Sonney could crash his car, then laugh it off and build himself another one."

Waterman is quick to add this: "He also had tremendous ability."

~

In 1968, the Utica-Rome guard was changing. Fewer New England cars showed up. The NASCAR-sanctioned Thompson Speedway was running more night races, so Vernon saw less of guys like Flemke—the track's biggest winner to that point—and Don MacTavish. For the first time since the track was built, the NASCAR national champion had not a single top-five finish at Utica-Rome. Bugs Stevens, en route to his second Modified crown, made a few appearances, but his late arrivals and subsequent tail-end starts hurt his results.

Only one New Englander captured a Utica-Rome victory, and he was almost an honorary New Yorker. Rene Charland, who had visited Utica-Rome when it was only a clearing, suffered through a miserable season at the track he once ruled. By mid-summer, he hadn't finished in the top five. But thanks to all those lousy nights and a handicapping system that started the top cars toward the rear, Rene had the pole for a 30-lapper on July 14. He led the whole way, stopping a final lunge by the fast-closing Lazzaro.

The gap between asphalt Modifieds and dirt Modifieds was growing wider. Specialty cars were clearly the coming wave. For hired-gun drivers like Charland,

Though he continued his winning ways elsewhere, 1968 marked the last Utica-Rome triumph for Rene "The Champ" Charland. (Bob Hunter Photo)

On June 9, 1968, Bernie Miller won over Cook, Evans, Lazzaro, and Flemke. "Pretty good group," said Bernie. (John Grady Photo)

that meant either finding a deep-pockets owner, or choosing one surface over the other. More and more, Rene was tilting toward the dirt. In 1967, he had won six features at Fonda, five of them in a row. Most of his future glory, which was considerable, would also come on dirt tracks.

He kept wandering more than most drivers, making occasional pavement Modified appearances well into the 1970s and, for a time, running Late Models with the NASCAR North series, where he was the darling of French-Canadian fans. But that July evening in 1968 marked the 19th and final Utica-Rome victory of Rene Charland's wonderful career.

In the eyes of many Vernon fans, he will always be The Champ.

~

This shortage of out-of-state invaders had an upside: Sunday after Sunday, the winner's circle was filled with New Yorkers. Most were veterans: Lazzaro took 30-lappers on May 26 and June 2; dirt ace Don Wayman showed his pavement chops by winning on July 7; Jerry Cook, now roaming more than ever in a hint of his upcoming NASCAR national assaults, won on Aug, 25; and Bernie Miller, the previous year's Sportsman champ, took his first-ever Utica-Rome feature on June 9, defeating Cook, Richie Evans, Lazzaro, and Flemke. "Pretty good group," Bernie chuckles in retrospect.

But the spotlight also shined on some new faces. New Hartford's Dick Fowler and Rome's Kenny Platt, both up from the Late Models, collected trophies. Romano won a dazzling Lou Smith Memorial 100 in June, holding off Cook and Evans as they rushed toward the waving checkered flag.

It was the first multi-win season at Utica-Rome for Evans, and the only one for Dave Kotary. On June 23, Kotary led the final lap of a 30-lap main that runner-up Bill Henry is still rerunning. "I was leading," Henry laments, "but I got a little sideways out of turn two, and David got by me." On Aug. 11, in a 50-lapper, Kotary

Richie Evans, fired from the Wright-Zautner #24, redeemed himself with two Utica-Rome wins in his own coupe. (John Grady Photo)

took home the trophy after what the papers called "a lap-after-lap duel with veteran Lou Lazzaro."

Evans had a rollercoaster season. Early on, he thought he'd caught a break when he accepted a ride in the Wright-Zautner coupe after its owners, to the surprise of many, sacked Kenny Shoemaker. But Richie's stay in the car was brief; he was soon replaced by MacTavish. "That's the only time I ever got fired," Evans would grin many years and many championships later, anytime someone mentioned his stint in the white #24. But in 1968, struggling financially, he was not smiling about having to return to his own orange coupe, by then carrying the number 6. Still, he beat his pal Seamon to the checkers on May 26, and won a second 30-lapper on July 28, this time edging Dave Lape.

~

The sentimental moment of '68 came on Aug. 4, when flashbulbs illuminated the great Pete Corey. Dark and enigmatic, Corey was that rarest of individuals, a legend in his own time. A maestro on dirt, he had won the 1955 National Open at Langhorne, Pennsylvania, precursor to the Race of Champions. Two years later he was the champ at his home track, Fonda Speedway. In the spring of '60, he lost a leg in a gruesome Fonda wreck, and many assumed his career had reached its end. But this was a man of extraordinary grit. He came back to earn Fonda titles in 1965 and '66, and won multiple features at Lebanon Valley and Stafford Springs, Connecticut.

His influence was huge. "Pete was my man," says Lape, whose paint schemes for years paid homage to the #22 cars Corey drove for owner Bob Whitbeck.

Eyeing new challenges, Corey began mixing more asphalt racing into his late-'60s repertoire. His only win at Utica-Rome—over Cook, Miller, Seamon, and Lazzaro—capped an incredible weekend; he had also won at Albany-Saratoga, and finished second at Fonda.

"People forget, because he was so great on the dirt," Lape says. "But Pete was also a really good pavement driver."

~

On Sunday evening, June 23, Chuck LeRicheux, one of the four partners who in 1964 had purchased the Utica-Rome Speedway from Joe Lesik, was taking tickets and greeting incoming fans at the front gate when he told a co-worker he felt ill. The co-worker suggested he sit and rest. LeRicheux walked a few yards, then was felled by a heart attack.

"I told him the [track] ambulance was coming to take him to the hospital," Waterman recalls. "This will tell you what kind of a guy he was: He said, 'No, you can't do that, because without the ambulance you won't be able to run.' Trying to humor him and keep him calm, I told him we'd have an intermission while he was gone."

Charles. E. LeRicheux, 50, died before reaching the hospital.

~

All summer, the local headlines blared the names of Norm Moyer and Buddy Thurston, tops in the Late Model field. When they were done swapping paint and victories, Moyer was the 1968 champion. And a new beginner's class called Chargers spiced up the weekly program. Bob Engler, like Modified champ Seamon a Vernon guy, wore that division's crown.

~

Lou Lazzaro could be beaten, but he couldn't be worn down. That was clear going back to 1962, when the big fellow won a Utica-Rome 150. In '63, of course, he took the first New Yorker 400, run straight through, no resting. The coupes of the day were tall, heavy, and unwieldy. Lazzaro wrestled them, and won.

By 1968 and the eighth annual New Yorker, the Modifieds had grown more sophisticated, but not by much. They were lower, their tires were wider, but

Nothing was beyond Pete Corey's grasp. A renowned dirt chauffeur, he scored on the blacktop at Utica-Rome and Malta in 1968. (Rod Nacewicz Collection)

The Mayor of Vernon Center

Lou Lazzaro swept both ends of the 1968 New Yorker 400, proving yet again that no one was tougher. (John Grady Photo, Rod Nacewicz Collection)

they remained crude, straight-axle warhorses. And Lazzaro could still make them do as he pleased.

On Labor Day weekend he was the fastest qualifier, and led every circuit of the first 200-lap segment, topping Flemke, Miller, Seamon, and Connecticut's versatile Ron Narducci. Though few drivers would have admitted it at the time, most welcomed the short mid-race pause.

"That halfway break refreshed everybody," says Miller. "It let us do some work on the cars, of course, but it was a good break for the driver."

If Lazzaro needed a break, it never showed. When the call came to return to the track, he slid back through the window of his maroon #4 and went back to work. He started 22nd, but rode a high, handsome line toward the front. By lap 150 he was sitting pretty, running second to Troy's Phil Spiak, very quick on this night. Then, on lap 172, Spiak's engine blew. Lazzaro inherited the lead, and beat Seamon, Fred Harbach, Narducci, and Fowler.

Lou's friends called him "Monk," a playful swipe at his premature baldness. On Sept. 1, 1968, the smart folks called him Mr. Lazzaro.

1969

Distant Tragedy, Local Sorrow, and Healing

For many in the Northeast, the 1969 season could not arrive soon enough. February had dealt a crushing blow: Don MacTavish, the 1967 NASCAR Sportsman champion and a winner at Utica-Rome and tracks across New England and New York, died in a Late Model Sportsman crash at Daytona. Just 26 years old, MacTavish had a young, enthusiastic following. He was also admired by his peers, who saw that he was more than just a helmet-carrying kid with a heavy right foot. Mac was a dirty-hands guy, wrenching his title-winning Circle J and, later, the L&R coupe.

1969 dawned with a devastating blow, the February death of Don MacTavish at Daytona. (Dick Berggren Collection)

All these years later, he remains highly regarded. "Don was a very talented driver," remembers Andy Romano. "But he was also an excellent fabricator. In fact, he built a car for me when he worked at L&R."

Somehow—who knows why?—roaring engines and cheering crowds always manage to salve this sport's deepest emotional wounds. Just as the Irish have their celebratory wakes, so do racing people gather, hoping to remember and to forget. But in 1969, winter would not let go. It stayed raw and damp well into April. Occasionally, the chill was broken by a bit of news. First Utica-Rome announced a purse increase; the Modified winner would now bank $500. Then Bill Wimble, so long a fixture in victory lanes around the region, announced his retirement. Dick Waterman promptly hired Wimble to join the Utica-Rome staff, assisting chief steward Ralph Ouderkirk. But what people needed was racing. Noise. Laps. Healing.

Finally, on the first week of May, came relief. Friday night at Albany-Saratoga, Jerry Cook beat Richie Evans and Lou Lazzaro in the Modified feature. Two days later, everyone reconvened in Vernon for the Utica-Rome opener, and after 30 laps the results were the same: Cook, Evans, Lazzaro.

For these short bursts, grief was put aside. Spring had sprung.

~

Cook was on his game as the 1960s closed. In '68, he had picked up the Hollebrand Trucking sponsorship he would carry through the rest of his career. For a racer like Jerry who captained his own ship, Pete Hollebrand was the perfect benefactor, a hands-off guy, more sportsman than sponsor. Hollebrand simply liked to see his cars do well, and, in the hands of drivers like Steve Danish, Jeep Herbert, and Ed Ortiz, they had done very well.

And they sure did well with Cook aboard. With his trademark consistency and a fierce persistence, he earned the 1969 Utica-Rome title. Counting that season opener, Jerry won three scrappy 30-lappers. And, as is always the case with championships, what mattered was how he did when he wasn't winning: four runner-up finishes, a third, some fourths and fifths …

It was also in 1969 that Cook announced his presence on the national scene, popping up everywhere

Right: One of Modified racing's unsung heroes, Pete Hollebrand, backed Jerry Cook to six NASCAR national titles and the 1969 Utica-Rome championship. (Rod Nacewicz Collection)

Bottom: The Cook brigade, loaded up and ready for the road. Next stop? Anywhere on the NASCAR Modified map! (John Grady Photo)

Lazzaro leads 'em through turn four on the tight, flat Vernon bullring. (Ron Ingraham Collection)

from Daytona (where he finished fifth in that tragic Sportsman race) to Martinsville (where he topped a 500-lap Modified grind) to Fonda (where in August he took the last of his seven career wins.)

At season's end, Cook was second in the NASCAR national points. He would play a role in the championship chase for the next 13 seasons.

~

All year, the amazing Lazzaro did what he did best: He amazed. Lou won seven times at Malta, went 11-for-16 at Fonda, and took both track titles. In a single August week he won five times: two at the Monroe County Fair, both halves of an Albany-Saratoga twinbill, and a Utica-Rome feature.

In all, Monk drove to eight Utica-Rome wins, including a sweep of the track's extra-distance races. In June he beat Cook in a 100-lapper, and in August, over the same distance, he held back Bugs Stevens. And on Labor Day weekend—again!—Louie and his trusty coupe drove all comers into the ground in the New Yorker 400. Just as he had done in '68, he set fast time and then won both 200-lap halves.

You can break down Lazzaro's 1968-69 New Yorker numbers any way you like. Toss them all into a cup, shake them like dice, spill them onto a table, and every roll looks impressive. There he is, leading every lap of those opening 200s; there he is again, twice outqualifying quality fields; there is his wrinkled coupe, dispatching of shiny rivals across 800 hard laps; there's Lazzaro in those two rugged nightcaps, starting 22nd in 1968 and 26th in '69 and passing everybody. This was a giant at play.

Three men in the '69 New Yorker had great results. Rebel invader Jimmy Hensley, chasing NASCAR points, finished the twin features second and third; Stevens was third and fourth; and Perk Brown, pride of Eden, North Carolina, collected two fifths. Brown and Hensley had hauled in from South Boston, Virginia, having finished second and third in another 400-lapper on Saturday night. But, hey, Lazzaro had a busy weekend, too. On Friday he'd beaten Stevens, and everybody else, at Albany-Saratoga.

~

Billy Hensley (23) and Perk Brown, were among the Southern stars who hauled from Dixie to Utica-Rome's special events. (John Grady Photos)

One of the biggest Utica-Rome stories of 1969 concerned a guy who barely ran there. Richie Evans finished second in the May 4 opener, got snowed out the next Sunday, and on May 18 won a heat race before rains postponed the feature. On May 25, it rained again. On one of those wet Sundays, Evans scrambled to Fulton Speedway for an open-competition Modified show.

Running an unsanctioned "outlaw" track in conflict with a NASCAR event had long been considered a punishable offense by the law in Daytona Beach. In the 1950s and early '60s, drivers got around this by painting their cars in watercolors and racing under nicknames, some bordering on the ridiculous. When entering non-NASCAR events, the great Jeep Herbert claimed to be Pete Moss, Flex Hose, or Bob Alou. In his earliest Modified days, Evans sometimes used the name Milt Carpenter, borrowed from a kid who pumped gas at Richie's Shell station in Rome.

Waterman says, "I don't think there was a driver who didn't sneak off once in a while." He jokes that when raindrops fell at the outlaw tracks, "you'd see the whitewash coming off the cars."

By the late '60s, things had eased a bit. So when Utica-Rome rained out, Evans never considered that running Fulton might cause problems. Nor, apparently, did anyone else suspect trouble. According to Evans crewman Wilbur Jones, "a bunch of" Utica-Rome regulars made the trip.

Evans won at Fulton. The next day, he learned he'd been suspended from NASCAR. No other drivers were disciplined.

Normally these matters were resolved through a fine, a loss of points, or a contrite apology. Evans, not at all contrite, took another course of action. He painted the word "outlaw" on the tail of his coupe, and for nearly three full seasons ran every unsanctioned race he could. Hauling to Fulton most Sundays, he did not return to Utica-Rome until September of 1971.

Richie Evans was big news at Utica-Rome, but not for winning. In 1969, he began serving a lengthy NASCAR suspension. (John Grady Photo)

Evans was popular, and he was gone. Many of his fans were, too. The episode "hurt us," admits Waterman. "There's no getting around that."

Though still a staunch NASCAR supporter, Waterman says, "If I had it all to do over again, that's one thing I'd do differently. I'd have let those guys go wherever they wanted to, with my blessing."

~

With seven races lost to weather, another to electrical woes—"a light pole that started sending off sparks," the papers said—and the dominance of Lazzaro and Cook, Modified trophies were in short supply. Bernie Miller and Sonney Seamon each got one. So did veteran Jerry Pennock, who in late August won a barnburner of a 30-lapper over Dave Lape. It was the only Utica-Rome victory of Pennock's fine career, though he took five at Fonda.

The support divisions continued to evolve. Don VanSlyke of Durhamville was the Charger division king, while Geneva's Al Golley was the boss in the Mini-Stock class.

The Northeast Midget Association breezed in for an August show, won by Massachusetts hero Dave Humphrey. But the local press paid more attention to Lou Fray, who flipped in turn one. Briefly pinned in his car, Fray "was pried loose and put in an ambulance, but escaped serious injury and was not taken to the hospital."

~

Racing flagmen are like baseball umpires: Nobody pays them any mind until they make a bad call. It's a compliment, therefore, to say that John Tallini's work at Utica-Rome went mostly unnoticed.

Tallini worked at the track so long he seemed to become part of the place. First hired by Joe Lesik, he remained on the starter's perch until 1978. Initially Tallini was assistant starter, but he had a long stint as flagger-in-chief. He popped up everywhere across the '60s and '70s, twirling his silks regularly at Albany-Saratoga and Riverside Park, and made spot appearances in flagstands from Quebec to Florida. But, always, he saw Utica-Rome as his home.

Years after his retirement, Tallini discussed his career with writer Ron Hedger, and Hedger couldn't resist asking what it was like to have flagged the New Yorker 400. Tallini replied, "It was horrible."

Surprised? Don't be. In those 400-lappers, the starter and his assistant were essentially on their own, with little communication and no scoreboard to guide them. Tallini counted laps on a hand-held clicker.

Six months before his death in 2007, John Tallini was inducted into the New York State Stock Car Association Hall of Fame.

~

Starter John Tallini (right) shared Utica-Rome's victory lane with any number of legends, among them Jerry Cook. (Mary Ellen Higley Collection)

Distant Tragedy, Local Sorrow, and Healing

Three-time NASCAR national Modified champion Bugs Stevens, seated in the Len Boehler #3, frequently visited Utica-Rome. (Dick Berggren Collection)

give a damn what his car looked like. He'd let dents and dings go untouched, but he'd spend hours tweaking the chassis or his homebuilt engine. And in 1969, Bugsy Stevens and Lenny's #3, which didn't look like much of a car, won their third straight NASCAR national Modified title.

Two trophies already on the mantle and another one on the way, Bugsy was right where NASCAR champions belonged: battling for the win at Utica-Rome.

One summer night—evidence suggests it was Aug. 3, 1969—a high school student from Edmeston took his seat in the bleachers behind Tallini. The kid's name was Paul Jensen, and he grew up to become a four-time champion on the Utica-Rome dirt track. But still fresh in his mind is the night he got his first look at a genuine asphalt Modified icon.

"It was a big show, maybe a 100-lapper," says Paul. "A guy sitting near us said, 'Keep your eye on that number 3. Watch him go.' Well, I saw the car he was talking about, a blue coupe. To be honest, it didn't look like much of a car, but I paid attention anyway. Did that car win the race? No. But was it fast? Oh, man."

Here, Jensen grins. "That was the first I'd ever heard of Bugs Stevens."

The blue coupe was owned by a backyard genius from Massachusetts named Len Boehler. Cost-conscious and wonderfully eccentric—he wore second-hand work shirts, so the name sewn above his breast pocket might be George, Bill, or Tom—Boehler didn't

1970

Heroes, Anti-Heroes, and Underdogs

An anti-hero, the Oxford English Dictionary tells us, is "a central character in a story or drama who noticeably lacks conventional heroic attributes." Webster's describes an underdog as the "expected loser in a contest or struggle," or "one in a disadvantageous position."

Throw together a bunch of these characters, and you have the makings of a fine short-track program. Of course, you'll need a hero, too.

What's that? You want to know what a hero is? Well, if it's 1970 and you're standing in the pits at Utica-Rome Speedway, there's an easy answer. Just go look at the guy in car #4, the maroon coupe with the wide ribbon of white on its flanks.

Lou Lazzaro, there's a hero.

Lou Lazzaro won four features, one of them a 100-lapper, in collecting his second track title. (John Grady Photo, Rod Nacewicz Collection)

According to *Gater Racing News*, New York's weekly short-track bible, Utica-Rome's crowd on Sept. 6, 1970 was "standing-room-only, the largest of the season." Those fans witnessed the most celebrated anti-hero triumph in Modified history. That Sunday, a car owner banished by NASCAR, not even allowed to set foot in the Utica-Rome pit area, unloaded his equipment and set up camp in the parking lot. His driver, very much welcome and quite amused by the whole thing, flashed his pit pass for the gate guard each time he headed toward the track to practice, qualify, and race.

Several hours later, keeping up with events over the public-address loudspeaker from his dark and dusty makeshift pit, the car owner listened as his driver, Ed Flemke, took the overall victory in the New Yorker 400.

The car owner's name was Richie Evans. Did he lack "conventional heroic attributes"? Did he ever. Evans had turned his 1969 NASCAR suspension into a defection, spending the better part of two seasons piling up victories at outlaw tracks like Fulton, Lancaster, and Spencer.

Tweaking NASCAR had become sport for the driver announcers were calling the Rapid Roman. When he won an All Star League race at Albany-Saratoga, what delighted him most was that right behind him came Bugs Stevens, the three-time defending NASCAR national champion. And while he was off running open-competition shows, Evans often sent a backup car to NASCAR tracks for his friend Flemke to drive. In August at Utica-Rome, Flemke steered an Evans coupe to victory in the Utica Club Beer 100, beating Fred DeSarro, the NASCAR national points leader and eventual champion, by a bumper.

On Saturday night, Sept. 5, Evans drove his orange Modified, now carrying #61, to a Lancaster Speedway win. Then he hustled back to Rome to finish preparations for the next night's New Yorker 400.

That Sunday evening, Flemke and the backup #61 were on rails, setting fast time in qualifying. In the opening 200, Steady Eddie beat DeSarro, Dave Lape, Robbie Kotary and Rene Charland. The halftime inversion placed Flemke 24th when the green waved for the second segment. He passed everyone but Lazzaro, who had started up front. Kotary finished third, followed by Virginia's Gerald Compton and Dick Fowler. Flemke's average finish made him the New Yorker 400 champion.

Strange, but true: Eddie Flemke really did win the New Yorker 400 despite his Evans team being banished to the parking lot! (John Grady Photo)

1970 was a great season for Dick Fowler, whose two Utica-Rome victories aided his top-five finish in the national standings. (Rod Nacewicz Collection)

Evans and his team were unable to join Flemke for the victory photos, but they did get a head start on the post-race fun. "Boy," recalls crewman Donny Marcello, "did we ever party that night!"

It would be another year before Evans returned to Utica-Rome as a driver. But, in an interesting twist, Maynard Troyer, another prominent outlaw, officially joined NASCAR to compete in the 1970 New Yorker. Down the road, he also would win big in Vernon.

~

Lazzaro's heroic season won him four Utica-Rome features and the track championship. His past success in extra-distance events had earned Louie a deserved reputation as a thinking racer, a survivor, but he could get scrappy when he had to. Three of his victories came in short 30-lappers, those quick dust-ups that favored the daring over the deliberate. Each time, he out-punched a different rival: Jerry Cook on June 14, Lape on Aug. 2, Charland on Aug. 23. But Lazzaro hadn't lost his edge in the marathons. On July 5, in a hot 100-lapper, he took the measure of Cook, Robbie Kotary, surprise New England entrant George Rettew, and Andy Romano.

The scuffle for the track crown was a dandy. Cook led the standings as summer arrived, but Lazzaro closed the gap by elbowing his way past Cookie to win that July 100. The following week, Cook slid over the third-turn banking while Lazzaro finished fourth. July 19 should have been a huge break for Lazzaro, since Cook was elsewhere chasing national points, but The Monk's #4 failed him and he had to bum a strange ride for the feature, finishing 11th. At the close of that evening, Cook led the standings by 18 points. But Lazzaro won on Aug. 2, tying things up. He never again slipped out of the points lead.

It was Lazzaro's second Utica-Rome title, and it was cheered by the Vernon faithful. "The fans loved Louie," says crewman Junior Bianco. "See, a lot of drivers would take off right after the races on Sundays, because they lived far away and some of them had to work in the morning. But Louie would stay late and sign autographs for anybody who came by."

Fowler, too, was a favorite. Though fondly recalled as a party guy from the Evans mold, he was also a solid racer. He opened the Utica-Rome season in style, beating Flemke in a 100-lapper on May 3, then won again on July 12. He was also strong at Plattsburgh and Malta. Finding himself well placed in NASCAR's national standings, Fowler now did some serious points-chasing. At season's end he was an outstanding fifth in the national rundown, behind DeSarro, Cook, Bernie Miller, and Flemke. "Dick was a good competitor," says Romano. "In that period, he was tough to beat."

Andy Romano, tough wherever he went, copped his second career NASCAR Modified main at Utica-Rome in June of '68. (AARN Photo Archive)

Heroes, Anti-Heroes, and Underdogs

May 31 was a beauty if your heroes were named Kotary. First on the program was a 30-lap Modified show held over from a previous rainout, and Robbie Kotary won it. In the nightcap, again covering 30 laps, Robbie's nephew Dave took the checkers. "Pretty good night," smiles Dave Kotary.

Second to both Robbie and Dave on that night was Cook, by now a Rome resident himself. Fired up, Cook won the very next Sunday. "Jerry was a good guy to race with," Romano declares. "It seemed like I ran against him every night back then. We ran the pavement at Malta and Utica-Rome, the dirt at Fonda, and we both traveled with the All Star League."

Like Charland before him, Cook was nearing that Dirt vs. Asphalt crossroads. Some, like Romano, kept a foot in both camps, but that made less and less economic sense. Cook had been terrific on dirt, and Fonda had been good to him. But he began phasing out his dirt program, opting for blacktop. His career NASCAR numbers show what a wise decision that was.

Romano himself had some big nights in 1970, none bigger than June 28, when he won his second and final Utica-Rome feature. His first had come two years earlier, also on the last weekend in June. Andy, fast and popular, was the second-tier Romano in a three-generation family that gave up an awful lot of Sunday dinners to go racing at Utica-Rome.

~

What a year for underdogs! 1970 Mod winners included John Kollar (#10%), Ron Newman (#44), Ray Sitterly (#C-88), and Bill Henry. (John Grady Photos, Rod Nacewicz Collection)

When Buddy Thurston was hot, as he was in 1970, the Charger division was his domain. (Utica-Rome Archive)

On May 24, Johnstown's John Kollar figured out a way to wring 100 percent out of his #10% coupe, and he beat Al Clark and Lape in a 30-lap main. It was the only Utica-Rome victory of Kollar's career. On July 19, Ron Newman captured his first feature over Fowler and that pesky Kollar. One week later, on July 26, Oneida's Bill Henry and his sharp #28 outran Fowler and Amsterdam's Ray Sitterly. And in the final feature of the season, Sitterly scored his maiden victory, over Lazzaro, Lape, and Cook.

Yes, it was a heck of a year for underdogs.

Henry, whose tire tracks are all over that 1970 campaign, is a great story. He says he saw his first race at the old Brookfield Speedway at age six, "and I've loved racing ever since." He apprenticed in Late Models at Utica-Rome and Brewerton, then jumped up to the Modifieds. At various times he was a regular at Albany-Saratoga, Shangri-La, and Plattsburgh, and he sometimes wandered into New England and Canada. But Utica-Rome, just "six or eight miles" from his home, was Henry's base.

Though 1970 was his Utica-Rome high-water mark, Henry spent several years rubbing wheels with the Modified gods. There was the 30-lapper in 1971 when he finished between winner Cook and third-place Stevens, and the summer night in '73 when the top five was Evans, Seamon, Troyer, Bill Henry, and Stevens.

"I was racing with the best," he says, his voice proud. "I was *there*."

As much as the competition, Henry loved the camaraderie. "On Sundays, six or eight [competitors] would stop at my place on the way to the track. Doc Blanchard, Andy Romano, Bruce Dostal, a lot of guys. We'd have a cookout and talk about wherever we'd raced the night before. We were all good friends.

"Take a guy like Sonney Seamon. I had always had Sonney in my corner. Not only did he build my cars, but when we used to haul down to Shangri-La we would double-tow, with his car on his truck and my car behind it on the trailer."

Bill's son, Scott Henry, eventually married the former Diane Seamon, daughter of Sonney and his wife, Rita. They met, as you'd guess, at Utica-Rome Speedway.

~

Heroes, Anti-Heroes, and Underdogs

Vernon's Buddy Thurston had always been quick in the Charger division, but by 1970 he had learned to blend in just the right amount of cool. Good thing. There he was, leading the points on the final weekend of the year, when it became clear that many of his rivals were intent on squeezing every last bit of excitement out of the season. They seemed bent on smashing every last nut and bolt off one another's cars. Thurston throttled back. Of the 26 starters, only eight finished, and Buddy was among them. His common sense clinched him a champion's seat at the awards banquet.

The Mini-Stock points battle also went right down to the wire, with Al Golley emerging as the kingpin over Lou Lanza.

~

Seven of the scheduled 21 events on the Utica-Rome schedule were rained out, an ominous sign of things to come. The bad weather impacted promoter Dick Waterman, naturally. But get him going about those days, and he talks not about Mother Nature but about all the great racers he saw. All those heroes and anti-heroes, and all those wonderful underdogs.

Waterman says, "John Tallini told me he used to look down from his flagstand on the parade lap, and he'd realize that a lot of the cars in that Modified lineup had already won a feature somewhere else that same weekend. See, they all ran their different Friday and Saturday tracks, but we had 'em all on Sunday. We had the best."

EYEWITNESS
1966–1970: JUNIOR BIANCO

"I did whatever Louie asked me to do. I saw his first race and his last race, and just about everything in between"

NOTE: Across Lou Lazzaro's glorious career, there were three constants: maroon stock cars, most of them battle-scarred, all of them bearing the number 4; a German Shepherd named Blackie, Lou's traveling companion for so many seasons; and Peter "Junior" Bianco, perhaps Lazzaro's closest ally. As teenagers they hung out at Vinnie Maugeri's filling station in Utica, admiring the stock cars housed there. Once Lazzaro established himself as a driver, he found in Bianco a trusted sideman. Admittedly more a helper than a crew chief in the classic sense, Bianco says he did "whatever Louie asked me to do." These days, Junior holds court at his Utica garage, reminiscing about all those nights with Louie. "I saw his first race and his last race, and just about everything in between," Bianco says with a grin. "And they were all exciting." None more so, perhaps, than the four straight 200-lap segments Lazzaro won in sweeping the 1968 and '69 New Yorker 400s.

Let me tell you, those New Yorker 400 races at Utica-Rome were tough. You'd run 200 laps, then they'd invert the field and run 200 more. And in that period in the late '60s, everybody was there: Richie Evans, Bugsy Stevens, Ray Hendrick, Eddie Flemke, Jerry Cook, you name it. Those two years when Louie won everything—all four 200-lappers—that was really something. Just look at the people he beat! You had the best of the best there, that's for sure.

My favorite part of the New Yorker 400 was always watching the second race, when the fast guys started in the rear. Louie's secret was to just let 'em all get single-file around the bottom, because that little track was so tight, and then jump up there on the outside and pass 'em one at a time. While they were all trying to run the shortest way around, he spent the early laps of that second 200 cleaning a groove for himself, sweeping off the dust and the rubber marbles, and as soon as there was a good outside lane he'd really start rolling. You know, he'd even put a different gear in the car so it would help him keep up the momentum out there. He'd pass 'em all–*boom, boom, boom*–until he was up front, and then he was gone. Oh, man, that was fun to watch.

The other thing he had going for him was that he was very strong, and I mean physically strong. He'd been like that since we were kids. So he didn't get tired, not even in a race like that New Yorker 400, when the weather could be hot sometimes and you always had to deal with a lot of traffic. You know, blacktop is hard to drive, and in those days no one thought about things like power steering. You'd watch some of the guys toward the end of that race, and you could tell they were tired by the way their driving changed. Not Louie. He'd still be going strong. One time we asked him how he was feeling after that 400, and he just laughed. "I could go another 200 right now," he said. And he wasn't kidding.

Yes, we always had a good car for that race, but we also had the right driver. Louie was strong and he was smart, much smarter as a driver than a lot of people ever knew.

Still, that 400 was no picnic, ever. One year, we blew the clutch late in practice. At first we figured we were all done, but then we thought about it and decided maybe we had time to change it. We parked the car up on the trailer so we could work on it—guys crawling underneath it, on top of it, all around—and we pulled out the old clutch while Louie went down to his old garage on Herkimer Road to get another one. Got the new clutch in, bolted everything together with the motor and the transmission, and pushed the thing to get it running because we didn't have time to hook up a starter. Then Louie drove it onto the track and won the first race, and later on he won the second one. That's a long night.

Even if you *didn't* have problems, those 400-lappers were long nights. The only way you could make life easier for the whole team was if you set fast time in qualifying. That way, at least you got to start up front for the first race.

You know, Louie was always a driver who knew how he wanted his cars set up. He'd come into the pits–whether it was after practice or after a heat race or even after the first 200 laps at the New Yorker races–and he'd tell us what to do. It was always his call. I always figured he was the only guy who really knew how the car felt, because he was in the seat. In the pits, watching, we might *think* we know, but compared to a smart driver we don't really know what that car needs. So he'd come in and say, "Change the gear, turn that bolt," or whatever, and we'd just do it. And, you know, that usually worked out pretty good!

Louie was very good on both dirt and blacktop. People think of him as a dirt-tracker, but even way back in the '50s, when we were still fooling around with the six-cylinder classes, he raced a lot on blacktop at tracks like Brewerton Speedway. So when Utica-Rome opened up, running on the asphalt was no big deal for him, where for some of the guys—say, the ones who came over from Fonda—it was a whole new thing.

Lou Lazzaro was, as Junior Bianco notes, "very strong. He didn't get tired." (John Grady Photo)

Lazzaro had a loyal army, but none more faithful than Junior Bianco and Blackie, Lazzaro's longtime mascot. (Rod Nacewicz Collection)

Look at what he did on the asphalt at Utica-Rome and Albany-Saratoga. What can you say? He was just a natural race driver. In those days, you didn't come out of any driving schools. You didn't take *lessons*. You learned by racing, and if you had some success you kept going. Louie had so much natural ability. He never really had a super car, but yet he won at just about every track he went to.

When we started going to Utica-Rome, and right through most of the '60s, they didn't have dirt Modifieds and macadam Modifieds. You just had *Modifieds*, mostly coupes, plain and simple cars, and you ran 'em everywhere. We'd run our car on the dirt at Fonda on Saturday nights, clean it up a little bit on Sunday–but not much!–and take it to Utica-Rome. And of course, we had probably already run the same car on Friday night at Albany-Saratoga, which was also asphalt in those days.

Eventually, it got to the point when you definitely needed separate cars for dirt and blacktop. The New England racers always had great asphalt cars, because all they had out there were paved tracks. And as the Southern guys started coming up for the big races, that meant even more really good asphalt cars, because that's all they ran down in Virginia and North Carolina. You know, when Ray Hendrick came up he had tremendous equipment, and when Louie battled with Jimmy Hensley in the (1969) New Yorker race, Hensley had a *super* car. I still remember that thing; it was a nice asphalt Modified, built low so Hensley could really *drive* the turns instead of sliding around them, and it sounded like he had just the right gear for that track. I can still hear the way it sounded. But, you know, Louie beat him with our big old coupe.

Of course, the New York pavement guys got better and better, too. That's when Richie Evans started coming on strong. Those two guys, Louie and Richie, were close friends for many years. We were *all* close, everybody on both teams. In the beginning, Richie would come to Louie and ask him what tires to run, what gear, stuff like that, and Louie always gave him the right advice. Why not? They were friends! Plus, you know, Louie was on top, and Richie was just getting started.

Eventually things changed, and now Louie had to chase Richie. That's because Richie had begun to race all over the place, and *win* all over the place, and he really caught on to the hot setups in pavement racing. He had a setup where the car basically worked off the right-rear tire, and he really got it working for him. So in a few years we went from Richie being able to run with Louie only sometimes, to both of them being about equal, to Louie chasing Richie. That's just the way it goes in racing.

Talking about Richie, and about Utica-Rome, reminds me about Jerry Cook. You know, Jerry lived in Rome for years, but he came from Lockport originally, and I had a cousin who lived out there. So my cousin introduced me to Jerry, and I got to know him before he ever moved out this way. I'd go over to his parents' house, where he kept his coupe in his father's little garage. He was just a teenager, but he already had a nice Modified, and Kenny Meahl was

The South's best came North for the New Yorker 400, including Ray Hendrick (11) and Jimmy Hensley, but Lazzaro beat 'em all. (John Grady Photos)

his driver. Of course, Jerry eventually started driving himself, and he obviously did a good job. I mean, just look at all the NASCAR championships he won! But it's funny that I knew Jerry when he was just a kid, and then pretty soon he was battling with Louie at Utica-Rome every Sunday night, and everyplace else we went, too!

Like I said, we eventually came to the point where a good dirt car was different from a good pavement car, and you either had to have one of each or just go racing at one type of track. We finally had Sonney Seamon build us an asphalt car. But, you know, even if the cars had changed, a good driver was still a good driver, and Louie was still tough wherever he went, including Utica-Rome. He won the championship there in 1970, so he obviously still knew how to get around that track, no matter what kinds of cars everybody ran!

Boy, Utica-Rome was quite a place back then. You had the best dirt drivers going up against the best asphalt drivers, and everybody got along so well. It was a special period, it really was.

1971

Stories, Stories, Everywhere

In 1971, a speedway named for its proximity to Utica and Rome crowned a track champ from Utica, and helped produce a NASCAR national champion from Rome. Utica-Rome also sent forth the unlikely winner of one of short-track racing's biggest events; was the site of the first asphalt victory by a future dirt-track icon; hosted key rounds in a rivalry for the ages; had a hometown champion in its homegrown support class; and saw the return of an exiled star who came home determined to win big, and did just that.

Yes, if you wanted to focus on Utica-Rome's pavement era and select its most dazzling, vibrant year, 1971 would do. There was such a buzz in the air that it couldn't possibly be contained in Vernon, or confined to the track's own schedule.

~

Even before the Utica-Rome season opened, good guy Bernie Miller was already a big winner. (John Grady Photo)

The season was supposed to kick off on May 2, but rain fell on three straight Sundays. It wasn't until May 23 that the Modifieds took John Tallini's green flag to begin a feature race.

It had been a glorious spring nonetheless. In late March, Bernie Miller, one of Utica-Rome's own, did the home folks proud by winning the NASCAR Modified portion of the Dogwood 500 at Martinsville, Virginia.

Traditionally, Martinsville was where the best Modified racers came out of hibernation and got on the gas, driving away from winter. Fans came in numbers, too, their loyalties broken down several ways: North vs. South, of course, but also state by state, and track by track. If your local speedway happened to be Utica-Rome, Bernie was one of your guys.

Rarely did underdogs leave Martinsville with the trophy, but this time one did. The same nose for survival that gave Miller the '67 Utica-Rome Sportsman title made him a Dogwood winner.

"I was lucky that day," Bernie says. "I was running good, up in the top five, and I was about to lap Lou Austin. I looked in my mirror and saw Bugsy Stevens flying up behind me, so I pulled over to let him go. When we ran down into the third turn, Bugsy got into Austin, which took them both out. I stayed on the bottom and got by. They piled up 13 or 14 cars."

He led the rest of the way, finishing ahead of Jimmy Hensley, New England star Bobby Santos, Austin, and Jerry Cook. "It was," Bernie says, "a big day for me." It was also a big day for Canastota, and every other town that supplied cars, drivers, and fans to Utica-Rome.

Miller went on to have a solid season, finishing fourth in NASCAR's national standings. On July 25, he beat Ray Sitterly and Stevens for a Utica-Rome victory.

~

Jerry Cook was going to be a NASCAR national champion. Lots of folks had come to that conclusion. It was simply a matter of when.

He had all the necessary ingredients. For openers, Cook never minded the travel, seeming to gain strength on the screwball weekends—Vermont to New York to Virginia to Connecticut to New York—that wore down so many others. His ability to finish races was both astounding and instinctive. If he realized he had a sixth-place car, he wouldn't wreck it trying to run third. Instead, by playing it smart and keeping a little something in reserve for the final laps, he might turn that sixth into a fifth.

Cook had finished second to Stevens in the 1969 NASCAR national standings, and second in 1970 to Fred DeSarro. If there was truth in the adage about a racer needing to lose a championship in order to learn how to win one, Jerry was doubly primed.

So no one was surprised when 1971 ended with Cook atop the standings, ahead of—again no surprise—DeSarro and Stevens.

Cook's title run started with that fifth at Martinsville, and ended there with a fourth in October. In between came seven months of combat up and down the East Coast, and three Utica-Rome victories. On May 23, Jerry outran Robbie Kotary and Sonney Seamon (who raced despite a broken left leg); on Aug. 1, Cook won over DeSarro and Ralph Holmes; and on Aug. 29, he beat Bill Henry and Stevens.

In 1971, Utica-Rome ran 17 features. Complete records are sketchy, but Cook likely skipped one or two while chasing national points. Even so, he ended up with 10 top-five finishes. Of such consistency, champions are made.

~

Lou Lazzaro did nothing out of the ordinary at Utica-Rome in 1971. In other words, he ended the season tied for most feature wins and out-pointed Cook and Dick Fowler to grab his second track championship in a row, and his third overall. Though he was in the mix all sea-

Oneida's Ralph Holmes was among the tough locals hustling the coupes every Sunday. (John Grady Photo, Rod Nacewicz Collection)

Top: Jerry Cook did Rome proud, bringing a NASCAR national title to his adopted hometown. In the process came three Utica-Rome wins. (John Grady Photo)

Left: Just another year in the storied career of Lou Lazzaro: Three Utica-Rome wins, and another track championship. (John Grady Photo)

son, a five-race stretch between June 13 and July 11 produced all three of his victories.

Louie was starting to look like the proverbial rock in the stream, embedded and solid, with Utica-Rome's history flowing past him. In his earliest years at the track, he had upheld the local honor against all invaders: Charland, Ortiz, Flemke, Gahan. Now, Sunday after Sunday, he was dealing with Cook, Fowler, Seamon, and this pesky kid, Dave Lape. The faces around him had changed, but Lazzaro, the rock, held fast.

~

In the summer of 1971, some no doubt thought they were seeing the next Lazzaro, the next Ken Shoemaker, the next Bill Wimble, the next … well, the next crossover hero, as tough on dirt tracks as he was on the blacktop. Things didn't work out that way for Dave Lape, but only because the times were against him. Racing on both surfaces was tougher than ever, and soon it would become darn near impossible. Lape eventually became a full-time dirt Modified racer, one of the best.

But on Aug. 8, here he came, off the final turn at Utica-Rome and headed for the checkers ahead of Holmes, Ray Sitterly, Fowler, and Cook. After four victories on the Fonda clay, Lape had won his first asphalt race.

"In those days we went to Utica-Rome a lot," he recalls. "And Malta, which was also paved. But I didn't know a thing about asphalt."

That's Lape being modest, and given his incredible career on dirt he can shrug off his blacktop days. Fact is, he scored six more top-five finishes at Utica-Rome that year.

With Malta, Fonda, and Utica-Rome all NASCAR-sanctioned, Lape crept upward in the national standings. Like Fowler in 1970, he became points-conscious;

Stories, Stories, Everywhere

Though a dirt-track legend, Dave Lape had lots of asphalt success. In 1971, he was fifth in the NASCAR national standings. (John Grady Photo)

he traveled more, even hauling to Martinsville at season's end. "Took forever to get there," he grins. In the final reckoning, Dave Lape, the young pride of Canajoharie, placed fifth in the NASCAR Modified rundown, behind Cook, DeSarro, Stevens, and Miller.

Sitterly (May 23), Fowler (June 6), and Ron Newman (July 18) also graced victory lane in the never-a-dull-moment year that was 1971.

~

When Utica-Rome fans caught their first glimpses of DeSarro and Stevens early in the season, there were double-takes galore. Bugsy was now in the white #15 coupe DeSarro had driven to the 1970 NASCAR national championship. Freddy was aboard the blue #3 which had carried Stevens to the same honor three years running, 1967-69. Huh?

In April, car owner Sonny Koszela had parted company with DeSarro, and offered Stevens the ride. When Stevens accepted, leaving Len Boehler's team, Boehler simply dialed DeSarro.

NASCAR Modified diehards still refer to the episode as "The Shot Heard Around the World." Though they were in fact good friends, DeSarro and Stevens were painted as fierce rivals, ginning up incredible excitement. Best of all, nobody directly involved—two great drivers, two great owners—missed a beat. On April 11, Stevens and Boehler won the New England opener at Thompson. One week later, back at Thompson but now driving for Koszela, Bugsy swept 25-lap features. The very next Sunday, same track, same format, DeSarro and Boehler won twice. By year's end, Stevens and Koszela had 26 victories, DeSarro and Boehler 19.

Both teams scored at Utica-Rome. DeSarro won a pair of 30-lappers in May and June, and on Aug. 15 he outran Stevens and Lazzaro in a blistering 100-lapper. His take-no-prisoners style still raises the eyebrows of old-timers. "Freddy was tough," says Dave Kotary. "I mean, *tough*.

On July 4, in another 100-lapper, Stevens beat Miller, DeSarro, Lape, and Cook.

"One night, Bugsy and I were in the same heat

Swapping rides, Bugs Stevens moved into the Koszela #15, Fred DeSarro switched to the Boehler #3, and both kept winning. (John Grady Photos)

race," remembers Lape. "He drove up inside me, but he didn't pass me. We ran side by side for about seven laps. We got the checkered flag, and I was thinking, 'God, I'm running good tonight.' Then I looked over at Bugsy, and he was sitting in that car, laughing. I thought we'd had a hell of a race going on, and he was just monkeying around. What a guy."

Though DeSarro and Stevens made occasional stops at Utica-Rome over the next couple of seasons, neither won there again. But their presence—and their big switcheroo—sure lit up the place in 1971.

~

Buddy Thurston lived not far from the track, right there in Vernon, so the weekly crowds were liberally sprinkled with friends and assorted family members. Buddy, being a nice guy, kept them cheering by winning another Charger division title. Louie Lanza, having just barely missed the Mini-Stock championship the year before, was first in class in 1971.

~

By the end of August, Richie Evans had stopped feuding with the NASCAR brass. Or maybe the NASCAR brass, rattled when lawyers suggested that the organization's efforts to corral drivers might not jibe with New York's right-to-work laws, had stopped feuding with Evans. In any case, his two-year-old suspension was lifted, and Richie was told he'd be permitted to race in the upcoming New Yorker 400. It was quite a switch from the previous edition, when he wasn't even allowed to buy a pit pass.

Back in the fold: Richie Evans (leading in turn four) rejoined NASCAR just in time to dominate the New Yorker 400. (Ron Ingraham Collection)

He came hungry for redemption. "I remember going all-out in warm-ups," Evans later told writer Pete Zanardi. "I was there to win, and I wanted them to know it."

They soon did. Evans dominated both 200-lap segments. In the opener, only runner-up DeSarro and third-place Lazzaro finished on the lead lap. In the second 200, Richie started 23rd and had the lead by lap 50.

Crewman Wilbur Jones remembers Ed Flemke standing in the infield, imploring his friend to pull back the reins. "Eddie was signaling Richie with his hands: *Slow down! Slow down!* Richie just kept on trucking. Finally, Eddie bent over and picked up a good-sized rock. He showed it to Richie, as if to say, 'If you don't slow down, I'm gonna throw this damn rock at you!' That got the message across. Richie slowed down."

He still lapped the entire field. DeSarro finished second again, with Cook third.

"I don't think I've ever been as psyched up as I was that night," Evans admitted to Zanardi. "I wanted that one badly."

1972

The Reformation of Richie Evans

His exile from NASCAR over, Richie Evans began the process of becoming—in pure statistical terms—the greatest champion the sanctioning body's Modified division ever had. Between 1972 and his death in 1985, no driver won more NASCAR Modified races, and no driver, before or since, equaled his nine national championships. You could also make the case, based on his nine Most Popular Driver awards, that he was NASCAR Modified racing's most effective ambassador. Pretty nice turnaround for an outlaw.

Richie's reformation began at Utica-Rome, where he won the first NASCAR track championship of his career. In 14 starts—counting the split New Yorker 400 as twin 200s—Richie finished in the top five 11 times. Three of those finishes were victories. Heating up with the weather, Evans won two straight, a 100-lapper on July 2 and a 30-lapper the very next Sunday. He also won the opening 200-lap segment of the New Yorker.

Richie Evans was at or near the front of the pack all season, winning the first NASCAR track title of his career. (John Grady Photo)

Without question, 1972 put Evans on the national map, signaling not only that he was back, but that he was now on equal footing with the likes of Bugs Stevens, Fred DeSarro, and Jerry Cook, NASCAR champions all.

~

Utica-Rome looked a bit different in '72, both from the grandstands and in the pits. The track underwent another facelift when Dick Waterman pushed out the backstretch by 15 feet and laid some extra pavement on the inside of the frontstretch. And, operating on the theory that a fox makes a fine guard for a henhouse, Waterman promoted Bill Wimble to the post of NASCAR chief steward. Wimble, whose résumé showed 11 Utica-Rome wins, had far more laps there than most of the drivers he was tasked with policing.

~

The season's other big winners were Lou Lazzaro and a wily veteran out of Crescent, New York, named Eddie Pieniazek.

Lazzaro's three victories, all 30-lappers, surprised no one. He'd had Sonney Seamon build a pavement #4 coupe; the days when a dirt Modified could reliably do the job on blacktop had passed, even with a hero like Lazzaro at the helm. "Things were changing, that's all," says Junior Bianco, Louie's go-to man. "Nothing you could do about it." Armed with his sweet blend of speed and experience, Louie defeated Evans and Ralph Holmes on June 11; Seamon and Cook on July 30; and Evans and Seamon on Aug. 6.

Pieniazek left his fingerprints all over New York motorsports. An ace mechanic, he turned bolts for the great Pete Corey. But he was also a skilled wheelman, versatile enough for nine wins on the Fonda dirt and a track title on the Shangri-La pavement. In 1972, he had Utica-Rome wired. On May 28, Eddie outran Al Clark, Mike Loescher, Lazzaro, and Cook. Two weeks later he beat Evans, Bernie Miller, Cook, and Ron Newman.

It was a great season for Bobby Santos. A June 100-lapper at Utica-Rome was just one of his big conquests. (John Grady Photo)

Opening-night winner Sonney Seamon was steady all year, and placed second in the track's Modified standings. (John Grady Photo)

Often overlooked, likely because he seldom stayed put for long, Pieniazek was a posthumous inductee to the New York State Stock Car Association's Hall of Fame.

~

On the afternoon of June 4, Connecticut car owner Art Barry unloaded his pretty #09 in the pits at Utica-Rome. Seven hours later he swung his ramp truck onto Route 5, with a smile on his face and a big trophy riding shotgun.

Bobby Santos, Barry's driver, qualified second-best in time trials, and started outside the front row in the evening's 100-lap feature. Pole winner Miller had encountered Santos at any number of Modified events, and knew he was fast. Idling around on the pace laps, Miller was aware that the start might be the whole ballgame. As they rolled toward the green, Bernie was quick on the trigger. Just not quick enough.

"Santos got by me right off the bat," Miller recalls, "and we ran nose-to-tail the whole race." Behind them at the checkers came Quebec's Denis Giroux, Evans, and Cook, "but they were a ways back from Bobby and me."

Rolling into the pits after a New Yorker practice session is the battle-scarred coupe of Ernie Gahan. (Ron Ingraham Collection)

The Reformation of Richie Evans

Santos—dubbed the "Frito Bandito" because he resembled the mustachioed character in the corn-chips ad—was in top form in '72. On Labor Day weekend, he finished second in the closing segment of the New Yorker 400. A week later, he beat Evans, Fred DeSarro, Ed Flemke and Geoff Bodine in a 200 at Lancaster. And as autumn slid toward winter and Utica-Rome sat cold and silent, Santos and Barry ended their season by winning the Modified half of Martinsville Speedway's Cardinal 500.

~

Seamon (May 21), Dave Lape (July 30), and Dave Kotary (Aug. 13) all reached victory lane in Utica-Rome 30-lappers in 1972.

Sonney's win in the season opener was an early display of the speed he'd shown all season. He finished second three times, and ended the year second in the Modified standings.

Lape's victory was his second, and last, on the pavement. He soon focused his attention on dirt racing, and in Utica-Rome's second life as a clay track he won six more features. Of that final asphalt win, Dave says, "Bernie Miller was right on me, and he was fast, but I just protected the bottom. Boy, what a nice guy Bernie was. I still remember him congratulating me, and being happy for me."

For Kotary, too, 1972 marked the last winning season at Utica-Rome. On Aug. 13, he led Evans, Lazzaro, Cook, and Giroux across the stripe. It wasn't easy. "Those guys raced for a living, three or four fights a week," says Kotary. "They were real *sincere* about wanting to win."

At one point in his career, Dave decided maybe he, too, should try racing professionally. With a wife and a growing family to support, it was an uphill climb. "The last race of the season, the motor blew," he recalls. "That Monday, I got a job." But his zeal for the sport did not diminish. For a while he toiled as a welder on the graveyard shift, 11:00 PM to 7:00 AM. "I'd come home, work on the race car all day, and at five o'clock my wife would call me in for supper. I'd eat, lay down for a couple hours, work some more on the race car, then go to my job. Did that year after year."

Denis Giroux, smiling and packed with potential, poses with the Emerick Associates #50, a coupe he drove to glory across the Northeast. (John Grady Photo)

Ray Hendrick and the Armstrong #1 were fast in the New Yorker 400, but couldn't catch Evans. (Ron Ingraham Photo)

With her husband's time stretched thin, Betty Kotary—like so many wives—resolved to make racing a family thing. "I just packed the kids in the station wagon, and wherever Dave raced, we were there."

Dick Waterman, who had a long look at the entire Kotary clan, says, "Dave never had what I'd call top equipment in the Modifieds. If he had the cars some of the other guys around here had, I'm sure he would have done even better. As it was, he was a better runner than Tiger Tom or Robbie."

Tom Kotary's career included five Utica-Rome wins. His brother Robbie pitched in two more. But Waterman is right: Their nephew Dave, the runt of the litter early on, had six victories there, best of the bunch.

~

On Aug. 20, in a short regular feature, Lape finished a close second to Denis Giroux, who had been doing great work all around the Northeast aboard the Emerick Associates #50. Lape thought the world of his Canadian rival, both as a racer and "a good friend."

Lape says, "Denny was a nice guy, a very good driver, and smart, too. He was one of the first guys to run a Scout frame, and he showed me how to build one. That was my pavement coupe, which was really good."

Giroux seemed to be walking a pathway to the stars. He turned heads at Malta, Plattsburgh, Martinsville, everywhere he went. Nothing seemed beyond him. Even when he tackled Daytona in a Late Mod-Sportsman car for the 1973 Permatex 300, Giroux finished a dazzling third.

In April of '74, a crazy chain of events changed everything. Giroux entered Stafford's Spring Sizzler with Connecticut owner Billy Corazzo, but mechanical woes parked their #9X in practice. Denis, full of desire, found another ride. At the start of his heat race, its throttle stuck. Out of control, Giroux's car jumped Leo Cleary's right-rear tire and crash-landed at the base of a concrete wall. He suffered head injuries that ended his career.

No one who saw Giroux at Utica-Rome in 1972—in addition to his victory, he had three other top-five finishes—has ever forgotten the fast, smiling kid from Canada.

~

Again, the Charger division had the joint jumping. George Caswell topped the win column with four, just ahead of Chip Lanz and Buddy Thurston with three apiece. And the brother combo of Russ VanSlyke and Dave VanSlyke each grabbed single wins. When they were all done slapping fenders, Thurston had his fourth championship, and his third in a row. Meanwhile, the top cat in the Mini-Stocks, with his first track title, was Doug Rundell.

~

The capper to Evans's track championship season was the New Yorker 400. Earlier in the year he had unveiled a new Modified, joining what was hailed as the "Pinto Revolution." The car was an immediate success, winning out of the box at Lancaster and Oswego. But come New Yorker time, Evans saddled up the trusty coupe that had carried him to those two July wins.

Crew chief Buster Maurer recalls that coupe being "a phenomenal car for Utica-Rome, *tenths* faster than the next guy. You'd watch everybody else let off going into [turn] three, and Rich would just drive right around 'em."

When Evans finished the first segment with a huge lead over Ray Hendrick—aboard the bright red #1 owned by flamboyant Massachusetts jeweler Dick Armstrong—the great Virginia driver was impressed.

"On the halfway break," Maurer says, "Ray came over with a big smile. He said, 'Man, Richie, we ain't gonna run the second 200 laps like we ran the first 200, are we?' Rich just looked at him and laughed."

In the finale, Evans knifed through traffic from his tail-end start, but could not repeat his all-conquering 1971 sweep. He ended up third, behind Stevens and Santos. Still, his combined finishes were good enough to give Evans his second straight New Yorker 400 crown, with Lazzaro, Cook, DeSarro, and Ollie Silva—a Supermodified legend and spectacular moonlighting Modified shoe—completing the overall top five.

Incidentally, Richie's Utica-Rome title had huge career implications. It gave him a guaranteed starting position in the following February's Permatex 300. Richie didn't have a Late Model Sportsman car, but a businessman from Batavia owned one that needed a driver. Turns out this same fellow also used to sponsor Modifieds driven by the great Dutch Hoag, and was looking for an up-and-coming shoe. Bill Wimble, who knew the gentleman, suggested Evans.

Wimble turned out to be quite the matchmaker. The businessman's name was Gene DeWitt, and he and Evans were about to start writing some history.

1973

Richie and Jerry, Part I

From the very start, Utica-Rome played a key role in NASCAR's national Modified and/or Sportsman points battles. This lent the track terrific regional importance, and was largely responsible for the wild mix of cars and drivers. It's possible that Ernie Gahan, Don MacTavish, Pete Hamilton, Bugs Stevens, and Fred DeSarro—all New Englanders, all NASCAR champs—might never have visited Vernon were it not for the points to be had there.

Yet in 1973, the chase for the NASCAR Modified crown was a local affair. Jerry Cook had won it in '71 and '72, and was looking to make it three straight. But another Roman, defending Utica-Rome champ Richie Evans, had his eyes on the prize. Evans had gone to Daytona with a Late Model Sportsman car owned by Gene DeWitt, whose interests were in concrete, sand and gravel, and trucking. Daytona was a get-acquainted race; if it went well, DeWitt had decided, he'd also back Richie's Modifieds. And Daytona went very well: Evans qualified the blue-and-gold Ford sixth and ran as high as second before exiting

Mature, experienced, and flush with his new DeWitt sponsorship, Richie Evans won the NASCAR national title and eight Utica-Rome features. (Ron Ingraham Collection)

with a blown head gasket. Now, backed by his first big sponsor, Evans made plans to chase the national title. It's safe to say that this caused something of a buzz in the Copper City.

In the spring of '73, Bill Payne and Randy "Buster" Maurer met for a beer. Payne worked on Cook's car, Maurer was crew chief for Evans, and they were close pals; Payne was best man at Maurer's wedding. Over that beer, Payne suggested that Evans couldn't possibly win the championship on his initial attempt. "Nobody wins it the first time," he said. To which Maurer replied, "I'm telling you right now, we're going to win that thing." Civility exited the conversation at this point. Laughing all these years later, Maurer says, "I think it was the first time anybody ever saw us arguing."

The struggle, intense all season, was settled in favor of Evans by his October romp in the Race of Champions at Trenton. At Utica-Rome, things were more lopsided. Richie took eight of the 14 features, including four straight in July. Along the way came a pair of 100-lap wins, on May 6 and July 8. He countered everybody's best punches: Seven different drivers—Bernie Miller, Roger Griffith, Stevens, Maynard Troyer, Cook, Maynard Forrette, and Sonney Seamon (twice)—finished second to Evans that season.

Cook, second in the national standings, was third in the Utica-Rome rundown, after Evans and Seamon. And Jerry hadn't lost his winning touch, taking the trophy home after a 30-lap feature on June 10.

~

It wasn't easy in 1973 to upstage Evans anywhere, but especially at Utica-Rome. Yet Troyer did it twice, and in a big way.

Maynard was a hot item. He'd made his name at the same outlaw tracks where Evans took refuge during his NASCAR ban, and his cars topped anything in Modified racing in the "wow" category. They had well-crafted bodywork, cutting-edge chassis designs, and a stance that was theirs alone. In an age when every car in the pits looked a bit different from the one beside it, you just couldn't miss Maynard's. (That's ironic, because years later, as the Northeast's busiest car builder, Troyer helped usher in the age of the "cookie cutter" Modified.) In 1973, he made several Utica-Rome appear-

Left: When Troyer parked in victory lane after the New Yorker 400, it capped a fine year for the Rochester shoe. (Ron Ingraham Collection)

Bottom: Maynard Troyer and his shapely Pinto breezed into Vernon and won big ... twice! (Ron Ingraham Collection)

Despite wheeling a new Seamon-built Valiant, Lou Lazzaro had a rare winless season at Utica-Rome. (Ron Ingraham Collection)

ances with his Nagle Ford #6, a low-slung red Pinto with a sculpted hood, coil-over front suspension, and plenty of speed.

Because he had so much seat time at Lancaster and Spencer—roomy half-miles—there was some question about how Troyer might fare at the Utica-Rome bullring. By mid-summer, it was safe to say he'd figured out the joint. On July 22, he finished second to Evans. Two weeks later, on Aug. 5, he beat Cook and Evans in a 100-lap special.

And on Sept. 2, Troyer grabbed the overall victory in the New Yorker 400, which drew its usual glitzy field. He finished second to Stevens in the first 200-lapper, then beat Cook and Stevens to win the finale. Troyer's combined finishes of second and first were just a tick better than the first and third posted by Stevens. (Evans, having set a new track record of 13.75 seconds, saw his night go downhill after qualifying; he finished a bent-up 15th in the first half, and spun off the track in the closer.)

Troyer's New Yorker win had a mission-accomplished feel. "Maynard raced with us a number of times that summer, but he wasn't going home with much money," Dick Waterman says. "One night I told him I felt badly about that, and he said, 'Don't worry about it. I've been coming here because right now, Richie is better in traffic than I am, and he got that way by racing here at Utica-Rome.' And, you know, Maynard must have figured it out, because he took home all the marbles in our biggest race!"

~

It was news when Maynard "Cyclone" Forrette won a 30-lapper, and bigger news when the season concluded without Lou Lazzaro winning at all.

Born up near the Canadian border, Forrette's early life was a bumpy road. He reportedly suffered from serious asthma, and that may have been the least of his problems. There are stories of young Maynard running away from home and living for a time in the woods, quite literally a wild child.

"Maynard did not have things easy," photographer John Grady says sympathetically. "But in his own way he was very intelligent, smart as hell mechanically. Maynard was competitive for many years, in many cars, at many tracks."

Grady isn't kidding. By the summer of '73 his trophy collection included a half-dozen from Fonda, so he knew how to beat the best. And on June 17 at Utica-Rome, Cyclone Forrette outran Evans, Miller, Dick Fowler, and Lazzaro. Later that summer, on Aug. 26, Forrette bagged a runner-up finish between winner Evans and third-place Cook.

Lazzaro, wheeling a trendy Plymouth Valiant—Geoff Bodine and George Kent drove Valiants elsewhere—finished second to Eddie Pieniazek on June 3, and third to Evans and Stevens in that July 100-lapper. But no valiant effort, and no Valiant Modified, could get Louie to victory lane. Not counting the track's abbreviated first season, 1973 marked only the second year in which Louie failed to win at his home track.

Pieniazek's victory was his third in two years, and his last at Utica-Rome. Mayor Seamon also notched a 30-lap win, on Aug. 12, when Sonney outran Troyer, Evans, Cook, and Andy Romano.

~

Vernon Center's Chip Lanz emerged as champion in the top support class, known officially as Street Stocks although many diehards still called them Chargers. Several drivers took turns trying to elbow Lanz off the top of the heap: In early June, Dave VanSlyke rattled off three wins in a row; John Coleman, Buddy Thurston, and George Caswell took two each, as did champion Lanz; and Russ VanSlyke, hot at mid-season, grabbed a single victory.

Meanwhile, Jim Brown grabbed the title in a newly minted entry-level class called Pure Stocks, although few of them passed for "pure" after a typical free-for-all feature. The fans approved.

~

Bill Wimble had quickly stamped his signature on his chief steward's role. He conducted the weekly pit meetings using the public-address system "as a way of enhancing interest" and pumping up fans. And folks began referring to the post-race payoff as the "Bill and Nancy Show," because of the friendly energy he and his pretty wife brought to an otherwise dull routine.

There were things about the job Wimble disliked. "It was an eye-opener, a *wide* eye-opener, to see how tempers can come into play. You'll hear your friends say things you can't believe they would even *think*. One night, Jerry Cook had to pit for repairs. Now, Jerry was driving for Pete Hollebrand, and they were both close friends of mine, so if I were ever going to favor anybody, I would probably have started with them. As it was, I probably kept the caution period going a couple extra laps, because you always want a guy to be able to get back into the race. But the fans were sitting there, waiting for a restart, so we went green, and Jerry was trapped in the pits. Well, Pete really took me to task. He was absolutely incensed that I hadn't given Jerry enough of a chance to get back out there. Some of the things he said, I just could not believe, because we had been great friends.

"That incident showed me how the heat of battle can impact your friendships. You'd better not take things to heart, or you can easily have your heart broken."

On the other hand, the job had some perks. "The racing was so good that it was fun just to be there," Wimble recalls. "We had talent coming in from all directions: Maynard Troyer from the West, Bugsy from the East, and of course all the local guys, starting with Richie and Jerry. I mean, we had every bit of talent you could ask for. It was wonderful stuff."

Besides, Wimble adds, "I would do anything Richard Waterman asked me to do, today or back then, so I did it."

For his part, Waterman speaks as if he was simply part of the band, rather than its conductor, offering generous, unsolicited praise. Like this, for example: "Having Jack Burgess as our announcer was great, because he was so well-known in this area. In addition to Utica-Rome he worked at Oswego, Albany-Saratoga, the Fairgrounds in Syracuse, and several other tracks.

And this: "There were jobs I knew I couldn't have done. I could never have been a good starter. I tried it once, and knew right away it wasn't for me. And I couldn't have been a good scorer. To be a good scorer, you might be better off if you don't like racing. Dorothy Baldwin, who worked for me for many years, was an excellent scorer, but she didn't care who won, who finished 10th, or who finished last. All she cared about was writing down the car numbers in the correct order when they crossed the line."

Here, Dick Waterman smiles. "Claude Hollinger, who looked after the men's room for the whole 15 years I had the track, became my good friend. He came to our home for dinner with me and my wife. Some nights after the races, we'd go out and have a beer together."

Yes, 1973 certainly did seem like another of Utica-Rome Speedway's high-water marks. The racing sizzled, the grandstands buzzed, the staff enjoyed their work, and the two most publicized drivers in NASCAR Modified racing, Evans and Cook, were hometown guys.

But just out of sight, over the horizon, were gathering storm clouds, literal and figurative. There were rough times ahead.

1974

Richie and Jerry, Part II...
Soggy Fridays... and Geoff Bodine

Thanks largely to the buzz around Utica-Rome, NASCAR made a serious push into upstate New York in 1974. Lancaster Speedway and Fulton Speedway, both long-time outlaw tracks, joined the Daytona Beach outfit. Lancaster retained its usual Saturday race night, but Utica-Rome's Dick Waterman, rolling the dice a bit, changed his to Friday. It was a leap of meteorological faith: Sundays had been awfully rainy over the previous seasons, wiping out four races in 1971, seven in '72, five in '73. Fridays, Waterman hoped, would be drier. Fulton's veteran promoter, Bub Benway, was happy to pick up the Sunday-evening sanction.

Richie Evans returns to the pits after a warm-up session. For the third straight year, he was Utica-Rome's champion. (Ron Ingraham Photo)

So what happened? Well, Fulton got rained out three times, and Utica-Rome *seven*.

"Poor Richard," Bill Wimble says of his friend and boss. "I remember him saying, 'I may not know how to run a race track, but I sure know how to run a rain-out.' He had the damnedest luck I've ever seen in my lifetime around race tracks, and I've been around a bunch of 'em."

Opening night was supposed to be May 3, with a main event of 100 laps. It rained out. The next two Fridays were also wet. Finally Waterman gave up on his 100-lapper and scheduled a normal weekly show on May 24. That one ran, and Dick Fowler grabbed the 30-lap Modified feature. Rain fell again on May 31, and then Richie Evans won on the first two weekends in June. Alas, the rains returned to cancel two more Fridays in a row.

By the end of June, Utica-Rome had run three race programs and suffered six rainouts. Another washout in mid-July rounded out the track's awful run of bad weather.

Well, sort of. There were 17 events scheduled. Waterman recalls 13 of those Fridays getting at least *some* rain. "We were able to run a few of those nights, but I'd have been better off not to," he says. "It would rain all over the area but not at the track, so we'd have almost no one in the grandstand. I remember that on one of

In 1974, quiet Geoff Bodine made big noise on the track, winning two weekly shows and a pair of 100-lappers. (Dick Berggren Collection)

One of Modified racing's nicest guys, Dick Clark, beat Lazzaro and Evans to the Utica-Rome checkers on August 23. (John Grady Photo)

those nights when we did run, we had 844 paid admissions. Today, promoters will call off a race on a day like that, with a bad forecast; back then, you just didn't do that. So you have all your help there, all the built-in expenses, and of course you still have to pay the purse."

He remembers that after his 844-ticket night, "Somebody said, 'Well, you probably made up the difference on your concessions.' Let me tell you, if you're expecting thousands of people, and you've got the food on hand to feed thousands of people, and you've got the help [in the concession stands] you need to feed thousands of people, there is no way you make it up."

These were not good days along Route 5.

~

Too bad, because the racing was electric. Evans won his third straight track championship over Jerry Cook and Sonney Seamon, but he certainly did not dominate. If you divide that '74 campaign into thirds, rain was the story of the first part, and Evans, whose three wins came within a five-week span, ruled the middle stretch. But the last third belonged to a 24-year-old from Chemung who kept mostly to himself. That is, when he wasn't designing, building, wrenching, and driving his very fast blue-and-white #99. The kid's name was Geoff Bodine.

Bodine—whose father, Eli, had built and operated the Chemung Speedrome—cut his driving teeth at the tail end of Modified racing's coupe era. But the dawning of the modern-body age seemed perfect for Geoff, as if he was a painter with a blank canvas. By 1972 he was winning with a Valiant rivaled only by Maynard Troyer's Pintos for new ideas. Bodine took his Valiant to Trenton that fall and captured the Race of Champions, at that time the cherry on the Modified sundae. He showed up at Utica-Rome in '74 with a sharp Vega that looks racy even today, in photographs.

"When Geoff first came around," says Junior Bianco, "I thought, Who is this short little kid? Sometimes I even gave him a hand, because he didn't have much help. But you know something? He had a really super car, and he did a great job."

Did he ever. On June 14, Bodine trailed only Evans at the end of a 100-lapper; behind him were Cook, Sonney Seamon, and Fowler. A couple more top-fives came next for Bodine, and by mid-summer he had figured out the track, found the setup he needed, and sized up his rivals. Beginning on July 26, he won four of the last five features of the Utica-Rome season.

"Geoff did a number on everybody, Richie included," Waterman remembers. "He had a line that was a little bit different; I remember Geoff running the inside groove coming out of the fourth turn, gaining about a foot per lap on the guys he was fighting until he was leading the race. There was a dogged determination to the way he did it."

Two of Bodine's wins were 30-lappers; he beat Evans and Seamon to win the first one, Miller and Cook to win the second. The other two were 100-lappers, the first on Aug. 2, when he again beat Evans and Seamon.

His final victory closed the season on the Friday of Labor Day weekend, in something called the Permatex New Yorker 100. After 11 runnings, the 400 and its split format was history. But the New Yorker 100 was still a big deal, still a NASCAR national championship event, still a draw. And when the checkered flag waved, Bodine took it first, beating Lazzaro, Cook, Evans, and Eddie Pieniazek. Local writer Vic Carucci reported that Geoff "was swamped after the race by autograph seekers."

~

Lazzaro's runner-up finish in the Permatex 100 was his second straight, and his late surge was one of August's two feel-good stories. He had taken a ride with Jerry Rose, out of Saratoga Springs, who fielded sharp, clean

Modifieds; in other words, the Rose car was very un-Lazzaro, but it was fast.

The previous week, Louie had run second in a 30-lapper won by the summer's *other* feel-good story, Dick Clark. One of the sport's true nice guys, Dick made friends wherever he turned up in the company of car owner Hugh Hedger and Hugh's supportive, enthusiastic family. Clark earned NASCAR's New York State Sportsman title in 1967, but his biggest achievement was simply racing at all. Childhood polio had weakened him—"I always had to have the gas pedal just so," recalls Hugh's son Ron Hedger, now one of the Northeast's leading racing journalists, "because his leg was weak and unpredictable"—and multiple sclerosis made his adult life a struggle. Yet Clark raced, Ron says, "until even carrying him in and out of the car didn't work." Clark's final triumph was his 1997 induction into the New York State Stock Car Association Hall of Fame.

His long, brave race ended in 2008, but Dick Clark's spirit and his smile still float above pit areas throughout the region.

~

For a second straight year, Cook and Evans chased the NASCAR Modified championship, hauling out of Rome often, headed for all points on the compass. Again, the Race of Champions essentially decided things. A strong September meant that heading into Trenton, Evans was 627 points in front; that sounds like an insurmountable lead, but in those days the points payouts for national championship events like the ROC was determined by a complex formula involving the race distance, the purse, and other factors. When Evans blew an engine at the race's midway point, the momentum shifted suddenly to Cook, who finished the race in eighth place. Just like that, Jerry had won his third national Modified championship in four years.

No Northeastern shoe—not Charland, the four-time Sportsman champion, or Evans, who would eventually win nine Modified tiles—ever worked NASCAR's complicated old points system as adroitly as Cook did, or understood it as completely. Consistency and determination were a title-chaser's best qualities, and Cook had more than enough of both. No, he didn't win like Evans did—or like DeSarro and Stevens before them—but Jerry Cook had a way of grinding, grinding, grind-

Jerry Cook won a 100-lapper in August, but the big news was his third NASCAR national championship in four years. (John Grady Photo)

Chip Lanz, wheeling this sanitary machine, was a repeat champion in the Street Stocks. (Jim Robertson Photo, Chip Lanz Collection)

ing out those points. For years he fed his family as a professional short-track racer in an era when that breed was growing rare.

"Jerry was a steady driver, a smart driver," says Dick Waterman. He didn't take home too much wrecked equipment. I saw Jerry as a driver who would take advantage of an opportunity if he thought he could do so without wrecking, but might not take that opportunity if it was too risky. He was always going to get that good finish; that was his goal. And, you know, he probably made more money in the end than most of the guys he ran with."

Cook's championship and his second straight points tussle with Evans generated plenty of noise about how "Richie vs. Jerry" was the sport's newest, hottest rivalry. But even when their relationship occasionally got rocky, as will happen in title fights of 65 or 70 races, the two shared a mutual respect. Each man understood and appreciated the hours and the effort the other was putting in.

"We got along pretty good," says Jerry. "Of course, at different times that was strained somewhat, depending on what had happened. But there were times when each of us needed something and went to the other one to get it, because we both basically had parts supplies stocked on shelves. So he could drive outside of town to my place, or I could drive downtown to his place."

Together, they were making Rome, New York, a NASCAR landmark.

~

Chip Lanz grabbed another championship in the Street Stocks, and did it in high style by also topping the victory chart. Lanz copped double features on June 7, then won again on July 5, July 12, and August 23. In a rain-shorted season of just 11 features, five wins will take a man a long way.

Buddy Thurston was his usual competitive self, bagging four Street Stock trophies, while George Caswell and John Coleman also made it to victory lane.

~

As autumn slid toward winter, Dick Waterman was doing some heavy thinking. His Friday-night experiment hadn't worked; the same bad weather that had dogged him in recent seasons simply switched nights when he did. You really can't fool Mother Nature. Ask Waterman.

"It took 150 people to run that place [on a race night]," he says. "And some of those people were paid pretty good money. For example, your announcers, your starters, and some of your other officials were certainly not working for minimum wage."

Thirty-five years later, his sigh is as heavy as the humid air on all those Friday afternoons. "The rain killed me," Dick Waterman mutters.

1975-1976

It Looked Good on Paper

The punches he took in 1974 led Dick Waterman to dramatically reshape his philosophy. For years Utica-Rome had been a magnet, drawing Modifieds from many directions, but competition from other tracks had diminished that pull. The fact that fewer drivers were chasing NASCAR national points also had an impact. Though occasional outsiders still added spice—Maynard Troyer in '73, Geoff Bodine in '74—the weekly rosters no longer sparkled with names from faraway places. The track still registered in the regional and even the national racing press, but mostly because those two NASCAR champions, Jerry Cook and Richie Evans, called the place home.

Things had changed. Utica-Rome had become a local show.

Waterman, taking the view that "local" didn't mean "bad," devised a card that focused on area drivers and might stem the track's financial bleeding. The speedway would again run Fridays, starting May 2. The program would consist of Street Stocks and Pure Stocks. The big news was that the Modifieds would run just four times—all 100-lap NASCAR national championship races—once a month from June through September.

It looked good on paper. The crowds would be smaller, but the payoff would be, too. Waterman's hope was that guys like Buddy Thurston, Chip Lanz, George Caswell, and John Coleman—popular racers from the fendered classes who lived within a 20-mile radius—would pull in enough fans to slowly nurse Utica-Rome back to health, with the Modifieds creating a monthly big bang. Think of it in baseball terms: lots of solid singles, jazzed by the occasional triple, maybe even a home run or two.

Verona's Caswell took the first two Street Stock features. The Pure Stock winners on those same Fridays were Terry Tubbs of Sherrill and Jim Brown of Vernon. The local drivers were doing their part. But there were signs that the local fans were not doing theirs. For race number three, on May 16, there would be a reduced admission price: just $1.00.

~

The first of Utica-Rome's four 100-lap Modified events was scheduled for Friday night, June 6. Predictably, cruelly, it rained out.

Waterman pedaled hard in preparation for the next week's make-up. Thursday's papers said that "Lou Lazzaro of Utica, Richie Evans of Rome, and Jerry Cook of Rome, three of the nation's most popular Modified drivers, are the favorites in tomorrow night's Goodyear 100." The report hyped a duel between "Cook, the current NASCAR champion" and "Evans, the classic hard charger," while teasing that Lazzaro "would like nothing better than to upset the nation's two best drivers." Dick Fowler, Sonney Seamon, Bill Henry, and Bernie Miller were also trumpeted as contenders.

"The largest crowd of the season is expected," the papers said.

~

Some details are fuzzy, but others are crystal clear to Wayne Seamon. He was just 10 years old in that summer of 1975, and the Goodyear 100 remains a great boyhood memory. He was in the grandstands with his family as his father's car, the sharp Cal Smales #41 Pinto, rolled onto the track.

"The race started, then it rained," Wayne says. "It was just a passing shower, so they dried the track. Then it rained again, so they dried it again."

He is right on the money. News accounts tell of a one-hour delay. When racing resumed, it was clear that the #41 was quick, and that its driver, Sonney Seamon, had things handled. He eased into the lead on lap 57, and that was that. The Mayor of Vernon Center was in office.

"My dad was really fast," Wayne says.

Seamon won over Lazzaro, Fowler, Cook, and Roger Griffith.

"I remember Richie and Jerry Cook got tangled up," says Wayne. Right again. Dueling for fourth with eight laps left, the two Romans collided. Evans cut a tire and did not finish.

Those were fine days for Sonney Seamon. He had a top-notch ride with Smales, and spent his weekdays tending to a nice little fabrication business. He didn't crank out Modifieds assembly-line style, but plenty of winning cars in the Northeast started as tubing on Seamon's shop floor.

"Sonney built a nice, nice Modified," says Billy Nacewicz, who joined the Evans team in 1975. The Evans #61 Pintos of that period were prime examples, as was the Smales #41.

Bill Henry, a winner with his Seamon-built coupe, says, "Sonney sure did a lot of engineering for a guy out of a little garage in Vernon Center."

That garage sat beside the home Sonney shared with his wife, Rita, and their four children, a few miles from Utica-Rome. The couple married in 1959, when the only racing he'd done was on a fooling-around level at the old Morris Speedway. As we've learned, Sonney was part of the work crew Joe Lesik hired to build the track, and Rita pictures an idea flashing in the young welder's head: "I think he probably told himself, 'As soon as this place opens, I'm going to be here, racing!'"

Every Utica-Rome veteran has a tale of Seamon dropping everything to come to the aid of a fellow racer. Bernie Miller recalls a New Yorker 400 in which one of the spokes on his steering wheel broke during the opening 200-lap segment. "During the break," Miller says, "Sonney drove over to his shop and brought back another steering wheel for me."

Rita says, "Part of that was just his nature." But there was something else: She recalls Sonney telling her how, in his early racing days, he had asked a well-known Sportsman driver for some pointers. "The way he told it, this fellow said, 'Get away from me, kid.' That really bothered Sonney."

He apparently reacted by going out of his way to be helpful himself. Writer Tom Boggie got a peek at that side of Seamon through driver Ralph Holmes. "He never locked his garage," said Holmes, who told Boggie a story about "borrowing" Sonney's hauler and his brand new coupe—and then crashing the car at Fulton—while Seamon was away at Martinsville.

Goodyear 100 winner Sonney Seamon, joined by rain-battered promoter Dick Waterman and starter John Tallini. (Skip Spink Photo, AARN Photo Archive)

Top: The Seamon family home and shop in Vernon Center were places where children played, adults hung out, and winning Modifieds were constructed. (Rita Seamon Collection)

Left: Everyone loved Sonney Seamon. This 1973 celebration with Richie Evans followed Richie's Trenton Race of Champions win in a Seamon-built car. (Dick Berggren Collection)

That open-door policy, by the way, extended to Sonney's home, and also went well beyond regular working hours. Adhering to old-school short-track tradition, he enjoyed wrapping up a race night at one tavern or another. "The bar," Rita says, "was where the guys re-ran the race and hashed over everything that happened." And since the rehashing wasn't always complete come closing time, an alternate site had to be found so that these deep discussions might continue. Sonney knew the perfect spot.

"Our home became a gathering place, the place everybody went for breakfast after the bars closed," says a smiling Rita.

If she had gone to the races that evening, she'd march into her home with the gang and start cooking. And if she hadn't, "they'd just wake me up. That happened a lot. One time at about three o'clock in the morning, a whole crowd came in. I'd been asleep, and I heard all these people yelling, 'Rita! Rita! We want breakfast.' I got busy cooking eggs. [Driver] Gene Kotary was there. He said, 'Rita, you don't have to cook mine. Just throw me one.' I tossed him an egg, and he cracked it and ate it raw. Well, Gene's friend Randy Schneibel said, 'I can do better than that.' Randy put a whole egg into his mouth, crunched it up, and swallowed it, shell and all."

Sonney would take in all this tomfoolery, grinning and eating his breakfast. When he reached the point where he'd had enough fun, "he didn't care what everybody else was doing," Rita says. "He'd get up and say, 'Goodnight, folks,' and go to bed." Whereupon the guests either left, or found a nice horizontal spot to conk out for the remainder of the night.

Other folks visited at more sensible hours. "Maynard Troyer used to come here on Sunday afternoons with [car owner] Dave Nagle and his wife Bonnie," says Rita. "We'd cook out before we went to Utica-Rome."

How sincere were Sonney's come-anytime offers? Well, Rene Charland spent his Saturdays at Fonda, while Seamon raced at Shangri-La. Sundays, for both men, meant Utica-Rome. "Shangri-La was farther away than Fonda," Rita says, "so we'd get home pretty late. And there would be Rene and his guys, sleeping on the couch, on the floor, everywhere." Sonney thought that was a hoot. Sonney thought *everything* was a hoot.

Sonney Seamon died in 1994, but remains among the brightest threads in the expanding tapestry that is the history of the Utica-Rome Speedway.

Asked if her husband knew how well respected he was, Rita laughs out loud. "Oh, of course. He used to say, 'Everybody loves me!' He'd laugh and tell me that all the time: 'Everybody loves me!' He was a happy guy."

~

Billy Seamon captured four Street Stock victories, and shared the 1975 division title with Bob Engler. (Willy Seamon Collection)

While track officials managed to overcome the dodgy weather and complete that Goodyear 100, the rain didn't do Waterman any favors. The event was not a home run, or even a solid triple. Quietly, the three remaining Modified events on the schedule were scrapped.

So, by virtue of winning that Goodyear 100, Sonney Seamon is in the books as the 1975 Utica-Rome Speedway NASCAR Modified champ..

~

Billy Seamon and Sonney Seamon were first cousins. Though Billy was much younger, just 18 during the 1975 season, they shared the Seamon go-fast gene. Billy won four Street Stock mains in '75, and when he wasn't winning he was usually harassing whoever was. At season's end, he and Vernon's Bob Engler, a three-time winner, were tied in the standings, giving Utica-Rome a rare set of co-champions. George Caswell, out of Verona, also won four times, so those three men combined to capture 11 of the division's 15 features. Four others shared the remaining trophies. Buddy Thurston, consistent enough on a weekly basis to finish third in the points, joined Lynn Morey, Gene Kotary, and John Coleman in visiting the winner's circle.

The Pure Stock division was a bit less democratic. Jim Brown ruled, with seven victories and a 50-point lead over Terry Tubbs in the final tally. In addition to that pair, Dick "Suitcase" Simpson, Mike Burth, Dave Jamieson, Rich Hall, and Jim Zabele were winners.

The Streeters and the Pure Stocks had fine fields, upwards of 35 cars each on some nights, but Utica-Rome hardly prospered with the cheap-cars-and-local-stars format. The local stars the fans wanted had names like Evans, Cook, Lazzaro, and Seamon, and those guys were racing at Fulton, Shangri-La, Albany-Saratoga … everyplace, it seemed, but at Utica-Rome.

The season finale was slated for Aug. 30, but it rained all day. The event was not rescheduled..

~

The Utica-Rome Speedway never opened in 1976. Fifteen seasons of color and sparks and outsized characters—from Charland to Stevens, Flemke to Fowler, Kotary to Kotary to Kotary to Kotary—had been undone by bad weather and a couple of well-intentioned promotional moves gone awry.

For more than a year, it was quiet, much too quiet, along Route 5.

EYEWITNESS
1971–1975: JERRY COOK

"In half an hour, you could be sleeping in your own bed"

NOTE: Few drivers from Utica-Rome's asphalt era remain as closely linked with the track as Jerry Cook, a six-time national champion of the NASCAR Modified division. Though he hailed originally from Lockport, New York, out on the state's western frontier, Cook relocated to Rome in the mid-'60s, and it was from there that he launched his annual quest for the NASCAR title. Though his point-chasing travels took him up and down the East Coast at a dizzying pace, a huge percentage of his weekly jaunts happily ended close to home, on Sunday evenings at Utica-Rome. There, Cook was the 1969 track champion, and the winningest driver of a thrilling 1965 season, a campaign that helped put Jerry on the Northeast's racing radar well before his first NASCAR national title in 1971.

It was always good to be at Utica-Rome, because that usually meant it was the end of a long weekend. Even better, we were close to home. Back when we were running for those championships, that didn't happen very often.

Our schedule changed quite a bit, sometimes from year to year. For quite a while we raced in Ottawa on Wednesday nights, and later at New Egypt, New Jersey. On Thursdays for several years we ran at Catamount, in Vermont. Fridays we usually went to Albany-Saratoga. Our Saturday tracks changed quite a bit, too; in the '60s we'd go to Fonda and run dirt, and in the early '70s we might run Shangri-La, Islip, Plattsburgh, or Stafford on Saturday nights. Naturally, if there was a big race down South, we'd load up and haul down there. But no matter where went on any given weekend, we almost always ran Utica-Rome on Sundays, and that was only 20 minutes from our home and shop in Rome. Racing at Utica-Rome meant getting home at 11:00 PM instead of 3:00 AM or 4:00 AM, and that was great.

Ken Dippel Photo

Jerry Cook navigates turn four, close to home at Utica-Rome, as another long, hard weekend draws to a close. (Ron Ingraham Collection)

For a while in the late 1960s and early '70s, a lot of us raced at Thompson, Connecticut, on Sunday afternoons, and then came straight to Utica-Rome to race that night. If you were serious about chasing points, you had to do it, because both tracks were NASCAR-sanctioned. Some guys flew in private planes and others came by car or truck, but no matter how you got there it was not an easy thing to do. At some point, Thompson switched from afternoon races to nights, and I was leading the points at both places! I remember somebody actually asked me which place I was going to run. I said, "Well, Utica-Rome is 20 minutes from my home and shop, and Thompson is four-and-a-half hours. See if you can figure it out."

Being able to end the weekend that close to home was especially nice after some of our Southern trips. There were times when we'd run Albany-Saratoga on Friday night, haul all the way to North Carolina for a Saturday-night race at Bowman Gray Stadium, then turn around and come right back to Utica-Rome on Sunday. In fact, I remember a few trips where we ran Albany-Saratoga on Friday and Utica-Rome on Sunday, with *two* Southern races in between: Martinsville on Saturday afternoon, and Caraway Speedway in Asheboro, North Carolina, on Saturday night. So we're talking about a lot of racing, plus over 20 hours of driving time, in a three-day period! When you got done doing all that, it sure felt good to load up after racing at Utica-Rome and realize that in half an hour, you could be sleeping in your own bed.

There were other guys in Modified racing before me who had traveled quite a bit. Rene Charland and Eddie Flemke ran down South a lot, along with Denny Zimmerman. But, like I said, that was before my time, or at least before I started racing fulltime. In the period when I did a lot of traveling, the only guys doing it were the ones who were going for the NASCAR championship, like Lenny Boehler's team with Bugsy Stevens in the '60s, and Richie Evans in the '70s.

Some of the things we did back then are just unbelievable to me now. My wife Sue and I sit and talk with people who were around back then and we wonder how we pulled some of it off. I mean, back then we ran 70 races a year or so just running for the NASCAR points, and on top of that you'd run some other races, too, which would put you up over 90 races in a year almost *every* year. There was one week when I ran eight races in six days. Like I said, you think about it now and it's like, "How did we pull that off?" We never got tired, and we did not know the word "quit.

Most of the time, I had at least one full-time crew member. There was quite a long list of them over the years: George Colwell, Jerry Bear, Steve Hmiel, Mike Ray, John McDowell, John Davis, and some others. And, of course, we also had volunteer help. But there were several trips when it was just the two of us in the truck, Sue and me, because it wasn't easy for some of the crew guys to pack up and leave for days at a time. They had fulltime jobs and families, and that didn't fit in with some of our crazier trips. Fortunately, I could always count on some help when we got to the track, from local guys we'd gotten to know over the years. But Sue and I made a lot of trips, particularly for those Southern races, by ourselves.

You know, I actually met Sue at Utica-Rome. Her stepfather worked at the track—he was the guard at the pit gate—so she'd be at the track quite a bit, and that's how we met. And, like I've said a lot over the years, if you've got someone by your side who enjoys what you do, like racing in our case, that's a hell of a lot easier than being involved with someone who doesn't like it and thinks you should quit. We have been a pretty good team.

Someone pointed out to me that a lot of guys don't get to go back to the place where they met their wives. I hadn't thought about that before, but it's true. Utica-Rome had a night in the 2010 season when they honored me and Dick Waterman, and that was something to think about while I was there: This was the place where Sue and I met.

She and the kids were able to travel with me quite a bit when I raced, but there were also times when that just wasn't possible. That was another good thing about Utica-Rome; they were always able to be there. In fact, if I'd been racing someplace far off that weekend, Utica-Rome might be the first place I'd see them when I got back, because I didn't always have time to get home first. Plus, a lot of our local family members and friends were usually able to be there, along with the families of the guys who worked on the crew. For them, just like for a lot of people in this area, that was what you did on Sunday nights: You went to Utica-Rome.

I can look back at that place and see how much my career changed in the period I raced there. In the early days, the big sponsor on the side of my coupe was Bayne's Liquor Store in Rome. That deal might have been just a few hundred bucks, but it was important at the time because it helped me get to the

Cook's familiar Falcon rolls off the track after qualifying for the 1972 New Yorker 400. (Ron Ingraham Photo)

When it came to chasing points, Jerry Cook didn't play around, as proven by the two #38 Mods in the pit area. (Ron Ingraham Collection)

race track. Later, obviously, I had Hollebrand Trucking with me for years, and Pete Hollebrand made it possible for me to accomplish just about everything I did, starting with those NASCAR Modified championships. Pete came on board with me in 1968, and, honestly, just prior to that I had been thinking, How much longer can we do this, and still make a living at it? It's hard to believe, but our first deal wasn't even a handshake agreement. It was done over the phone! We talked, and Pete sent me some money, and we started building a new car. And, you know, he never even saw that car until the spring, when it was sitting on the track at Martinsville!

We ended up being together for 14 years. I always ran the team as if Pete's money was my own money, and that's probably why our arrangement lasted so long. He was a racer. He absolutely loved the sport. He couldn't get to all of our races, because he was looking after the business, but Utica-Rome was one of the places he would always come.

Even though I enjoyed racing there, Utica-Rome was a very tough place. It was a tight track—not as tight as, say, Islip, but still tight—so you really had to pay attention. If you wanted to avoid the crashes, you had to drive *ahead* of your own car, and not just off your front bumper. And, of course, you had to deal with the handicapped starts, which meant that we almost always started deep in the pack. It was important to know the people you were racing against, and to understand them. That's something you *have* to do; every driver is different, so you have to have a good idea of what you need to do to pass each guy when you get to him. I suppose that was more difficult if you traveled like I did, simply because you were racing against more drivers. But I knew enough about most of the guys at Utica-Rome, and that helped me a lot. When you're starting at the back of the pack in a 30-lap feature on a tight race track, you don't have a lot of time to figure things out!

We had a lot of good times at Utica-Rome. It was hard racing, and it was a tough place to win, but it was like being at home. Those are good memories, for sure.

1977

New Faces, Same Old Sinking Feeling

What a strange year 1977 was for Utica-Rome: A pair of enthusiastic rookie promoters brought in a new sanctioning group, and something called a "track tire"—a relatively new concept in those days, particularly in the Northeast—which, at least for a while, had the effect of locking out one of the speedway's top names. Then the sanctioning body had a major political meltdown and withdrew from Utica-Rome, leading to a "split" schedule which created enough confusion that, all these years later, there is still debate over who was the track's Modified champion. A place that had been around for 17 seasons suddenly looked a baby colt, wobbly, trying to find its footing. For Utica-Rome, all this newness was, well, *new*. Yet the year closed on a miserably familiar note when rain washed away four of the last seven scheduled events, keeping Utica-Rome's future up in the air.

~

This chain of events was put into motion when Steve LoPiccolo and Mike Talerico, two young pals from Utica, decided to try their hands at the race-promotion game. LoPiccolo, 26 years old, was a policeman; Talerico, 25, owned an auto repair shop. Though their lease agreement certainly seemed like a last-minute thing—the announcement was made on June 7—they must have appeared as knights in shining armor to track owner Dick Waterman, whose recent seasons had been so brutal. Yet Waterman insists, "They came to me. I didn't go looking for someone to take over." The duo leased the oval, with Waterman retaining the concessions. (The drag strip, still under Waterman's control, was not part of the arrangement.)

From the grandstands, not much would appear different; Modifieds, Street Stocks, and Pure Stocks remained weekly staples. But on the other side of the pit fence, things were very different. For the first time, Utica-Rome would not operate under the NASCAR umbrella. Talerico and LoPiccolo cast their lot with the year-old Northeast Auto Racing Association (NEARA), which in 1976 had sanctioned the Lancaster, Spencer, Fulton, Shangri-La and Chemung tracks. Headed by Lancaster's Jim Vollertsen and Fulton's Bub

Benway, NEARA aimed to rein in short-track racing's rising costs through gear rules and a durable, less expensive Hoosier spec tire.

Maynard Troyer and George Kent were two of NEARA's top drawing cards, along with an interesting addition: Richie Evans, who in 1975 had jumped off the NASCAR highway to do his racing closer to home. Evans, a Firestone loyalist, disliked the tire rule but seemed genuinely supportive of NEARA's effort to revive asphalt Modified racing in his home state. So while he stayed on Firestones for his NASCAR outings, Richie bolted on the Hoosiers to run with NEARA. And he was thrilled that Utica-Rome, the track that had set him on the path to stock car stardom, was back in action.

The new promotional team announced a June 12 opener featuring its standard weekly show, headlined by a 50-lap Modified main paying $600 to win out of a $3,600 total purse.

~

Things did not get off to a banner start. Oh, at night's end the Evans #61 was parked in victory lane—having beaten Sonney Seamon, Dave Nichols, Mike Loescher, and Roger Griffith—which had to please the local fans. The big problem was, there weren't many of them to please. Tepid press reports said the show attracted "more than 1,000 spectators," which seemed a nice way of saying "much less than 2,000." Whatever the number was, it had to be a letdown for those hoping for a glorious resurrection. Worse yet—strictly from an excitement standpoint—was that Evans started from the pole and led the entire distance. Sure, things might change a bit once the season progressed and the normal handicapping system kicked in, but a dull first race in front of a small crowd was no grand opening, popular winner or not.

The next two weeks had much more spark. On June 19, Maynard Troyer started close to the front, and the show had the makings of another runaway. But Maynard's car had a softening tire, and soon Seamon, up from seventh, was putting on the pressure.

Seamon slipped into the lead on lap 42, but Troyer fought back. As they tussled, third-place Nichols pounced; a real comer on the New York scene, Nichols drove past both Modified heroes. Then Seamon regained his rhythm, went back to work, and retook the lead with the white flag waving. The finish was Seamon, Nichols, Troyer, Dave Kotary, and Griffith. On June 26, in another thriller, Seamon made it two straight. He took the lead from George Kent at halfway, just after Troyer and Evans ricocheted off the wall, bending Maynard's car and breaking Richie's. At the checkers, Sonney led Nichols, Kent, and a rebounding Troyer. It would prove to be Sonney Seamon's last Utica-Rome triumph.

Among the missing, you'll notice, was Jerry Cook. Though still on the road piling up NASCAR points,

Sonney Seamon grabbed his final Vernon victory in '77, and might have been track champ if not for an odd points setup. (Rita Seamon Collection)

Geoff Bodine and car owner Dick Armstrong were a controversial pair, but, boy, did they ever win. (Dick Berggren Collection)

Cook had a strange hole in his weekly calendar. A half-dozen years earlier, Sundays had been hectic for Jerry, with Thompson's afternoon shows and Utica-Rome's nightcaps; now Thompson was running unsanctioned small-block programs, and Utica-Rome had aligned with NEARA. And Cook—like Evans a Firestone man—was dead-set against buying NEARA's spec Hoosier tires simply to squeeze a few more races into his schedule.

Then the weird season got even weirder. Benway, the Fulton Speedway boss and NEARA's vice-president, had opted against scheduling Modifieds on a regular basis at his track; come summer, however, he decided to run them weekly, *on Sunday evenings*. To facilitate this, NEARA revoked Utica-Rome's sanction. The move infuriated Evans, who voiced his support for Talerico and LoPiccolo. "Here these two kids are trying to do something good," Evans told writer Andy Fusco, "and NEARA goes and screws them."

Utica-Rome's traditional Independence Day weekend 100 became an open-competition affair, paving the way for Cook's return. The crowd was decent, but the show was another artistic flop: Evans lapped the entire field. Second through fifth were Seamon, Cook, Griffith, and a promising pup named Randy Hedger, son of the veteran car owner Hugh Hedger.

The season was completed under the open-comp format, highlighted by three more 100-lappers, a mini-series of sorts: July 31, Aug. 14 (rain-delayed to Aug. 28), and Sept. 4. Geoff Bodine, now living in Massachusetts and driving Dick Armstrong's #1 Pinto, beat Evans and Loescher to win the first one; for an encore, Bodine topped Evans and Seamon in August's 100-lapper. On Labor Day weekend, Evans won over Bodine, Cook, Seamon, and New England visitor John Rosati.

The remainder of the schedule had some surprises (Nichols beating all the stars in a July feature), some nail-biters (Troyer and Evans banging wheels in another July main, won by Troyer), and some snoozers (the papers kindly described how Evans "breezed to victory" in one event). And it also had lots of rain, canceling the events of Aug. 7, Aug. 14, Aug. 21, and Sept. 11, which otherwise would have been the season finale.

Though not a red-ink tsunami on the scale of Waterman's 1974, the season was another a poor one, financially. "LoPiccolo said the track lost money," reported the *Observer-Dispatch*.

~

At a glance, the Street Stock results looked a lot like those from the Overheads and Flatheads, those infamous jalopies that spawned so many heroes in the early '60s. One week it was Kotary and Seamon finishing one-two, and the next week it was the other way around, but now it was Billy Seamon (Sonney's cousin) battling Gene Kotary (Dave's cousin, and a nephew to Cliff, Tommy and Robbie). They owned the division in 1977, with Billy winning six times to Gene's four.

Two years earlier, Seamon had shared the Street Stock title with Bob Engler. In '77 he wanted it for himself, and he got it.

Jim Brown, so dominant in the Pure Stocks in 1975, hadn't gotten rusty while the track sat silent. He out-muscled everybody again, and grabbed himself another division championship.

~

The Modified track title was a whole different ball of yarn. Here and there you can still find references to both Bodine and Seamon reigning as Utica-Rome's 1977 kingpin. Geoff's title is actually based on those final three open-comp 100-lappers. "Otherwise," notes dogged New York racing historian Doug Zupan, "it appears Sonney Seamon would have been the track champion."

Fans of each driver, of course, claim the 1977 title for their man, which is how it should be. What is short-track racing without a good debate over heroes, races, and seasons gone by? Besides, seeing two different men listed as champion looks odd, and that is only fitting for this very odd year.

~

The cold late-autumn winds blew in a dramatic development. It arrived on Thanksgiving Day, in the form of an item in the *Utica-Observer-Dispatch*. It began: "Four area men, one of them a supervising principal for the Westmoreland school district, have secured an option for the purchase of the Utica-Rome Speedway."

The head man was Clifford W. Baker, the educator mentioned in the story. He and his group, Auto Snow Racing Inc., had ideas of digging up the asphalt oval and laying out a half-mile dirt track that would see action year-round: stock cars, motorcycles, and snowmobiles were in the mix. Auto Snow Racing Inc., having secured the purchase option in a non-refundable, $2,000 deal with Dick Waterman, was offering common stock at $2.00 a share "as a vehicle for financing the project."

This was big news in what was normally a quiet, catch-your-breath month at the start of the off-season. It turned out to be a false alarm. The purchase option was valid through the last day of the year, and when 1978 dawned the track still belonged to Dick Waterman. Still, the whole episode was watched with great interest by both the dirt and asphalt camps, which, by the middle '70s, were two different Modified worlds.

Dave Lape, twice a Utica-Rome winner in the early 1970s, had been long gone for years, doing his thing on the dirt. In '77 he was the hottest thing in the Empire State, winning everywhere and earning the coveted Mr. DIRT crown. As busy as he was hoisting trophies at places like Fonda, Weedsport, and Rolling Wheels, Lape paid little attention to Utica-Rome that summer. But in hindsight, he sees that the Vernon track was ripe for a change. Albany-Saratoga, for so many years a sister track of sorts to Utica-Rome, had been covered with clay in 1977 by its new owner, Vermonter C.J. Richards. With Malta gone from the pavement Modified loop, could Utica-Rome be far behind?

"Everything was pointing toward dirt back then," says Lape. "That's the way it looked to me, anyway."

Clifford Baker and Auto Snow Racing Inc. had stepped away, but they'd be back.

1978
Black Days for the Blacktop

The failure of Auto Snow Racing Inc. to pursue its purchase option left Utica-Rome's future in doubt, but not for long. In March, track owner Dick Waterman announced that Mike Talerico and Steve LoPiccolo had again leased the track. Immediately, they sought and secured a NASCAR sanction.

"Race Promoters Think Positive," read an April headline in the *Utica Observer-Dispatch*, above a story noting that promotional dollars from the R.J. Reynolds Tobacco Co.—whose Winston brand helped NASCAR tracks to market their programs through the 1970s and '80s—would be helpful to Talerico and LoPiccolo. They announced plans

Nine times in 1978, starter John Tallini greeted Modified winner Richie Evans, including the 200-lap asphalt finale. (Terry Bourcy Photo, Dick Berggren Collection)

to "spruce up the property," no doubt by splashing around some of the free red and white Winston paint which came with the sanction.

The newspaper's Mark DeCotis noted that "with some of the sport's hottest Modified drivers, like Richie Evans and Jerry Cook of Rome, Sonney Seamon of Vernon, and Roger Griffith of Clinton committed, the promoters are optimistic their latest venture into racing will be successful."

Their exuberance may have flagged on May 14, when a driving rain cancelled their scheduled opener.

~

Seamon was not in the field when the season fired up on May 21, with Evans winning a 50-lapper over Chip Lanz and Griffith. Back surgery had put Sonney down, and finances kept him there. "The costs kept going up," Rita Seamon recalls. "It was almost impossible to be an independent racer. The guys doing well were the guys who had backing."

One of them was Geoff Bodine, now dividing his Sundays between Utica-Rome and Connecticut's Thompson Speedway. Geoff's car owner, Dick Armstrong, was an interesting character. He funded his racing through his business, Nu-Style Jewelry, and wanted his Modifieds to sparkle like the bangles and beads he

Right: Geoff Bodine, ready for battle. His celebrated feud with Richie Evans was sparked at Utica-Rome. (Terry Bourcy Photo, Dick Berggren Collection)

Bottom: Included in Geoff Bodine's tally of 55 feature wins in 1978 were three at Utica-Rome. (Dick Berggren Photo)

Maynard Troyer's brief but impressive Utica-Rome résumé was capped by a 100-lap score in 1978. (Terry Bourcy Photo, Dick Berggren Collection)

sold. Gleaming red, heavy on the chrome, the Nu-Style #1 became a serious force when Bodine took the ride in 1975. In '78 he was the hottest driver in Modified racing, eventually winning 55 of his 84 starts. Three of those victories (100-lappers on May 28 and July 2, and a 50-lap show on June 25) came at Utica-Rome.

When Bodine wasn't winning there, Evans was. The pair ruled Utica-Rome so completely that by August, Geoff's three wins and Richie's six accounted for all nine features the track had run. In that stretch, some fine drivers ate their dust: Cook finished second six times; Griffith had a second and a third, Dave Kotary and Dick Clark each had five top-fives; and Long Island's Wayne Anderson finished fourth three times. But Evans and Bodine kept victory lane to themselves.

Finally, on Aug. 6, Maynard Troyer won a 100-lapper over Evans, Cook, Clark, and Bernie Miller. Having split with longtime owner/sponsor Dave Nagle, Troyer was now wheeling his own white #6, and operating the Rochester chassis shop that would revolutionize Modified racing.

~

Evans and Bodine are two of Modified racing's most celebrated rivals, having waged war in the late 1970s and early '80s. To those close to the situation, that came as a bit of a surprise. Brett Bodine, who worked with his brother before becoming a winning driver himself, says, "For a while, Geoff and Richie were actually very friendly. They sort of hung out a little bit."

But feud they did, and the whole thing may have started in 1978 at Utica-Rome. On June 25, Evans was leading a 50-lap feature, with Bodine applying fierce pressure. As they exited turn four to complete the 35th lap, Bodine, charging hard, made an outside bid. Suddenly, in a shower of sparks, Evans was in the wall, his car a mess.

"I was coming off the corner," Richie told *Utica Daily Press* columnist Vic Carucci, "and he [Bodine] hooked into me somehow and turned me into the wall."

Geoff had a different account. "[Evans] just squeezed into me," he told Carucci. "He was trying to stay low, but he didn't expect me to get that far [alongside] him. There was no way I could have backed off."

Track officials deemed it a racing accident, and Bodine went on to win the feature. But the whole thing stuck in Evans's craw, and his mood probably did not improve when the following Sunday saw them both back at Utica-Rome for a 100-lapper. The results? Bodine first, Evans second.

From there, the rivalry became real: Evans vs. Bodine, Bodine vs. Evans. Their tussles—most famously their crashing Martinsville finish in 1981—were absolutely explosive. But the fuse may have been lit in that all-but-forgotten 50-lapper at Utica-Rome.

~

Chip Lanz, a Vernon Center kid, had more than paid his dues in the support divisions. When he graduated to the Modifieds in 1977 and poked himself into the top five in a late-season 100, everyone was impressed. And why not? That night he trailed only Bodine, Evans, Seamon, and Miller, all Utica-Rome heavyweights.

In 1978, Lanz raised his game. He was second to Evans in the opener; third to Evans and Cook on June 11; third to Bodine and Cook on June 25; fifth behind Bodine, Evans, Cook, and Dave Kotary in a July 100-lapper; and third to Evans and Cook on July 30.

"Chip was one of those guys who never had the best equipment," says Dick Waterman. "His father, Barney, always liked to run a Ford engine, and in my opinion that engine never kept up too good. But Chip got to the point where he'd had a number of top-five finishes."

Vernon Center's Chip Lanz, a popular underdog, drove his low-budget Modified to several fine finishes and an August victory. (Lanz Family Collection)

Pushing 50 years of age but still a steady top-fiver, Bernie Miller closed his long career after Utica-Rome's September 200. (Utica-Rome Archive)

On Aug. 20, Lanz had another, and it was a beauty. He topped Clark, Randy Hedger, Gordie Smith, and Miller to win the 50-lap feature.

His victory fell on a night when Utica-Rome's top stars were out of town; Evans, Bodine, and Cook were at New Hampshire's Monadnock Speedway, where Evans won a 100-lap NASCAR special. But Waterman insists there's no way that made Lanz's victory any less valid.

"We had nights over the years when the top names were elsewhere, chasing points," Waterman says. "The first time it happened, I thought it was the end of the world. Instead, I saw that a lot of the regulars came in—guys who were very good drivers, but didn't have the best cars—and you could tell right away they were thinking, 'This could be my night.' And because they were all hungry, you'd have some of the best racing you ever saw."

~

Gene Kotary kept the family name in lights by winning the Street Stock championship, his first. Gene was fast all year long, spreading out his four wins: one in May, one in June, one in July, and one on Labor Day weekend, Bob Engler also won four, but seemed to be a bit more streaky, grabbing back-to-back features on two different occasions. And Billy Seamon was still fast, picking up three trophies.

~

Like everyone in the area, Evans heard the whispers that Utica-Rome's days as an asphalt track might be numbered. But those rumors certainly weren't new; besides, there wasn't much he could do about it. So he kept the throttle down and closed out the season with two straight wins, the first a 50-lap win over Cook and the surprising Chuck Frisbie.

Then Richie came back on Labor Day weekend and dominated the New Yorker 200. After he'd led from the start, an overheating engine forced an unplanned pit stop when a caution waved on lap 92. Evans restarted from the rear, but just 25 laps later was back out front. Cook placed second, with Lanz a strong third, followed by veteran Ken Canestrari and young Joel Thomas, who would be part of the Utica-Rome scene for years to come.

It was a big autumn for Evans. Not only did he sew up another track title, his fourth, but he was also cruising toward his second NASCAR national championship.

No one knew it for certain at the time, but that '78 New Yorker ended up being the last time either Evans or Cook turned a wheel at Utica-Rome. In retrospect, they ended up bringing it as much notoriety as it brought them.

"We had a lot of knockdown, drag-out battles there," Jerry recalls. Though winless at the track in '78, Cook finished second to Evans seven times. Right to the end, they were a solid one-two punch in Vernon.

~

The 200 also marked the final race in the long, distinguished career of Bernie Miller. The former Utica-Rome Sportsman champ was pushing 50, but still showing plenty of savvy.

"I liked that track," he says. "For some reason, it kind of suited me."

On the six Sundays leading up to Labor Day weekend, Miller had finished fifth, fourth, fifth, third, fifth, and fifth. He was geared up and ready when he unloaded his #41 Pinto for the 200. He won the first heat race and therefore started the feature from the pole, with Evans alongside.

"The car was running great," Bernie recalls. "But I ended up getting two flat tires, and that was that."

He pulled into the pits and climbed out of a stock car for good. "I hated to quit," he says, "but it was time."

His 1967 Sportsman cup and the grandfather clock from Martinsville in '71 were nice, but his real trophies were the friends he'd made. Bernie Miller was more than a good racer; he was a good guy.

~

Like Miller, Dave Kotary remains forever linked with Utica-Rome. Oh, he raced elsewhere after 1978, and sure wowed the troops down at Shangri-La in '79. "They had a bounty on George Kent, because he was winning all the races," he recalls. "We went down there and beat him."

But it is Utica-Rome you think of first when someone mentions Dave Kotary, or *any* Kotary, from 1961 until the present. "Any race you won there, you earned it," Dave says. "Think about the names who showed up: all the guys from around here—Sonney, Richie, Bernie, Cookie, Lou Lazzaro—plus Bugsy Stevens, Denny Giroux, Rene Charland, Eddie Flemke, Kenny Shoemaker, Don MacTavish. That's a tough group, boy.

"I had a lot of fun there. And a lot of hard years."

He recalls feeling a tinge of sadness as the track slouched through its last few troubled seasons as a pavement track.

"There were less cars in the pits," Dave Kotary says. "Let's face it, most of the tracks in New York were dirt, so anybody coming along was going to build a dirt car. The asphalt Modifieds were just fading away."

~

All the doom-and-gloom speculation about Utica-Rome was put into stark, sad perspective in December, with the awful news that Paul Seamon, the 18-year-old son of Sonney and Rita, had lost his life in a highway crash. In addition to his parents, Paul left a brother, two sisters, and a huge number of friends he'd met on a hundred Sundays at Utica-Rome Speedway.

1961-78
The Pavement Era

Billy Rafter. (John Grady Photo, Rod Nacewicz Collection)

Lee Millington. (John Grady Photo)

Vern Angell, 1962. (John Grady Photo, Rod Nacewicz Collection)

Speedy Williamson. (John Grady Photo, Rod Nacewicz Collection)

Frank Mathalia with flagger Cliff Kotary, 1962. (John Grady Photo)

Tom Kotary, 1963. (John Grady Photo, Rod Nacewicz Collection)

Steady Eddie Flemke, 1964. (Alan Weaver Collection)

Wild Bill Slater, 1963. (John Grady Photo, Rod Nacewicz Collection)

Buddy Thurston, Late Model hero. (John Grady Photo)

Denny Zimmerman, Eastern Bandit, 1963. (John Grady Photo)

Jerry Cook hauls in. (Utica-Rome Archive)

Lou Lazzaro's "reverse color" coupe. (John Grady Photo)

Popular Doc Blanchard. (John Grady Photo)

Big Lou Smith. (John Grady Photo)

Lou Lazzaro in a Richie Evans car! (John Grady Photo)

Robbie Kotary. (John Grady Photo)

Daytona Dave VanSlyke. (John Grady Photo)

Eastern Bandits leader Ed Flemke, 1963. (John Grady Photo)

Pete Hamilton, 1965. (John Grady Photo, Rod Nacewicz Collection)

The Pavement Era

L&R Speed Shop boss Len Bosley. (John Grady Photo)

Phil Spiak. (John Grady Photo)

Tom Kotary and his Studebaker. (Rod Nacewicz Collection)

Don MacTavish, 1967. (John Grady Photo)

A star in the making: Richie Evans, 1967. (John Grady Photo)

Rene Charland. (John Grady Photo)

Bernie Miller. (John Grady Photo)

Kenny Shoemaker. (Alan Weaver Collection)

Lucky #13, Joel Thomas. (John Grady Photo)

Long Island ace Fred Harbach.
(John Grady Photo, Rod Nacewicz Collection)

Maynard "The Cyclone" Forrette. (John Grady Photo)

Colorful Dick Fowler. (John Grady Photo)

The Pavement Era

Don VanSlyke, 1969. (Rod Nacewicz Collection)

The great Pete Corey. (John Grady Photo)

Bobby Adams and his Mustang Modified. (John Grady Photo)

Bugsy Stevens with starter John Tallini. (John Grady Photo, Mary Ellen Higley Collection)

Dick Clark in the Hedger sedan. (John Grady Photo)

The Champ, Mr. Charland. (John Grady Photo)

Ralph Holmes. (John Grady Photo)

Ron Newman, ready to roll. (Rod Nacewicz Collection)

Bruce Dostal. (John Grady Photo)

Maynard Troyer, ever-stylish. (John Grady Photo)

Ron Fazio. (Rod Nacewicz Collection)

Bill Henry. (John Grady Photo)

Two Evans coupes: One for Richie, one for Ed Flemke. (John Grady Photo)

Robbie Kotary. (John Grady Photo)

The Pavement Era

Jean-Guy Chartrand's Hemi Cuda, 1971. (John Grady Photo)

Virginia's Paul Radford. (John Grady Photo)

Richie Evans, 1978. (John Grady Photo)

Denis Giroux, 1972. (John Grady Photo)

1973: Miss Utica-Rome and the Javelin pace car. (Utica-Rome Archive)

Grand entrance: Sonney Seamon and Bill Henry. (Utica-Rome Archive)

The Straight and Narrow... and the Fun!

Fast, Loud Times at the Utica-Rome Dragway

The vast bulk of Utica-Rome's notoriety, and thus the vast bulk of this book, revolves around the facility's oval, whether in its original configuration as a tight asphalt bullring or its present position as one of the Northeast's top dirt tracks. But there are those whose Utica-Rome memories are of a less-circular nature, who recall that plot of land along Route 5 offering the best of an entirely different form of motorsports.

Wow! The Vega of famed engine wizard Ron Hutter meets the Gapp & Roush Pinto steered by Wayne Gapp and tuned by Jack Roush. (Carl Gross Photo)

Traces of the Utica-Rome Dragway can still be seen today. The one-eighth-mile strip, running from southeast to northwest, once angled past the outside rim of the asphalt oval's second turn, its finish line beyond the third-turn end of the current backstretch. The 1979 expansion of the speedway buried the strip, though there has occasionally been talk of replacing it.

Conceived by the track's first owner, Joe Lesik, but ultimately opened in 1965 under the four-way partnership of Dick Waterman, Bernie Ingersoll, Chuck LeRicheux, and Lou Brando, the strip was an immediate smash with local hot-rodders and regional drag stars from tracks like the ESTA strip in Cicero, north of Syracuse. Before long, some of the top names from the National Hot Rod Association—or NHRA, then and now the sport's leading sanctioning body—were bouncing in and out of Vernon.

With the oval track operating mostly on Sundays—save for the Hobby division's Thursday experiments in the early '60s and the Friday experiment in 1974—the drag racers took center stage on Saturday evenings, often attracting terrific crowds.

"We ran everything, from the amateur street-car classes right up to the pros," says Dick Waterman, who eventually had sole control of both the oval and the drag strip. He's not kidding; the strip hosted everything from "run whatcha brung" events for weekend-warrior gearheads right up to staged appearances by the biggest names in the sport.

Its glory came in loud, short bursts lasting just a few seconds. Yet more than 30 years later, mention of the place still conjures knowing nods and nostalgic smiles.

Ah, what times those were ...

∽

No question, a handful of special-guest appearances by top NHRA stars helped put Utica-Rome on the map. Some ran in heads-up competitions, as part of regional meets; others took part in the wildly popular "match races" which swept the nation as drag racing gained traction with the American public. The match-race concept was simple: A promoter lacking either the funding or the facility to host an NHRA "national" meet—and with Utica-Rome short of the quarter-mile distance required for a national event, Waterman fell into that category—would arrange for two or more of the NHRA's headline drivers to appear. Then, rather than battling an entire field of cars in the same division, the drivers faced off in a pre-determined series of rounds, usually a two-out-of-three affair.

"We had all the hot dogs at one time or another," Waterman says. "We had Don 'Big Daddy' Garlits, Gene Snow, Tommy Ivo, and lots of other big names. Art Arfons ran there many times for me.

"And, of course, Shirley Muldowney."

Ah, yes, Shirley. Born in Vermont, she later called Schenectady home, and it was there that she discovered drag racing. At first, it was of the illicit variety; before she was old enough to earn a driver's license, she and her 1951 Mercury went against the local tough-guy hot-rodders. In the vernacular of the day, they raced for "pink slips," registrations; in other words, if you lost the race, you also lost your car. "School had no appeal to me," Muldowney told *Sports Illustrated* years later. "All I wanted was to race up and down the streets in a hot rod." Soon enough she moved to organized events—many fans recall seeing her run at Fonda, on the old drag strip bisecting the dirt oval—and obtained an NHRA license in 1965. In her long career she won big in both Funny Cars and Top Fuel dragsters, taking three NHRA championships in the latter class.

Shirley—who went by the brassy nickname "Cha-Cha"—was a perfect fit for the match-race era. She was a big enough NHRA name to attract every guy who loved major-league drag racing, but now those guys could bring along their wives, girlfriends, sisters, and mothers, who rooted for the spunky brunette to whip all the he-man heroes. Cha-Cha Muldowney was a huge draw.

Likewise, Garlits and Ivo were in the racing stratosphere. Both were quick to recognize that there was as much money to be made on their "off" weekends, via deals with match-race promoters, as there was on the NHRA circuit. Legend has it that in a single season, Garlits and Ivo went head-to-head 72 times at 72 different drag strips! Of the two, Garlits had the better career numbers, by far: "Big Daddy" won 144 NHRA national meets and three NHRA Top Fuel championships, plus 10 titles with the American Hot Rod Association (AHRA) and five with the International Hot Rod Association (IHRA). But whatever Ivo—

Eyes on the prize: Shirley Muldowney in her office, ready to "cha-cha" down the eighth-mile strip. (Tom Loughlin Photo)

dubbed "TV Tommy" for his stint as a child actor—lacked in numbers, he made up for in showmanship. He traveled constantly, often with a *glass-sided* 10-wheel truck toting his two dragsters and a matching Corvette push vehicle.

Arfons, while a drag racer of considerable repute, was better known for setting land speed records on the Bonneville Salt Flats, and for his jet-powered "Green Monster" rail, which made several exhibition runs in Vernon. For years Art drove the Monster himself, but when injuries ended his career he hired other drivers and kept right on touring. In 1969, with Garth Hardacre at the wheel, the Monster topped 180 MPH at Utica-Rome, then sailed off the end of the runoff road after a parachute failure. Thankfully, Hardacre was unhurt.

And there were other great names—Mickey Thompson and Don Schumacher among them—who roared down the Utica-Rome strip.

Over time, the match-race system developed some flaws. Since the racers were guaranteed lump-sum payments, there was little incentive to perform, on-track or off, once the money was pocketed. At times a promoter could feel stung, as Waterman attests. "Some of those people were awfully good to deal with, and some were awfully bad," he says. "For example, Tommy Ivo was great; he got there on time and did the promotional work you wanted him to do. A few others were not as reliable."

Tommy Ivo was a one-man show, hauling his dragsters around the country in a trailer with glass side panels! (Lynn Morton Photo)

Waterman tells of one top-level shoe, in on a paid deal, who "didn't show up for any of the promotional things we'd planned in the afternoon. That night, we had him scheduled to run three rounds. He basically laid down in his first round. In the second he ran very fast, and may have even set a record. Then he said he couldn't get his car ready for the third round. I felt like I got one round out of him. I never had him come back."

But, overall, the match races were terrific for promoters, and also for fans, who otherwise wouldn't have seen the era's stars at places like Utica-Rome. And they were pretty good, too, for the racers. "The first time Shirley Muldowney came to my race track, she paid to get in," Dick Waterman says. "The last time she came, I gave her $2,500 to show up! But she was great."

Though Empire State fans claimed her as one of their own, Muldowney was clearly much more than a local draw. Shirley's fans came to Utica-Rome from all points on the map: from Canada, from New England, from Pennsylvania. Ditto for those who came to see NHRA stars like Garlits and Ivo, as well the speed demon Arfons. They were among the top motorsports celebrities of the era, featured often in the glossy magazines and thus known even to the most casual of car buffs.

But the NHRA pro who really got the Utica-Rome crowds jumping was Phil Castronovo. A Utica resident, Phil was already an accomplished guy before Waterman and his partners opened their strip, having traveled with a good bit of success, but racing close to home made him a sensation. The local papers

Right: Utica's own Phil Castronovo and the Custom Body Shop Funny Car gave the locals something to holler about. (Lynn Morton Photo)

Bottom: Wherever she went, Ms. Muldowney drew crowds. Having lived for years in Schenectady, she had plenty of New York fans. (Lynn Morton Photo)

watched him closely; in the spring of 1967, one tipped that Castronovo was constructing a new Funny Car, "a fuel-burning, altered wheelbase, Hemi-powered Barracuda under the sponsorship of Custom Body Shop." The article said the car was "being built mainly for match races at a cost of $10,000," an eye-popping sum at the time.

Folks around greater Utica jumped onto the speeding Castronovo bandwagon. Even promoter Waterman—who knew a good draw when he saw one—pitched in, allowing the team to utilize Utica-Rome as its private test track. When necessary, Phil and his boys would haul the car over to Vernon and make a few passes. Waterman's only stipulation was that they confine these experimental runs to the early-afternoon hours on Saturdays, before the regulars began showing up.

"Since we ran the drag cars on Saturday night, our insurance policy was good for that whole day," Waterman explains. "So I'd let Castronovo come over and test on Saturday afternoons."

Shrugging, the promoter adds, "Where else are you going to test a car that goes *that* fast?"

Though Castronovo is best remembered for his successes—including a 1971 score in Amarillo, Texas, that designated him the NHRA Funny Car "world champion"—one of his losses has stuck with Waterman, who says the whole thing happened because Castronovo was playing the good guy, trying to make a good show out of a mismatch.

"A guy came in from somewhere down around Binghamton with what he said was a Funny Car," Waterman says. "It was actually the worst cobbled-up mess I'd ever seen. Anyway, he went up against Castronovo, who obviously had terrific equipment. Well, Phil let him get too big a lead; honestly, he just sat there too long before he took off. At the end of the strip, Phil went past him like a shot, but not before they crossed the line.

"Castronovo and his guys tried to get me to have a rematch. I told 'em the only way I can do that is if the *other* guy wants a rematch, too. After all, the fellow won fair and square. Well, the other guy didn't want to know anything about a rematch. He went on to the next round, where he was beaten badly, the same as Phil would have beaten him badly if only he hadn't been playing games."

Dubbed the "Utica Flash," Castronovo competed at the Vernon strip in standard elimination-type events and, as his popularity grew, in match races. He and the Custom Body machine—which remained a hot NHRA ride even after Phil climbed out of it—were prominent among a handful of drivers and cars spreading the growing reputation of Utica-Rome.

Another Utican, Ron Walsh, made a big regional splash wheeling a Funny Car built by New England chassis builder Pete Tropeano. On the quarter-mile strips like ESTA, Walsh topped the then-magical 200 MPH mark. Not surprisingly, he was a big hit at Utica-Rome.

Waterman recalls being on a trip and bumping into a fellow from Cragar, the California manufacturer whose "mag" wheels were coveted by hot rodders. Making conversation, Waterman began explaining a bit about his facility. To his surprise, the man from Cragar grinned and interrupted.

According to Waterman, "The guy said, 'You don't have to tell me about Utica-Rome Dragway. I go to a lot of national meets, and when I ask some of these new hot dogs where they came from, they talk about Utica-Rome.' I thought that was pretty good."

∽

Not all the memories are pleasant. The Ken Poffenberger crash—though it had a satisfactory ending—was a terrifying affair.

Born in New Jersey, Poffenberger passed his teenage years in the 1950s, when hot-rodding and drag racing were on the upswing. Once he saw his first organized event at a converted airfield in Montgomery, New York, the hook was set. With a series of homebuilt cars, Poffenberger climbed the drag ladder, graduating from dual-purpose street/strip cars to Altereds and Gassers. His first famous ride was a wild Funny Car featuring a fiberglass Corvair body draped over a Logghe chassis. Later, he did well with an ex-Don Prudhomme Barracuda. Certainly, "Poff" was among the most popular drag racers on the East Coast.

There came a night when Poffenberger and Gene Snow—famed for his series of "Rambunctious" and "Snowman" Funny Cars—squared off at Utica-Rome. Snow was victorious, but losing the round soon be-

Here is the very essence of Utica-Rome Dragway: Two amateur "door-slammers" jump off the starting line. (Lynn Morton Collection)

came the least of Ken Poffenberger's problems. "His throttle stuck," says Waterman. "You could just hear that engine running wide open."

Gaining speed as it passed through the shutdown area, the car got airborne, perhaps after running off the side of the pavement or hitting a bump. Waterman says, "A farmer happened to be driving down the road [adjacent to the runoff area]. He told me later, 'I will never drive there again while you're running. I heard a *screaming* noise, and when I looked up I saw a car as high as the trees. It looked like it was coming right at me!'"

Adding to the drama, Poffenberger's supercharged engine, revving even more wildly once the car left the ground, blew in mid-air.

Waterman remembers hopping into the ambulance and imploring its driver to go faster, even as they approached the remains of Poffenberger's car. "The man said, 'I don't want to kill him, if he's still alive!'"

When the rescue vehicle skidded to a halt, Poffenberger "was just regaining consciousness," says Waterman. "He asked what happened, and I told him he'd been in an accident. He said, 'How bad is my car?' Well, he was sitting there in what was *left* of his car, which was just the roll cage." Amazingly, Ken Poffenberger was merely shaken up.

Waterman says, "I asked Snow, 'How fast do you think he was going, maybe 180? And he said, 'Dick, he was doin' a deuce!' In other words, 200 miles per hour. I could tell it had thrilled Gene a little bit, seeing that crash."

All these years later, Waterman remains a little bit thrilled himself. "I never forgot that line: 'He was doin' a deuce.'"

∽

The visiting superstars—Snow, Garlits, Muldowney—were treats, sugar cookies served up only occasionally. The meat-and-potatoes weekly fare at the Utica-Rome Dragway was provided by the amateur classes. Running an assortment of "door-slammer" divisions, either street-legal cars or vehicles on the lower end—no disrespect intended—of the drag-racing food chain, they packed the pits, servicing their cars on the paved oval track.

"There were nights when we had more than 300 competitors," says Waterman. He and his staff, often assisted by officials from ESTA, worked tirelessly to get all those cars inspected and placed in the proper divisions. Waterman adds, "If a fellow didn't know what class his car fit in, we'd find him one. Once in a while, a man might question the classification his car was put in, but that could be straightened out fairly easily."

Once that bit of pre-race business was out of the way, those Saturday nights tended to go rather smoothly. "We had very few problems from the drag folks, very little stress," says Waterman. "It was a nice change from the oval side. Over there, we had guys complaining about the scorekeeping, the handicapping, all kinds of things. With the drag races, the clocks told it all; you either won or you lost, and that was that."

The amateur nature of those shows, sadly, makes it impossible to compile an accurate record of all that occurred on that hot little strip. A guy might drive three cars one night; another car might have three different drivers on three successive weeks. Today, most of the wild-eyed folks who raced at the Utica-Rome Dragway have faded into the shadows of time. Some have passed on; others may still frequent the region's remaining drag strips. And it's a good bet that a few, their hair now silver, get their automotive kicks on cruise nights, rather than at the track.

But the spirit of the strip lives on in a most unlikely place: the Internet. Enter the words "Utica-Rome Dragway" into any search engine, and you'll find a number of websites referencing the joint. Particularly cool are the message-board posts of former Utica-Rome fans who can clearly still hear the rumble of those long-ago Saturdays. Their language is informal and their grammar might need polish, but there is no mistaking their passion.

"I raced there in the early '70s," wrote a poster who gave his name as Rich Freitag. "I ran my '69 AMX 390, 4-speed, posi. Back then I drove my car about 40 miles, raced it and drove home hoping nothing broke … $5 to get in and $1 to race. That is what it cost at Utica-Rome. Let's take a walk in the pits. Over here is Bob Hertline's SS/HA Camaro, there's Bill Russell's Chevy wagon the Magic Buss, Roger Forbes's SS Matchmaker Camaro, the Blue Venom Camaro, Charlene Wood's "Tons of Fun" Pontiac Wagon, Ralph Conte and Herm Schremmer's Mighty Mopars, and so many more. Moving on, the Modifieds: Moe Hall's "Hangman" '55 Chevy, Richie Forbes's "Kong" Camaro, Curt LaShure's Opel, Gordy Hmiel's Pinto, Pete DeSalvo's Mustang II, and Bob Newbury's Vette. All these cars are making me hungry, which brings me to their famous hotdogs. Best dogs ever..."

A poster identified as Bret Kepner wrote, "Every once in a while, I'll spot a Utica-Rome Dragway class winner decal on a drag car. Take good care of yours … it's rare!"

And then there was this chunk of a post from someone giving his name as Brien Radley, clearly caught up in the time-warp that only fine nostalgia can produce: "What a place! I used to haul my '70 Cuda on a 1967 International flatbed truck [to Utica-Rome] on Saturdays and then to ESTA on Sundays. Wasn't that long ago, was it?"

Hundreds of racers, and thousands of crewmembers and fans, times all those eighth-mile blasts toward either victory or defeat. How many great times does that equal?

Looking every inch the prototype late-1960s NHRA recruitment tool, Bob Newberry's Corvette awaits another run. (Lynn Morton Photo)

~

Racers being a restless lot, it's not surprising that more than a few ended up sampling from both sides of the Utica-Rome menu, dabbling in the drags *and* the stock cars.

Jon Button may have been the most successful of the crossover artists. The "Chittenango Cheetah" made his name at the drags, winning assorted championships and state titles. But almost as soon as his mastery of the strip had become an accepted fact,

Button changed directions. In 1968 he was still screaming triumphantly down the eighth-mile on Saturday nights, but also showed the circle-track fans a thing or two by topping the Mini-Stocks on the oval next door. And crafty Jon proved just as adept on the bigger, half-mile dirt track: Obscured by the crazy managerial mess of the 1980 Utica-Rome Speedway season was Button's championship in the small-block Modified class. Later, his sons, Mike and Gordy, were among the track's most dynamic dirt shoes. Still kicking, still full of great stories, Jon Button can tell you a thing or two about what it took to go fast at Utica-Rome, whether turning left or in mash-the-gas, "Point A to Point B" style on the drag strip. He remains one of the area's most delightful racing characters, and is a New York State Stock Car Association Hall of Fame inductee.

Also proficient at both disciplines was Ralph Holmes, patriarch of the fabulously successful racing clan from Oneida. Though known best for blasting around the paved oval in a NASCAR coupe, Ralph fondly recalls a brief period in the mid-'60s when he "drag-raced on Saturdays, and ran twice a week in my Hobby car."

And, make no mistake, he was quite a stud in those amateur brawls on the strip. "At one time I won 83 trophies in two summers," Ralph says.

All that Utica-Rome action got Holmes well-acquainted with Dick Waterman, and with Dick's wife Dorothy, who worked in the popcorn concession on drag nights. Mischievous racer that he was, Ralph figured that entitled him to pull rank on his competitors every now and again.

"I had a little truck I drag-raced, and Dorothy loved that thing," he chuckles. "So anytime I saw her walking back up through the dusty pits from that concession stand, I'd whip over there with that little truck and say, 'Get in!' Then I'd roar right up through the pits with those headers wide open. It drove everybody crazy, but what were they going to say? I mean, I had the boss's wife with me!"

୭

Interestingly, though Dick Waterman was a circle-track fan when he bought the place and became an even bigger one as the years passed—he still gets excited talking about NASCAR Modified heroes like Bill Wimble, Geoff Bodine, Richie Evans, and Jerry Cook—he never had any great love for the straight-line stuff.

"I'm not sure why," Waterman says. "To this day, I go to Daytona every year, and go to the NASCAR races at Bristol and Pocono. But I sold Utica-Rome in '79, and I have never been to another drag race since. Don't get me wrong, I don't *dislike* it; I just never developed any real emotion for drag racing."

But he was a sharp businessman, and everything about the dollars-and-cents part of drag racing rang his chimes. For one thing, the talent pool was constantly refilled; in the car-crazy 1960s and '70s, there were new hot-rodders born every day. He recalls keeping the names and addresses of those who competed there, as a way of notifying them of any news or scheduling changes. "At one point I had almost 4,000 names on that mailing list," he says, "and every single one of those 4,000 people had raced there at least once."

And while bringing in a Muldowney or a Garlits meant forking over serious money, on a regular Saturday the purse was negligible: a 1965 advertisement lists the winner's payoff for the Top Stock, Junior Stock, Middle Eliminator, Street Eliminator, and Top Eliminator classes at $50.

"The drags worked out very well for me," he says. "Even on a terrible night, when it rained all around you but not at the track, you still broke even with the drags. With the stock cars, on a night like that you went in the hole."

A bit wistfully, Dick Waterman says, "Had I kept the place, I think we could have built that into the premier drag strip in the state."

Instead, when he sold the facility to Cliff Baker in the spring of 1979, Waterman could only shake his head at the first step in the oval track's conversion from asphalt to dirt: "He tore up the drag strip."

In The Margins

Airplanes, Open-Wheelers, Wild Animals, Demo Derbies, Vampires, Hippies, and Other Utica-Rome Oddities

When is a drag strip more than a drag strip? Well, how about when it doubles as an airport? In the days when every NASCAR-sanctioned race a fellow ran counted toward the championship in the Modified and Sportsman divisions, drivers took great pains to squeeze in extra events whenever possible. Often that meant running two races on Sundays, with the second of those often coming at Utica-Rome. The first could come just about anyplace, though in the late 1960s and early '70s was usually the Thompson Speedway in the northeast corner of Connecticut.

Using the drag strip as a runway, Bugs Stevens and other NASCAR points chasers made Utica-Rome the nightcap of their busy Sundays! (John Grady Photo)

For a time, the adventurous racers would load up as quickly as possible after the Thompson feature and hit the highway, hammer down. If promoter Dick Waterman knew a group was on the way, he would do his best to delay the consolation event, giving those gypsies a chance to make the Utica-Rome feature. Make no mistake, it was a serious hassle. But before long, someone—no one is sure which driver did it first—talked with someone else who had a friend with a private plane, and the travel dynamics changed immediately. Instead of 250 road miles and close to four hours driving, the journey of 200 air miles could be done in about 90 minutes in a stout single-engine plane. Now, with backup cars already positioned at Utica-Rome, these double-duty drivers could arrive in time for the heat races, thereby earning better starting spots in the main event.

All that was needed was an airport close to the track in Vernon. Or maybe an airport right *at* the track in Vernon. It was determined that Utica-Rome Dragway could indeed function legally as a private air strip, and before long it seemed like every serious NASCAR points-chaser had buddied up with someone who was a pilot.

"It was not uncommon to have four or five planes land on Sunday evening," Waterman remembers. "We'd have to turn off half the lights on the oval to divert that power to the lights on the drag strip, so they could see to land and take off."

For the local racers, it was quite a sight. Modified veteran Andy Romano says, "I remember Don MacTavish, Bugsy Stevens, and a few other guys landing on that drag strip in the '60s, coming in from Thompson."

Stevens recalls also flying in from Pocono in the early '70s, by which time Jerry Cook and Richie Evans had joined the NASCAR Modified frequent-fliers club. Says Romano, "Jerry and Richie might have been just about anywhere on Sunday afternoon—hell, even Virginia—and this was the only way they could get to Utica-Rome in time."

Waterman says, "We always had to be sure that the pilots knew there was a wire running above the track about halfway down the strip. If they were landing they had to get down before that point, and if they were taking off they couldn't bring it up too soon."

Stevens, who says he "always had a couple of planes available" in his points-chasing days, remem-

Among those wheeling Sprinters on the Utica-Rome dirt was the driver of car #86, current Fonda Speedway boss Ric Lucia. (Don Edds Photo)

Joyful Jessica Zemken beams from atop her car's wing after a 2010 ESS Sprint Car score (Images by DC)

bers those Utica-Rome takeoffs being especially nerve-wracking, with trees looming at the far end of the strip.

"I flew out of there pretty often, and I could never get comfortable with that departure," says Bugsy. "Even today, I can picture those green trees getting closer and closer, and praying we'd pull up in time."

⁂

Though known best as a stock car track, Utica-Rome Speedway has hosted some dynamite open-wheel racing, with various touring groups stopping at the Vernon track. Sadly, the transient nature of those visits, coupled with the frequent changes in track management, made record-keeping a less than exact science. But this much is irrefutable: Utica-Rome's victory lane has been graced by some of the Northeast's finest Sprint Car and Midget drivers.

Of those two classes, the Sprints have visited far more often, with at least 50 features in the books. The first, under the sanction of the grand old United Racing Club (URC), was run in August of 1963, and it was topped by New Jersey's Bill Brown. That was, as near as can be determined, the only Sprint event held on the old paved quarter-mile.

But since Sprint Cars and dirt go together like peanut butter and jelly, it's no surprise that the flyweight brutes have rolled into town often since the track's conversion to an earthen surface. Most of those events were sanctioned by Empire Super Sprints, starting in 1987, when Gordy Button and Mike VanDusen won features.

Other ESS winners have included George Sifo, Robbie Hart, and Mal Lane in 1989; Bob Podolak and Jeff Thomas in '90; Lance Yonge in '92; Bobby Parrow in '94; Mike Woodring, Hart, and Parrow in '96; Steve Dow in 2001; Dan Kaszubinski and Doug Emery in '02; Mike Lutz and Justin Barger (twice) in '03; Jeff VanDusen, Kaszubinski, and Yonge in '04; Kaszubinski, Mike Stelter, and Yonge in '05; Steve Poirier, Chuck Hebing, and Jeff VanDusen in '06; Barger, Hebing, and Poirier in '07; Jason Barney (twice) and Poirier in '08; Jessica Zemken, Kaszubinski, and Barney in '09; and Zemken (twice) and Hebing in 2010.

Between 1997 and 2000, Utica-Rome welcomed the Eastern Limited Sprints sanctioning body, and the ELS winners included George Ely, Lee Sanders, and Mike VanDusen in 1997; Jeff Thomas and Gordy Button in '98; Button (twice) and Rich Wood in '99; and George Suprick, Mike Lauterborn, and Doug Emery in 2000.

More recently, in 2010, the ridiculously fast 410 Sprints of the All Star Circuit of Champions rolled into Vernon, and all the chatter was about two of America's finest racers: Fred Rahmer, the Sprint Car Hall of Famer who captured the feature, and Tony Stewart, the two-time NASCAR Sprint Cup Champion (and four-time USAC open-wheel champion) who made a surprise appearance and finished seventh in the feature in his first visit to the track.

The Midgets, too, have danced on both surfaces at Utica-Rome. As mentioned in the 1962 chapter, New Jersey's Tony Romit scored big in an ARDC feature during Joe Lesik's tenure. Dick Waterman also

NASCAR champ Tony Stewart thrilled the Utica-Rome crowd as a late entry to a 2010 All Star Sprint event. (Jay Fish Photo)

hosted the Midgets, but he booked NEMA, the Northeast Midget Association. Again, our exhaustive research may not be all-encompassing, but it's certain that in four NEMA visits between 1965 and '72, three giants of Eastern Midget racing emerged victorious: Dave Humphrey (1965 and '69), Johnny Kay (1968), and Johnny Mann (1972).

Once the track was converted to dirt, ARDC was back. Its two 1981 events were won by steady Lenny Boyd and thrill-a-minute Nokie Fornoro; a decade later, in 1991, the two ARDC events were split by Pennsylvanians Lou Cicconi and Johnny Heydenreich.

∽

The popular Lucas Oil Late Model series visited Utica-Rome in both 2009 and 2010, giving area fans a chance to see a great collection of racers made familiar by that tour's terrific television exposure. North Carolina's Ray Cook was the winner of the debut race in the summer of '09, while in 2010 the checkers waved over the menacing black machine of Scott Bloomquist, who actually hauled twice from his Tennessee base to Vernon: first to test tires, and then to blow off some of the best dirt-track shoes in America.

∽

In several seasons in the asphalt era, Utica-Rome ran Figure 8 events on a course that sliced across the infield. Though the history of those events is also sketchy, it's worth noting some of the Figure 8 contestants who were better known for racing in the track's traditional oval divisions. Dick Fowler, who achieved plenty of success in the Modifieds, was a frequent Figure 8 winner and the 1965 class champion. In 1974, Utica-Rome ran five Figure 8 events, and three of the winners were established Modified aces: Fowler, Sonney Seamon, and Robbie Kotary. And Dave VanSlyke, a star in the Hobby cars, was also a repeat winner in the Figure 8 class; one of Dave's wins came on May 29, 1966, when he topped Dick Delaney and a second-year Modified driver by the name of Richie Evans.

It's not hard to imagine Fowler, Seamon, and Evans, three fun-loving guys, laughing as they dodged traffic through that "X" in the infield.

∽

When Jim Bechy operated Utica-Rome in the '80s, he decided to make a stab at running "mud bogs," essentially drag races for all-terrain vehicles down a 200-foot-long pit of slop. Something of a cousin to tractor-pulling, mud-bogging has had brief flings with mainstream popularity. Bechy was sold on the sport to the point where in 1987 he assumed the presidency of the new North American Mud Bog Association. The group staged a handful of events at Utica-Rome in '87 and again in 1988, when legal woes saw the track hold just one program for stock cars.

Bechy's stay at Utica-Rome was rocky, but the motive behind his mud-bog experiment was sound. He told Paul Loughridge of the *Utica Observer-Dispatch* that his facility was in "the outdoor entertainment business," so it made sense to "diversify into other areas of motor racing." Many track operators have similarly fattened their revenue streams by hosting sideline events on non-racing nights, or in their off-seasons.

But that hasn't always gone well at Utica-Rome. Noting the rising popularity of snowmobiling, Waterman twice held events for the sleds in the early '70s. "The first time was to prove to myself that it would lose money," he chuckles today, "and the second time was to be sure I was right."

A regional snowmobile club watched Waterman take his two strikes, "and they were sure they knew exactly what I did wrong. So I leased them the track for a weekend, and kept the concessions. It worked beautifully. They made a few dollars, and so did I. They tried it again, and this time they had no snow. They had to truck snow in, and that's a big extra expense. So they didn't do so well, but I did great with the concessions. Come the third year, I offered them the place rent-free, and they weren't interested."

༄

And how about those Powder Puff derbies? A fad that seems to reoccur occasionally in short-track racing, Powder Puffs generally feature support-division cars with amateur female drivers, often the wives, girlfriends, or sisters of the regular drivers. In theory, they are supposed to be "fun" events; in reality, the girls sometimes get as racy and brave as the guys.

Powder Puffs were particularly popular on the old pavement track. The first was held in August of 1962, and it showed how feisty the ladies could get. Sue Duncan was awarded the trophy after the feature was red-flagged with just seven laps complete, thanks to a flip—*a flip!*—by Joan Hennessy.

Four Powder Puff derbies were held in '63, with Lucy Boratyn winning twice. Clearly, Ms. Boratyn had some real skills. In 1969, Utica-Rome hosted three Powder Puffs, and she won 'em all. She was so quick, in fact, that in 1971 she had the rare distinction of having a bounty placed on her head: A cash bonus was offered to any woman who could top Leadfoot Lucy in a July feature. The papers told of "17 daring Mohawk Valley beauties" starting that race, and its eventual winner was one Wanda Stevens. But, alas, the bonus went uncollected; Lucy Boratyn's car would not start, and she sat out the event.

༄

Want to determine in a hurry if a Utica-Rome fan is a true old-timer or a Johnny-come-lately? Ask if he or she remembers when Baron Daemon made occasional guest appearances. If the immediate answer is a wide smile, you've got yourself a dyed-in-the-wool Utica-Rome lifer.

The Baron—a clownish vampire character—was in fact Mike Price, a broadcaster who had worked at a couple of Syracuse radio and TV stations before

The much-traveled Lou Cicconi cruised to an ARDC Midget feature victory in 1991. (Don Edds Photo)

Airplanes, Open-Wheelers, Wild Animals...

spending several years at WSYR. He was a weatherman, a sports anchor, a news reporter, and a talk-show host. But his most enduring and endearing role was Baron Daemon. Initially, the Baron served as a host introducing late-night horror movies, but an interesting phenomenon developed: Parents began contacting the station with complaints that their children wouldn't go to bed until they'd seen Baron Daemon do his bit at 11:00 PM. Sensing an opportunity, the station created a daily show at an hour that better suited the kiddies, and made moms and dads much happier.

Now, the Baron—"Central New York's coolest ghoul," the station called him—became a sensation. In 1963, Price and some backup musicians, billed as Baron Daemon and The Vampires, released a 45 RPM record of a gag song called "The Transylvania Twist." To borrow a modern term, its popularity was viral. Every kid had to own a copy. (A half-century later, "The Transylvania Twist" still gets lots of airplay around Halloween.)

Price, in full Baron Daemon regalia, paid several visits to Utica-Rome, where he clowned with drivers and officials, mugged it up for the cameras, and did his best to scare and/or amuse the kiddies.

The young folks who loved him are, of course, aging Baby Boomers today. But just the thought of that spooky vampire cavorting on the speedway frontstretch makes them again grin like children.

And the Baron wasn't the only media personality to have his time in the Utica-Rome spotlight. Take the night in 1973 when a 25-car demolition derby was held for the press corps. Woody Maurer of Rome's WKAL radio ended up winning, outlasting *Rome Sentinel* staffer Pete Waters. Third and fourth were two names familiar to New York race fans: Norm Patrick, editor of *Gater Racing News*, and longtime Oswego Speedway race director Dick O'Brien, who also covered motorsports for the *Syracuse Herald-Journal*.

On a few other occasions, the track hosted what were billed as "disc jockey demo derbies," featuring "the top record-spinners and newsmen from area stations." Think of all the free publicity: You can bet that for weeks leading up to the derby, every DJ who planned on entering gave Waterman's track plenty of free plugs between spins of Iron Butterfly's "In-A-Gadda-Da-Vida" and "Jumpin' Jack Flash" by the Rolling Stones, that summer's hottest singles, and Steppenwolf's brand-new hit, "Magic Carpet Ride."

Rock on, Utica-Rome!

On at least two occasions, Utica-Rome gave local lawmen a chance to act as unruly as that portion of the citizenry they dealt with on their day jobs. In 1971 there was a 15-car demo derby, "with cars being driven by deputy sheriffs." Two years later, a 20-car derby involved teams from the Utica, Oneida, and Rome police departments, as well as Oneida County Sheriffs.

Waterman understood what many short-track promoters did not: that banking this sort of goodwill within the community, and particularly with local law enforcement, might one day pay off should problems arise over things like engine noise, rowdy crowds, or late-night traffic.

Some tales need no embellishment. "Ask Dick Waterman about the time he oiled down the place," suggested one NASCAR Modified old-timer. The story that resulted, though nightmarish at the time, brings belly laughs from all who tell it today, including the former track owner and promoter.

"For a long time, I had been using oil to keep down the dust in the pits and the parking lots," Waterman begins. "Well, apparently the guy I bought the oil from had been selling me something that was mostly water, because one Saturday we put this stuff down and found out what *real* oil was.

"Saturday afternoon, all the drag cars rolled in. Remember, it was not uncommon for us to have 200 or 300 competitors. Many of them raced the same cars they drove to the track, so the first thing they always did was unhook their mufflers. Well, when these guys crawled out from beneath their cars, they were *covered* with oil. Naturally, their cars tracked all that oil onto the drag strip, and that made for a hell of a slippery night.

"Keep in mind, a lot of the drag cars would pit on the oval, so of course they tracked a lot of oil onto the oval, as well. So, come the next night, the stock car guys were skidding and sliding all over the track.

"But the worst part came late Sunday night. Just as the races ended it started raining, so all the cars in our parking lot dragged that oil onto the wet highway. Naturally, that made the surface of the road as slippery as ice. Oh, I could hear the cars crashing out on Route 5! It was a terrible, terrible night.

"I tell people that this was the only time they ever had to sand Route 5 in July. But, at the time, this wasn't funny at all. I was scared to death that I was going to get into legal trouble."

Eventually the whole thing blew over, but not without a stern warning from on high. "I got a call from an official in Albany, with the DOT or some other agency, telling me never to use oil that way again," says Waterman. "I told that fellow, 'If you only knew the problems that stuff caused me, you'd know better than to think you have to tell me that!'

"Boy, that was one awful mess."

❦

June 6, 1971 was a terrific night for journeyman Modified driver Bill Nelson. He finished fifth in the Utica-Rome feature, behind Dick Fowler, Sonney Seamon, Lou Lazzaro, and Robbie Kotary.

Nelson doesn't look the part today, but 40 years ago, when he was a young pup out of Tribes Hill— "between Amsterdam and Fonda"—he had a wide anti-establishment streak. And, like many a rebellious youth in the late '60s and early '70s, he was not exactly making regular trips to the barbershop. One evening at Utica-Rome, his shaggy mane made him the center of attention.

"It was a hot summer night, and they had to red-flag the feature because of a crash," Bill says. "All the drivers were getting out of their cars, and of course the fans cheered as different guys climbed out. I was running decent, and I thought that was pretty cool, to hear people cheering for me.

"Like I said, it was really hot, so I took off my helmet. When I did, my shoulder-length hair fell out. And it was like half the crowd turned on me! I could hear, 'Hippie! Hippie!' A couple of people threw beer cans."

Nelson's story recalls the 1973 Charlie Daniels tune, "Uneasy Rider," in which the longhaired protagonist, laid low by a flat tire "in Jackson, Mississippi, on a Saturday night," tucks his hair under his hat and walks into "a redneck-lookin' joint called the Dew Drop Inn" to call a tow truck. While he's waiting, "some guy walks in and says, 'Who owns this car with the peace sign, the mag wheels, and four on the floor?'" As he's easing toward the door, our hero is met by "five big dudes" and "one old drunk chick."

If you owned a radio in the early '70s, you know the next lines: "I was almost to the door when the biggest one / said, 'You tip your hat to this lady, son' / And when I did, all that hair fell out from underneath."

Nelson shrugs. "It was the height of the Vietnam War, and all the protests. And my car had a peace symbol [painted] on it."

Different times.

❦

You'd think that keeping several dozen unruly racers in check would be enough disciplinary work for one man, but former speedway owner Dick Waterman also had a fondness for animals that were at least high-spirited, if not downright wild. For a while he had a guard dog, "a black Great Dane that weighed 212 pounds." The dog once had a major dispute with a horse. The horse did not survive.

And in 1968, as a door prize to a lucky Utica-Rome ticket holder, Waterman gave away a five-foot boa constrictor!

But a lion? *A lion?*

In the spring of 1969, he says, "we had a thrill show coming in, and their advance man paid us a visit. He couldn't believe the size of that dog, and we got talking. I said, 'You know, I've always wanted a lion, but I've never been able to find one.' The guy said, 'I've got a friend who's got three. Maybe he'd sell you one.' So he called this fellow, and I bought myself a lion right over the phone."

The lion was in Rochester, so Waterman hopped into the Utica-Rome Speedway pace car and headed west to pick up his new pet.

"The guy met me at the Thruway exit, and he had the cat on a chain," says Waterman. "It was little then, only weighed something like 35 pounds, so I put him in the car and took off for home."

Cute scene? Well, yes. For a while. "Pretty soon,

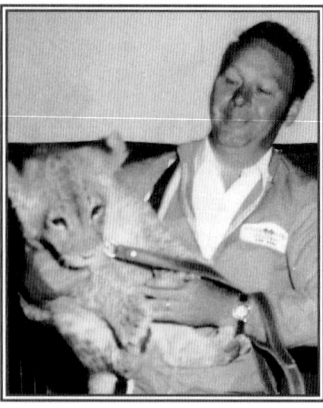

In 1969, promoter Dick Waterman adopted a lion cub he named Teddy. Though friendly, Teddy grew a bit intimidating! (John Grady Photos, Dick Waterman Collection)

that cat was going crazy. He got up under the dashboard, trying to pull out the wiring. He chewed up the Thruway ticket. I was having quite a time just managing to drive. Finally, I thought that if I could just hold him in my arms, maybe he'd sleep. So I did that, and, sure enough, he went right to sleep."

The cub was still snoozing when Waterman steered the pace car off I-90 at the Canastota exit, stopped at the tollbooth, and prepared to explain to the toll-taker why his ticket was in shreds. Leaning out of his booth, the toll-taker noticed the furry little bundle in Waterman's lap.

"The fellow said, 'What's that, a teddy bear?' Well, when the lion heard that voice, he woke up and looked at the guy, and right away he was all teeth! The guy in the tollbooth said, 'Mister, if you've got a problem with that thing, don't look for any help from me!'"

After the toll was paid—with arms fully extended, no doubt—Waterman headed home. He had already decided on a name for the cub: Teddy, in honor of the toll man's mistake.

Growing rapidly, Teddy lived with Dick and Dorothy Waterman "until, when he weighed 175 pounds, he climbed from the floor to the ceiling on the drapes," Dick chuckles. "Dorothy decided right then that it was time for him to go."

Relocated to the Waterman family's upholstery shop, Teddy spent his Sundays at the speedway, lounging in an oversized cage beneath the announcer's tower. He grew to a healthy 325 pounds, yet Dick Waterman continued to walk into the cage to groom the lion and feed him raw meat "right from my hand."

Phew! How could a driver or a car owner angry about a race-night ruling ever hope to intimidate a promoter who fed a lion by hand?

Oh, and one last thing about Waterman and his animals: That boa he gave away one Sunday night in 1968? It bit the fellow who won it!

1979

Saturday Night Jive

Leave it to Louie. Somebody had to restore order, slow things down, help things make sense at the end of the most chaotic off-season in Utica-Rome's history. The perfect "somebody" for the job was Lou Lazzaro, and there he was on May 30, a familiar face in a familiar place: victory lane.

He hadn't won there since 1972, in the heart of the track's pavement era, and between his own focus on dirt racing and Utica-Rome's 1975-76 troubles, it had been a while since he'd made news in Vernon. But that didn't matter a bit. Lazzaro had been part of the joint from the start. He was now on his third promoter and his third or fourth track configuration—counting subtle tweaks to the asphalt track—and there's no telling how many pit stewards, starters, assistant starters, and various other officials he'd been through. The Monk was Utica-Rome bedrock.

So seeing him win the season opener was a race fan's version of comfort food, as reassuring as Mom's meatloaf. All was right with the world, at least for this one moment.

But it sure had been crazy right up until then, and it would get crazy again shortly.

The size and surface had changed, but the great Lou Lazzaro hadn't lost his winning touch. (Bob Maneri Photo, Dick Berggren Collection)

~

Dick Waterman's winter had involved a lot of thinking. For two seasons, Mike Talerico and Steve LoPiccolo had leased and operated his speedway. They were young, ambitious, good guys. But they hadn't exactly hit the jackpot, for a variety of reasons: the weather, the NEARA debacle, and the region's steady tilt toward dirt-track racing and away from asphalt.

Besides, leasing the oval hardly left Waterman worry-free. As long as he was landlord, he was tied financially to the track's ups and downs. Bill Wimble, tight with Waterman and his late wife, Dorothy, says, "I admired the fact that Richard was always resilient. I know there were times when poor Dorothy was beside herself, because she'd seen the track have so much bad luck that she'd have liked him to get out of it. I think Richard finally came to that conclusion, too."

Enter Clifford W. Baker. Well, make that *re-enter* Clifford W. Baker and Auto Snow Racing Inc., which in late 1977 had demonstrated its interest in purchasing Utica-Rome. Baker, for six years the superintendent of the Westmoreland Central School District, had not given up on the idea.

"For two years he kept coming around, talking about buying the place," says Waterman, who at last was ready to listen.

Baker claimed to have been a snowmobile racer, but as for any solid links to auto racing Waterman says, "To my knowledge, he had none. He was more interested in snowmobiles. He thought he was going to make his fortune in snowmobile racing."

In time a deal was struck, and Auto Snow Racing Inc.—a five-way partnership including Baker, Westmoreland High School principal Richard Stanley, Oneida educator Paul Stratton, and Utica businessmen Louis DiOrio and Ralph Ventura—became the first new owner the speedway had seen since Waterman bought the place from Joe Lesik in 1964.

On Feb. 23, the *Utica Observer-Dispatch* carried a long story beneath this headline: "Baker Leaving Westmoreland Post to Manage Speedway." The piece was hardly a kiss on the cheek, noting that during Baker's tenure as superintendent, the school district had "experienced a controversy nearly every year," including a petition from parents calling for his removal. Asked by the newspaper about this, Baker replied, "I never lost sleep over any of it." If nothing else, he seemed to have the thick skin a track operator needs.

He still had plans to replace the paved bullring with a half-mile dirt track, with the pits in the infield. New spectator amenities would include 3,000 more bleacher seats and a concession building 100 feet long.

Rebuilding virtually every aspect of the track, cultivating a new crop of racers and fans, and planning out a busy racing program seemed a bit much for a rookie promoter to tackle in the few months before the season would start. Waterman suggests he said as much to Baker.

"We sat around talking after the whole deal was consummated," he recalls. "I said, 'Why don't you run it [as is] for a year, and see what's good and what's bad, and what changes you want to make.' He told me [the track] was his, and he had his plans, and he was going to do it his way. So he did."

~

Problems surfaced immediately. One week after the Utica paper detailed Auto Snow's plans, a headline in the *Oneida Daily Dispatch* didn't sound very sunny. "Track Changes Opposed," it read. Seems 170 local residents had filed a petition at the town offices—what was it about Baker and petitions?—voicing worries over what was happening at Utica-Rome. Their primary questions were about noise and "dust which could be created by the clay track," the paper said. There was also speculation that calcium used to alleviate dust "could kill trees and crops on adjoining property."

The *Daily Dispatch* quoted Baker as saying, "We understand their concerns and are hoping that we will be able to satisfy them."

But a Mrs. Frederick Gerow said, "Mr. Baker does a lot of talking to appease us. The problem is that we have no faith in his talk."

No, Baker's road was not smooth. Even though construction was well underway, with the old track plowed under and most of the new track graded, Vernon leaders made him apply for what the *Daily Dispatch* called "a permit to install a half-mile clay oval." The permit was issued on April 9.

Weather and construction delays bumped the opener from April 21 to April 28, then May 5, and so on. The politics and delays were a reality check. All along, Baker had talked of operating three nights a week: drag racing on Thursday, motorcycles on Fridays, stock cars on Saturdays. By April's end, Auto Snow was tamping down expectations, declaring that Saturdays would be the focus "for an indefinite period." That still left plenty of room for doubt, since this put Utica-Rome in direct conflict with the ever-popular Fonda Speedway. But, as has been established, the new owners seemed bent on following their own path, however perilous it looked.

~

May 30: Just a month after telling the press that Utica-Rome would run "only on Saturday nights," Baker finally opened his gates on a Wednesday. It was instantly clear that this was no place for the timid. The new dirt track had been touted as "a big half-mile," and it was definitely all of that. Ten feet off the pole, a common method of measuring track length, it was said to be six-tenths of a mile around.

Crafty Dick Schoonover topped the undercard for Late Models. Then came a 60-lap Modified feature, and Lazzaro's comforting victory.

Andy Romano, another guy with long ties to Utica-Rome, placed second, followed by Bob Savoie, Andy's son Mike Romano, and Ron Miller.

The regular Saturday schedule began June 2. The weekly show would include a 35-lap Modified feature paying $1,000 to win, supported by Late Models and an entry-level Amateur division. The Amateurs ran for trophies only, no purse, and with pride the only motivator the action was wild. In no time, a typical Amateur field looked like wrinkled shirts on laundry day. The early fan favorite was Vernon's own Gerry Newman, a woman mixing it up with the toughest men.

The Modifieds, of course, were the main attraction. Wally Warburton grabbed the first two Saturday-night mains before Leroy Hurlbut won the first feature of his career. Already, some interesting names were in the mix. Jimmy Winks, terrific on dirt but better known as an Oswego Supermodified star, was second to Warburton one night, and Rene Charland was back, gassing it hard enough to run third on the night Hurlbut won.

Lazzaro—jumping between Fonda and Vernon—returned to Utica-Rome in style on June 30, charging from a 21st-place start all the way to victory lane. Next came a midweek 50 on July 4, with young Tommy Wilson stepping up to win. And Larry Dalmata was often quick, winning on July 7 and eventually finishing second three times.

The second half of the year belonged to Maynard Forrette and Bob Savoie. Forrette, the Cyclone, won two straight in July and another in mid-August. Savoie, on his stride in a marvelous career, beat Warburton to the finish on Aug. 4 and then grabbed the last two features of the season. Only the invading Jack Johnson—taking

Jimmy Winks, a star on both blacktop and clay, gasses his Pinto at Utica-Rome. (Utica-Rome Archive)

Sitting tall in the saddle, Louie preps for some Vernon action. (Utica-Rome Archive)

Tommy Wilson drove to a terrific win on the Fourth of July, just a sign of things to come. (Utica-Rome Archive)

The Amateur class was supposed to be the domain of rough-and-tumble men. Then Gerry Newman showed up, and earned the championship! (Don Edds Photo)

At the top of his game, which included Utica-Rome's 1980 season, Tommy Williams was the region's Late Model king. (Utica-Rome Archive)

advantage of Fonda's early closing date—broke the Forrette/Savoie stranglehold, beating Mike Romano on Sept. 1.

Savoie was steady all season, adding five third-place finishes to those three wins, and come autumn he was Utica-Rome's first dirt-track Modified champion. The Gloversville resident, popular with area fans, topped Bud Hinman, Rick Gray, Fred Brooks, and Bob Simons in the standings.

~

Waterville's Tommy Williams, a marquee player in area Late Model racing, topped the points in that division. His dominant season included four straight wins in June, one in July, and one in August. Bill Roese, another guy who would be heard from for years, took three Late Model features. Other winners included Dick Schoonover, backing up his opening-night victory with a July score, and Jack Cottrell, whose winning spanned decades, took the checkers on July 4.

Few folks who watched the bare-knuckles racing on display in the Amateur class would have predicted a female champion, but there was Gerry Newman, holding the big trophy at season's end.

~

Sadly, the story of 1979 was not on the track, but in the front office. Almost nothing went as planned. In April, the brass had announced three Modified specials: a Memorial Day 100-lapper on Monday, May 28, a "summer championship" 100-lapper on Aug. 4, and a special season finale of 50 laps on Sept 29. Not one of those events ran as planned. The track opened two days after Memorial Day, with the Mods running 60 laps; the summer 100 was changed to a regular show; and Utica-Rome closed two weeks before that scheduled finale.

Certainly Cliff Baker never expected the day-to-day pressures to prove more than he could shoulder. But on July 10 he resigned as Auto Snow's president, informing the Utica-Rome staff that he was leaving "for health reasons." His partners took up the slack and slogged onward.

By then, Dick Waterman had long since reached a sad conclusion. He says Baker was "a very nice man, and a brilliant man, well-educated," but adds that he "was just totally unprepared for owning a race track."

Lou Lazzaro had made things feel so right on opening night, and there were a few other bright spots. But 1979, starting with the Auto Snow purchase, was a catastrophe.

Dick Waterman says, "If you had *set out* to ruin something—with a plan *how* you were going to ruin it—you couldn't have done it better."

1980

All the News Was Bad

Anyone hoping 1979 would go into the books as Utica-Rome's low point was forced into a quick rethink, because 1980 showed things could sink lower. Across most of '79, Auto Snow Racing Inc. had proven incapable of operating the track. But having sunk large sums of money into the place, it was in no position to bail out on the property. A "For Sale" sign would have been seen as a distress flare, and any offers would likely have amounted to pennies on each Auto Snow dollar. Its best option was to sit tight; maybe down the road a buyer would appear. And maybe—though this seemed a long shot—Utica-Rome could be leased to a third party in the meantime.

Chuck Mahoney sure had some fine days as a stock car racer. His 1980 promotional stint at Utica-Rome went less well. (John Grady Photo)

Against all odds, that long-shot scenario materialized, and a lessee signed on to operate the track in 1980. In mid-July, newspapers brought the word home to the area's race fans: "Utica-Rome Speedway to Open."

But any giddiness was replaced in track-record time by question marks, concerned frowns, and, ultimately, exasperation.

In 1979, Utica-Rome had been driven into the ditch by a manager who hadn't known much about auto racing. In 1980, its crack-up was caused by a fellow who talked as if he knew it all. His reign was marked by political blunders, postponements, officiating gaffes, and a wave of bad publicity.

~

Chuck Mahoney was big and tough and bold in an era when racing rewarded big, tough, bold men. There was no denying his driving ability. He bulled stock cars around with a style made for the times, stiff-armed and aggressive. Intimidation was not something he had to rehearse; it came naturally. In the posed-portrait photos so popular back then, he's often smiling as if he knew victory was a sure thing. Many times, it was.

Even when he stepped up to the big time, his talent carried him. In 1950, Mahoney ran 11 races in NASCAR's top-tier Grand National division. On friendly turf at the Vernon Fairgrounds, Mahoney qualified on the pole and finished third, ahead of giants like Lee Petty, Bill Rexford, and Herb Thomas. At the half-mile Charlotte Speedway dirt track, he placed second to the great Curtis Turner. In Darlington's inaugural Southern 500, Mahoney finished fifth behind winner Johnny Mantz, Fireball Roberts, Red Byron, and Rexford, and ahead of Petty and Cotton Owens.

Though he slid out from behind the wheel in the early '60s, retirement did not quiet Mahoney. He still made the rounds of tracks and garages, and in 1962 did a stint as NASCAR chief steward at Utica-Rome. That same year, Mahoney helped persuade a young drag racer named Richie Evans that he ought to give this circle-track stuff a shot.

Mahoney had paid his dues. So maybe it made sense—from a distance—when he declared himself the managing half of the duo holding the Utica-Rome lease. His partner was Charles Kotary, another brother born on the same branch of the strong family tree that produced Cliff, Tom, and Robbie.

But Mahoney was not management material. Cocksure, impulsive, he attacked every obstacle as if it were a car in his way on the white-flag lap. Rules and procedures? They were for other people. Mahoney hustled, took chances. Dick Waterman, Utica-Rome's owner from 1964-78, grew up with Mahoney. "I knew him very well," Waterman begins. "And let me say this: Chuck Mahoney should have been one of the wealthiest men in this area, because he had so many golden opportunities."

Waterman recalls that "in the Kaiser-Frazer days"—late 1940s, early '50s—Mahoney "had a car dealership. He told me himself he'd made something like $2,800 in one day, and that was a lot of money back then. Well, he ended up blowing it."

Even when he raced, things sometimes went screwy. That 1950 GN race at Vernon, in which he'd finished third, was a fine example. Mahoney was out front, charging hard, when he spotted a wheel another car had shucked. Waterman says, "In those days, they didn't always stop a race for a mere tire and wheel laying out on the track. Chuck passes by that tire a couple times, and everything is OK. Then he comes around again, and hits it!" A bent axle cost him any chance at victory. Waterman sees that goof as a metaphor for Mahoney's stiff-armed and aggressive charge through life. "Chuck," he sighs, "just could not seem to do things 100 percent right."

This was the man now operating Utica-Rome, crowing to the press, "I'm confident I can get things back to where they were in 1962."

~

That seemed to be a big thing with Mahoney, this harkening back to 1962. Though archived clippings from that year refer to him only as chief steward, he insisted his role had been much bigger. "I ran the track for Joe Lesik in 1962," Mahoney told the *Boonville Herald*. "I ran everything. We had 5,000 people here twice a week, and had to shut the gates at 6:00 PM because there wasn't room for any more people." He imagined those glory days returning. Mahoney laid out a Thursday-night card of Late Models, Street Stocks, and Modifieds, with Sundays slated for small-block Modifieds and Street Stocks.

This rosy picture remained in the air for maybe 10 minutes.

Everything that followed is best summed up by a series of headlines from the *Oneida Daily Dispatch* and the *Utica Observer-Dispatch*. They all appeared between July 16 and Sept. 12, a remarkable flood of bad ink in an eight-week stretch.

"Speedway Opening Postponed by Health Inspector"
"Starting Flag Falls at Speedway … Finally"
"Thursday Racing Cancelled"
"Arrest in Speedway Incident"
"Speedway Promoter Charged"

Every bold letter in that bad-news barrage led back to missteps by the track brass. The inspection debacle began when an agent from the Oneida County Environmental Health Department paid a July visit to test the water supply. Learning that the track's well had not been used for months, the inspector recommended it be disinfected, said the *Daily Dispatch*. Lacking a water sample, the inspector could not give the facility a passing grade. One old-timer close to the situation claims that when asked later to submit a sample, Mahoney, presumably irked by the whole affair, "took one straight from the sewer." That story may be apocryphal, but it's telling that no one seems to doubt that it *could have* happened. Rules? Procedures? Who needed them? Mahoney termed the water problem a misunderstanding.

When the track opened on Aug. 3, the night was a disaster. Angry because he felt the starter was too quick to wave yellow flags, Mahoney fired the fellow after the heats. Come the 25-lap small-block main, the replacement flagger mistakenly dropped the checkers after 10 laps. An animated discussion followed, on the front straightaway, between Mahoney, his officials, and several drivers. The "solution" was to run a second feature, 15 laps long, and divvy up the purse based on combined finishes.

Things got no better. One of the Thursday postponements was due to Fonda's Syracuse Qualifier having rained out on Tuesday, forcing Fonda to a Thursday rain date. "Mahoney said he would not be able to get the drivers because they would be racing at Fonda," reported the Daily Dispatch, which said little for Mahoney's foresight. Another Thursday night was scrubbed—with fans already seated—"due to the small number of entries."

The capper came on Sept. 7, when state police arrested Mahoney for reckless endangerment. According the *Utica Observer-Dispatch*, the races "were apparently terminated because of problems with the public address system, and the crowd became angry because patrons were not permitted a refund." Mahoney said he had refunded money to fans holding tickets for the Sept. 7 program, but not to those who had used rain checks from an earlier cancelled race. A number of fans became unruly. State police, according to the Oneida paper, alleged that Mahoney "attempted to run down people with his car." The Utica paper quoted one trooper as saying Mahoney allegedly drove his car "in a reckless manner toward another person."

Mercifully, the 1980 Utica-Rome Speedway season concluded shortly thereafter, as did the management of Charles Kotary and Chuck Mahoney.

~

Overlooked in all this chaos, sadly, was the racing. That is partly because the real news, and thus the focus of the local press, was the track's operational woes. And with Mahoney presumably too busy treading water to worry about things like public relations, a short-term lapse in preserving records left a long-term hole in the track's year-by-year narrative. In his relentless research for this book, historian Doug Zupan spent untold hours scouring microfilm and chasing down leads pertaining to each of Utica-Rome's 50 seasons. Time and again, he ran into dead ends concerning 1980.

"That's the one year I wish we knew more about," says a frustrated Zupan. "But you just can't find the information."

What is known is that on that controversial opening day, Chuck Kennison of Watkins Glen got the win in the short 10-lap "feature," and Weedsport's Donnie Wetmore grabbed the hastily-scheduled 15-lap nightcap. Street Stock honors went to Bob Engler, fast as ever.

Kennison came back to win another small-block show a few days later, this time over the proper 25-lap distance, and the next event went to Wetmore, so the two of them had obviously figured out the hot Utica-Rome setup. No surprise, because both men were quick wherever they roamed in their long careers. And throwback hero Gary Iulg, whose versatility carried him to numerous wins on both dirt and pavement, hauled east from Sanborn to steal a 25-lapper on Aug. 17.

On Aug. 24, Tommy Williams picked up another Late Model trophy, and Dave Carrington collected the Street Stock victory. From there, the season seems to have petered out thanks to rain, low car counts, and Mahoney's brush with John Law.

Steady Jon Button won the small-block Modified title, and Williams took his second straight Late Model championship.

~

There's no getting around this: History will not be kind to Chuck Mahoney's stint as boss man at the Utica-Rome Speedway. That's the price of sitting in the big chair: You get the glory, or you get the grief.

But it's necessary—not just fair, but necessary—to give the devil his due. Clearly, Chuck Mahoney loved racing, because he stuck around it in various roles for most of his life. The fact that his passion for the sport sometimes manifested itself in ways that others found distasteful does not diminish that passion. His death in 1999, at age 79, marked the passing of a major figure in New York motorsports.

Racing needs big, tough, bold men, stiff-armed and aggressive. The record books are full of them. They sometimes make champion drivers, winning team owners, and innovative mechanics. Best, however, not to hand them the keys to the front office.

EYEWITNESS
1976–1980: ANDY ROMANO

"I was not surprised to hear it was going to become a dirt track"

NOTE: Younger fans recognize the Romano clan as one of the region's premier dirt-track families. That's understandable, because in the last 20 years they've seen plenty of A.J. and Mike Romano running up front at various clay-topped tracks, But before that, papa Andy, himself the son of renowned area car owner Joe Romano, was a solid shoe in the asphalt Modifieds, running with the NASCAR big dogs at Utica-Rome, Albany-Saratoga, Plattsburgh, and at the Devil's Bowl Speedway in West Haven, Vermont. Always a self-reliant racer—"Drove my own cars, took care of 'em mechanically, everything"—Andy scored his first Utica-Rome victory on June 30, 1968, and what a show that was: In the closing stages of the 100-lap Lou Smith Memorial 100, he held off Jerry Cook and Richie Evans. But Andy was a fine shoe on any surface: On the day Utica-Rome reopened as a dirt track in 1979, he finished in the Modified feature. These days, Andy lends help and advice to son Mike, who, with Jake Spraker, operates Fultonville's Glen Ridge Motorsports Park.

Fred Smith, *AARN* Archive

When Utica-Rome was at its peak—I'm talking now about its peak as an asphalt track—it was the best. You'd go there on a Sunday night, and depending on which particular period it was, you had to deal with Richie Evans, you had to deal with Eddie Flemke, you had to deal with Rene Charland, you had to deal with Lou Lazzaro, you had to deal with Bill Wimble. Different guys had different times when they were *the* toughest, but right below them you had guys that were also really great drivers. It was just a star-studded field, every week. And the crowds were always good, too. That area has always had a lot of dedicated race fans, and those Sunday-night shows brought in a lot of people.

For a while there in the late '60s and early '70s, we had Albany-Saratoga on Friday nights and Utica-Rome on Sundays. On Saturdays everybody went off in different directions; some of us went to Plattsburgh, some of us ran the dirt at

Fonda, and some of the New England guys ran all the way back to race at Norwood Arena, near Boston, or later on to Stafford. But every Friday every Sunday, you had the best of the best.

It was a tough little circuit in those days. When you won a race at Albany-Saratoga or Utica-Rome, you beat the very best. At the other asphalt tracks around here, like Plattsburgh or Devil's Bowl, it wasn't a great big deal to win, because they didn't draw fields that were as good. But if you could win on a Sunday night at Utica-Rome, you had really done something.

I still remember the first time I won there, in that 100-lapper. Beat Jerry Cook and Richie Evans. One thing that stands out is that Richie was driving the #24, Cliff Wright's Modified car, and not his own car. There was a yellow flag with just a few laps to go, and as we were riding around slowly under caution I checked the mirrors to see who was going to be behind me on the restart. Well, I saw that white 24 back there, and Cookie as well. I thought, Boy, it's gonna be a tough couple of laps. And I ended up winning, which was great, because when you beat those two guys in a 100-lap race at a place like Utica-Rome—their home track!—you knew you had earned that win. It was not *given* to you.

Like I said, to win there anytime was special, so if it was a big race, like that 100-lapper, you had every right to puff your chest out.

When you look back, you can see how everything changed and led up to the track being changed to dirt. It wasn't a quick thing; it took several years. What happened was, in the very beginning at Utica-Rome, most of the guys around here had cars that had been built to race on dirt. But you also had a few cars that were built especially for asphalt, like Rene Charland's and Eddie Flemke's, and they beat up the local guys pretty good for a few years. Before long, there were more and more pavement-only cars showing up; several came in from New England, and of course there were guys around here who had figured out that stuff, too, like Sonney Seamon. It got to where if you had a dirt coupe and you brought it to Utica-Rome, you basically were driving an antique, like a Model A or something. So now, if you wanted to keep up, or if you were from around here and you wanted to do a lot of racing under NASCAR— because, remember, Fonda was a NASCAR track back then—you needed two cars. Some guys went ahead and built an asphalt car, or bought one, and used their older cars on the dirt.

In his pavement days, Romano wheeled some rough, powerful iron, including this coach with a fuel-injected big-block engine. (John Grady Photo)

Though never truly a Utica-Rome dirt-track regular, Andy knew his way around. Here, he hikes the left-front wheel in 1994. (Don Edds Photo)

So now you had to keep two cars running, one for dirt and one for the pavement. I did that myself. That's not an easy thing, and eventually a lot of guys had to decide, one way or the other, if they were going to be pavement racers or dirt racers. It's not that you *wanted* to choose, but it was just getting too hard and too expensive to have two cars that were completely different.

For most guys it was an easy decision to choose dirt, because that just gave you more options. Plattsburgh and Devil's Bowl had switched over and become dirt tracks, and of course there were a number of tracks in New York State that had *always* been dirt. So there were more dirt tracks than pavement tracks in this general area, so if you wanted to race at more than one place, this was the way to go. In my case, I went dirt racing, and I ran nothing but dirt for a lot of years. I did buy an asphalt car much later on, in the late '80s, and I raced that quite a bit. But in the period we're talking about, I was just like most of the guys around here: I raced dirt, and only dirt.

When Albany-Saratoga became a dirt track in 1977, you knew that Utica-Rome was in a difficult position. It was now the only asphalt track in the area, and it had a couple of tough years. And that was a sad thing to see, because here you had a track that was once one of the top places in the Northeast, with big crowds and great fields of cars, and now it was really struggling, mostly because of the changing times. So I was not surprised when I heard that Dick Waterman had sold the place, and I was not surprised to hear it was going to become a dirt track. I think a lot of people in this area saw it coming. But it was definitely the end of an era.

When Utica-Rome reopened as a dirt track in 1979, it was a longer track than it is today. Turns one and two were way over where the pits are now. I guess it's a half-mile now, and they called it a five-eighths then. And, man, that place had some *long* straightaways.

I can't say I was ever a regular at Utica-Rome Speedway as a dirt track, not in the way I was when it was paved. I did run there for a while on that long track, and later I was back there again, running on the track the way it is configured today. But I was never really a steady, every-week competitor there for any long period of time on the dirt.

But, you know, in the first race ever run there as a dirt track, I finished second to Lou Lazzaro. That was really something. I mean, we had raced together so many times there on the asphalt, and there were again, finishing one-two at the same place, but as a

Driving a car backed by his speed shop, Mr. Romano hustles around the Utica-Rome oval in 2001. (Post-Time Photo)

dirt track. I really don't have any memories of the race itself, but I seem to remember that it was a good crowd. Like I said earlier, that area's got plenty of race fans, and when the track has been stable, they've supported it.

The strange thing is, that track did have a few periods where different promoters just could not make it work. This might not be the proper thing to say, but in those early days as a dirt track it was kind of a run-down place. They were trying to get it going again, and that's not an easy thing. I've got to say, Gene Cole, who owns it today, has made it one of the premier tracks in this region. It is a really nice place, especially for a dirt track, and that has been good to see. I like to see *every* track do well; being involved with my son Mike and Jake Spraker at Glen Ridge has given me a whole new outlook on that. I've been involved in racing forever, but it's only been recently that I've learned a lot about how things work on the other side of the fence.

You know, my son Mike was still in his early days as a driver when Utica-Rome reopened as a dirt track, and he had some really good finishes in those days. In fact, we ran together there quite a bit. That was always interesting for me; I've raced with both my boys, Mike and A.J., and that can be a tough thing. Fun, but tough. I mean, it's hard for a father—at least for me—even being in the pit area and watching your kids when they're racing. Mike had back surgery a while ago, so he's retired, but A.J. is still out there, and of course I'm right there watching. But, you know, I'm lucky: I had two sons who both became very good race drivers. And, you know, both of the boys have won at Utica-Rome, so we're all there together in the record book. That makes me feel good.

1981

Fresh Start: The Brothers Compani, and DIRT

How many years had it been since the warm breezes of spring delivered high hopes to Utica-Rome fans? Recent seasons had brought late openings, rookie promoters, radical schedule changes, and an extensive and risky remake of the entire facility. Even under the relative stability of Dick Waterman's pavement years, the second half of the '70s had been rocky; recall 1975's "local show" experiment, the track sitting in total silence throughout '76, and the struggles of the Talerico-LoPiccolo management in 1977-78.

Honestly, Utica-Rome hadn't had a feel-good kickoff since 1974, when Jerry Cook and Richie Evans were turning the annual chase for the NASCAR Modified title into an all-Rome affair. And of course, the spring fever that year did not last: The first three races rained out.

Optimism had been a long time gone. In 1981, however, it came roaring back. Ron Compani, the veteran promotional face of the Saturday-night juggernaut called Fonda Speedway, rode into Vernon as the chief of a new leadership team.

This classic "moment in time" shot shows the Fonda pace car alongside the freshened-up sign along Route 5. (Biittig Photo)

New promoter Ron Compani brought great enthusiasm and a DIRT sanction to Utica-Rome. (Dick Berggren Collection)

Now, the word "new" was ominous to those who loved Utica-Rome. Unfamiliar faces had popped up in the track office like dandelions on a fresh lawn, and proved just as pesky. But Compani was different. For starters, his plans were set in late April and made public by early May, a stark contrast to the mid-July headlines announcing Chuck Mahoney's lease one year earlier. Then there was the fact that Compani was already talking long-term, telling the *Utica Observer-Dispatch* that he was in the process of buying the track. (This involved more than the usual amount of paperwork. When Auto Snow Racing Inc. hit the skids, the Bank of Utica foreclosed; the loan had been guaranteed by the Small Business Administration of Syracuse, which paid off the debt and took possession of the property. Thus, Compani was dealing with the SBA in his efforts to purchase the track.)

Plus, Compani had more promotional experience than anyone who had steered Utica-Rome in years. He had served at Fonda in a number of capacities, from teenaged track-crew worker to top dog. First with Jim Gage Jr. and later with brother Ralph Compani and friend Seymour Hayes, Ron Compani had led Fonda through some of that track's finest days. He'd also endured just enough trouble there to give Utica-Rome fans confidence that this was a man who could navigate a crisis.

And, make no mistake, Utica-Rome was in a serious crisis. It was bad enough that racers and fans were upset about what had recently gone on there; it was *worse* that many locals seemed to have been in the dark about the Utica-Rome Speedway almost since Dick Waterman sold the place. In an *Observer-Dispatch* story dated May 3, 1981, writer Ed Ruffing mentioned the track had "been closed for about two seasons."

Compani was going to have his hands full. He wasted no time in rolling up his sleeves.

~

Ron and Ralph Compani, who would run Utica-Rome together, had solid connections. Fonda had joined Glenn Donnelly's Drivers Independent Race Tracks (DIRT) outfit in 1980, and the Companis inked a DIRT sanction for Utica-Rome as soon as they took over. This virtually guaranteed that the track's special events would draw New York's biggest names.

But the real ace up their sleeves was the pool of Fonda talent they could tap. A decade earlier, in Utica-Rome's asphalt heyday, it had enjoyed an informal "sister track" relationship with Albany-Saratoga, and that association had benefited both tracks. Now the dirt version of Utica-Rome had a truly familial relationship with Fonda, and an unspoken assurance that many of that track's stars would do their Sunday racing in Vernon.

Even before the season started, the association was paying off. Jack Johnson, Dave Lape, Lou Lazzaro, and young Tommy Wilson—Fonda regulars all—planned on running Utica-Rome, as did the racing Romanos, papa Andy and his son Mike, and the Dalmata brothers, Ray and Larry. No question, the "Fonda West" theme was going to help.

"We came [to Utica-Rome] just because of Ronnie and Ralph," Jack Johnson recalled nearly 30 years later.

Still, for Johnson and Lape, heading to Vernon on Sundays was hardly a no-brainer. After all, their prior Sunday track had been the Weedsport Speedway, DIRT's home base, operated by Donnelly himself. While Donnelly certainly had an interest in the success of a DIRT-affiliated track like Utica-Rome, losing established Weedsport winners had to concern him. While Lape admits to feeling "a little bit of pressure"—for more, see Dave's "Eyewitness" reflections on page 165—Johnson could not recall any.

"Glenn knew we were Fonda guys," Jack said. "I had started there, and Ralph and Ronnie were friends of ours. So if they had another track, especially one that paid good and was pretty close to home, it was just nat-

Left: Lape gets a handshake from Ron Compani as crew, family, and friends celebrate one of Dave's four wins. (Lape Collection Photo)

Bottom: What a pair of giants! Jack Johnson, at left, grabbed six victories, while Dave Lape earned the 1981 track championship. (Clancy Miller Photo, Lape Collection)

ural that I would be there. I think everybody understood that."

A mid-May opener was scheduled. The weekly-show admission was $5.00 for adults, $2.00 for children 11 and under. For opening night, the new Utica-Rome brass announced that they would waive that two-buck kiddie charge, and let the youngsters in free.

Ronnie Compani sounded like a proud parent as he spoke to Joe Mecca of the *Oneida Daily Dispatch* just days before the first green flag.

"When we took this place over, it was a complete mess," Compani declared. "We've refurbished every building on the grounds and removed every piece of rock, by hand, from the track."

All was in readiness.

~

The first DIRT Modified season at Utica-Rome became a Johnson vs. Lape affair, which the new management, wooing those Fonda fans, had to love. Jack emerged as the top winner, bagging six wins: four 30-lap weekly mains, and two 50s, one in July and the other on Labor Day weekend. Though the track's layout in those days confounded many drivers—some were never sure if they were actually running downhill into that first turn, or if it just *felt* like they were—Jack enjoyed the place.

"It was a big track, at least a five-eighths, and fast, *real* fast," he recalled, adding that the Compani prep team normally "made the track pretty good. I actually had a lot of fun there."

But Duanesburg Jack had nothing for Canajoharie Dave in the battle for the track championship. Lape backed up his four wins—three weekly shows and an Independence Day 100—with two runner-up finishes and four third-places. Interestingly, Johnson and Lape each had 10 podium finishes, but Jack was more hot-and-cold; his only top-fives were those six wins and four second-place finishes. Either he ran up front, or he rolled snake eyes.

Only two other Modified men stood in the winner's circle. Underdog Art Kiser had a happy night in the opener on May 17, outrunning Andy Romano and Ken Hanson for his only Utica-Rome victory. (Art did poke into the top-five on three more occasions, including a fine fourth behind Lape, Johnson, and Mike Romano in that 100-lapper on July 4.)

The pleasant surprise of the year had to be Tommy Wilson. He had won a 50-lapper at the Vernon track in 1979, and had always showed good speed wherever he went. In fact, in '78 he won a championship at the Can-Am Speedway, up north in LaFargeville. But Tommy really turned up the wick in 1981. On three Sundays, he and his Fred Burrows-owned Modified took the checkered flag, with Utica-Rome's most famous names pressing him hard each time. On May 24, Wilson passed Lazzaro for second, and then, in a great tussle, *twice* passed Johnson for the lead. On Aug. 9, Tommy outran Johnson, Lape, Romano, and Ray Dalmata for a

Fresh Start: The Brothers Compani, and DIRT

50-lap score. And on Aug. 30, Wilson gassed it hard to hold off the ever-charging C.D. Coville.

In a season best remembered for the Lape/Johnson dominance, Wilson shook things up. He died young, of natural causes, but diehard New York Modified fans still recall him hustling that Burrows car with style.

And just imagine what Tommy's 1981 Utica-Rome season might have looked like had it not been for Jack Johnson and Dave Lape! See, in addition to those three victories, Wilson finished second to Lape in a pair of regular Sunday features, and second to Jumpin' Jack in two 50-lap specials.

When he was hot, Tommy Wilson ran with the very best.

~

All these years later, in 2011, you still run across message-board posts about Wilson, and in some of them he gets mixed up with Tommy Williams, who was shining in the Late Models as Wilson did his thing in the Modifieds.

With all due respect and forgiveness to aging memories—and the two names are awfully similar—Williams deserves his own place in his sun. At the dawn of the '80s he had a hot hand in the Late Models, but even by his own standards his 1981 Utica-Rome campaign was spectacular. He won on opening night, then steered his Howe Camaro to seven more consecutive victories on his way to the division title. He was just 22.

"I was just getting better, maturing and driving smart," Williams says in retrospect. "We had good equipment, and we were right on top of it." And Utica-Rome was right up his alley. "That place was *huge*, and I liked the big tracks. I liked being out there, just sailing.

"If you won a lot in those days, you started way back. Seemed like my starting spot was always ninth row, outside. And if you're starting 18th in a 20-lap feature, you'd better work fast. Concentrate, look for a hole, dive in."

Randy Glenski, Fonda's Late Model champ that season, must have memorized the tail end of the Williams car, finishing second to it four times. But talented Randy did manage to collect one of the three trophies Williams did not take home. The other two went to Paul Holic and Jim Rothwell.

And the Amateur class was back, and noteworthy because its winners—two-timer John Kiskiel, Gerry Newman, Sonny Platt, Randy Davis, Lloyd Drake, Craig Henry, and Rod Morgan—included many surnames familiar to area fans. Healthy blood was again coursing through the speedway's veins.

~

This upswing would not last forever, of course. Nothing seemed to last back then, not at Utica-Rome. But what the 1981 season accomplished was significant; it returned the old track in Vernon to a place of prominence. Fans followed who won and who lost, rather than snickering at the latest screwball promotional move. People cared again.

Most of all, everybody caught their breath. The dizzying downward spiral of their local speedway had been checked.

"This is a racing area," Ron Compani had said earlier in the year.

And in 1981, it felt like one again.

1982

The Tide Never Turned

The impression that 1981 was a triumphant season for Utica-Rome lasted through the following winter. There had been so many reasons to feel good, not least among them the weekly presence of so many big-name drivers, the terrific racing they produced, and the positive publicity the speedway had gotten following so many seasons of being justifiably kicked around in the press. Yes, Utica-Rome was again on solid ground.

Or was it?

Fans, racers, and the local media had looked for gains in '81, and they got them. Ron Compani saw gains, too, but while he was a fan of the highest order, he hadn't gotten involved with Utica-Rome just to see big stars and close racing, or to rehab the track's lousy image. He and brother Ralph also viewed Utica-Rome as a business opportunity, particularly if positioned, as it was in 1981, as sister track to their Fonda Speedway. But Ron Compani's post-season numbers-crunching did not reveal a facility awash in black ink.

Come April of '82, in a piece headlined "Utica-Rome Speedway Hoping to Turn Tide," Compani told the *Utica Daily Press*, "Last year, we didn't really make any big dollars." That meant zero profit, he claimed. But Compani did not panic. Stressing that it was not realistic to expect a reversal of fortune in a single season, and adding that those weren't boom times in the Mohawk Valley in general, he added, "With the economy the way it is, we're happy with Fonda. We're satisfied with Utica-Rome."

But not satisfied enough to just hope for better luck in '82. Surprising many, Compani changed Utica-Rome's race night from Sunday to Friday. Sundays, he decided, were "family nights," he told the *Daily Press*. Though likely upsetting traditionalists, the move had some logic. Forgetting '81, not since 1978 and the track's final pavement season had Utica-Rome been truly successful on Sundays, so it's not like Compani trashed a solid program to start anew. Something else to consider: Running Fridays rather than Sundays avoided another year of conflict with Weedsport, flagship of Glenn Donnelly's DIRT organization. Any way you viewed it, that made good political sense. Plus, Compani pointed out, fans from the Syracuse area, "just 38 miles from Vernon," might be tempted to support both Weedsport and Utica-Rome, instead of choosing between the two.

Was this an admission that trying to lure *Fonda* fans to Utica-Rome hadn't worked? And if the eastern front had been a letdown, did Compani's salvation—and thus Utica-Rome's—lay with those DIRT fans to the west?

Question, questions. It had become a typical Utica-Rome spring.

~

In short order, Compani's Friday move enticed a handful of Weedsport stars east, giving Vernon fans long looks at drivers who previously visited only for major events. But it also had the entirely unexpected consequence of costing Compani a driver with whom he had been linked for years.

Sundays at Utica-Rome in '81 had been comfortable for Dave Lape, providing a nice weekly postscript to his beloved Fonda Saturdays and giving the popular Canajoharie veteran a track championship. But Lape and car owner Dick Putman didn't find Friday nights in Vernon as appealing as Friday nights in Malta, where they had already found a sweet setup for the Albany-Saratoga Speedway. So Lape sightings at Utica-Rome were rare in '82, limited to biggies like the Super DIRT Series show in August. He finished fifth on that Wednesday evening, his only top-five of the year at Compani's new track. (On Saturdays, Dave did collect plenty of his friend Ronnie's payoff dollars, winning seven Fonda mains.)

But the Weedsport influence was felt immediately when Alan Johnson—"A.J. Slideways" in those days, a youngster just reaching the peak of his powers—grabbed the Modified 30-lapper on April 23. Randy Glenski, up from the Late Models, was second on that cool Friday, cheering the Fonda partisans, but third was Sanborn's Gary Iulg (a Utica-Rome winner in '80, you'll recall), adding to the Western flavor suddenly new to Vernon. In the course of the season, drivers from towns "left of Syracuse" continued to dot the top five, including John Birosh and late model grad Jeff Kappesser.

Alan's win on opening night was just one of six at Utica-Rome in 1982. And check this: when *Alan* Johnson wasn't winning, *Jack* Johnson—no relation, of course—was. In the first 11 features run that season, either Alan or Jack emerged victorious. Certainly, the duo was the on-track story of the season; with Jack in his familiar #12A and Alan aboard Tico Conley's #14J, they finished one-two on six occasions, with Alan winning five. The April 30 main showcased the extreme talents of both men. In 30 hair-raising laps, they swapped the lead *six* times. Alan was in front from laps 3-6; Jack took over for 7-8; Alan owned 9-16; Jack led lap 17; Alan nosed ahead on laps 18-20; and Jack reassumed command for the final 10.

The 1982 season gave Utica-Rime fans a good look at electrifying Alan Johnson, who won on opening night and never throttled back. (Clancy Miller Photo)

Jumpin' Jack Johnson had eight wins and seven second-place finishes. Guess who was the track champion? (AARN Photo Archive)

Interestingly, when their dominance was finally broken, on July 23, the Modified feature went to *Danny* Johnson, Alan's very fast kid brother, who outran—who else?—Jumpin' Jack.

Johnsons, Johnsons, Johnsons everywhere.

Danny Johnson was among three one-time winners, the others being the very accomplished John Podolak (who had seven other top-fives) and Mike Romano, keeping alive his family's strong Utica-Rome history.

And Merv Treichler, another Sanborn guy, spiced up the last five weeks of the season. Though he had a mild-mannered look—maybe, as with Bill Wimble, it was the eyeglasses—Treichler gave Northeast race fans some of their most electrifying moments, winning the biggest Modified races on both pavement (Langhorne '70) and dirt (Syracuse, 1981-82). Marvelous Merv brought his act to Utica-Rome in a big way, winning a 30-lapper on Aug. 6 as a tune-up to a 100-lap score on Sept. 17.

But the man of the year in Vernon was Jack Johnson, who, after trading those early victories with Alan, took control. Jack ended up winning eight features in '82, including three straight in August, one of them that Wednesday Super DIRT 82-lapper. He also placed second seven times, adding up to 15 top-two finishes in 19 Utica-Rome starts. That astonishing run of speed made Jack the track's Modified champion.

Reflecting on '82 while at the Utica-Rome pits in 2010, Jumpin' Jack smiled and said, "Alan came over and won quite a bit, and I remember Merv winning, too. But we were really fast."

Yeah, he really was.

~

It was a transformative season for Utica-Rome's second division, as the brass—echoing a DIRT trend—integrated small-block Modifieds into what had previously been the Late Model class, while keeping separate point standings for each. The low-slung offset Late Models running with the upright center-steer small-block Mods presented an odd image, indeed.

Paul Jensen, poised to make Utica-Rome headlines for years to come, topped the small-block points in 1982, winning a pair of features and generally serving as the poster boy for consistency. And Jim Rothwell, another future fixture at the Vernon track, was the Late Model champion. Jim won but a single race, but always seemed to be harassing whoever did win; seven times, Rothwell was the runner-up.

Top winner in this hybrid class was the previous Late Model king, Tommy Williams, who saw five checkered flags. Now retired and living in South Carolina, Williams still relishes what he did at Utica-Rome on July 9, 1982, in a qualifying race for the Syracuse Super DIRT Week small-block Modified event. Williams aced it with his Late Model, creating a dilemma for DIRT. Tommy says, "I beat Paul Parker, who had been really hot in the small-blocks. He got a wheel under me in every corner, but he couldn't get by. So we had the only full-bodied car ever to win a guaranteed starting for Syracuse," where it would have had a decided aerodynamic advantage.

"They called us up and told us not to bother bringing the car."

Lonnie Riehlman scored four times in LM/small-block action, while Parker and Bob Podolak each took two and George Hoffmier had a solo win.

The Amateur division ran a dozen feature events in 1982. Gerry Newman, by now the undisputed Queen of Utica-Rome Speedway, won *nine* of them. And she still had an awful lot of good seasons left.

Tommy Williams blitzed the Late Model field, and even won a Syracuse qualifier against the area's top small-block Modifieds! (Clancy Miller Photo)

~

It ended up being another puzzling year at Utica-Rome, not appreciably better or worse than 1981 had been. But it was certainly not the great leap forward Ron and Ralph Compani had hoped for. They pulled the plug when the '82 campaign closed, ending what had seemed to many to be a perfect match of venue and promotional team.

A story in the *Utica Daily Press* in April of '83 illustrated just how much the track had confounded Ron Compani, pointing out that in just 12 months he had gone from flatly declaring, "The Utica area can support a race track" to conceding, "I don't think the economy of the Utica-Rome area can handle that race track."

Fonda West hadn't worked. Nor had Weedsport East.

Perhaps Dick Berggren, most widely known as a NASCAR broadcaster but at his core a motorsports journalist with a short-track heart, has the best take on the whole thing. His years in the sport have convinced Berggren that what works well at one track cannot simply be transferred to another. He recalls that Lindy Vicari, considered the promotional wizard of Pennsylvania's Reading Speedway, could not replicate Reading's buzz when he opened nearby Penn National. "Opening night brought a huge crowd," Berggren recalls, "but thereafter the crowds thinned and the track ultimately failed." He adds that Tom Curley, the charismatic asphalt Late Model guru, could not make Plattsburgh work the way his wildly successful Thunder Road facility in Barre, Vermont, always had.

"In both cases, it was the same drivers, same program, same agenda, same management," Berggren says. "I don't know of any promoter who has been successful moving the magic of an 'in' track to another track."

1985

A New Venture

Thank heavens for dreamers. Every time Utica-Rome has seemed to bottom out, along has come an optimist who looked at the place not as what it was at the time—just another troubled short track—but as what it *could* be.

After 1983, when not a single engine cracked the summer air, three dreamers began kicking around ideas. Like Ron and Ralph Compani before them, they were dreamers with credibility. Trucking company boss Fred Burrows was a longtime racing enthusiast, and sponsored Tommy Wilson's winning Modified; Jack Johnson, the track's most recent champion, was in the midst of a career as one of the Northeast's most decorated racers; and Jim Bechy had been connected to racing in a variety of ways, including as a partner with Johnson in Jumpin' Jack's Pro Speed, the parts business they'd purchased from one of the area's great racing gentlemen, Frank Trinkhaus.

"We'd all known each other, of course," Johnson remembers. "Well, I don't know how this all came up, but one day Fred said, 'Why don't we buy Utica-Rome?' It was for sale, and it could basically be bought cheap."

Promoter Jim Bechy hands the CRC Series trophy to Dave Lape, who was champion of New Venture's abbreviated 1985 Modified season. (Bill Moore Photo, Lape Collection)

It sure could. According to the *Utica Observer-Dispatch*, the trio, doing business as New Venture Speedway Inc., assumed ownership from the Small Business Administration for the sum of $80,001, with Bechy serving as front man. The sale took place in June of '84, and word soon spread that Utica-Rome—uh, make that New Venture—was in the midst of yet another rebirth. As optimists will, Burrows, Johnson, and Bechy tore right into things, splashing around fresh paint and spending a reported $70,000 on new lighting. "We even built [a branch of] the speed shop out front," Jack recalls.

But they wisely kept tight reins on their enthusiasm. For 1985, they scheduled just four DIRT Modified events—all long-distance shows, one a month between June and September—and a couple of low-cost, (hopefully) high-profit programs consisting of Street Stocks and run-whatcha-brung Enduro events. Slow but steady was the game plan.

"We don't intend to *run* right away," Bechy told the *Observer-Dispatch* in January. "We intend to *crawl* and do things right."

DIRT president Glenn Donnelly endorsed that plan, suggesting to the *Utica Daily Press* that New Venture had "a lot of potential … with a schedule of major events four or five times a year."

Making things easier was the fact that many of the events were sponsored, the result of an arrangement between New Venture management and Ralph Stoppiello, in those days a regional food broker and later a friend of the sport who helped coordinate several major marketing packages. The extra flash would, in theory, attract fresh blood to the speedway. "We're going to bring fun back to New Venture," Bechy declared.

It all looked good on paper. But on dirt? That answer would take time.

~

NASCAR star Bobby Allison, fast in anything he sat in, qualified for a Tuesday-night 100-lapper before rain spoiled things. (Bill Moore Photo)

Alan Johnson, with Bechy beside him, copped the Miller 100 in July. Hours later, Alan placed third in the 85-lap Syracuse qualifier. (Ken Dippel Photo)

Interestingly enough, by the time the track reopened in 1985, Johnson and Bechy were no longer partners in the speed shop, which went to Johnson, or the speedway, which fell to Bechy and Burrows. Stepping away from the track-management game, Johnson reminisced in the summer of 2010, gave him one less thing he had to worry about in those hectic days. "I was just along for the ride, to be honest with you," he said.

Jumpin' Jack's history with Utica-Rome/New Venture went back further than most folks realized. Way back in 1969, when Dick Waterman reigned in the front office and NASCAR Modifieds ruled the Vernon asphalt, area fans were a bit surprised to see young Mr. Johnson at the pit sign-in shack with his Fonda Speedway ride, the Tom Douglas #91 out of Amsterdam. Though he was still two seasons away from his first victory at Fonda—where he ultimately became the biggest all-time winner—Jack already had a reputation as a kid who didn't spare the throttle.

But on that Sunday in '69, he was a stranger in a strange land. The Douglas car, Falcon-bodied, was every inch a dirt-track machine, and by then the black-top-only Modifieds engineered by the likes of Sonney Seamon and Len Boehler had made it all but impossible for a dirt car to do any serious business on the macadam. Plus, Utica-Rome was a stacked deck in 1969, its pits teeming with asphalt stars: Bugsy Stevens, Jerry Cook, Bobby Santos, local boys Dick Fowler and Bernie Miller, and …

"*Everybody*," Jack Johnson grinned.

The particulars of the evening have been fogged over by time, and by all the success that came later. "I really don't remember a whole lot about it," Johnson chuckled. "I was just starting out, and we were looking for another place to run. I know we probably didn't fare too well, or I would have remembered *something* about it.

"Really, I didn't have a whole lot of interest in running pavement at that time. I had started on the dirt, and that was where my heart was."

So on dirt he stayed, and on dirt he became a legend.

~

A New Venture

The "big-show" format brought all the stars to Vernon. Here, Jack Johnson pokes his #12A beneath Bob McCreadie's #9. (Ken Dippel Photo)

Rain ruined the first planned Modified special on Tuesday night, June 25. Too bad, because NASCAR superstar Bobby Allison was on hand for the 100-lapper, underwritten by his Cup series sponsor, Miller Beer. A race-anytime, race-anywhere hero, Allison drove a Jimmy Horton backup car to fourth in his heat race, good enough to make the feature cut before Mother Nature intervened.

The Miller 100 feature was eventually run as part of an incredible card on Tuesday, July 16. Alan Johnson won it, topping Jack Johnson, Horton, Joe Plazek, and Will Cagle. As soon as that race concluded, there began a complete program of racing headlined by an 85-lap CRC Series Syracuse qualifier. That one went to Dave Lape over Bob McCreadie, Alan Johnson, John Birosh and Horton. Track management claimed a crowd of 9,212.

On Aug. 14, a Wednesday evening, another DIRT 100-lapper saw Jack Johnson beat out Lape, Brett Hearn, C.D. Coville, and Richie Burgess. Wet weather earlier in the week got that program off to a late start, and a pre-feature concert delayed things further, to the dismay of many on hand.

But New Venture rebounded well, pulling in "nearly 4,500 fans" for its season-ending Blue Bonnet Butter Blend 200 on Sunday, Sept. 29. It ended up being a heartbreaker for Danny Johnson, leading with 17 laps left when his car conked out. Freddie Brightbill, up from Delaware, romped home the winner ahead of John Hewitt, Lape, and Ray Dalmata.

Lape's three podium finishes in the four Modified events gave him the 1985 New Venture championship, his second in the track's most recent three active seasons.

~

Oddly, two events that should have been headache-free moneymakers caused the loudest ruckuses of the New Venture season. First came the June 2 opener, which drew more than 4,200 fans for a slate of Street Stock racing and a 100-lap Enduro. Nick Ryan appeared to have won the Street Stock main, but was later disqualified for illegal cylinder heads. By the time that conclusion had been reached, Ryan had posed for the winner's photos, collected his trophy and the $1,000 payoff, and left for his Middleburgh home. Promoter Bechy forked over a second $1,000 to official winner Scott Noel and, according to the *Daily Press*, would "ask Ryan to return his share." Third-place George Hartshorn was also DQ'd for engine violations and, the paper said, spoke of taking "legal action" against the track.

Then a fellow named Dave Razey took the checkers in the Enduro feature, also paying a grand to win, only to be told after a scoring recheck that he was actually a few laps down, and that a pal of his named Dave Burt had won. Razey, said the *Daily Press*, "was not visibly upset," but that soon changed. It seems "Razey and other Enduro drivers said they had seen promotional material that indicated the top 20 drivers would be paid," when in fact it was, as most Enduros were, a winner-take-all affair. Not surprisingly, a spirited discussion ensued.

And on July 28, another Enduro produced a near-riot. A seven-car wreck produced a major fire—two drivers were taken to the hospital, one with minor burns and one with a neck injury—and led officials to halt the proceedings after 36 of the scheduled 100 laps. This did not sit well with many on hand, as Paul Loughridge of the *Utica Observer-Dispatch* reported. "About 175 drivers, fans and pit crew workers surrounded the track's [scoring] tower, demanding a refund" of their ticket and pit-pass money. "Oneida County sheriff's deputies and State and Vernon police had to be called to make sure things didn't get out of hand."

So much for easy-money fun races.

"A promoter takes a lot of flak," Bechy told *Daily Press* columnist Marty Lyons, "but he has to contend with it."

~

Though it happened far from Utica-Rome, and in a form of the sport no longer relevant to the goings-on there—asphalt Modifieds as opposed to the dirt variety now in vogue in Vernon—the area's motorsports community was rocked to its core when Richie Evans died on Oct. 24 at Martinsville. Just one week earlier, at Thompson, Connecticut, Evans had sewn up his ninth NASCAR national championship.

Freddie Brightbill surprised everyone in the Blue Bonnet 200, including runner-up John Hewitt (right) and third-place Dave Lape. (Ken Dippel Photo)

A New Venture

Top: New Venture's two Enduro events packed in the crowd, but were not exactly headache-free moneymakers! (Clancy Miller Photo)

Right: This huge conflagration, which interrupted an Enduro event in July, was the least of Jim Bechy's problems that day. (Clancy Miller Photo)

Starting in 1962, Richie had centered his career around Utica-Rome. Between 1965 and '78, he won 33 Modified/Sportsman races there, tops among all pavement drivers, including the final asphalt feature, a 200-lapper on Sept. 3, 1978. Additionally, he was the track champion in 1972, '73, '74, and '78.

In the beginning, Utica-Rome helped put Richie Evans on the map. By 1978, things had flipped completely; people came from far and wide to see him race there. He became its ultimate home-track hero.

Though absolute numbers are hard to pin down, Evans won something in the neighborhood of 500 feature races in his career. But his impact could not be measured in terms of mere trophies; just as weighty were his nine NASCAR Most Popular Driver awards.

Tributes to Evans flowed, and still do. One of the best was delivered in the emotion of the moment by a man he greatly admired, Cliff Kotary. The Copper City Cowboy may have been Rome's most accomplished race driver until the '70s rise of Evans and Jerry Cook, and in retirement he had served stints as Utica-Rome's flagger and gray eminence. Asked by the *Rome Sentinel* for his thoughts on Evans, Cliff said, "I used to win 30 to 35 races a year myself, and I couldn't shine his shoes."

EYEWITNESS
1981–1985: DAVE LAPE

"The racing was close, the competition was tough, and I had some success"

NOTE: Two-time Utica-Rome champion Dave Lape is a hall-of-fame racer in anybody's book, with victories throughout the Northeast and track titles at the Fonda and Weedsport speedways to go along with his kingpin trophies from Utica-Rome. He's also one of only three drivers—Maynard Forrette and the great Lou Lazzaro, one of Lape's heroes, being the other two—who managed to win in both the pavement and dirt incarnations of the Vernon oval. A hometown boy made good, he made tiny and distinctively-named Canajoharie, New York, famous for more than just its Beech-Nut baby food plant; for better than 40 years, race fans passing its Thruway exit have known they were speeding through the hometown of the great Dave Lape.

Ken Dippel Photo

That early-'80s period at Utica-Rome was interesting for me. It had been a really popular place as a pavement track, and I ran there quite a bit in the late '60s and early '70s. Then, of course, it was sold in '79 and changed over to a dirt track. But even though I was running nothing but dirt myself by then, I really didn't think much about the place when that first happened. That's the truth. I was racing at Weedsport Speedway on Sundays at that point, so Utica was just another town, another city I drove past on the way to Weedsport. I didn't think much about what was going on at Utica-Rome, or about who was running the place or who was racing there. And I don't mean that in any kind of a bad way; it's just that I was so busy, and I was having so much success at Weedsport and elsewhere, that I just drove right past Utica-Rome every Sunday without thinking about it.

What changed all that for me was Ronnie and Ralph Compani taking over as promoters in 1981. I knew Ronnie and Ralph really well from Fonda,

163

Always popular, Dave Lape won two track championships during Utica-Rome's rocky 1981-85 period. (Bill Moore Photo, Lape Collection)

and we were all buddies back then, really. I was glad to hear that was going to happen. They never consulted with me, or anything like that, but I heard a few things about it and thought it was a good idea. It was nice for me, personally, because even though Weedsport isn't very far away, maybe 120 miles, it was only about half that distance to Utica-Rome. If you're a professional racer, all that stuff counts. But in the bigger picture, it also gave this area a really nice two-track circuit. In the pavement days, Albany-Saratoga and Utica-Rome had been kind of like sister tracks, and that helped both places. Now you had the same kind of a situation on the dirt with Fonda and Utica-Rome.

Right away, a bunch of us from Fonda started going to Utica-Rome on Sundays, where in the past some of us might have gone to Weedsport instead and some others would have just stayed home. You had Fonda guys like C.D. Coville, Louie Lazzaro, Andy and Mike Romano, and Ray Dalmata there. Art Kiser and Tommy Wilson, who was driving for Fred Burrows at the time, were also Fonda guys, and they both won races at Utica-Rome. I think a lot of us from Fonda showed up to support the Companis, and to support the idea of this two-track thing they had going on.

And, of course, Jack Johnson also came to Utica-Rome. Jack and I had some really good battles at Utica-Rome in '81, which was nothing new for us. We've battled all our lives, before and after those years. It didn't matter where we were—Fonda, Weedsport, Malta, you name it—we always seemed to both be competitive. So, you know, Utica-Rome added another chapter to that; it's another place we can look back and say we fought for wins. I know I won the track championship there in 1981, but he won more races than I did, so, like I said, it was just another place where the two of us were competing hard.

Utica-Rome was a big dirt track in those days, *huge*, with some kind of a crazy dog-leg going into turn one. It was a fast, crazy track to drive; you'd be wide-open one minute and then almost stopped the next, just so you could get turned back and going the other way.

My memories from those years aren't all perfectly clear, because we're talking about a long time ago and I've run a lot of races since then. The seasons kind of start blending together. But I'm sure that in 1981 there must have been a pretty good battle for cars going on between Ronnie Compani at Utica-Rome and Glenn Donnelly at Weedsport. I mean, even though Utica got a lot of Fonda cars, it was also taking some away from Weedsport, and Glenn couldn't have liked that.

I did feel a little bit of pressure in those years about where I was going to race on Sundays. Like I said, I was friendly with Ronnie and Ralph, so it was a natural thing for me to go there in 1981. But I'm sure Glenn didn't like it, because—especially back thenhe wanted to control *everything* that went on in the DIRT Modified world. And, you know, Weedsport was his home track, his main deal, so I'm sure it bothered him.

In 1982, Utica-Rome went to Friday nights, which left me free to go back to Weedsport on Sundays. I wanted to run for the overall DIRT championship, which we ended up winning, and I'm sure it was in the back of my mind that running Weedsport put me back in good graces with Glenn. I guess I just figured it would be easier, if we wanted to run for his overall championship, to run at his home track, too. Anyway, I won that DIRT title and the Weedsport track championship, and 1982 turned out to be one of the very best years of my career. I went to 105 races that season and won 30 of 'em, driving for Dick Putman. But what was strange about '82 is that instead of being on Glenn's bad side, I ended up having a little bit of friction between myself and Ronnie and Ralph. See, when they moved Utica-Rome to Fridays, that put them up against Albany-Saratoga, and Dick chose to run at Albany-Saratoga instead; in fact, we had a great year there. As I recall, I explained my position to the Companis the best I could, but it's always tough when you're dealing with your friends. And it's nothing we didn't get over; I'm sure they didn't like it, but I think they understood. We all got past it.

I have to say that in my mind, Ronnie Compani was one of the best guys we've ever had around here when it came down to the actual business of promoting a race track. If there was a weekly show at some other track, you'd see him there with that Fonda pace car, talking to people, keeping up the interest in his

Dave and Jackie Lape enjoy a 1985 New Venture score, in the company of promoter Jim Bechy. (Bill Moore Photo, Lape Collection)

The final ride? Lape in 2000, ready to roll out for what just might have been his last Utica-Rome start. (Post-Time Photo)

place. He knew how to deal with fans, he knew how to deal with racers, and he knew how to handle the event itself: Get the show going, make sure everything runs smoothly, and keep everybody happy. He did that at Fonda for years, and from everything I could see he did the same thing at Utica-Rome.

Those guys only had Utica-Rome for those two years, 1981 and '82, and then they were gone. I've never really understood the story behind that. I guess either they weren't making money at Utica-Rome, or trying to promote two tracks at once turned out to be too much for them. Maybe having both tracks rely on the Fonda stars didn't work because the fans from that area just didn't follow us all over to Utica-Rome. All I remember is that all of a sudden, Ronnie and Ralph were out of there. But I thought they had done a good job at Utica-Rome, so it was too bad they couldn't keep going there, especially because no one else came in and took their place. The place just shut down for a couple years. But, again, that didn't really impact me at the time, because I still had Weedsport. I was back to just driving past Utica again every Sunday, and not even thinking about it.

I went back to Utica-Rome in 1985, when it was taken over by Jim Bechy, Fred Burrows, and Jack Johnson. When I first heard they were going to reopen the track, I wasn't sure what to think, really. Utica-Rome had gone through a lot of changes, and this was just another one. That's how I looked at it; like, let's see what happens. But it worked out well for me, because I got another track championship there that season. They only ran four races, all big ones, and we were able to win one of them and run pretty good in the others. And, you know, it was also at Utica-Rome in '85 that I really got to know Fred Burrows, who I ended up racing with for, what, 16 years? We used to park beside his car at in the pits at Weedsport when Tommy Wilson drove for him, so I knew him a little bit already, but at Utica-Rome we became even better friends.

Somewhere in all this—I guess maybe it was when Fred, Jack, and Jim had the track—we actually used to run both Weedsport and Utica-Rome on the same day, one in the afternoon and one in the evening. A bunch of us would scramble out of one track, and hurry up to get to the other. That's a lot of work, but it's also fun, and it gave us one more race to run.

By the way, watching how things went with those three guys in charge also got me thinking even more seriously about promoting. I think I could see pretty early on that their deal was not going to work, for a few different reasons. But it made me look at the promoting end of things, and of course Andy Fusco and I ended up doing that at several different tracks.

Like I said, it was an interesting period for me, and for Utica-Rome. The racing was close, the competition was tough, and I had some success there, so the memories are good.

1986

A Good Year for All, Especially Brett Hearn

Having fulfilled their promise by crawling, then walking—and even running a bit—in fairly impressive fashion in 1985, the New Venture management team stepped up its pace for 1986. The schedule was expanded, with seven DIRT Modified events planned (though only six were run, thanks to that all-too-familiar race-night nemesis, rain). And the previous season's outreach to sponsors had paid off handsomely; for '86, there were race nights and various programs backed by P&C Markets, Planters Peanuts, Ragú, Miller Beer, and Sun Country Cooler, among others, as well as companies which came via the DIRT organization, such as Skoal and Ground Round Restaurants.

Those sponsorships, co-promoter Jim Bechy told the *Utica Observer-Dispatch*, "have made it more favorable to do special shows for higher purses. That means more opportunities for drivers." The P&C link was interesting, in that the supermarket chain directed most of its New Venture push toward a weekly schedule for the Street Stock division, shoring up the competitor base while at the same time boosting interest among local grassroots racing families.

For the DIRT Modified division, the slate included a single event in May, two in June, one in July, two in August, and the second annual Blue Bonnet 200 in late September.

"All of our events will have more significance," said Bechy.

It was a lofty goal, and one which, in hindsight, was achieved.

~

Brett Hearn had a stellar 1986 season at New Venture, winning five of his six starts. (Ken Dippel Photo)

The '86 season is a memorable one in Utica-Rome lore—OK, New Venture lore—simply because it gave another Northeast superstar his crack at Vernon dominance. From its very beginnings as Joe Lesik's little asphalt bullring, some of the region's top names have had killer seasons at the track on Route 5: Rene Charland, Lou Lazzaro, Eddie Flemke, Jerry Cook, Richie Evans, Dave Lape, Jack Johnson, right up until the 21st-century rise of heroes like Pat Ward, Willy Decker, and Stewart Friesen.

But in 1986, New Venture belonged to Brett Hearn, who went five-for six against some of the biggest Modified names of the era, or any era, for that matter.

"It was one of those years where we just couldn't do anything wrong," Hearn recalls. "For the short season we had there, I remember pretty much having my way [at New Venture]."

Ain't that the truth? Brett the Jet won the 50-lap opener on Friday, May 9; the 86-lap Super DIRT Series show on Tuesday night, July 15; another 50-lapper on Sunday, Aug. 3; and a pair of 100-lappers on Wednesday, Aug. 13 and Friday, Aug 22.

Even on the one night he didn't win, June 6, he managed to steal the show. In the early going of a 40-lap main, Hearn and John Birosh collided while battling for second. Restarting at the tail end, Hearn put on what *Gater Racing News* called "one of his infamous charges through the pack," and furiously tracked down Bob McCreadie, who had led from the opening green flag. Hearn actually slipped past McCreadie for the lead with five laps remaining, but Barefoot Bob, ever crafty, rose to the occasion and gassed his way back into the lead for keeps. Second place on this night was Hearn's worst finish of the New Venture Modified season.

"No matter what we tried that year, it seemed like it was the right thing," says Hearn. "I remember getting to the track late once and having the completely wrong gear in the car, and still winning our heat race. I remember having some driveline issues on another night, having the driveline basically grind itself apart, and winning the feature anyway."

His luck may have baffled Brett, but his speed confounded many of those he raced against. "Some of the competitors were pretty upset," says Hearn. "I still remember that after one of those races, we were forced to take the heads off the engine [for inspection]. We got protested. It was a situation where we had a race either that night or the next day at Weedsport, and it was kind of like they were just busting me. And the heads were fine.

"You know, it's aggravating to be torn down, but I think ultimately it's *more* aggravating to the person who tore you down [once the car passes]."

It was a season of accolades for Hearn, who also won the Super DIRT Series championship—his first of seven—as well as the fifth of his amazing 15 track titles at the Orange County Fair Speedway in Middletown, his Saturday-night home for so many years. He was also named "Driver of the Year" by the Eastern Motorsports Press Association. Yet there is no mistaking his pride in what he accomplished that summer in Vernon, when he was still very much an up-and-comer; he turned 28 that September, and in those pre-Jeff Gordon days any driver under 30 was still viewed as something of a cub.

"For us, going up there for those races was pretty big," Hearn reminisced in late 2010. "That was kind of in my early days of traveling, when I was starting to stretch out and get away from just running Nazareth and Middletown. [New Venture] was a little bit bigger than it is now. In those days it had long straightaways and pretty broad turns. And it was in great shape; it was a really nice place to go [in that period], as it is today.

"It seemed to be almost like a resurgence of that track. I don't remember exactly who ran in the top five on each night—I don't have that Will Cagle kind of memory—but I remember so many good guys being there. You know, in that period Bob McCreadie was really tough, and Alan has always been tough, and Dave Lape was winning a lot. We're talking about people who are the 'best of all-time' kinds of guys, so to go upstate and beat them at that particular stage of my career was very, very special."

Barefoot Bob McCreadie was the only man to beat Hearn at New Venture in 1986, winning a June 40-lapper. (Bill Moore Photo)

Hearn sure beat the best. On this night in July, he topped Danny Johnson (center) and Charlie Rudolph. (Ken Dippel Photo)

Interestingly, Hearn's five victories came at the expense of five different runner-up finishers. C.D. Coville, Danny Johnson, Steve Paine, McCreadie, and Alan Johnson all played second fiddle.

"Pretty good lineup, huh?" Brett quips, his satisfaction still evident.

And he relishes the fact that all of his victories in that special season came in extra-distance events. "You know, we were so strong that year, I don't think it would have mattered if they were all 10-lap races," he says. "But I liked the longer races. I really liked the idea that they were high-paying races, for that time. And when you win a long race, it gives everyone ample time to get a shot at you, so it's more special in that way, too."

~

As if not content with elbowing around the biggest names in Modified racing, Hearn also ended up as champion of a New Venture mini-series for DIRT's 320-Modified division. The small-block guys were originally scheduled four times, but one was cancelled after twice being rained out. Hearn won two of the three events that did run, beating Mike Ricci and Maynard Forrette in a 50-lapper on July 27 and then topping Alan Johnson and Billy Schinkel Jr. over the 86-lap distance on Oct. 9.

The remaining feature, a 30-lap show on June 15, saw A.J. Romano outrun Roger Horvath and Steve Behrent.

Hearn is certainly one of the acknowledged masters of jumping back and forth between big-block Modifieds and their high-revving mouse-engined cousins, having authored numerous same-night sweeps of both divisions, most notably at Middletown's Orange County Fair Speedway. At New Venture in '86, he had the rare luxury of being able to concentrate on the Modifieds and the 320-Mods on different nights, since none of the races coincided. Still, he had to master the different setups required by each, not to mention the largely different fields of racers.

"It's never been easy to do that," says Hearn, though on many nights he sure made it look that way.

~

Nick Ryan won the P&C Street Stock division championship, boosted by three victories, four runner-up finishes and a pair of thirds in 14 starts. Only Bobby Taylor was in the same league; Taylor won four times, but lacked Ryan's consistency.

With that duo gobbling up half of the division's trophies, their competitors were unselfish enough to spread the other hardware around amongst themselves. Taking single Street Stock victories were Dave Werber, Todd Hoffman, Bobby Knipe, Ed Kuck, Kevin Blacken, Fred Tauss, and the wonderfully (and almost suspiciously) named Dan DeLine.

~

So where exactly did New Venture, or Utica-Rome, stand in 1986? Had the place truly bounced back? Was it merely in the process of bouncing back? Or was this just another false blip in what had been a spotty, troubled history?

The real answers were still down the road a bit. But there's nothing like some "in the moment" commentary to bring back the feel of the day, and a 1986 issue of *Gater* sheds a bit of light on the positive vibes surrounding the track in its second year under the Bechy/Burrows banner.

After visiting the track for the Syracuse qualifier on July 15, columnist Jerry Skibinsi wrote the following in his "Niagara Frontier" space: "It was difficult not to be impressed with the well-prepared New Venture facility and hard-working promoter Jim Beechy [sic]. Due to the difficulties experienced by the old Utica-Rome Speedway, Beechy is not just running the track with the hope of making a few dollars and seeing what happens. But rather Jim has devised an intricate five-year building plan which strives to develop a broad base of fan and driver support. Jim's goal of assuring that any fan

The mid-1980s saw several new stars emerge in the DIRT Modified world, and Doug Hoffman was among the brightest. (Ken Dippel Photo)

who comes to New Venture once will receive a positive impression and might therefore return is promoted by running a professional show, having neatly manicured grounds, freshly painted buildings, sponsor's billboards, and bleachers and accommodations for everyone including a plainly marked family section and a much-appreciated raised flat with a ramp for those confined to wheel chairs."

Yes, New Venture was a good place to be, and to race, in that summer of '86 … even if your name wasn't Brett Hearn.

1987-1988

Tremont Shines; New Venture Fades

The headlines that rang in 1987 were bold and beautiful: "4,378 See Races at New Venture," one read. That was on Monday, April 27, the day after the track opened with a 100-lap feature for DIRT Modifieds, won by Jumpin' Jack Johnson. It was an upbeat kickoff to what looked to be another positive baby-steps season for the Bechy/Burrows ownership team.

On the Modified side of the slate, there were seven nights planned, but with 10 total features, thanks to a couple of interesting promotional twists: twin 25-lap features on Friday night, June 12, and triple-25s on July 31, also a Friday. Elsewhere on the calendar were two 100-lappers, one on opening night and the other on Tuesday, June 16; a 50-lapper on Friday, May 15; a Super DIRT Series 87-lapper on Tuesday, July 14 (rescheduled to July 22 after what was, happily, the season's only rainout); and the 61-lap Richie Evans Memorial on Wed., Aug. 12.

The familiar Tremont family #115 was a great addition to any speedway's pit area. (Ken Dippel Photo)

And so pumped up was Jim Bechy with way things were going at that stage that he added two more Modified events, 30-lappers on consecutive Saturday nights, Aug. 29 and Sept. 5.

The racing was intense all the way. After winning that opener, Jack Johnson authored a May 15 victory dripping with bravura; trailing leader Alan Johnson and stifled in many earlier attempts, Jack tried a Hail Mary outside pass on the final corner of the final lap. It worked. Never down long, Alan had things go the other way in the June 100-lapper, when leader Kenny Tremont Jr. slowed with a broken brake caliper on lap 74. A.J. Slideways and his red-hot Billy Taylor Modified ride parked in victory lane.

But by that point in the year, it was clear that Tremont had something going for him. Second to Jack Johnson in the opener, Kenny scored a win and a second (to Jack again) in that twin-25 program in June. And after giving up that June victory to Alan Johnson, Tremont went on a New Venture rampage. He won the Super DIRT Series race; placed first, fourth, and third in those wild triple-25s (Jack Cottrell and Ray Dalmata were the other winners); and outran Dave Lape to win the Evans Memorial.

Lape and first-time winner Tim Dwyer aced the two Saturday-night specials tacked on at season's end, but Tremont had already iced the New Venture championship. Though not often associated with the Vernon track—he hadn't often strayed there prior to '87 and would soon be robbed of more opportunities—his title became one more interesting jewel in his glittering crown. On the quiet side, and too often overlooked because of it, Kenny has certainly been loud when it mattered most. Were he the bragging type, he could make the truly rare boast of having won a dozen championships each at two different tracks, Albany-Saratoga (including one on the new asphalt in 2010) and Lebanon Valley, where he is also the all-time Modified winner.

Tremont and his family, headed by father Ken, a New York State Stock Car Racing Hall of Fame inductee, have brought class to every track they've visited. In 1987, it was simply New Venture's turn.

~

The support-division scene in '87 was, in a word, weird. Bechy attempted to run four events for the DIRT 320-Modified championship series. All four were lost to either rain or freezing temperatures.

The Sportsman guys did get in its four events, with Stu Sheppard and Alton Palmer each winning twice. But Palmer's consistency—he ran second and third on the nights Sheppard won—gave him the crown.

Todd Hoffman's six wins in 11 starts propelled him to the Street Stock title. Fred Tauss copped three trophies, with the other two snagged by Bubba Tanner. Top cat in the Pure Stocks was three-timer Steve Lockwood, with Jerry Holmes (twice) and Craig Henry also earning popular victories.

Top: Ray Dalmata, highly respected along the Mohawk River corridor, bulls his #643 around New Venture (Ken Dippel Photo)

Left: Kenny Tremont, quiet, classy, and fast, was the 1987 New Venture champion. (AARN Photo Archive)

Top: Todd Hoffman was on the hammer in the Street Stocks, winning six features and the division title. (Utica-Rome Archive)

Left: Dave Lape celebrates a late-August feature win with car owner Fred Burrows' daughters Brenda (L) and Bonnie. (Bill Moore Photo)

There was something about that 100-lap Modified opener that harkened back to a certain 30-lapper in the track's days as an asphalt NASCAR Modified beehive. The chapter in this book covering 1966 recounts the great mix of talent that comprised the top-five finishers on June 12 of that year: Ken Shoemaker, Richie Evans, Pete Hamilton, Eddie Flemke, and Bill Wimble, a diverse group of personalities we called "emblematic of its times."

Well, in that 1987 opener, Jack Johnson was chased home by Tremont, Kenny Brightbill, Lape, and Alan Johnson, another interesting and diverse collection. Jack and Lape are Mohawk Valley legends, Tremont might be the hottest east-of-Albany racer in New York history, Alan won everywhere but especially in the central and western portions of the state, and Brightbill will always be identified with Pennsylvania's revered Reading Fairgrounds and his fast, basic, homemade string of #19 Modifieds. By '87, Jack, Lape, and Brightbill were established vets, while both Tremont and Alan, though big winners for a while already, were still fresh-faced enough that a trade paper report that season called them "youthful speedsters."

You could comb through the archives of every feature rundown at every dirt Modified track that season and maybe find a top-five that was just as good. But it would be impossible to find one *better*.

Yeah, Utica-Rome had a lot going for it in 1987.

And then it all came crashing down.

~

Every kid who visits a carnival and has even an ounce of curiosity will eventually feel a desire to peek behind the fences, to see how this stuff all really happens. And though it may take a while—weeks, months, years—he or she will one day wish that urge had remained suppressed. Sometimes in life, it's just easier to not know exactly how things work.

Partnerships can be a lot like that. What looks smooth and easy from a distance can be a mess up close. And in the spring of 1988, the Northeast racing community got an up-close look at the mess that had become of the New Venture Speedway management team. Fred Burrows, the longtime racing enthusiast, Modified sponsor, and quiet half of the partnership that owned the track, filed suit against Bechy, the out-front guy in the team from the days when it had been a trio involving Jack Johnson.

At issue was what court documents and press reports called "an interest or lien on the premises in the sum of over $113,000" held by Burrows. Ron Moshier, the top-notch motorsports scribe for the *Utica Observer-Dispatch*, reported at the time, "According to Burrows, over $107,000 of that total is for work and materials for grading and excavating done between November, 1984, and October [of 1987]."

It was easy to read between the lines and conclude that Burrows had put more dollars into track ownership, and taken fewer dollars out, than he'd planned on. Now he had drawn a line in the sand. "Just the money," he told the newspaper. "That's all I want." And while it's always tricky to guess at the tone of a conversation via

Track co-owner Fred Burrows takes Rome mayor Carl Eilenburg for a spin in the pace car. (Utica-Rome Archive)

printed quotes, Burrows sure seemed to be well past the partnership-honeymoon stage when he told Moshier he and Jim Bechy would not be running the speedway together in the days ahead.

"It's either him or me," Burrows declared.

At stake was more than just the not-inconsiderable amount of money Fred Burrows felt he had coming. The 1988 New Venture season was also clearly in jeopardy, despite Bechy's protestations—again, quoted by Moshier—that, "The track will open. There is no doubt in my mind."

According to Bechy, he and Burrows remained partners in the corporation that owned the speedway, with Burrows owning a third of the stock. But, surprising many, Bechy disclosed that since February of 1987, operating independently, he had been leasing the track. "I leased the property from the corporation that owns the land," he told the *Observer-Dispatch*, "so I own one hundred percent of the [racing] operation."

And *Area Auto Racing News* columnist Dean Reynolds quoted Bechy as saying, "I have New Venture. Not Fred Burrows."

Keeping his distance was DIRT's Glenn Donnelly, whose outfit now viewed New Venture as an "associate" track rather than a full-on member. "When you're an associate, we really don't get into any of your problems," Donnelly told Moshier, adding, "We're taking a wait-and-see attitude."

To watch this affair play out was to wish that the whole thing had stayed hidden behind that carnival fence. Race fans had seen various Utica-Rome bosses derailed by boredom (Joe Lesik), weather (Dick Waterman), inexperience (Talerico and LoPiccolo), arrogance (Cliff Baker, Chuck Mahoney), and financial constraints (the brothers Compani). Now they saw their speedway treated like the unfortunate child in a contested divorce, its parents suddenly antagonistic after what had seemed to be happy times.

Resolution came at last when Bechy and Burrows settled out of court that summer. "I bought Fred out," Bechy told Ron Moshier. But the fears of those who loved the track proved well-founded; it was too late to put together any kind of a serious racing schedule for the season.

There was but a single stock car event held in 1988 at New Venture, and—with no disrespect to the participants—it was hardly befitting a venue which in 1986 and '87 had headlined the Hearns, Johnsons, Lapes, Tremonts, and McCreadies, the royalty of Northeast dirt-track racing. On Sunday, Aug. 21, Late Model grad Jim Rothwell topped a meager 10-car Sportsman field, Bobby Knipe hauled in from Connecticut to grab the Street Stock checkers, and Dan Riffenburgh took home the Pure Stock trophy.

Two similar programs set for Sept. 11 and Oct. 2 were later cancelled, and Jim Bechy began easing toward the same door through which Fred Burrows—and all those before them—had shuffled away from Utica-Rome.

~

Recently, Brett Hearn was musing about the earliest days of the New Venture period, when Bechy, Burrows, and Jack Johnson—three racers—had just assumed ownership, full of plans and optimism.

"I thought that was the perfect setup," Hearn reflected. "They had the speed shop out front on the property, they had a Troyer dealership, and it could have made for an unbelievable test track. To me that was like a racer's dream: To be able to sell parts to the guys who are racing at your track, to be able to use the track to test whenever you want …

"It was kinda crazy that that fell apart."

Here, Hearn sighed. Back in 1988, a sigh was all anyone who loved Utica-Rome—no matter what they called the place—could manage.

1989

Bub Saves the Day

Anybody who honestly saw Millard "Bub" Benway as any sort of motorsports visionary prior to the late 1980s would almost have to have been a motorsports visionary himself. Benway was not a Glenn Donnelly, forging his own vision for stock car racing in the region. He wasn't a Joe Lesik, restless for new challenges.

No, Bub Benway, at least viewed from afar, was the picture of a contented man. In 1960, operating on a dream and utilizing equipment on loan from the construction business he co-owned with his brother Ray, he began carving into the ground in Fulton, New York, a track he dubbed Mil-Ray Speedway. Built on land abutting the Oswego River—fitting, because Bub had been inspired by the action at nearby Oswego Speedway—the track sat in a natural amphitheatre, its racing surface in a bowl of sorts and its seats built into the hillside. Three-eighths of a mile around and paved, it opened in 1961 and was soon renamed Fulton Speedway. Across its history came waves of regional stock car stars: Billy Rafter, Jackie Naum, Johnny Michaels, and Jack Murphy; Dutch Hoag, Lee Osborne, Maynard Troyer, and Sonney Seamon; Richie Evans, Geoff Bodine, Jim Shampine, and George Kent. Then came Supermodifieds, and they brought their own heroes: the great Shampine, of course, along with Eddie Bellinger, Bentley Warren, Jimmy Winks, and more.

Benway did take the occasional sideways step, including a brief early-'70s promotional stint at Canandaigua. But, always, Fulton was his baby. When Dick Waterman owned Utica-Rome, the two tracks often ran in conflict, particularly in the '60s, with Utica-Rome as a NASCAR facility and Fulton the archetypal "outlaw" Modified track. In the '70s, first under NASCAR and later during the short heyday of the NEARA sanctioning body, Utica-Rome and Fulton sometimes co-existed peacefully.

They also entered hard times together: Benway closed Fulton briefly in 1978, plotting his next move, while Waterman leased his track to Steve LoPiccolo and Mike Talerico. The general slide of asphalt Modified racing in New York, coupled with the rise of dirt (and DIRT), had both speedways on the skids. They would reopen as dirt tracks in '79; the difference was, Waterman had flown the coop, selling Utica-Rome that spring, while Fulton still had Bub Benway—and his wife and best friend, Victoria—in charge.

Success came slowly to the clay-topped version of Fulton Speedway. The earliest races for Late Models and Strictly Stocks were light on cars and fans, and it was far from big news when, on May 6, 1979, a kid named Alan Johnson won the track's first dirt Modified feature. But success surely *did* come, and while Utica-Rome staggered and lurched with a kaleidoscopic array of promoters and formats, Fulton gained ground with a homespun weekly recipe: small-block Modifieds, Late Models, Street Stocks, Mini-Sprints. That, of course, spawned homegrown heroes: Donnie Wetmore, Paul Jensen, and Bob Podolak were among the Fulton's first dirt stars.

The two tracks were less than 60 miles apart, an hour's drive, and in hindsight it seems entirely natural that when the New Venture brass sailed away and left Utica-Rome with no captain at the helm, Millard Benway might hop on board to steer the ship. But it *wasn't* a natural assumption to make at the time. Bub, nearly 70, was no kid, and, again, he seemed a thoroughly contented man. But in his head, there were indeed visions, visions of expanding what he'd started at Fulton. And he now had some young blood in his corner, thanks to his niece Gisele and her husband, Eric Kingsley, who had studied at Benway's knee at Fulton.

In the spring of '89 came the announcement that Benway had leased the Vernon track, rechristening it New Utica-Rome Speedway. Kingsley would serve as race director, with Marcia Wetmore, Fulton's effective public relations rep, filling the same role at its new sister track.

Immediate changes were announced: The lead division would be small-block Modifieds, setting up what became a Fulton/Utica-Rome Outlaw Modified circuit (soon joined by Brewerton) that flourished for years; the weekly race night would be Sunday, restoring an old Vernon tradition; and the track would be shortened to something close to a half-mile from its previous size of five-eighths or more.

Turned out ol' Bub had lots of energy left. It also turned out that he was the right man for the moment, and, really, for years to come.

~

Right: Kingsley, officially the race director under the new regime, also played several other roles, including grader operator. (Don Edds Photo)

The initial plan was to launch the New Utica-Rome Speedway in late May, but a wet spring ended up pushing the opener back to June 11 because the new clay surface hadn't had the proper chance to settle.

"We want all factors to be right for the grand opening," said Kingsley, striking exactly the proper optimistic tone.

When the gates finally were swung back, things were grand indeed. A crowd estimated at close to 3,000

Construction site: Shortening "New Utica-Rome" to its present length turned out to be a change for the better. (Don Edds Photo)

Track savior Bub Benway, flanked by his niece Gisele and her husband, Eric Kingsley. (Don Edds Photo)

filed in—"We were thrilled with the number of fans," said a cheery Marcia Wetmore—to see Modifieds, Street Stocks, Pure Stocks, and the visiting Empire Super Sprints.

The most immediate impact of the Benway team was a complete change of the race-night cast. Out were the DIRT big-block names, and in was a feisty group of small-block Modified racers who'd built a cult following at Fulton. In addition to the aforementioned Wetmore, Jensen, and Podolak, there were Roger Phelps, Ted Lamb Jr., Jim Mahaney, and Doug Fuller, all of them fast, and a teenaged kid named Dale Planck, who was in the opening laps of a stellar career. And a smiling guy named Gordy Button, who had dabbled successfully in many different divisions, settled in with this small-block Mod group and quickly got with the program.

All of them and more went at it every Sunday, with the regular weekly feature running a taut 25 laps. It was certainly a contrast with the slew of extra-distance events run in the New Venture years, but there was no denying the rush of seeing all those hungry small-block dudes scrapping and clawing their way to the front, with no time to spare.

The shortened track was also a boon. For one thing, it put New Utica-Rome closer in line with Fulton, a speedy three-eighths, than the old track would have been. For another, the budgets of the average Fulton/New Utica-Rome small-block team were certainly less than, say, Brett Hearn's or Jack Johnson's, and the previous track configuration's long straightaways were brutal to engines. Paul Jensen, who'd made several Utica-Rome appearances prior to Benway's arrival, remembers, "On that big track, you'd just sit there and listen to the motor scream."

~

Across the marathon season—17 race dates scheduled, 14 completed, three lost to rain—Jensen emerged as track champ. The quiet man from Edmeston was also the top feature winner, with five to his credit. As is always the way with champions, it was what Jensen did when he wasn't winning that paid dividends: Two runner-up finishes, a third, and a fourth meant that he had finished in the top-five nine times. And he closed like a champion, too, winning the season's last two features and three of the last four.

Jensen's principal competitor, Donnie Wetmore, got off to a flashier start, grabbing the year's first two features, and won twice more as the season progressed. Interestingly, though they combined to win nine times, the pair finished one-two just twice (July 17 and Oct. 1),

Paul Jensen had a stellar season. His five feature wins earned him the 1989 New Utica-Rome Speedway Modified championship. (Don Edds Photo)

Mike Rolewicz was as steady as a heartbeat, piling up points on his way to the Pure Stock title. (Don Edds Photo)

with Jensen coming out on top both occasions. Still, they saw an awful lot of each other while slicing through traffic in those weekly get-it-done-now 25-lappers.

"We had a lot of fierce battles," Jensen says of those days with Wetmore, "but I think we also had a lot of respect for each other."

Wetmore's downfall was his lack of consistency, though this was as attributable to the odd mechanical breakdown and the inevitable contact from the close-quarters racing as it was to any fault on Donnie's part. But, blameless or not, he managed only three top-five finishes—two seconds and a fifth—aside from those four victories.

The only other multiple winner was Button, who in addition to two checkers had two second-places, three thirds, and a fourth, and was a factor nearly every Sunday evening. His progress was dramatic.

"Gordy came out of Sprint Cars, and for a while I think he had a little too much Sprint Car in him to suit these [stock] cars," grins Jensen. "What I mean is, the Sprint Car guys tend to drive too sideways when they run Modifieds, and that's not the way to get these things around, especially when the track is slick. Now, when the tracks suited that style, Gordy could be *bad* fast, but other nights he wasn't. But he figured things out and started running straighter and smoother, and racing him was tough going."

Also breaking into the win column were Mike Arminio, John Podolak, and Ted Lamb Jr. It was a terrific season for Lamb, that year's Fulton Modified champion, but it came very close to being a whole lot better: Four times at New Utica-Rome, he ended the feature in second place.

~

The Street Stock championship went to four-time winner Tom Sears Jr., though three-time victor Tom Kinsella showed some glimpses of the glory days he would have down the road. And the Pure Stock crown ultimately rested on the head of Mike Rolewicz, whose steady season was highlighted by two consecutive feature scores in early June.

~

The season's momentum was palpable. Crowds were good, the action was exhilarating, and the assimilation of Utica-Rome into the Fulton scene—they had basically been two very distinct camps just a year earlier—was nearly seamless, for fans and racers alike.

"We hope to develop the following here at New Utica-Rome that we have back in Fulton," Marcia Wetmore had told the *Oneida Daily Dispatch* back at the season opener. "Based on the enthusiasm of the crowd tonight, I think we're well on our way."

And all year long, that's the direction in which things flowed.

In the background, quiet and tending to business, stood Bub Benway. In the space of that single year, things had changed as much for him as they had for Utica-Rome. His Fulton track was rock-steady, the product of his years of hard work there, and the success of his second track was the talk of the region. He had breathed new life into a track that had so often been comatose. He was praised as a man of action; his previous contentment was now just a memory.

Utica-Rome had been revamped, revitalized, and rehabbed in the past. But this time, things seemed different. This time, things *were* different.

1990
Who Wants to Win?

Just one year into the life of the New Utica-Rome Speedway—and its new track surface—it seemed as if everyone in the pit area had suddenly stumbled across its secrets. Ten different drivers won small-block Modified features, the biggest collection of top-class winners since 1970 and the height of the paved track's NASCAR Modified era, when 11 different drivers stood with trophies in hand.

The '60s and very early '70s had, in fact, been filled with seasons boasting long lists of winners. There were also 11 winners in 1965 and '68, and in four different seasons—1963, '66, '67, and '71—there had been 10 Modified winners. But for some reason, most likely the spiraling cost of competition increasing the gap between the "haves" and "have-nots" across the 1970s and '80s, that era seemed to have disappeared.

Is there a better sight in racing than a grandstand full of enthusiastic fans? (Don Edds Photo)

But it had sure enough returned in 1990. Nineteen different Modified features were run, and only two men—Gordy Button in July, and Donnie Wetmore in August—were able to win on consecutive Sundays. Paul Jensen did technically win two straight features in May, but between those triumphs came a pair of rainouts.

A third and final Jensen victory, on the Sunday of Labor Day weekend, helped ice his second New Utica-Rome track championship in as many years, and there would be more to come. But the real story was the way Paul and his peers spread around the wealth, and how it ended up signaling the dawn of a four-year period in which large numbers of drivers shared in the Vernon glory: There were 10 Modified winners in '91, nine in '92, nine again in '93.

"That was a good period, a challenging period," says Jensen. "If you were the top guy the previous year, or even the previous *week*, that meant nothing."

Ted Lamb Jr. won the season opener on April 22, then won in June and again in July. Button, best man on Sunday number two—and sporting one of the era's truly high-profile sponsorships, from Wheels Auto Supply Stores—ended up atop the win column with four after adding a June victory and those two straight in the summer heat. Donnie Wetmore also loaded three trophies along with his small-block Modified after a win in June and that pair in August. And winning singles were rookie Tom Kinsella, Jim Mahaney, Roger Phelps, John Ramsey, Doug Fuller … and a roaming gunslinger named Billy Pauch, about whom you will learn more shortly.

This bare-knuckles, free-for-all season was typified by two explosive laps at the end of the 25-lap weekly feature on June 3. With three laps to go, Lamb soared around leader Button with an impressive fourth-turn pass. As soon as they reached the other end of the track, Button stole the lead back. Thus the order remained until, heading toward the white flag, Lamb headed for turn four's cushion again. Button, no dummy, was already high, occupying Lamb's fast lane. But Lamb suddenly changed direction—he explained to writer Ron Moshier that he "hit the brake to knock my corner speed off just enough"—and dove to the bottom, grabbing the lead and this time keeping it. The

Paul Jensen, here joined by wife Stella and wide-eyed son Eric, picked up his second straight track championship. (Don Edds Photo)

Popular Gordy Button (Right) snagged two straight features in the July heat. Ted Lamb (far right) won three features, and his flair made him one of the New Utica-Rome fan favorites. (Don Edds Photos)

battle thrilled both drivers as much as it did the fans.

"That's one of my favorite moves," Lamb told Moshier.

Button, who'd done all he could, countered, "If he hadn't done that he'd have been a fool."

It was a moment of great drama in a season full of such moments.

Jensen, the kind of workaday racer who signed on for a full shift and doggedly got the job done, was tough to beat over a full season. He won the title rather handily, with a surplus of 78 points. But behind him came a tight four-way scrap featuring, in order, Fuller, Wetmore, Lamb, and Phelps.

Oh, and here's something to think about: It rained on four Sunday nights, or who knows how many more drivers might have lined up first at the payoff window?

~

In August, New Utica-Rome got the sort of gift no management team can buy, especially one in its early make-or-break seasons. A freelance writer named David W. Hollis spent a Sunday night in the pits and the grandstands, obviously taking plenty of notes, and produced a long, splendid feature story which ran prominently in the *Utica Observer-Dispatch*, in the "Accent" section—the *lifestyle* pages—as opposed to simply the sports pages. There's no telling how many people read the piece, but there was no getting around this: Focusing on the people he met, rather than simply describing the racing he watched, Hollis made a night at the speedway sound fun for fans and competitors alike. He made it sound addictive. Racing is both those things, of course, but Hollis explained it in layman's terms in a way few racing journalists ever could. Anyone who'd never seen a short-track event but bothered to read the feature had to come away at least a bit more interested in stock car racing than he or she had been before opening the newspaper.

Of such intrigue, new fans are made.

Hollis focused on a handful of support-division guys, letting their individual Everyman tales tell the story of every racer who toiled all week long to bring his homebuilt car to the speedway. When he wrote of one such fellow "slogging through his work days at a normal job so he can pursue this dirt-laced hobby with as much fervor as unpaid help from friends and relatives," Hollis was describing more than half the competitors on the grounds.

Among those the writer chatted with was Dave Herb, a young Canastota racer who said he liked racing because, according to Hollis, "he can do here what he can't do on the road as a meter reader for Niagara Mohawk." And he tracked down Jerry Holmes of Oneida's racing-rich Holmes clan, who was having the sort of hectic evening every racer eventually does. Jerry's Street Stock broke in practice, so he hustled to the shop of woman driver Charlotte Jordan, who'd skipped the night's racing because of other commitments, and hauled her car back to the track. Holmes made the feature through the consi, and then told Hollis, "I don't care what they put me in as long as I get to race."

And one driver's girlfriend acknowledged, "I'm scared to death while he's driving," adding thankfully, "There are a lot of crinkles on his car, but none on him."

It was great stuff.

Hollis wrote, "Some 3,000-4,000 local souls pack the grandstands, drink sodas and beer, cheer for their

Top: Even winners have tough nights. Donnie Wetmore copped three features, but had his tin wrinkled on New Yorker night. (Don Edds Photo)

Left: Billy Pauch had a stunning September weekend, winning both the Victoria 200 at Fulton and the New Yorker 50 at Utica-Rome. (Ken Dippel Photo)

favorite drivers … more than likely someone they know, or feel they know …"

And come the night's end, he said, fans and racers alike "head out and home, mostly to addresses within a half hour's drive."

You read that clipping even today, and you wish it was 1990 and you were sitting in Bub Benway's grandstands, cheering for Herb and Holmes, not to mention all those terrific Modified shoes. Yes, these were good times, *good* times, at New Utica-Rome.

~

Back in 1986, Victoria Benway, Bub's beloved wife and confidant, had passed away, prompting him to memorialize her with a spectacular Fulton Speedway race he called the Victoria 200. It was the biggest and richest event anyone had ever conceived for the small-block Modifieds that had brought Fulton back from the brink, and it was a classic from its very first running that October. Billy Pauch, a New Jersey hotshoe who raced—and still races—where the money is, hauled up to Fulton and won that first Victoria after a thrilling duel with Pennsylvania's Ronnie Tobias.

Then Pauch went out and won the *next four* Victoria 200s, his dominance adding to—as opposed to subtracting from—the race's mystique. Every autumn, the best dirt-track Modified guys in the country, from big-block DIRT invaders to Benway's sizzling small-block regulars, threw their best punches at Billy Pauch, who slipped them all.

In 1990, Benway decided that New Utica-Rome could use its own major small-block Modified event, one which would build a little bit of a Victoria-style tradition while at the same time reviving an old brand name. The New Yorker 50 was scheduled for September in the manner of the old New Yorker 200s run in the track's best pavement years, but rather than Labor Day weekend it was placed on Sunday, October 16th, the night after the Victoria 200. The New Yorker did what Benway wanted it to, filling the grandstands and enticing some of the finest driving talent on the East Coast to partake of a second night of high-stakes small-block racing.

And so it was that one night after winning his fifth straight Victoria trophy, Billy Pauch outran Richie Tobias, Pete Bicknell, Roger Phelps and Donnie Wetmore to grab his first New Yorker cup. It would not be his last.

~

The Street Stock warriors, like their Modified cousins, did a good job dividing up the hardware in 1990. Steve Hulsizer, who would stick around for a while, was the top winner with six, although one of them was sort of a shared victory, having come in a stunning side-by-side finish with Bret Belden. Scorers, officials, announcers, and everyone else whose opinions were solicited hemmed, hawed, and ultimately shrugged, and the finish was officially ruled a dead heat, the only "tie for the win" in Utica-Rome's long history. And it was fitting, because it put the season's winningest driver in the spotlight with the division's track champion, Belden, who captured three features. Other winners were Bob Goutermout (four), Scott Moyer (three), and Jim Smith and Mike Rolewicz with one apiece.

Left: Steve Hulsizer took six Street Stock wins in 1990, and became a familiar face at the Vernon oval. (Don Edds Photo)

Bottom: The family that races together: Street Stock champion Bret Belden with wife Brenda and daughter Ashley. (Don Edds Photo)

Now, in the Pure Stocks, Rick Miller wasn't playing nice. He won 11 of the 18 features contested, coupling a fast car with a level of daring that was a cut above. But it was Dave Mannise—a name you will get used to as this book rolls onward through the years—who managed to eclipse Miller and win the Pure Stock title. Mannise only won twice, but he was always in the fray, finishing second five times, third on four occasions, fourth once, and fifth once. Miller, on the other hand, had only a single runner-up finish—in addition to all those wins, of course—on his résumé of top-fives for the year. For want of a few thirds and fourths, a championship was lost.

Rick Miller flexed his muscles in the street stocks, winning 11 of his 18 starts! (Don Edds Photo)

EYEWITNESS
1986–1990: RON MOSHIER

"As both a fan and a sportswriter, dirt-track racing was fun again"

NOTE: As weekly short tracks go, Utica-Rome Speedway has generally been blessed with fine support from the area's daily newspapers. While diehard race fans will always proclaim that there's never enough coverage no matter where they live or what speedways they're interested in, our extensive archival research revealed that going all the way back to 1961, the sports pages of the papers from Rome, Utica, Oneida, and other surrounding towns almost always carried the results from Utica-Rome, and regularly ran blurbs on upcoming events as the weekends neared. Sure, there were periods of weak coverage and negative press, but those not-so-curiously coincided with periods when the track's management was in chaos and the media was as ill-informed and frustrated as fans and racers were. But through good times and bad, one fellow whose coverage could always be counted on was Ron Moshier of the Utica Observer-Dispatch. Ron has both a fan's passion for the sport and a reporter's nose for what makes a great story. As a result, he not only knows what the fellow in the grandstands might want in terms of subject, he'll also load his longer pieces—and the fight for space is a newspaperman's constant battle—with driver quotes and other details that bring the reader behind the scenes. That was never more true than in the topsy-turvy transition period of 1986-90, when Moshier's coverage of yet another Utica-Rome regime change saw him playing both sportswriter and court reporter. Through it all, and right up to the present day, he has been a credit to his profession and a huge asset to motorsports in the region.

Matt Becker, *Utica Observer-Dispatch* Photo

Growing up as a Saturday-night regular at Fonda Speedway back in the 1960s—and living just a few minutes away from longtime car owner Frank Trinkhaus of Fly Creek—got me hooked on dirt-track stock car racing as a kid. Twenty or so years later, after graduating from college and moving back to the Mohawk Valley area, that same dirt track fan found himself covering the area auto racing scene as a sportswriter for the *Observer-Dispatch*, Utica's daily newspaper.

For starters, anyway, it wasn't nearly as much fun as I had hoped, or as much fun as I had remembered. At least not for a year or two, back in the mid-1980s, when our circulation area's only race track was Vernon's New Venture Speedway... formerly known, of course, as Utica-Rome.

The New Venture years were full of promise, but when the management team unraveled, the tracks' future was in jeopardy. (Utica-Rome Archive)

What really had looked like a promising "new venture" when car owners Jim Bechy and Fred Burrows and driver Jack Johnson joined forces, renaming and reopening the track in 1985, did little to rekindle the short-track racing fire that for so many years had made Utica-Rome a roaring success. The partnership did make it work for a short while, but when Burrows filed a lawsuit against Bechy, and then Glenn Donnelly's DIRT organization jumped from what obviously was a sinking ship, I wasn't the only one feeling like the speedway's racing future was in doubt. Again.

No, from a fan's point of view, or even a sportswriter's, it wasn't a fun time, certainly not at all like Utica-Rome's "good old days." There was an uneasy feeling around here that local short-track racing was on the road to ruin, one more time. We all could sense that area racing was again on shaky ground with Utica-Rome on the rocks, and it was going to take something or someone to keep the race track up and running and win back the fans, many of whom clearly felt alienated. Much damage had been done.

Fortunately, the winds of change blew Vernon's way again, and this time it quickly became evident that this was going to be a change for the better; a better way of running a race track, good enough to reestablish a solid driver and fan base that breathed new life into what had been a dying venture.

I must admit, this all happened before I ever made my very first trip to Fulton Speedway. But I certainly did know who Bub Benway was, and I knew of

The Outlaw Modified circuit brought back many old fans, and lured in many from Fulton and Brewerton tracks. (Don Edds Photo)

Drivers like Tommy Kinsella, new to Utica-Rome, had the joint jumping as the 1980s gave way to the '90s. (Don Edds Photo)

what Bub had accomplished. So when he and Fulton race director Eric Kingsley announced they were going to take over the weekly operations of New Venture International Speedway—eventually buying it and renaming it New Utica-Rome Speedway—I think many Central New York fans and drivers knew from past experience that this new team meant business.

As a fan and a member of the media, I found that out right away. The folks at the top of this new regime had already proven themselves, winning over drivers and fans at Fulton and Brewerton Speedway. And with Kingsley and a seasoned public relations director like Marcia Wetmore running things, the show went on at New Utica-Rome.

And, boy, what a show it was.

It was immediately obvious to me—and more importantly, it was obvious to the drivers, teams, and fans—that as a team Utica-Rome's new leaders were efficient; that they were committed to racing; and that while they were in business to make money, which I am pretty sure they did, they were also out to make the racing as good as it could possibly be. Kingsley, no doubt, was a whiz at preparing the track surface, something that had been a problem in the past under different promoters. He also shortened the speedway a bit, tightening up turns one and two, which the competitors seemed to like. And there was no one better in that period than Marcia Wetmore when it came to the public-relations side of promoting the race track.

When you add it all up, it was no wonder that crowd and car counts were soon on the rise again.

I'll admit that having been a big-block Modified fan for so many years, I was even pleasantly surprised at how much I enjoyed Kingsley's switch to weekly "Outlaw Modified" brand small-block racing. Obviously, many New Utica-Rome Speedway fans felt the same way. It was a gutsy move that instantly worked wonders for a troubled track that desperately needed some sense of stability, some consistency.

In 1990, the "Outlaw Circuit" took off, running Fridays at Brewerton, Saturdays at Fulton and Sundays at Utica-Rome. The Modified roster boasted a colorful cast of characters that included well-known veterans like Paul Jensen, Donnie Wetmore, Doug Fuller, Gordy Button, Tommy Kinsella, and Ted Lamb Jr. Those guys had all been popular drivers at Fulton in particular, but they quickly caught on with the Utica-Rome fans, too.

And the competition was as keen as anything the track had ever seen. I will never forget Lamb once telling me, "You start in a 24-car field, and 18 or 20 of those guys can win." He was right. And that's what the fans came to see.

That, and a show that you knew was going to go on. With Benway and Kingsley behind the wheel, even Mother Nature seldom got in the way of a Sunday-night program. If there was any chance that the races could be run, they'd make the effort. That's how committed they were.

By the end of the 1980s, this bunch of so-called "outlaws" had helped put Utica-Rome back on the stock car racing map. From my point of view, as both a fan and a sportswriter, dirt-track racing was fun again, thanks in large part to Benway and Kingsley and Wetmore, and their commitment to a sport that around these parts had more than once been on life support.

Without them, and without the changes that were made in the late 1980s, Utica-Rome Speedway may have never gotten to be 50 years old ... and still counting.

1991

Kinsella Comes Alive

In 1991, in just his second full season driving Modifieds—he had been, you may recall, a Street Stock terror—Tom Kinsella captured the New Utica-Rome Speedway Modified championship. And this was not the story of some careful kid just being steadier than his more experienced rivals, and happening to outpoint them while learning the ropes. Oh, Kinsella was certainly consistent across the long campaign; he had 16 top-five finishes in 23 features. But five of them were victories, and this, of course, was in that era when every Sunday evening meant a big pile of names scrapping for the Vernon gold.

Mod champ Tom Kinsella's five wins included the Richie Evans Memorial. He's joined by Richie Jr. and Tara Evans. (Don Edds Photo)

Kinsella was absolutely terrific in '91. Sure, Donnie Wetmore topped his win total by one, leading all drivers with six, but young Tommy handled pretty much everything the competition showed him. In copping those five victories, Kinsella relegated five different men to second place, and they were some of the absolute toughest men in the game: He beat Alan Johnson (in a special 40-lapper) on May 12; defeated Paul Jensen in the second half of a twin-20 program on July 21; edged Doug Fuller on July 28; held off Wetmore himself on Aug. 18; and outran the speedy Canadian Pete Bicknell on Sept. 8.

Heading into the season, the book on Kinsella was that he was fast, aggressive, a winner. Was his championship material? Only time could answer that. Exactly how much time? Well, about five months and one week, or the length of the 1991 New Utica-Rome Speedway season.

"We had learned a few things in terms of tires and setups," Kinsella recalls. "And I had certainly learned some patience. I was pretty aggressive early on, and at times was criticized for it. You know, when you watched Kyle Busch at the beginning of his career, you saw that maybe he didn't finish some races because he should have been a little more patient. I did the same thing, like any young driver does. So some people learn faster than others, and some people never learn."

Kinsella learned, and it all happened so fast. It was a dusty, down-home duplication of a feat pulled off in 1979-80 by a driver in the NASCAR Cup Series. Dale Earnhardt—fast, aggressive, a winner—had been the tour's top rookie in '79; one season later, he was its champion. Earnhardt drove car #2 in those two seasons, but soon enough he joined Richard Childress and began flying the #3, which eventually amounted to his calling card.

Hmmm … Tommy Kinsella's Modified was also #3.

In the summer of '91, in a questionnaire appearing in the "Outlaw Outlook," a souvenir program covering the action at New Utica-Rome, Fulton, and Brewerton, Kinsella was asked if there was any special meaning to his car number. His reply was straightforward: "It's Dale Earnhardt's number."

It's one thing to simply *have* a role model. To match his early strides is a whole different matter.

~

As mentioned, the mushrooming Outlaw Modified circuit was covered by a single souvenir program in '91,

A promoter's dream: A full parking lot, and people lined up to buy tickets to the stock car races! (Utica-Rome Archive)

Jeff Walton's win in July was the first of his fine New Utica-Rome career. (Don Edds Photo)

which both showed solidarity among the track managements in Vernon, Fulton, and Brewerton, and offered fans an easy way to chart the progress of their favorite racers. In August, "Outlaw Outlook" columnist Bob Connelly authored a piece charting the progress of New Utica-Rome itself.

"The 1991 season has found the grandstand area the healthiest in the three years of operation [under Bub Benway and Eric Kingsley]," wrote Connelly. He praised the weekly program's efficiency, "which usually finds 15 races conducted in less than three hours."

Connelly's assessment of things on the action side of the catch fence was equally rosy: "The overall car count has also risen ... Usually over 90 cars crowd the pit area ... [and] the competition has been very keen in all three divisions, with no driver showing dominance."

Granted, you wouldn't have expected a truly critical report to appear in the "Outlaw Outlook," had one been warranted. This was an official publication, underwritten by the tracks, and hardly a place for hard-hitting motorsports journalism. But the point is, the facts and figures in Connelly's column—the car counts, the bit about the quick Sunday shows—were right on the money, and they reflected a speedway that definitely had its act together. Things at New Utica-Rome were still trending upward.

~

Wetmore's six wins and Kinsella's five outclassed the rest of the Modified field, but there sure were some interesting stories on the rest of that win list. Two-time track champ Jensen won twice even in what had to be considered an off year, and both Gordy Button and Roger Phelps were back in victory lane, once apiece. And both Bob Podolak (on June 23) and Jeff Walton (July 7) took their first New Utica-Rome victories; Walton would win four more across the next several seasons, while Podolak, though at times so close to winning more, would end up with that sole Utica-Rome trophy.

And a pair of young, free-spirited brothers out of Baldwinsville buoyed the Vernon crowds when both of them scored their first wins at the track that summer. J.J. Michaels and his kid brother Lou were second-generation track brats whose dad, Johnny Michaels, had wheeled pavement Modifieds and Supermodifieds throughout the area. And their cousin, A.J. Michaels, had become one of the best Supermodified runners at Oswego before tragically losing his life there in May of 1990.

It was clear that J.J. and Lou took to racing naturally, and also that they took it seriously, but—to the

Kinsella Comes Alive

Lou Michaels, part of a great New York racing family, grabbed his sole Vernon victory in August of 1991. (Don Edds Photo)

delight of their friends and fans—not *too* seriously. Interviewed by Cathy Connelly for the "Spotlight On" page in the program, both J.J., born in 1962, and Lou, who came along five years later, were at their humorous best.

Quizzed about his most embarrassing moment, Lou said, "There are too many to list." Asked if he would change anything about himself, he replied that he'd "start over and proceed with caution."

J.J., just as playful, listed his hero as Al Bundy, the hard-trying but perennially bumbling dad on the TV sitcom "Married With Children." Pressed to finish the sentence, "I hope I never have to," he responded, "Answer another question like this."

Rocking the mullet hairdos in vogue at the time, both Michaels kids stood on the gas in '91. On June 16, J.J. busted into victory lane at New Utica-Rome for the first time, topping Kinsella and Jensen; two months later, on Aug. 18, he beat Kinsella and Tom Juhl Jr. to win again. And just a week before J.J.'s second triumph, there was Lou, grinning and posing with the trophy after having defeated Jensen and Walton.

Lou never did make it back to victory lane in Vernon, though he did come tantalizing close, scoring a number of second- and third-place finishes in the seasons ahead. And J.J.? Well, he had 19 more Utica-Rome wins and a track championship ahead of him.

~

One other driver took a Modified checkered flag at New Utica-Rome in '91, and it was in the season's biggest race, the New Yorker 50. Though his five-year win streak in Fulton's Victoria 200 had been snapped the night before by Frank Cozze—Pauch finished fourth—Billy wasn't about to sit around moping. He salved the pain of losing Benway's richest race by scooting down to Fulton's sister track and winning Benway's second-richest race.

Pauch exacted his revenge in the New Yorker, winning the event for the second straight year. But it was certainly a good showing for the home team, with Kinsella and Jensen filling out the second and third spots ahead of Billy Schinkel and Button.

~

Speaking of checkered flags, the one that signaled victory for Pauch—and everybody else in 1991—was waved by Dick Sweet, the head starter at all three Outlaw tracks. A former driver who had raced Late Models at the old Midstate Speedway, Five Mile Point, Penn Can and Brookfield (where in 1978 he was track champion), Sweet later played car owner to guys like Dick Schoonover and Bret Belden and unofficial aide to many racers, among them Lou Lazzaro and Randy Glenski. In 1986 he took another stab behind the wheel—though not his last—and ended up flipping his new small-block Modified ride down the Brewerton Speedway frontstretch.

He ended up in the flagstand, first at Fulton, then at Brewerton, and later with the traveling Empire Super Sprints troupe. When the Outlaw Modified circuit coalesced, someone had the bright idea that the only guy to have on the starter's perch was Dick Sweet.

He loved the gig, though it very nearly cost him dearly. *Twice.* In 1990, a wild frontstretch crash at Brewerton had Sweet diving for cover, if not for his life; the flying car of Will Smith destroyed the flagstand. Two weeks later, at Fulton, Sweet had to do the duck-and-scoot act again when Tom Kinsella's car took air, though thankfully with less destructive results.

"I guess my number isn't up get," Sweet quipped to writer Bob Connelly in the early days of the '91 season, "so all the drivers will have to put up with me for a while yet."

Years down the road, he would fill even larger shoes at Utica-Rome, and even do another short stint in the cockpit, winning two Street Stock mains at New Utica-Rome in 1993.

Some guys are in this sport for the long haul. Dick Sweet, waving those flags in 1991, was in the middle of his.

~

There was drama in the Street Stock ranks, most of it surrounding Steve Hulsizer, who romped to eight victories at Utica-Rome and many more at Fulton and Brewerton. By the first weekend in August his overall win total was 17, prompting a certain amount of grandstand speculation that Hulsizer's car was less than totally legal. Program columnist Bob Connelly defended Hulsizer, pointing out that (A) his car had been through countless post-race inspections, and (B) not one of Hulsizer's competitors had officially protested his #88 Nova. "I think the bottom line," suggested Connelly, "is that Steve can really drive a race car." Interestingly, the very week that column was published, Hulsizer crossed the

New Yorker 50 winner Billy Pauch ducks low in this battle with the ever-tough Donnie Wetmore. (Don Edds Photo)

finish line second at New Utica-Rome, but was awarded the victory when apparent winner Craig Henry refused to submit his car to a teardown.

Oddly, while other Street Stock multiple winners included Mike Rolewicz (four) and Paul Carey, Ron Holmes, and Craig Pritchard (each with two), the champion was again Bret Belden, who copped but a single victory. But Belden, sneaky-fast, had 10 other top-fives, and piled up the points while his primary foes were running hot and cold. Few would have disputed the assessment of steady top-five man Scott Moyer, who deemed Belden "probably the smartest driver in our class."

The Pure Stock champion was Jerry Sehn, whose consistent season sure spiked in early June, when he won two straight.

1992

Jensen's Career Year?

With three New Utica-Rome seasons behind them and a fourth underway, Eric Kingsley and his management team were firing on all cylinders. For 1992, though, they focused mostly on their proven program—Outlaw Modifieds, Street Stocks, and Pure Stocks. They did take the bold step of adding a fourth weekly division: Outlaw Sportsman, essentially a slightly tamer version of the headlining small-blocks and similar in concept to the various of 320-Modifieds and Sportsman cars run by the DIRT organization.

When Paul Jensen and his #57 squared off against Dale Planck's #77, Vernon fans were watching something very special. (Don Edds Photo)

Certainly, the Outlaw Modifieds remained the darlings of both fans and the track brass. Specials for the top class included a pair of midweek 40-lappers, both offering their winners guaranteed starts in the Victoria 200, and an oddball Sunday-night show in July with twin features of just 15 laps in length. And a June program offering double points in all divisions was a great way to spice things up and grab some extra press attention.

There was also a "Richie Evans Remembered" night in honor of the track's most iconic asphalt champion, and two designated events that spoke to the way Kingsley and his staff—principally Marcia Wetmore—made sure to reach out to the community: A Military Night in May, and a Scout Night in July.

~

By now, the Outlaw Modified circuit had developed its own stars. They were no longer confined to Fulton, which only seasons earlier had seemed so distant to fans from the Mohawk Valley, and no longer relegated to the shadows in which Brewerton had so long operated. Just as Bub Benway's brand of small-block Outlaw Modifieds had been good for Utica-Rome, Utica-Rome had been very good for them. Guys like Paul Jensen, Roger Phelps, Donnie Wetmore, Tommy Kinsella, the Michaels brothers, Dale Planck, and Gordy Button were no longer just names out of *Gater Racing News* who raced someplace else, and each was fast enough or colorful enough to make it into the headlines and the columns. Now their talents were on wider display and given an extra dimension of credibility because they were, after all, racing on a piece of property which, however troubled it had been at times, had also been consecrated by Lazzaro, Charland, Wimble, Flemke, Evans, Cook, Bodine, Lape, and various winning Johnsons.

Fulton always had a certain respect attached to it, but there were also times that it seemed a secondary location; when it hosted Supermodifieds, for example, there was no denying that it played second-fiddle to Oswego. And while Brewerton had long been a place local diehards pointed to as the site of wild action, the plain fact was that it never truly caught on with a larger audience until it became part of this Outlaw Modified circuit, a circuit weirdly legitimized by the presence of a track which had so often fought for its own legitimacy. And that, of course, was Utica-Rome.

Paul Jensen was among the first beneficiaries of all this. Though he had been kicking around for several years and clearly possessed great talent—he had won four times in the DIRT 320-Modifieds at Fonda, not the kind of place where you back into multiple victories—it took the Outlaw Modified circuit to bestow upon Jensen, and drivers like him, the regional respect they deserved. No longer could they be dismissed simply as guys who ran well at their home tracks; they were established winners on a tri-track circuit that was becoming more established with each passing year.

In 1992, Jensen took his third New Utica-Rome championship in the four seasons the track had been operated by Benway and Kingsley. Five times that year, he hauled home on the winding roads between Utica and Edmeston with the winner's trophy in his truck. And, as usual, he displayed an invaluable knack for making the most of whatever a particular evening was ready to offer him; in addition to those victories there were 14 other top-five finishes (seven second-places, three thirds, three fourths, and a fifth), adding up to a remarkable 19 in 23 starts.

Though the New Utica-Rome season remained live through Sept. 26—leaving room for the New Yorker 50 and a couple of open shows—the final points-paying event was run on Sept. 6. On that Sunday, Jensen clinched his track championship in a most authoritative manner. Starting 15th in the 25-lap main, Jensen gassed it from the green flag as if his very life depended on that race and that title. Before anyone could blink, he was in the top 10, and then the top five. Incredibly, he moved into second place on lap *four*. With more time on his hands than he'd perhaps expected, Jensen could afford to be a bit patient in sizing up leader Button; it took until lap 10 for Jensen to take the lead with his Gates-Cole Insurance #57 (sponsored by a fellow named Gene Cole, who down the line would play a larger role in the lives of every Utica-Rome racer). From there, Jensen held off a closing Wetmore to grab the win. In victory lane, he celebrated his win, his Utica-Rome title, and his overall Outlaw Modified circuit championship; he'd also been Fulton's track champ, and placed sixth in the Brewerton points.

The track's follow-up press release termed it "a career night" for Jensen. In hindsight, it probably was, at least in terms of the accolades it heaped upon him all at once. Then again, Paul Jensen's tenure behind the wheel—which continues even past Utica-Rome's 50th anniversary—has been full of evenings that would have been career nights for tens, hundreds, thousands of American short-track racers.

~

The previous season's champ, Kinsella, was this year's runner-up. But Tommy had a hot hand again, winning a season-high nine races: three straight in May, one in June, two in July, three in August (including one of those Wednesday-night 40-lap Victoria 200 qualifiers).

By now, he and Jensen had a bit of a "young gun versus grizzled veteran" thing going, which is exactly the kind of rivalry every good weekly short-track program is built upon. Oh, there were other rivalries on view every Sunday night in '92 at New Utica-Rome, but this one had the best storyline: two champions, one at the top of the heap and the other doing his best to knock him off. All was fair: hard driving, overt espionage, mind games, you name it.

Both men look back with what are clearly fond memories.

According to Jensen, Kinsella "was as tough as there was. We used to park next to each other in the pits, and he had no qualms about looking over our car, or even stabbing the tires to see what we had. And so I figured, If he can do that to us, I can do that to him."

Kinsella says, "Paul was always a good, hard racer, so we battled hard, but we respected each other for that. And even though I was still the new kid on the block, I think I was fortunate enough to establish a little respect there pretty quick. And, yeah, there was some harassment. We had a lot of fun with each other. Even though we battled hard, we could still have a beer and a couple laughs after the races. Well, most of the time!"

Tom Kinsella missed a second straight track title, but nine feature wins gave him reason to smile! (Don Edds Photo)

~

Seven other Modified drivers—including one new face—stood in victory lane at New Utica-Rome in '92. J.J. Michaels had another stout year, winning twice (and beating brother Lou in a memorable one-two Aug. 23).

And the rapid ascent of young Dale Planck, another two-timer, continued apace. One of Planck's wins we'll detail in a moment; the other came in the remaining Victoria 200 qualifier, on July 1, and what an affair that was. Jensen was leading the show handily with just over a lap left, eyeballing the white flag, when he made an uncharacteristic bobble exiting turn four; while Paul was all arms-and-elbows inputting a couple of major corrections, Planck rocketed past to steal the lead and the win. Among those greeting Dale in victory lane was his beaming wife Leslie; it happened to be the second anniversary of their wedding.

Pete Bicknell took the 40-lap opener (delayed by two rainy Sundays) on April 26, while Phelps, Wetmore, and Button each grabbed a 25-lapper.

The new face in the win column belonged to Dave Donath, who got it done in one of those wild twin-15s on July 19. It was quite literally a topsy-turvy year for journeyman Dave, who flipped his Donath Iron Special at Brewerton in May but just two months later picked up his only career victory at New Utica-Rome.

~

Nice N Easy Grocery Shoppes signed on as title sponsor of the speedway's big dance, the third annual New Yorker 50. And while there was certainly nothing easy about it, the race ended up being plenty nice to the Outlaw Modified circuit's regulars, particularly Planck, who led a top-four sweep that also included runner-up Wetmore, third-place Bicknell, and Kinsella. The first invader to cross the stripe was Randy Glenski, back in fifth. Though he would soon have some fine moments aboard Outlaw Modifieds—specifically, for our purposes, at New Utica-Rome—Randy was still a DIRT big-block guy in '92, centering his activity around his home track, Fonda.

Planck, just 22 years old and racing out of Homer—though in time Cortland would become his home—was on top of the world. And his good days were just beginning.

~

The addition of the Outlaw Sportsman division certainly spiced up the weekly action. Most of the drivers had never before raced New Utica-Rome, and for some it was the fastest joint they'd ever tackled, though others—like the year's leading feature winner, Ray Zemken—had logged their share of track time at Fonda.

Zemken, whose toddler daughter Jessica would grow up to become a Utica-Rome champion herself, grabbed five Sportsman wins in Vernon that season, while Ken Johnson took four, Pete Campione three, and Jim Smith two. But back there among those who won just a single feature—along with Guy Sheldon, Tim Clemons, Ron Richardson, Geoff Plis, and Jim Rothwell—a dude by the name of Larry Bezner showed

Top: J.J. Michaels won twice, solidifying his position as one of Utica-Rome's most popular racers. (Don Edds Photo)

Left: Earl Walrath hopped the wall, taking out a light pole in the process, but happily emerged unscathed. (Don Edds Photo)

Top: Pete Bicknell was one happy Canadian after collecting the winner's hardware in the season-opening 40-lapper. (Don Edds Photo)

Leftt: Continuing his rapid rise to stardom, Planck picked up a cool five grand for winning the New Yorker 50. (Don Edds Photo)

Jensen's Career Year?

everyone how championships were won. Steady but far from slow, Larry finished second five times, and ended up with more top-five showings than even Zemken. Come autumn, Bezner edged Johnson by a scant two points to wear the crown.

In the Street Stocks, Rick Miller duplicated his Pure Stock trick from 1990; that is to say, he won the most races, seven, but could do no better than second in the final standings, behind top man Craig Pritchard.

And in the Pure Stocks, Dave Mannise took his second New Utica-Rome championship, but far from his last. Dave copped an even dozen features, leaving table scraps for his competition, led by points runner-up and four-time winner Wayne Archer.

1993

Jensen, Pauch Star; So What Else Is New?

Across 1993, they were spreading the Sunday-night wealth around again in the Outlaw Modifieds. Oh, Paul Jensen solidified his status as the period's best blend of race-night brains and brawn, winning another New Utica-Rome championship—his fourth in five years—in the style he had made his own. He ran up front plenty, and won three times, but on the nights when others happened to be faster—Tom Kinsella and Randy Glenski each won five features—Jensen just kept his head down, grinding out those points. Come season's end, he had top-fived everybody into submission, clocking a pair of runner-up finishes, four thirds, three fourths, and two fifths. The guy was a dirt-slinging metronome, racing to his own beat, his own champion's rhythm.

Other guys blew hot and cold; Gordy Button, for example, won the first two races and then cracked the top three only twice in the next 19 features. But Jensen, even on his off nights, seemed to stay pretty warm.

"I wasn't necessarily better [in seasons like '93], but I was more consistent," Jensen says. "In other years, it might have been the other way around."

Two of 1993's stars: Paul Jensen won another points title, while Randy Glenksi drove his #28 to five wins. (Don Edds Photo)

Never truly flashy, yet displaying great style, Randy Glenski added New Utica-Rome to the list of tracks he'd conquered. (Don Edds Photo)

Jensen and Button, who finally won again in September, were joined in 1993's three-timers club by Doug Fuller, who earned a trophy per month in May, June, and July. Dale Planck, just visibly getting better by the week, won twice in the warm air of June and July.

Other weekly-show winners included Roger Phelps, always a threat, and teenaged Billy Whittaker, who in the opening feature of an Independence Day twin-20 program held off J.J. Michaels to score his only career victory at New Utica-Rome.

~

More and more frequently, stopping in at the Jensen pit on race nights was a fellow who, like Jensen, lived for a time in Edmeston. Gene Cole had done a bit of race-driving as a teenager, and did a bit more after a stint in the service, but had given it up as he focused on a career in the insurance business, first as an on-the-road salesman and then as the owner of a thriving young agency.

"But you know, once you love racing, it's a hard thing to get away from," Cole says. "Even when I was working for Nationwide and based in Rochester, I would still go to Fonda almost every Saturday night. As a matter of fact, I was there the night [in 1965] when Pepper Eastman was killed, which bothered me because I had actually raced against Pepper in the '50s at the old Brookfield Speedway."

Jensen says, "Gene Cole is a guy I've known forever, it seems like. When I was a kid I actually saw him race a few times, and I met him not long after I moved to Edmeston in '71."

One thing led to another, and eventually Cole began sponsoring Jensen, who had a reputation as a hard-working guy who would really shine with competitive equipment.

"It wasn't any kind of formal thing at first," Cole recalls. "Paul would need something for his engine, or maybe he'd need a tire, so I'd help him in that way. Little things. As time went on and I had my own agency, I'd help him a little bit more. When he first suggested that we put Gates-Cole Insurance on the car, I told him I'd pay him even more to leave it off because I didn't want to deal with all that; I just wanted to help him. But eventually we did put the name of the agency on the car, and since then it's been on a lot of different cars."

Cole and his wife Gloria became smiling fixtures at the Outlaw Modified tracks. "For about eight years, she and I rarely missed a race at either Fulton on Saturday nights or Utica-Rome on Sundays, and on Fridays I would often go to Brewerton. I enjoyed those times, I really did."

Gordy Button sure knew how to come out of the starting gate, stealing the season's first two features. (Don Edds Photo)

Remember the name. Gene Cole's enthusiasm for dirt-track weekends would mean very big things down the road for the Utica-Rome Speedway.

~

The annual New Yorker special, now in the fourth year of its revival, was bigger, better, stronger. Its distance had been doubled, and its official title therefore changed to the Nice N Easy Grocery Shoppes New Yorker 100. There would be a red-flag stoppage for pit service at the midway point.

The New Yorker had earned its upgrade, because by now it had built up a little bit of tradition. In the weeks leading up to each September, there would be speculation about which big-block guy might find a ride, or who among the red-hot collection of small-block racers from Pennsylvania and New Jersey might haul north for the combined Victoria/New Yorker weekend. And even after all the chatter about who might be steering what, you never knew until race night exactly who was going to show up. There was always a surprise or two, and some fan would hustle from the pit area to the grandstands to tells his friends, "Hey, guess who's here?"

In a lot of ways, the Outlaw Modified-era New Yorker had matured much the way the original New Yorker 400 had back when Utica-Rome was a paved quarter-mile. The 400 had its fourth running in '66, and although NASCAR was the sanctioning body things were a lot looser back then. Though the serious points-chasers had likely pre-entered, numerous teams pulled in unannounced from Connecticut, Massachusetts, New Hampshire, New Jersey, Quebec, just about everywhere, and those last-minute entries gave the race its mystique. The 400 was, of course, a twin-200 affair in 1966, and Bill Wimble's combined finishes of first and third made him the overall winner. But the guy who grabbed everybody's attention that night was Don MacTavish, a motivated traveler from just outside Boston who had already gained a reputation as a guy who could drop into anybody's back yard and make some noise.

And that, really, was Billy Pauch in the early '90s. He had put in his years as the young prince of Flemington Speedway in his native New Jersey, and later his career would have a remarkable second act in which he was a dominant winged Sprint Car shoe on the rugged Central Pennsylvania circuit. But what made Billy Pauch an icon—what made him *Billy Pauch*—were those in-between years in which he'd dip into town for a race like the Victoria 200 at Fulton, or the New Yorker 50/100 at New Utica-Rome, and just kick everybody's tails.

They called him Billy the Kid back then more than they do today, but even then he had some age on him, and lots of laps; Pauch was 34 years old in September of '91, and had been a champion many times over. But the handle had stuck because he really was a short-track gunslinger, a 20th-century William Bonney or a 1990s Don MacTavish.

In that 100-lapper in September of '93, Pauch was content to spend the early laps evaluating his competition. He even slipped back a bit from his starting spot outside the second row, hovering for a while in fifth as Randy Glenski led the scuffling trio of Jensen, Pennsylvania runner Duane Howard, and Wetmore, who by lap 12 had charged all the way to second from 11th on the grid. Then Pauch eased past Howard and Jensen, and Glenski popped a tire, and it came down to Donnie Wetmore and Billy the Kid.

Pauch took the lead on lap 24, and held it at the halftime break. Allowing him time to fiddle with his tires and his chassis only made him tougher, and for the rest of the night he continued to show the field his rear bumper. Oh, Glenski rebounded for a while, and both Jensen and Wetmore surged late to claim second and third, but the night belonged to Pauch, whose winning haul came to a bit over $10,000.

Jensen probably didn't feel too bad, though. In addition to his $5K check for second, he was still beaming about the $23,000-plus he'd earned for winning the previous night's Victoria 200. And, don't forget, the

Doug Fuller, here showing terrific form, sailed to victory lane three times in 1993. (Don Edds Photo)

New Yorker capped his fourth championship season at New Utica-Rome, so he was truly first in class—behind Pauch, but ahead of his Outlaw foes—on this night.

Yes, the New Yorker 100 seemed to have everything going for it. It was a recognizable brand at a resurgent track, and it drew the attention of traveling stars while serving as something close to an obsession to those who called Utica-Rome their home track. And yet, between a change in philosophies the following year and a management change soon thereafter, the New Yorker went on hiatus after its great 1993 edition. Though there were occasional extra-distance shows booked by various promoters in several seasons, not until 2007 would the New Yorker label return. Sad.

~

The support-class headlines were loaded with familiar names, and one significant new one, although even his handle had a very familiar ring to it. That fellow was Steve Kotary, another in the long, tangled vine of Kotary brothers, uncles, nephews, and cousins from Rome who right from 1961 had added to the track's color and drama. Steve emerged as the Pure Stock champion after a season in which he and Dave Mannise conspired to make the class a virtual two-man show. Of the 22 features run, they won 20; even more incredibly, they'd have split that total dead-even, winning 10 apiece, had it not been for Mannise getting disqualified after a May 30 teardown ... which handed that evening's trophy to Kotary! (By the way, the answers to the obvious Pure Stock trivia question from '93 are Stan Clark and Butch Reiter; they won the only two features Kotary and Mannise left on the table.)

Billy Pauch was again a winner in the New Yorker event, this time over the 100-lap distance. (Don Edds Photo)

Larry Bezner was again crowned champion in the Outlaw Sportsman ranks, though this year he showed more outright speed, topping the winner's tally with five features. In what amounted to a season-long brawl, also winning Sportsman features were Ron Holmes and Jim Smith (three each); Ray Zemken, Jim Rothwell, Dan Yankowski, and Ron Richardson (two each); and single winners Pete Campione, Jimmy Phelps, and Steve Hulsizer.

And Rick Miller, so often fast in the fendered classes in previous years but stymied in his attempts to earn a New Utica-Rome track championship, got one in 1993, taking top Street Stock honors. Rick won three of the season's first four features and later added two more. From there, the championship was a matter of Miller staying smart and smooth. Mission accomplished.

Steve Kotary added to his colorful family's racing legacy, winning 11 features and the Pure Stock championship. (Don Edds Photo)

1994

A Star Is Born

Change arrived in a big way in 1994. Eric Kingsley, Marcia Wetmore and the management at the New Utica-Rome and Fulton tracks—you'd have to include Bub Benway, by now semi-retired, as at least a serious consultant in all this—had signed on with a major sanctioning body, but it certainly wasn't the first one that leapt to mind when you thought about dirt-track Modified racing.

No, rather than linking up with Glenn Donnelly's DIRT outfit, the dominant player in New York and indeed the Northeast, Kingsley cast his lot with NASCAR, joining the Daytona Beach organization as part of its growing family of Winston Racing Series weekly-track operators.

Both Utica-Rome and Fulton, of course, had historical ties with NASCAR. From 1961 through '75, first under track founder Joe Lesik and then with Dick Waterman, and again in 1978 under Steve LoPiccolo and Mike Talerico, Utica-Rome had played a cen-

Dale Planck, here running the outside, proved himself the equal of Paul Jensen and everyone else in 1994. (Don Edds Photo)

tral role in pavement Modified racing under the NASCAR banner. And Fulton, though most often an open-competition joint and later a key track for the short-lived NEARA group, did have a short alliance with NASCAR in the mid-'70s.

But what made this arrangement so interesting was that since the lines between asphalt and dirt Modified racing were defined in the early '70s, NASCAR had shown little interest in the dirt-track variety. In the minds of most fans in the '90s, the term "NASCAR Modified" conjured visions of low-slung, offset machines and the pavement stars of the day: Mike Stefanik, Reggie Ruggiero, Tony Hirschman, Steve Park. Now, with Kingsley's bombshell announcement, there was a harkening back to, say, 1969 or '71, when both Don Wayman's burly Fonda Speedway coupe and the squat Utica-Rome coupe of Sonney Seamon could properly be termed NASCAR Modifieds.

Alas, the days of the "crossover" Modified—think all of all those weekends when Louie Lazzaro drove the same car to victory on both surfaces—were never coming back.

(Interestingly, in order to maintain a little bit of their identity in the region, the cars that ran at New Utica-Rome and Fulton were to be termed NASCAR Outlaw Modifieds. That might have drawn a chuckle from the late Richie Evans, who, in the days when that term would have been the ultimate racing oxymoron, drew the ire of the suits in Daytona by painting the word "Outlaw" on his coupe and winning all over New York State while he was suspended from NASCAR from early 1969 through much of '71.)

Starting in 1982, the Winston Racing Series divided the nation's NASCAR-sanctioned short tracks into specific regions, with the goal of naming individual champions and using set parameters to honor what the Winston marketing folks called "a true national champion of weekly racing." Back in '94, there were eight such regions; New Utica-Rome and Fulton were folded into the Mid-America region.

As spring sprung, there was new Winston signage being installed, and some red-and-white paint sprucing up the state's two newest NASCAR facilities. And, though nobody knew it just yet, a brand-new champion was just about to light up the area racing scene for several years to come.

~

Reflecting on the rise of his '90s rival Dale Planck, Tom Kinsella says with a bit of a chuckle, "When he first started racing, his father would only let him run on Saturday nights; Sundays were family nights. And he would also only let Dale run the bottom of the race track. So when Dale finally did start coming down to Utica-Rome, he really didn't mix it up with us because the bottom was never the fast way around."

Here, Kinsella's tone grows serious. "But, God, all of a sudden he got some combinations going there, and he was *tough*. You just couldn't beat him."

Well, it could be done, but it sure wasn't easy. Planck won 11 Utica-Rome features in 1994, twice stringing together streaks of three in a row. The track's first NASCAR Outlaw Modified championship was his, too. Dale himself says, "It really was an exceptional year."

Why the sudden burst of excellence? Planck credits "a little bit of everything." His driving, he says, had been steadily improving. Plus, "I had gotten a lot more familiar with the cars, and the Troyer stuff we were running was hot right at that time. We came into that '94 season with a little different package than some of the other guys. We had kind of a new suspension in the back, and we had a really good engine program. Up until '93 or '94, I'd always had trouble with engines staying together, but all of a sudden that wasn't an issue anymore.

"So the things we were doing with setups worked really well with the track, the engines stayed together,

This scene would be played out 11 times in 1994. It's track champion Planck with the checkers in victory lane. (Don Edds Photo)

Top: *In the season-opening 40-lapper, Paul Jensen edged Roger Phelps, who joined him in the victory portrait. (Don Edds Photo)*

Left: *Roger Phelps hustles his sharp #99 as he tussles with Planck. Roger grabbed himself a feature trophy in July. (Don Edds Photo)*

and I was getting more experienced with the tires. I guess I was just learning more about *all* the different parts of making the car go fast, instead of just throwing it on the scales and going to the race track. I was finally understanding *everything*."

This learning process can be traced right back to the father Tommy Kinsella mentioned. For years, the late Denny Planck was an overachieving underdog in both big blocks and small blocks; folks in the region still talk about the night in 1979 when, in grabbing his only Rolling Wheels Raceway feature, Denny beat that track's all-time winner, Will Cagle. Son Dale, an admitted garage brat, watched every move Denny made, absorbing lessons passed on by word, by deed, and by example.

"He definitely taught me everything I know," says Dale. "Taught me the things you need to do to be a successful racer. That means understanding the car, the engine, all aspects of the operation, from rebuilding a rear end or a transmission to knowing what a track is likely to do. He was a strong believer in the idea that if I knew the ins-and-outs, and could do everything on the car myself, I would be a better racer.

"And I think all of that really started to show right about then, in '94."

Boy, did it ever. And now that he had found his pace, Dale Planck would prove to be a difficult man to slow down.

Paul Jensen won four Utica-Rome features in 1994, including the longest one, the season-opening 40-lapper on April 24. Kinsella was victorious once in May and once in July, though off his winning form of the past few seasons, Tommy did finish second five times. And both Roger Phelps and Gordy Button made it to victory lane, Phelps in July and Button in a special season-ending 25-lap open-competition show.

~

Planck was also the 1994 NASCAR Winston Series Mid-America Regional champion. The points system—too complicated to explain in a few words, though as simple and fair as NASCAR officials could make it—required a driver to designate a "home" speedway, with his place in the regional standings weighted toward his results at that facility. Planck's home track was Fulton, but his championship also cast a positive light on New Utica-Rome, which certainly must have encouraged Kingsley, Benway and the other front-office folks.

And it sure wasn't a bad deal for Planck's team. The title came with a $40,000 check from R.J. Reynolds.

His chances at the overall Winston Racing Series national title, on the other hand, were quite literally handicapped. Unlike many areas of the country, where time trials determine the weekly feature line-ups with little or no inversion, most Northeast tracks have traditionally used a handicapping system based on the recent finishes of each driver, or the money he has recently earned. Generally speaking, three weeks is the period examined. Simply put, the hottest driver of any

A Star Is Born

The 1994 Sportsman title was just one of Jim Rothwell's many achievements at New Utica-Rome. (Don Edds Photo)

"The races at all the tracks were short—25, 30, 35 laps—so you had to get to the front quick," says Tom Kinsella, "You couldn't screw around. And you knew your best chance to pass guys was early, in traffic, because once things got strung out you sometimes can't get by 'em."

Here, Kinsella pauses. "It was hard, hard racing."

~

Jim "Rocky" Rothwell, part of the Vernon racing scene even in the present day, wrapped up the Sportsman division championship in style: He led all competitors with six victories, including April and September wins that served as bookends to the season. Four-time winner Steve Hulsizer and Larry Bezner, with three, kept Rothwell honest, as did fellow winners Geoff Plis and Jim Smith (two each) and one-hitters Bill Trexler and Jimmy Phelps, Roger's fleet nephew.

Street Stock honors went to Wayne Archer, celebrating his first New Utica-Rome title. Others won more—topped by Joe Slawiak with seven, and Rick Guernsey with four—but Archer was best across the broad season. His single victory was boosted by enough top-fives to make him king for a season.

Dave Mannise, beginning to make a habit of such things, won his third Pure Stock track championship after an eight-win season. Like Dale Planck, Mr. Mannise was just getting warmed up.

three-week period starts the next feature behind all the other cars that qualify through their heat races, with the next-best guy just ahead of him. In other words: Fast guys to the back!

"It seemed like I was starting 18th, or somewhere close to that, every time out," Planck recalls.

So while Dale's season was truly spectacular, it was always going to be all but impossible for him—coming from the tail almost every night—to match wins with drivers who regularly started in the first two or three rows.

But, hey, Planck's loss in that department was the race fan's gain. Northeast fans have never fully appreciated exactly how good they've had things—imagine how miserable it'd be to live in a region where the fast guys start in the front few rows every week?—but, to their credit, they usually knew good racing when they saw it.

Heck, even the drivers, though they surely must have found the handicapping system frustrating at times, knew how special the resulting action was.

Sportsman ace Larry Bezner is at the center of this happy group after one of his three trips to victory lane in 1994. (Don Edds Photo)

1995

Planck Repeats in a Year of Change

The more things change, the more they stay the same. Well, sometimes. See, sometimes when things change, they *really* change. For the New Utica-Rome Speedway, 1995 opened with word of a big change that turned out to mean … well, not much at all.

But the year ended with a change that really *was* a change, a move in an entirely new direction. Those who followed the speedway's fortunes had gotten used to the occasional cataclysm, but this one came without the usual fears for the track's future. No, this one was actually kind of exciting.

~

The first change was in the rules. Two things that had come to distinguish Outlaw Modifieds from their DIRT cousins were looser body restrictions—so the Outlaw cars sprouted huge sail panels, adding cornering stability—and tires that were taller and wider than what had become the standard elsewhere. Drag rubber, that's what everyone called the bigger tires. Years earlier, it had been the hot tip at certain tracks on certain nights, but by the early '90s you didn't often see drag rubber on a Modified unless you happened to be at a place like New Utica-Rome.

That changed in 1995, and, in truth, this made life easier for the average team owner, who now had fewer sizes and compounds to stuff into his tire rack. But it threw a curveball to the mechanics when it came to setups, and to the drivers whose duty it was to deal with the fruits—including the lemons—of those decisions.

None of this was easy stuff, said Paul Jensen, a four-time track champ and a guy who turned both the wrenches and the steering wheel. "If you had a fast Outlaw Modified and you talked to a guy running the standard smaller tires and the DIRT-style bodies, you'd find you had very different ideas about what was working," Jensen recalls. "And, of course, they had a very different feel from the driver's seat."

Jensen was most concerned with his own situation, of course. But what had many folks talking was how all this might affect Dale Planck. Certainly, rules are made with more than just one driver in mind, and, yes, they are the same for everybody. But Planck, who had hit his competitive stride in the more liberal drag-tire era, headed into the '95 campaign intent on repeating his NASCAR Winston Racing Series Mid-America Region championship, and, no doubt, his New Utica-Rome title. He didn't necessarily have more on the line than the next guy in the pits, but he certainly had more to lose.

~

As it turned out, Planck had everything under control. He ended up grabbing another NASCAR regional title—still listing Fulton as his home track—and his efforts at New Utica-Rome were spectacular. Winning eight features, tops again in the Outlaw Modified class, he closed the season with his second straight track championship.

Yes, he had worried about tires, and whether they might muddy the magic he'd found in '94. "We knew what the car would do with the big rubber," Planck said mid-season. "We didn't know what was going to happen [using the new tires.]" But come Sunday evenings, he was generally the toughest cat in the alley.

It was a season of short features. The longest, the opener on April 23, ran 40 laps, and Planck won it. There were three different nights offering twin 20-lappers, and Planck won four of those six quickies. Over the normal 25-lap distance, he won on April 30 and twice in a row in early July.

Jeff Walton leads Paul Jensen. On May 21, they finished a New Utica-Rome feature one-two, in this order. (Don Edds Photo)

Ronnie Holmes, here nosing his #82 past Mike Romano, did his clan proud by winning a July feature. (Don Edds Photo)

Tom Kinsella had another fine year, bagging five mains and winning on three straight Sundays in late August. (But not three features in a row, because on one of those weekends he split a twin-20 program with Planck.) Jensen took two victories, while Jeff Walton, Gordy Button, Donnie Wetmore, John Barker, and Mike VanDusen each saw the checkers once. And so did Ron Holmes, who returned a great local name to the headlines while notching his first top-division victory. More would follow.

Several guys who didn't crack the win column still had nice years. John Barker Jr. had a runner-up finish and two thirds, John Ramsey placed a fine second (between Planck and Kinsella) on July 2, Mike Romano poked into the top-five seven times, and others threatened when things went right.

Yes, when the green flag fell on Sunday nights—now serving as chief starter was Joe Cole—New Utica-Rome was a beehive. Announcer Jim King had a thorough vocal workout, calling the forward marches of Planck, Kinsella, Jensen, and whoever else happened to be fast that weekend.

"They don't give you an inch," said Planck. "And they're working as hard as I am, which makes it more rewarding."

Jensen says, "When Dale got on top of things, he was tough, *really* tough. He had good equipment, good help, and he did a good job himself. And he paid attention to things, working on the cars. I think Dale dug really hard at that part. He had learned the ropes, and he was coming on strong."

~

These were happy times for Dale Planck, whose successes close to home brought him national acclaim. (Ken Dippel Photo)

Research can be tedious or rewarding, depending on the material and the subject. When both parts of the equation are interesting, research—even reading a souvenir program 15 years old—can transport you back in time.

Toward the end of the 1995 season, Planck sat for an interview with writer Kevin Rice. Today the piece offers a glimpse at the stresses Planck felt as he worked through his second straight season winning both the New Utica-Rome and NASCAR Mid-America championships. He told Rice that 1995 had been "quite a bit tougher" than '94. "Last year was like a dream season," said the champ, "and this year is a reality season."

Chasing NASCAR points, he admitted, had been hard work. He was now in the habit of hauling two cars to the track, and the logistics of that have never been easy. "Sometimes it's kind of a pain," Planck said. "But the one time you don't bring the second car is the time you'll need it."

As for the pressure: "I'd say [that] I wish it was easier, but if was easier I'd probably want more challenge, so competition is always good."

No longer discussed as a rising young star, Planck was an established champion. He even *talked* like a champion, confident but aware that nothing could ever be taken for granted.

If such deep archival evidence dated back to 1961, we'd likely learn that Planck's thoughts echoed those of all the other NASCAR champions who passed through Utica-Rome in their title years: Bill Wimble, Rene Charland, Ernie Gahan, Don MacTavish, Pete Hamilton, Bugs Stevens, Fred DeSarro, Jerry Cook, and Richie Evans.

Dale was in pretty fine company.

~

Steve Hulsizer picked up his first New Utica-Rome Sportsman title in 1995. The Bridgeport driver won six times, spreading them across the full season. Jack Miller, though winless, had his solid season pay off when he placed second in the standings. Dan Yankowski, second in the win column with three, was third in points. And in the mix again, winning twice, was Jim Rothwell, as reliable in the summer as snow in winter.

Eight drivers scored single Sportsman victories: Greg Doust, Ron Richardson, John Kinsella (Tommy's uncle), Pete Campione, Jamie Christian, Bob Utter, Joe Slawiak (on the heels of his monster '94 Street Stock season), and Jeff Kotary. Yes, *another* Kotary in victory lane in Vernon! And Jeff would stick around a while, competing at Utica-Rome even as the track entered its second 50 years.

Rick Miller—who'd taken a sabbatical after his terrific '93 season to attend to real-life matters like building a home—earned another championship in the Street Stocks. Miller won the opener, the closer, and five more main events. But Dave Bruno also had a heck of a year, driving into victory lane six times.

And in the Pure Stocks, Steve Way earned a satisfying track title, swapping victories with Dave Mannise and Ed Kotary all year long. Dave ended up with five, while Steve and Ed took four each. But Way was the steadiest among them, topping Mannise by a 10-point margin.

~

Planck Repeats in a Year of Change

The bombshell at year's end was one few saw coming until it exploded. Both the Utica-Rome and Fulton tracks had a new ownership team, in the form of Alex Friesen and John Zemaitis. New Yorkers knew a lot about Friesen but far less about Zemaitis, although hardcore fans recognized John as a fellow who for years had sponsored Modifieds and Sprints in his native Pennsylvania. Just a year earlier, in 1994, Billy Pauch had won the Sprint Car portion of Super DIRT Week at Syracuse aboard the Zemaitis #1Z.

Friesen, on the other hand, was a high-profile young man. Soon after the sale was announced, he was named Northeast Promoter of the Year by the respected *Racing Promotion Monthly* newsletter. He was a race-promotion prodigy, having learned the game first by watching his father, Stan, who from 1973 had owned the Ransomville Speedway. "When I was eight years old," Alex told Ron Moshier of the *Utica Observer-Dispatch*, "I was selling programs and picking up garbage at Ransomville." Later, Friesen watched everybody else; an avid reader and a collector of informed friends, he seemed to know what was happening at every major short track in the Northeast, dirt or asphalt.

Dave Mannise was getting to be a fixture in victory lane, wrapping up five Pure Stock wins. (Don Edds Photo)

Rick Miller's short sabbatical sure didn't make him rusty. On seven Sundays, Rick was the Street Stock winner. (Don Edds Photo)

At 32, he seemed to be everywhere. He and Andy Harpell, another promotional up-and-comer, had started a series for pavement Modifieds, capitalizing on NASCAR's slide in the region. They'd even purchased the Race of Champions brand, moving that prestigious asphalt show from New Jersey's Flemington Speedway to Oswego. And Friesen had a hand in five weekly tracks: Ransomville, which he owned with his brothers; Lancaster, which he operated himself; Pennsylvania's Mahoning Valley Speedway, in partnership with DIRT Modified ace Doug Hoffman; and the two he'd just purchased, Fulton and New Utica-Rome, whose name he promptly shortened to simply Utica-Rome.

In a written statement, Friesen said, "I can't say enough about Bub Benway, as well as Eric and Gisele Kingsley. In just four short months, this entire project of purchasing both speedways was initialized and finalized."

This was the first management change at Utica-Rome with smiling faces all around since Dick Waterman bought the place from Joe Lesik in 1964. Sales are happiest when financial calamity is not part of the deal. This wasn't any "run for the hills" exit by one promoter, or a new guy picking up the joint at distress-auction prices. This was one party selling a good business to another party hoping to build a better one.

Credit for that belonged to Benway, the Kingsleys, Marcia Wetmore, and the rest of their organization. They had shown Friesen and Zemaitis—they had shown *everybody*—the possibilities that exist.

EYEWITNESS
1991–1995: PAUL JENSEN

"I was fortunate enough to be pretty steady, year-in and year-out"

NOTE: *Paul Jensen's roots in racing were as basic as basic gets. "It wasn't until I was 23 or 24 that I drove, and even then it was not a planned-out thing," Jensen says. "A few of us put a car together, and when we started talking about drivers all their fingers were pointing at me." His friends made a wise choice, because Paul became one of his generation's best. When the Outlaw Modified era was in high gear at Utica-Rome, he won four track championships (1989-90, '92-93) in five seasons. Interestingly, throughout that time Jensen was sponsored by current Utica-Rome Speedway owner Gene Cole, a fellow Edmeston resident. "We were friends long before he sponsored me," says Paul, "and we're going to be friends long after all this racing stuff is through." For his part, Cole calls Jensen "the Smokey Yunick of this area, a guy who knows how to do everything and has helped out so many people."*

My secret? That's easy: I was racing three nights a week, Friday, Saturday, Sunday, and no matter where you're at or what you're racing, that will make you a better driver. The more you go, the better you get, I know that. I'll give you some proof: Today I'm obviously a lot more experienced than I was back then, but I've cut back to running just once a week, and I'm rusty compared to a lot of the younger guys I'm running against who race a really busy schedule.

Now, I hadn't always raced so much. Like everybody else, I guess, I started with one night, then two. Started at Fonda, then later went to Fulton and Brewerton. And when Utica-Rome re-opened in 1989, we figured we'd try it. I wasn't sure right away if it was what I really wanted to do, but we raced there regularly for 10 years or more.

I had run Utica-Rome a few times on the big track in both Late Models and Small-Block Modifieds, but I never raced there on a regular basis until after Bub Benway took over the place and

Don Edds Photo

Sideways through turns one and two, Paul Jensen displays his championship form at New Utica-Rome.

shortened it. Bub had the track, and then Eric Kingsley took over, but there was no real change there because it was the same family. At the time, of course, they also operated Fulton, and it was nice to be dealing with the same management people a couple nights out of your weekend. Even if you don't always agree with them, you kind of know where they're coming from, and so a respect builds up. For example, Eric and I didn't see eye-to-eye a few times—which is probably the way it always goes between racers and promoters—but we're still friendly today. It was pretty much the same with the competitors; a lot of us who showed up at Utica-Rome in that period had been running together at Fulton, so it wasn't like going to an all-new track where you didn't know anybody. It felt like I already knew half the guys I was racing against.

That first season, 1989, got rolling late. They had redone the track and changed a few other things, so the season didn't start until June. But we did have a pretty good year there, and we ended up winning the track championship.

I think maybe I took to Utica-Rome faster than some of the other Fulton guys because I'd had a pretty good amount of experience on bigger tracks. See, Fonda is pretty fast, so Utica-Rome didn't really feel big or intimidating to me. I can't speak for anybody else, but if all you had ever raced was Fulton, I can see where Utica-Rome would have seemed awfully fast.

You know, you need a whole different mindset when you're racing small tracks and big tracks. On a small track you're close all the time, always in traffic, and I think that's something everyone ought to learn about when they're first getting started because it's something that helps you anywhere. On a big track, you're thinking more about being smooth and precise. It's not that you run either one with more aggression or less aggression, but you definitely need to bring that different mindset.

We ran what they called Outlaw Modifieds, with the rules pretty relaxed. We could use alcohol fuel and big tires, and they allowed us to do a lot of different things with the bodywork. They gave us very basic outlines on things like height and width, but everything else was pretty loose. Some teams took advantage of that and got pretty creative, and others stuck to what they were used to. In the beginning I ran pretty standard stuff, basic DIRT-style bodies, and then, like a lot of guys, I started doing things a little differently; add a panel here, a panel there. Then we built a car that was a little bit different *everywhere*; I had a guy build the body for us, but I told him how I wanted everything. I had different ideas where I asked myself, "Will *this* work? Let's try it." And, you know, that ended up being probably the best car I ever had, so apparently some of those things did work!

It was interesting trying to come out with the right setups in that period, because the different aerodynamics and the big drag tires changed things quite a bit. The cars stuck a lot better because of both the tires and the extra downforce. And, of course, with the alcohol fuel you had what felt like instant power; you could take the exact same car and engine on regular racing gas, and it would feel like a dog. There were a few times when I ran back-to-back, first on alcohol and then on racing gas, and I'd be sitting there thinking, Man, what *happened* to this thing? And I'm like any driver: I love that extra power, especially at a place like Utica-Rome!

There's two ways to look at rulebooks, I think. As a racer, you always want to build a car the way *you* want it, no matter what the rules say. From that standpoint, nobody likes rules. But, you know, if you run things under an "outlaw" kind of format long enough, you just keep pushing things further and further, until they get out of hand. Some of the cars in that period were weird enough as it was, I think. So it's good to have *some* limits, even though there are always things in the rulebook that I'd like to change.

I'm not sure we ever had any one special thing that made us so good at Utica-Rome. It couldn't have been a single setup, because in that time period we had a few different cars and they each required very different setups. It's not like we found, say, one particular combination of springs or cross-weight that worked all the time. I can tell you that from the time we won our first championship there in '89 to our last one in '93, things had changed so much that those two cars were completely different, not even close. In fact, maybe one of the things that helped us was that I've always been able to adapt to new things, rather than just sticking to what I knew. And that's very important. Over the years I've told a lot of guys, "Once in a while you're going to find a great setup through dumb luck. You'll be so fast that it's gonna feel like everyone out there is in your way. But just remember, that setup may not work a bit the very next week. So it's OK to keep that setup in your mind and work off it, but don't stick to it too long."

No matter which drivers got hot in any given year, sooner or later they all dealt with Jensen, here leading Tommy Kinsella. (Don Edds Photo)

Even champions must take their lumps. On this night in 1994, Jensen's Gates-Cole Modified absorbed many! (Don Edds Photo)

In that period we're talking about, there were so many guys who ran good, but it seemed like some of them were tougher than the rest on different years. For example, one year it might be Donnie Wetmore, the next year Tommy Kinsella, the next year J.J. Michaels, the next year Dale Planck. I was fortunate enough to be pretty steady year-in and year-out, but every year you just knew one of those guys and his team was going to be at the top of their game, and that meant every season was tough. Nobody really *dominated* that era. You might win the track championship in a given year and have another guy win more races. That happened at Utica-Rome with me in 1992, when I won the title even though Kinsella won more races. With things as close as they were, every finish counted.

It was a nice period, really. The purses were good and everything cost less than it does now, whether you're talking about fuel for the race car or gasoline for the tow vehicle, and you've got to think about all those things.

But you know something? Racing is always a challenge, no matter what period you want to discuss. I mean, I had some great years when we won a lot, but it was a challenge. And I'm sure Pat Ward and Stewart Friesen, who have been really tough up there for a few seasons now, would tell you the same thing today.

I liked Utica-Rome, I really did. It was 45 miles from my shop; not an easy 45 miles, because it's mostly back roads, dragging a trailer up and down the hills, but it was still pretty close to home. There was a lot of good racing, and a few nights where we hung out way too long after the races, having a beer. Met a lot of really good people in that period.

Good times. Fun times.

1996

Alex, Here and Gone

It wasn't supposed to be the story of one man, this 1996 season. It should have been a tale of Utica-Rome's forward progress, of a new management team taking something that worked very well and attempting to make it work even better. But the sheer *rah-rah* drive of Alex Friesen's personality, and the tragic fate that awaited him, overshadowed everything else that happened in '96. Even the superlative season of track champ Mitch Gibbs and the third consecutive NASCAR regional title for Dale Planck were shoved into the margins of that season's notebooks.

Utica-Rome had been lapping at a comfortable clip for a few seasons, but from the moment Friesen and partner John Zemaitis purchased the place—along with its sister track in Fulton—it was if everything had suddenly shifted into a higher gear, one few even suspected was in the transmission.

Promotional dynamo Alex Friesen, who had such big plans for Utica-Rome's future. Alas, he was gone too soon. (John Grady Photo, AARN *Photo Archive)*

Friesen came into 1996 talking about a campaign he called "Vision 2000," a collaborative effort that would include "drivers, crew members, media and press, track officials, spectators, and car owners [in] an extensive communications program that will help direct dirt-track racing into the year 2000." Vague? Sure. But who else in Northeast short-track racing was even talking about this sort of thing? Friesen's zest for promotion just glowed.

He told *PerforMax Motor News* he believed in what he called "the basics." Friesen said, "Let's keep it simple. [Fans] enter the turnstiles for a two-and-a-half- to three-hour-show that's fast-paced, reasonably priced, and entertaining."

The program in place over the past few years, centered on the Outlaw Modified class, had been a success, so Friesen wasn't changing things, just sharpening them a bit. Marcia Wetmore, who had briefly headed south to take a job with Richard Childress, returned as general manager, joining Jennifer Fidanza in the front office. On the marketing side, Friesen brought in Joe Foy, who had done a stint with Buffalo Bills quarterback Jim Kelly. Track prep fell to Lyle DeVore, highly praised for his dirty work at Albany-Saratoga and Devil's Bowl.

And NASCAR would still be part of the picture, raising the eyebrows of some who saw Friesen as too free-spirited to fit into the sanctioning body's structure. It was no secret that the NASCAR brass in Daytona Beach occasionally misread and mishandled ambitious, strong-minded promoters; everyone in the region knew the story of Tom Curley, who in 1977 walked onto the moribund Late Model Sportsman scene based in Vermont—then called the Northern NASCAR circuit—and within a few years whipped it into the dynamo known as NASCAR North. In *Stock Car Racing* magazine, the respected Herb Dodge wrote that Curley "used a psychology major, an iron will and countless hours of labor to build NASCAR's once-dying stepchild into a $1 million-a-year business." Curley wooed sponsors (Skoal, Coors, Valvoline), introduced innovative rules (weight breaks for smaller engines, green-flag finishes), and ran his own tight ship, always colorfully. Some suggested he tone down his act, be more of a company man; Curley shrugged them off. "I bought hook, line, and sinker the idea that we were isolated from Daytona," he told Dodge. But late in 1985, on the heels of two controversial rulings he'd made—one of which was overturned in Daytona Beach—NASCAR abruptly dropped his series. Curley subsequently formed the American-Canadian Tour, still going strong today.

It was not hard for some to imagine similar frictions erupting between NASCAR and the energetic Friesen.

But in what he called a "welcome message" in his *Raceday* newsletter, Alex wrote of NASCAR, "I'm looking forward to developing this relationship to its potential for both the speedways and race teams. When you look at Dale Planck receiving almost $100,000 in year-end cash bonuses for running two nights a week in just two years, you've got to be happy with NASCAR on your side."

Jerry Cook, the six-time NASCAR national Modified champion and former Utica-Rome kingpin who had retired in 1982 and was now a NASCAR competition administrator, returned the compliment in an April feature in the *Utica Observer-Dispatch*. "Alex is young," Cook told writer Ron Moshier, "but he has been in this business a long time. He's got good ideas, he knows how to get things done and he has a professional attitude."

Of Utica-Rome specifically, Cook declared, "There is no doubt that the track is in good hands."

Everything seemed in order. In his newsletter, Friesen bubbled, "I have never been more excited about the start of a new racing season."

~

Mitch Gibbs, one of his generation's best, won four times en route to the Utica-Rome Modified title.
(Don Edds Photo)

Top: Tom Kinsella won two features, but his season was not all peaches and cream, as evidenced by this rough landing. (John Clifford Photo)

Left: Dale Planck won a third straight NASCAR Winston Racing Series regional title, boosted by seven Utica-Rome scores. (Don Edds Photo)

Mitch Gibbs, bullet-fast for several years in the Modified wars at the Afton Speedway and Thunder Mountain Speedway, a pair of dirt joints on New York's Southern Tier, blew into Fulton and Utica-Rome in 1996 with one goal in mind. "The big one," he called it.

Gibbs, 33 and out of Sherburne, was talking about the NASCAR Winston Racing Series gold he'd seen Dale Planck win twice. (The two tracks were shifted to the New England Region in '96, but the glory and the rewards were the same.) And Gibbs sure gave it his all, putting together a dream season that rewarded him with both track championships … and second, to *Planck*, in the regional scuffle. Huh?

In tweaking its Winston Racing Series rules to make things as fair as possible—no easy task, given the nation's variety of cars, tracks, and lineup procedures—NASCAR had taken to rewarding victories within each region, rather than examining only home-track results as had been done in the past. Hence Mitch's puzzled quip in *PerforMax Motor News*, "If you win [championships] at both tracks, how the heck don't you win the region?"

Smilin' Steve Hulsizer kept right on chugging, and wrapped up another Sportsman division championship. (Don Edds Photo)

Local boy Willy Decker took the Street Stock points title. In the years ahead, he would become a star. (Don Edds Photo)

Looking for more action than his front-office job provided, promoter Alex Friesen dabbled as a Sportsman driver, and a good one. On Sept. 1, he won at Utica-Rome, then promptly disqualified himself to avoid any hint of favoritism, handing the win to Rick Miller. (Don Edds Photo)

Well, because Planck's 15 total victories (eight at Fulton, seven at Utica-Rome) beat his nine (five and four, respectively).

At Utica-Rome, Gibbs and his Mirabito Fuels #2g—built by retired Modified shoe Jon Birosh—notched 17 top-10 finishes in 20 starts. He won on June 2, twice straight on June 23 and 30, and again on Aug. 25, all of them 25-lappers. Planck won the April opener, won a feature per month in May, June, and July, and strung together three in a row in mid-August.

Mike Romano, Tom Kinsella, and Paul Jensen each won twice, with victory-lane solos turned in by Ron Holmes, Bob Sitterly, and J.J. Michaels.

Steve Hulsizer repeated as champion in the Sportsman division, and Dave Mannise was back at the head of the Pure Stock class. And in the Street Stocks, here came a name we'll hear again: Willy Decker. Winning five times to lead that division, Decker out-pointed Steve Kotary on the way to his first Utica-Rome title. Willy was on the ladder to bigger things.

~

On these weekends, an area businessman and team sponsor kept a curious eye on this new Outlaw Modified promoter, young Mr. Friesen. "Alex and I were friendly," says Gene Cole, then backing Paul Jensen's #57. "I met him through racing, of course, and we'd always talk. He was putting together deals to operate different tracks, and you could see that he had plans."

And Friesen was kicking those plans around. By autumn he voiced doubts whether NASCAR was the right fit for him and his tracks; he enjoyed the extra exposure provided by the Winston link, but the new-romance feel appeared to have faded.

"At this point I really have to look at the plusses and minuses of staying with NASCAR," Alex told the *Syracuse Post-Standard* for its Oct. 8 edition, "and I don't have that answer yet." He suggested that huddling with NASCAR officials at November's Winston Racing Series banquet might push him toward a decision.

It was a very different tune than the one he had sung in the springtime.

There were whispers that Friesen might jettison NASCAR and join DIRT. While that union might have presented the same sort of constraints he felt under NASCAR, the smaller scale of Glenn Donnelly's Weedsport-based group could have made them more manageable. Plus, the Friesen family, through their Ransomville Speedway, already had a working relationship with DIRT, so guiding Utica-Rome and Fulton in that direction would hardly have been stepping into uncharted territory.

Friesen told the *Post-Standard* that he'd met informally with racers, seeking their opinions about the pros and cons of both NASCAR and DIRT.

And there loomed the real possibility that—perhaps in '97, perhaps down the road—Friesen might form a dirt-track Modified circuit of his own, effectively pulling a Tom Curley. On Nov. 23, 1996, Alex convened a meeting of 15 Northeast promoters to air some ideas he had for what the Post-Standard called "a series of 14 long-distance, high-paying races for 358-Modifieds." He already had a name for the enterprise: STORM, for Short Track Organization for Racing and Marketing.

That so many came to hear his ideas showed just how much influence Alex Friesen already had in the business. It also showed why he might never have been a good fit, long-term, with either NASCAR or DIRT.

He was a go-his-own-way guy, unafraid to try new things, sure to kick up a storm, or a STORM, in the years ahead.

~

It's not clear which way Friesen was leaning on this whole sanction issue when, taking a break from the sport, he retreated with friends to Old Forge for some post-season snowmobiling. Just after 7:00 PM on the evening of Dec. 5, a Thursday, everything went terribly wrong. The *Post-Standard*, citing police accounts, said Friesen's sled "failed to negotiate a turn on Joy Tract Road in the town of Webb, went off the road and hit several trees." Its rider was thrown from the snowmobile.

Alex Friesen, just 33, was pronounced dead at the scene.

News of his passing sent shock waves through the racing world. Marcia Wetmore, having worked at Friesen's side for a busy year, told the *Post-Standard*, "His enthusiasm for life was contagious. He had ideas for the betterment of racing ... and that seemed to motivate everyone he met and talked with."

Kevin Enders, one of the area's top engine builders, told the paper Friesen was "a young Glenn Donnelly," characterizing his death as "really tragic, a great loss."

And Corky Stockham, publisher of the *Parts Peddler*, kind of a printed flea market for those looking to buy, sell, and swap racing gear, said, "Alex Friesen is going to be missed greatly. He was a mover and a shaker ... who was doing some great things for the sport."

That he was.

Police declared that "excessive speed was a factor" in Friesen's accident. Well, of course it was. Alex was a young man having fun, and he was always—*always*—moving forward in a hurry.

What his loss might mean to Utica-Rome would be something to worry about in the New Year. As 1996 closed, those who knew Alex Friesen were simply grieving a friend gone too soon.

1979-2001
Utica-Rome's Turbulent Middle Age

Mike Romano. (Utica-Rome Archive)

Hike that left-front wheel, Alan Johnson! (Ken Dippel Photo)

Charlie Rudolph, 1985. (Ken Dippel Photo)

Deek Decker in action. (Utica-Rome Archive)

John Barker. (Utica-Rome Archive)

New Jersey's Ken Brenn Jr. (Ken Dippel Photo)

New Venture, Old Lazzaro! (Ken Dippel Photo)

Much-traveled Kenny Brightbill. (Ken Dippel Photo)

C.D. Coville. (Ken Dippel Photo)

New Venture-era contender Rich Burgess. (Bill Moore Photo)

Track employees Carl and Dianne Smith say "I do."
(Dianne Smith Collection)

Tom Kinsella in his full-fendered days. (Don Edds Photo)

Marcel LaFrance. (Bill Moore Photo)

1987 New Venture champion Kenny Tremont. (Utica-Rome Archive)

Promoter Jim Bechy greets NASCAR visitor Bobby Hillin. (Bill Moore Photo)

1985: Freddy Brightbill and the Blue Bonnet Milk Maids. (Ken Dippel Photo)

Two great invaders: Chuck Akulis low, Jimmy Horton high. (Ken Dippel Photo)

Oneida's Lonnie Rood, circa 1986. (Bill Moore Photo)

Utica-Rome's Turbulent Middle Age   227

Gerry Newman, one fast female! (Utica-Rome Archive)

Off to war! (Don Edds Photo)

Randy Glenski's winning smile. (Don Edds Photo)

1993 New Yorker 50 winner Billy Pauch. (Don Edds Photo)

Billy Pauch at speed, 1993. (Don Edds Photo)

Good guy, fast guy: Roger Phelps. (Don Edds Photo)

Jim Mahaney, 1990. (Don Edds Photo)

Support-class heroes Bill Shantel Jr. and Jerry Holmes mix it up. (Post-Time Photo)

Ronnie Holmes, 1996. (Don Edds Photo)

Veteran Bob Sitterly. (Don Edds Photo)

NASCAR rep (and former track champ) Jerry Cook congratulates Dale Planck. (Don Edds Photo)

A happy Tommy Kinsella climbs out after a win. (John Clifford Photo)

Utica-Rome's Turbulent Middle Age

Underdog hero J.J. Michaels. (Post-Time Photo)

Mother's Day, 1997: (L-R) Runner-up Brett Hearn, winner Dale Planck, third-place Kenny Brightbill. (Post-Time Photo)

Pro Stocker Tom Denton looks under Dave Meeks. (Post-Time Photo)

Mitch Gibbs was OK after a violent '97 tumble. (Post-Time Photo)

Full-time promoter, part-time racer: The late Alex Friesen. (*AARN* Photo Archive)

Clowning around: Ralph Holmes, 1997. (Don Edds Photo)

Jimmy Horton (#M1) with Ray Zemken looking low. (Post-Time Photo)

Louie Lazzaro in 1998. (John Grady Photo)

Dale Planck, always a factor. (John Clifford Photo)

Pileup! This 1997 Sportsman wreck was a biggie. (Post-Time Photo)

Jeff Walton, 1997. (Post-Time Photo)

1998: Ron Holmes (82) and John Barker Jr. (Post-Time Photo)

Utica-Rome's Turbulent Middle Age

Promotional icons Bub Benway (left) and Dick Waterman. (Biittig Photo)

(L-R) Dick Waterman, Bill Wimble, and John Tallini celebrate the track's 40th anniversary. (Utica-Rome Archive)

40th Anniversary: Dick Waterman and track official Vern Angell. (Utica-Rome Archive)

Pro Stock hero Bret Belden. (Post-Time Photo)

2001: Danny Johnson wins a 100-lapper. (Utica-Rome Archive)

2001: Rene Charland and racing historian Doug Zupan. (Zupan Collection)

Jessica Zemken gets after it. (Post-Time Photo)

1997

Dale the Dominant

After a respectful idle as friends and the greater racing community mourned Alex Friesen, there was an easing out of the clutch in January. Details began to emerge about the tracks and plans Friesen left behind.

Regarding Utica-Rome and Fulton, little would change, though there would be a new face for some to get used to. According to columnist John Hill of the *Syracuse Post-Standard*, co-owner John Zemaitis would play a bigger part in 1997 than he had when Friesen was there to oversee things. "Zemaitis had been a silent partner in the deal," wrote Hill, "but he will now take a more active role in the operation."

Stan Friesen, Alex's dad and the man who first sparked his managerial and promotional fires way back when at Ransomville—and who was now overseeing things at the

Dale Planck was on the gas right from the start of the season, winning seven Modified features and his third championship. (Post-Time Photo)

John Zemaitis, previously a silent ownership partner to Alex Friesen, was forced into a more active role in 1997. (Mel Stettler Photo, AARN Photo Archive)

paved Lancaster track—would be available to assist Zemaitis when needed. The two of them were fortunate enough to rely on some familiar standbys: Jennifer Fidanza and Marcia Wetmore were back as director of operations and director of racing, respectively. Joe Foy returned to handle the marketing. Lyle DeVore was promoted to manager, and was still prepping the track. Gary Lamberton held forth as technical director.

And back on the flagstand was Dick Sweet, who in 1997 would twirl the silks at both Utica-Rome and Fulton, as well as at the downstate Afton Speedway, where he would work alongside that track's new promoter, Roger Heroux. The destinies of both men would continue to be interwoven with those of Utica-Rome, but we're getting ahead of ourselves.

NASCAR was still the sanctioning body at the two Outlaw Modified tracks, providing a helpful stability in 1997.

Stan Friesen, shown here in his driving days, has done it all in New York racing. In '97, he helped fill the Utica-Rome void left by Alex's death. (Rod Nacewicz Collection)

But in a holding pattern of sorts was the STORM mini-series for small-block Modifieds, with Wetmore telling John Hill that Alex Friesen was "the only person who really could have pulled it off the way he'd envisioned it."

The Utica-Rome schedule was built around 22 features for the Outlaw Modifieds. Mother Nature would eventually claim two of them. When the gates opened on May 4, the rest were up for grabs.

~

From the start, the action was spirited. Dale Planck captured the season's first two Modified features—both 40-lappers—and thus previewed what his rivals and Utica-Rome's fans were in for in 1997. Seven times that year, Dale's Sunday evenings ended with flashbulbs blinding him as he accepted the spoils of victory. And when September passed and the racing was through, he had earned his third track championship in four years.

It seemed like everyone else took turns in their attempts to knock Planck from his pedestal. The May 4 opener was a seesaw affair, Planck and Mitch Gibbs swapping the lead a few times before finishing in that order. Come the regular-season stretch of 25-lappers, three different men—Ron Holmes on May 25, Ted Lamb Jr. on June 15, and Jeff Walton on July 13—finished runner-up to Planck. And J.J. Michaels ran second to Planck twice, first on Aug. 10 and again in the season finale on Sept. 14. The champ handled all comers.

Three of the greats! Paul Jensen leads Ronnie Holmes (#82) and Dale Planck, each taking a slightly different line. (Post-Time Photo)

Michaels, meanwhile, had a stellar '97 season, his personal best at Utica-Rome in terms of win production. Five times, J.J. powered to the front and stayed there, winning on May 18 and then taking three of the four checkered flags waved in July. The last win of that mid-summer streak sent the folks home chattering. On July 27, Mitch Gibbs and Donnie Wetmore were having a wing-ding fight for the lead when, in an incredible burst of momentum on lap 14, Michaels caught and passed the two of them on the extreme outer edge of the track. A month later, J.J. made the nightcap of a twin-20s program the final conquest of his season.

Wetmore grabbed two main events that season, making him the only other multiple winner. Doug Fuller, Mitch Gibbs, Jeff Walton, Paul Jensen, and Roger Phelps copped a single win each, as did Steve Hulsizer, who grabbed his first career Utica-Rome Modified feature after having been a frequent winner in Street Stock and Sportsman action.

But the year belonged to Planck, adding to his remarkable run at Utica-Rome. Since his first win there in 1992, Dale had visited victory lane 36 more times, giving him an average of just over *six wins per season* at one track alone.

His shining moment in 1997 came on May 11. On that Sunday evening, the track hosted something called the "Big Block/Small Block Challenge," a 40-lapper with $3,000 in the winner's kitty and a pretty relaxed rulebook. A number of heavyweight outsiders towed in, but Planck led every lap. Oh, it was no gimme; Brett Hearn shared the front row with Planck on a mid-race restart, and late in the running Kenny Brightbill moved into second and threatened to close in.

The podium photos from that event, with 26-year-old Dale Planck flanked by Brightbill and Hearn—two of the dirt Modified giants of his lifetime, guys who had been champions everywhere—were proof of the heights he had already reached. And he wasn't done winning yet at Utica-Rome; heck, he wasn't even done winning *championships* at Utica-Rome. But in the years to come, anyone who wants to know just how tough a racer Dale Planck was needs only to look back upon May 11, 1997, when everybody came calling, and everybody lost.

In his day, on his game, Planck was as good a racer as has ever passed through Vernon, New York.

~

Mitch Gibbs emerged unscathed after a nasty spill in his Mirabito-backed Modified. (Post-Time Photo)

On May 11, Planck topped Kenny Brightbill (right) and Brett Hearn in a 40-lap tussle. By 1997, clearly, Planck could handle all comers. (Post-Time Photo)

Wetmore's two victories deserved combat-pay bonuses. On May 4, date of the season opener at Utica-Rome, he had a big Sunday planned. He would run an afternoon big-block DIRT show at Weedsport in the afternoon, then hustle on over to Vernon for an Outlaw Modified nightcap.

Ah, the best-laid plans ...

Donnie was loading up that morning when a steel cable on his trailer snapped. It whipped and cut his left forearm to the bone. Ever the racer, he bandaged and taped the wound, finished loading, and drove to Weedsport. With some time to kill before practice, he checked in at the trackside ambulance, and an attendant gave the sliced wing a proper dressing. "She told me I should have it checked," he would recall later.

By that point he was worried the arm might be broken, but since he was already at the track he figured he'd go ahead and run the feature. He led wire-to-wire. Wetmore later told the *Post-Standard* that the injury "didn't really bother me a lot. When you're running up front like that, you don't think about it." It's also likely that adrenaline—first released by the trailer incident, and then by leading and winning that feature—had done a fair job masking the pain. When he'd arrived at Utica-Rome he was hurting, and the rough opening-night track didn't help. He trailered early and headed home. The next morning, X-rays revealed a broken bone.

It was still bothering him in June, but on the final Sunday night of that month he held off a fierce attack from Planck to take the checkers in a 25-lap weekly

Despite playing hurt, Hall of Famer Donnie Wetmore won his final two Utica-Rome features in the summer of 1997. (Post-Time Photo)

show. Six weeks later, professing to be healed but no doubt still tender—you don't slice through flesh, muscle, and bone without lasting reminders—he outran Ron Holmes in the hot opener of a twin-20 program.

Those two wins were the last of Donnie Wetmore's stellar Utica-Rome career. Dating back to 1980—though for several seasons he was not a regular—he grabbed 21 features there, winning on the big five-eighths and later on the more sensible half-mile.

And he won so much elsewhere—68 times at Fulton, 67 at Brewerton, and enough here and there to push his lifetime total over 200—that he was a lock to make it into the New York State Stock Car Association Hall of Fame as soon as he was eligible. That happened in 2005. Incredibly, he was the third member of his family to be enshrined, joining his brother Stanley, a Lebanon Valley veteran, and their mother, Ethel Searing Wetmore, inducted in 2000 for her years of service to the sport in an era when dirt-track racing was anything but a ladies' game.

Oh, and you may have noticed another Wetmore connection at Utica-Rome. Though by '97 they had been separated for seven years, Donnie and Marcia Wetmore had already been married 20 more, and much of that had been spent at area speedways. Now Marcia helped run the show at Utica-Rome and Fulton, Donnie was running well, son Donnie Jr. was cutting his racing teeth in one of his dad's rides, and daughter Bridget was aiding her mother on race nights.

Sure, maybe other couples—or former couples—might find all that a bit awkward, and in a great 1997 *Post-Standard* feature story writer Nolan Weidner naturally asked Donnie and Marcia about this. "Both said they get along fine at the race track," Weidner reported. Which was nice, because stock car racing in New York was the richer for having the two of them involved.

~

Dan Yankowski had been a familiar face on the Utica-Rome grounds for several years, and in the Sportsman class his name had been in the win column since 1993. But the driver from New Berlin really had his act together in '97, collecting his first track championship.

Marcia Wetmore, so prominent in New York racing circles, in a typical pose: radio in hand, conducting business. (Ken Dippel Photo)

Top: Winning never grew old for Dave Mannise, who charged to his fifth championship in the Pure Stocks. (Post-Time Photo)

Left: This enthusiastic young fan of Dan Yankowski had to be happy when Dan clinched the Sportsman title with a victory. (John Clifford Photo)

Dan collected points in drip-drip-drip fashion, with 11 top-five finishes heading into the Sept. 14 season finale putting him in title contention. Then Yankowski, showing one terrific finishing kick, closed the year with his only feature win, stealing the big trophy away from Jim Rothwell, who finished as division runner-up.

And turning lots of heads in the Sportsman class was Rick Miller, who had worn the 1993 and '95 Street Stock crowns. Few probably guessed when Rick climbed into a Sportsman in '96 that within a year he'd contend for the title in that variety of car, but he won a division-high four features and finished third in the standings.

Oneida fans, and indeed all old-school Utica-Rome fans, were whooping it up over the Street Stock championship of Jerry Holmes, brother of Outlaw Modified shoe Ron and son of coupe-era crowd-pleaser Ralph Holmes. Jerry had six victories, as did his closest pursuer, Joe Palmer, but Holmes had a slight edge in the consistency department.

In the Pure Stocks, a season-long tussle between Dave Mannise and Stan Clark—another case of two men winning six times each—was ultimately decided in Mannise's favor. It was the fifth division title for Dave, and he was just getting warmed up.

And Stan Clark, by the way, was another guy with racing roots. His parents, John and Barb, were longtime stock car devotees, and down the line Barb would have a management role at Utica-Rome. Small world. Tight world.

1998

An(other) Irregular Season

Even by Utica-Rome standards, 1998 was a peaks-and-valleys year. In so many ways it seemed almost a microcosm of the track's history. There was a crisis in the front office, there was inclement weather at inopportune moments, there was a savior there when one was needed, and, ultimately, there was some very good racing.

And the racing, really, was what redeemed 1998. When the green flag was unfurled, the rhythm of those laps—the pack rumbling out of turn four, blasting down the frontstretch, slowing for turn one, gassing out of turn two—would shove aside all thoughts of trouble, for however long the event took. It was hard to give much consideration to lawyers and mortgages while watching Roger Phelps and J.J. Michaels slice through traffic in their Modifieds, or Dave Mannise carve up another Pure Stock field. It was only between heat races, or at intermission, or perhaps leaving the track, that folks would discuss whatever they might have heard about the goings-on behind the scenes.

And, for better or worse—it varied from week to week, it seemed—there was a lot to discuss.

Utica-Rome's two 1998 Modified champions, NASCAR titlist J.J. Michaels (#31) and open-comp kingpin Roger Phelps. (Post-Time Photo)

Eric Kingsley's return as Utica-Rome track boss was not easy, but he did a fine job stepping into a tangled situation. (Don Edds Photo)

~

There was no way to sugarcoat the uncertainty surrounding the Outlaw Modified circuit in the winter of 1997-98. John Hill, writing in the *Syracuse Post-Standard*, didn't even try. The lead to his column on Wednesday, February 25, 1998 got right to the point: "The chances of the Fulton and Utica-Rome speedways opening in April are slim."

The aftershocks of Alex Friesen's death were still being felt.

Alex's father, former driver and promotional veteran Stan Friesen, had assumed many of his son's responsibilities. Among those was Alex's partnership with John Zemaitis in the ownership of Utica-Rome and Fulton. But things between the two apparently were never as smooth as they'd been between Zemaitis and the younger Friesen, and before long this schism was more like a chasm. Published reports had the pair disagreeing over exactly who owned exactly what, and at some point in 1997 they stopped making mortgage payments on the two properties. Had this been a simple bank loan, the matter might have been resolved rather quickly, but the mortgage holders in this instance were Bub Benway and Eric Kingsley, the former owners of both tracks. Eventually they grew tired of not being paid—who wouldn't?—and initiated foreclosure proceedings, which kicked in during the winter. In no time, the newspapers and trade publications were full of speculation about what might happen to a pair of tracks that, less than two years earlier, had appeared rock-solid.

It seemed inconceivable that the tracks might not re-open, with plenty of suggestions that Benway and Kingsley could simply pick up where Zemaitis and the Friesens, father and son, had left off. But while Benway and Kingsley had long since proven their love of racing—Utica-Rome might not have been worth haggling over in '98 had they not saved it back in 1989—neither of them was particularly keen to get back into the promotion game. Eric had business involvements, including a heavy equipment concern in Phoenix, New York, and a water park in Tampa, and Bub wasn't getting any younger. Kingsley essentially said that if he and Benway did return to leadership positions, it would be out of a sense of obligation to the area's race teams. "Bub is sick about it," Kingsley told John Hill. "If we'd known this would happen we never would have sold the tracks. It's hurt the racers who don't know whether they'll have a track to run."

By March, little had been resolved, with Kingsley professing agitation over the speed at which things dragged along. "I've made 70 calls to Zemaitis's lawyer in the last month," Kingsley told the *Post-Standard*, "and he hasn't called me back once." In time things picked up: a foreclosure sale for Utica-Rome was set for April 21.

On that date, the situation took an odd turn. Kingsley, reportedly the only bidder for the property, retained ownership … and within days sold the facility to Zemaitis! (Fulton's foreclosure sale was scheduled for late May, at which time, Kingsley declared, he would similarly purchase that property and sell it to Zemaitis. That deal, however, never got off the ground.)

All very strange, but certainly not the strangest set of circumstances to ever involve the ownership and management of the Utica-Rome Speedway.

Zemaitis announced a mid-May opening for Utica-Rome, confirming that the track would continue to be part of the NASCAR Winston Racing Series. He and his son James would have roles in running the place, with Bob Connelly and Roger Heroux, both familiar names, lending a hand.

All seemed well again. It was not.

~

J.J. Michaels opened the season strong in the Modifieds, topping Billy Wilcox and Ron Holmes to win the opener on May 17 and then beating Holmes and John Barker Jr. to the checkers a week later. Rain fell on May

31, and on the first weekend in June, Michaels ended up third behind winner Holmes and Paul Jensen. After another wet Sunday, racing resumed on June 21; Jensen won over Holmes and Michaels.

In four races, then, J.J. Michaels had an average finish of second. So did Ron Holmes, although he had one fewer victory.

June 21 was one of those nights when folks in the know were whispering again. There was talk that things in the Zemaitis camp were not going smoothly. Crowds had not been stellar, and the fact that rain ruined two of the first five scheduled events—at a track where Mother Nature had scuppered more than a few promotional dreams—did not go unnoticed.

Where there was smoke …

That week, something came unglued in the sale agreement between Kingsley and Zemaitis. The offshoot was that Eric Kingsley, for the second time in two months and the third time in less than three years, was the man in charge at Utica-Rome Speedway. His first order of business was to announce that the speedway would be shuttered for one Sunday—June 28—thus creating a window of nearly two weeks in which to attend to legalities such as permits, to make adjustments to the staff, and to bring in folks to replace those who had left, among them Connelly and Heroux.

Kingsley announced he would allow big-block Modifieds in to compete alongside his small-block Outlaw cars, a bit of an insurance move in the event that all the uncertainty scared off some of the previous regulars.

Oh, and there was this: Effective immediately, Utica-Rome would no longer carry a NASCAR sanction. Points were reset, and the 11 remaining open-competition Sundays would count toward their own championship. Given the rules change, and Kingsley's hopes of attracting additional teams, restarting the points battle seemed a fair thing to do.

It did, however, have the unfortunate result of torpedoing what had been stellar opening runs by Michaels and Holmes. And to this day, 1998 is in the record books as a Utica-Rome season with two Modified champions; there's an asterisk noting that the NASCAR Modified title of J.J. Michaels was based on just those first four events. Although the asterisk is necessary to help with the explanation, J.J. deserved better in 1998. And if the season had run its normal course, he might have gotten it.

~

The "other" Modified champion at Utica-Rome that year was Roger Phelps, who announced his intentions right away by winning the first two features after the track reopened on July 5. (For that show, Kingsley's group brought in a huge fireworks display, a smart, fan-friendly move.) Ron Holmes blasted from the tail up to second in the opener, with Mitch Gibbs third in a big-block car. On the second Sunday, Gibbs placed second, just ahead of Steve Hulsizer.

On the remaining nine nights, eight different drivers won Modified features. Only Gibbs could repeat, winning a standard 25-lap main on Aug. 30 and a 35-

Top: Phelps aims low in this tight battle with Mike VanDusen's #24 as they round turn two. (Post-Time Photo)

Right: J.J. Michaels low, John Barker Jr. high, and the fans no doubt paying close attention. (Post-Time Photo)

An(other) Irregular Season

Ted Lamb is all smiles after grabbing an early-August Modified victory. (Post-Time Photo)

lapper, the only extra-distance show of the year, on Sept. 13.

Ted Lamb grabbed the trophy on Aug. 9, and John Barker Jr. drove into victory lane on Sept. 6. And for three other men, their lone Modified wins of 1998 became milestones in their colorful careers. Jim Rothwell's big score on Aug. 2 was the first of his two career Modified victories at the track; Gus Schmidt Jr. won for the first time on Aug. 23, and would eventually win five more features; and Jeff Walton's triumph on Aug. 16 was the last of his four victorious Sundays as a Modified driver at Utica-Rome.

And speaking of milestones ...

Roger Phelps, like J.J. Michaels, merits more recognition than that split '98 season provides. A solid chunk of racer, Roger's interest in the sport was piqued when, as a youngster, he was hired to wash a street car belonging to the great track announcer Jack Burgess; part of Jack's tip was a copy of *Gater Racing News*. Young Phelps was literally off to the races, becoming a fan of Dutch Hoag, a crewman for Late Model shoe Chuck Kerfien, and a winning driver himself in Late Models and Modifieds. He had eight career victories at Utica-Rome, the final two in July of '98, on the way to his only track championship there.

Always popular, Phelps had a soft spot for kids. The reason was simple and warm. "When I was little," he told writer Kevin Rice, "I would go up to the fence [at different tracks] and Dutch Hoag would talk to me. That meant a lot."

Roger Phelps meant a lot, and still does, to racing in New York.

~

Three-wide action in the Street Stocks. On the inside is the #71 of Stan Clark, another son of a longtime racing family. (Post-Time Photo)

There are weird asterisks, too, in the support-class records from that two-part '98 season. Tony Buffa, twice a winner early on, was the NASCAR Sportsman champion; Jack Miller, winless but steady, was the open-comp Sportsman king.

Tom Denton took the NASCAR Street Stock crown with Joe Palmer taking the post-June championship. Both men had terrific seasons, Palmer grabbing four wins and Denton three.

Dave Mannise earned another Pure Stock title, his sixth. Dave won eight features, though six-time winner Jeff Thorp kept him hustling.

A six-race mini-series was run for the IMCA-style Modifieds so popular in the American Midwest and gaining steam elsewhere. Cory Fachini won two times, but George Cantanzano topped the title fight.

~

In November, Eric Kingsley announced that Utica-Rome would operate under a DIRT sanction in 1999. Though the Vernon track had been part of Glenn Donnelly's organization in the past—in 1981-82, and in the 1985-87 New Venture era—Kingsley's move was noteworthy in that it put him and Bub Benway, whose circuit had been a sizable thorn in Donnelly's side, under Glenn's vast umbrella. The Outlaw promoters were now part of the establishment.

But, hey, in the wake of all that had happened since 1996, being a part of something big, something stable, seemed like the best thing that could happen to Utica-Rome.

1999

Lemonade, Anyone?

All those trucks rumbling in and out of the track property in late 1998, and all that racket in the first warm days of '99—the happy hammering of construction—belied the fact that less than one year earlier, Eric Kingsley wanted nothing to do with the day-to-day operation of the Utica-Rome Speedway. He was a guy who had more than paid his dues to the sport; if you asked him in the early months of '98, he'd probably have told you that his plans included tending to his businesses outside of racing, taking a bit of a breather when possible, and, when the spirit moved him, attending events at Utica-Rome and Fulton with the detached enthusiasm of an interested fan.

But, as we have seen, everything had gone a little bit haywire, and the track in Vernon he believed he'd sold was his again. What's that old proverb? Ah, yes: "When life gives you lemons, make lemonade." In other words, make the most of a situation. Eric Kingsley's situation was a half-mile dirt track—he was back to calling it the New Utica-Rome Speedway—and he clearly had his heart set on making the most of it.

As soon as the snows thawed, the spectator areas were abuzz with construction. (Doug Zupan Photo)

Those trucks had hauled in more than 5,000 yards of "new rock-free red clay." It was spread over the track surface before the ground froze, giving the new clay months to bond with its base, like a casserole's flavors melding together in the refrigerator of a New York winter.

Come springtime, Kingsley and his helpers had projects in the works everywhere. The concession stand was enlarged, and buildings in the grandstand area got new roofing and siding. Outside turns one and two, in the overflow paddock commonly called the upper pits, land was cleared to help accommodate the larger transporters coming into fashion among touring racers and even the better-heeled local teams. And a new catch fence went up to help keep the odd bit of flying debris out of that area.

The weekly program would feature DIRT 358-Modifieds, Sportsman, Pro Stocks—new handle for the former Street Stock class—and Pure Stocks.

"We are very excited about the improvements to the speedway," Kingsley said in an April press release, "and we are committed to more improvements over the next few years."

He sounded like a guy whipping up a big, tasty batch of lemonade, and getting ready to ladle it out to thirsty race fans every Sunday night.

~

The DIRT sanction signed by Kingsley was looking to be as good a move as he'd ever made. Outsiders began to eyeball the place as a nice Sunday workout for their 358-Modifieds, and even the prior Utica-Rome regulars—those Outlaws—seemed to consider the switch to DIRT a fine idea.

Oh, things might take a bit of adjustment, because they were now racing under rules that trimmed the once-exotic bodywork of their cars—no more sail panels!—and had everybody running spec Hoosier tires and gasoline rather than alcohol fuel. But, what the heck, *every* spring involved a bit of adjustment even when rules remained unchanged, owing to evolutions in setups; besides, the track surface itself would be new, so every driver and team in the place, whether ex-Outlaws or DIRT devotees, would be feeling out the place together.

When Ron Moshier of the *Utica Observer-Dispatch* visited the track for a midweek practice session in late-April, the folks he talked with all seemed to relish the challenge.

"Everybody's even now," said Jeff Walton, who had four Utica-Rome Modified trophies at home. "You're going to have 15 guys, instead of maybe five, who are capable of winning every night."

Three-time track champ Dale Planck, back at New Utica-Rome as a regular after a season on the DIRT trail, told Moshier, "The way the rules are set, everybody's got the same thing now. It's going to come down to who has the best setup. That's going to be the deal."

Mike Romano saw nothing but good coming from the changes. "What they've done is open it up for more guys to come here," Romano said in the *Observer-Dispatch*. "These fans are going to get to see a new group of guys racing against the same nucleus of drivers who've been here for years." For instance, Mike said, "You're going to see a lot of Fonda guys come here."

And you just had to love the bring-'em-on attitude of Oneida's Ron Holmes. "Let's just put everybody on the race track and duke it out," the second-generation racer told Moshier. "I don't care who comes here. I'll race anybody."

~

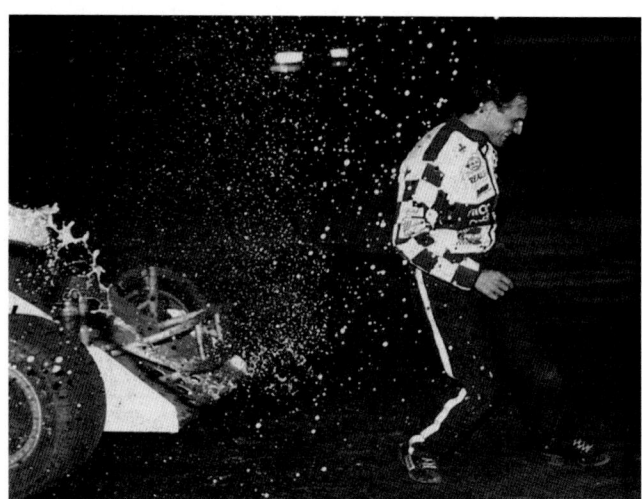

Dale Planck, here ducking a champagne shower, won his fourth Utica-Rome title, tying him with Paul Jensen and the late Richie Evans. (Post-Time Photo)

A standing ovation awaited Gus Schmidt Jr. when he scored an upset victory over Planck in August. Atta boy, Gus! (Don Edds Photo)

Rave reviews were just around the corner. To this day, the history page of Utica-Rome's website declares 1999 "the most successful racing season ever at the speedway. Large crowds week in and week out came to the speedway to see some of the finest racing action in the Northeastern United States."

Opening night was May 2. The DIRT 358-Modified feature, key moment in this exciting rebirth, was a doozy. Mike Romano, his predictions of outside invaders having proven accurate, handled all of them and the Outlaw holdovers, too. Bypassing guys like Planck, early leaders Holmes and Rocky Rothwell, and legendary Maynard Forrette, Romano had the lead just past the halfway mark of the 30-lap main and held it until starter Chip Burdick unfurled the checkered flag. Planck settled for second ahead of Rothwell, John Barker Jr., and A.J. Romano, the winner's brother. There were compliments from the drivers for the new clay, and from the fans for the show they'd seen.

And so it went, all season long. Great crowds, great racing, great fun.

Having the *most* fun were a couple of past track champions who were really airing out their small-block mills. Mitch Gibbs, the 1996 Utica-Rome kingpin, was Mr. Speed in '99, romping to six feature wins, all of them get-up-and-go 30-lappers. But Planck, who had won his 1994, '95, and '97 titles by running everybody else into the ground, topping the win column each time, showed he could do it the hard way, too. In 1999, Dale won just twice, but he also had a dozen *other* podium finishes. That's 14 top-three results, four more than the electric Mr. Gibbs. When they tallied up the points at year's end, Dale led Mitch by a relatively comfortable 46 points.

It was Planck's fourth track title, moving him into a three-way tie with Richie Evans and Paul Jensen atop the roll of repeat champions.

The list of men who joined Planck, Gibbs, and Romano in winning features was awesome. J.J. Michaels proved especially adept at running where the competition wasn't. He won four times and finished up front regularly, defining both his style and his love of a good scrap with his post-race remarks after beating Ted Lamb and Planck on Aug. 15. "Wherever you wanted to race—inside, outside, in the middle—it was a lot of fun," exulted J.J., who had used all those lanes on the way to victory.

The season's three biggest events fell to non-regulars. Todd Burley—gearing up for more Vernon success in the future—dropped in and out of New Utica-Rome all year, but made his July 29 visit count when he topped Planck and Michaels in a 50-lapper. Danny Johnson grabbed a midweek Super DIRT Series 358-Modified win on Aug. 25, besting Steve Paine, Michaels, and everybody else. And on Sept. 24, Brett Hearn took the measure of Paine and Danny Johnson over the 100-lap distance. Brett clearly hadn't lost his winning touch at the track; then again, did he ever lose his touch *anywhere*?

Ron Holmes backed up his pre-season boldness, winning in mid-June and mid-July, and for Ronnie, too, more great days awaited. Steve Hulsizer was everybody's All-American, winning on July 4 over Planck and Burley.

And when little guy Gus Schmidt Jr. edged big star Planck by less than a foot on Aug. 1—David beating Goliath after a restart on the final lap—the crowd rained down applause, rewarding Gus with a rare standing ovation. Son of a hotshot drag racer, Gus Jr. was as good as any circle-tracker alive that night.

~

Jamie Christian was the man of the year in the DIRT Sportsman class, emerging as track champ. Incredibly, Jamie was the leading winner with just three victories; in all, 11 drivers split up the 18 trophies, with Jim Smith, Ron Richardson, Willy Decker, Kevin Crave, and Tim Clemons each scoring twice.

A racer to the core, Pro Stock champion Tom Denton posed for photos like this one eight times in 1999.

Racing lifer Tom Denton—"I've been around it since I was in diapers," he told the *Observer-Dispatch*—won eight times en route to the Pro Stock title. That was more than double those won by next-best Jerry Holmes, who took three.

And for Dave Mannise, 1999 marked his fourth straight Pure Stock championship at the track, and his seventh overall. So far, that is.

~

That blast of personality splitting the Sunday-evening air was the amplified voice of Shane Andrews, who in 1999 became the track's head announcer. A kid out of nearby Oriskany Falls, Andrews had been doing some announcing for Roger Heroux down at Afton Speedway in the mid-'90s when Dick Sweet and Marcia Wetmore heard his work. They introduced him to veteran announcer Jim King, and King—"a great mentor," says Andrews of the man he respectfully calls "Kinger"—took the young man under his wing for a few seasons.

At 28, he assumed the leading role in the New Utica-Rome booth. He loved the people he worked with—"There were some characters in the mix"—and his enthusiasm for the racing itself could not be missed. Blessed with an energy that translates easily into his on-air persona, Andrews could make the lunch-hour crawl at a fast-food drive-thru sound like the lead draft at the Daytona 500. It didn't hurt that he had plenty to describe; outside his window was some of the wildest Modified racing anywhere. He was in residence at Utica-Rome through 2005.

In the years that followed, Andrews would get some serious TV time, working with "This Week on DIRT" and doing lots of dirt-track pit reportage for SPEED-TV. These days, some see him as something of a celebrity when he shows up around his home tracks. Truth is, Shane Andrews is still very much the race fan he was long before he ever held a microphone. Check this out: In the stat-crammed notebook he carries to various speedways—and he has now announced at more than 20—he carries an autographed photo of one of his boyhood heroes, the great Late Model racer Tommy Williams, taken (and later autographed) at Utica-Rome "in 1980 or '81." Andrews says, "I still remember the battles he had with Randy Glenksi. That picture goes everywhere with me when I'm on the road."

With veteran scorer Jerry Brooks to his left, announcer Shane Andrews calls the action on a Sunday in 1999. (Utica-Rome Archive)

2000

Hot Shoe, Indeed

Talk about spreading the wealth around! In 2000, the DIRT 358-Modified division at New Utica-Rome was so tight that the two winningest drivers in the class, Ron Holmes and Todd Burley, had just two victories each. *Two!* Nine other drivers made single visits to victory lane, making it not only one of the most competitive years the track had ever seen, but also one of the most democratic. Everybody had a say in the outcome; no one enjoyed an unconditional rule. No dictators in Vernon, not this year.

There was, however, a track champion.

~

Hard-driving Ronnie Holmes, the 2000 Utica-Rome champion in the DIRT 358-Modified class. (John Clifford Photo)

Ron Holmes was a second-generation racer; his father, Ralph, was a fan favorite in the NASCAR coupes during Utica-Rome's pavement era. Across the 1990s, the speedway's second dirt decade, Ronnie had more than come into his own, winning a half-dozen top-class features. He was very much an old-school dude, putting in a full week at Ralph's Collision, the family business in Oneida, plus working nights on stock cars and then hustling them hard on the weekends.

So it made sense that when Ron won himself the DIRT 358-Modified track championship in 2000, he did it the old-school way, fighting and clawing. He won twice, placed second twice, finished third twice and fourth once. In a short season of just 13 features—seven more Sunday nights were rained out, including three straight in June, a flashback to the wet '70s—that was a good enough combination to give Ronnie the title.

He was in the hunt right from opening night, May 7, when he finished second in a 40-lapper to a 24-year-old Massachusetts kid named Andy Bachetti, whose thrill-a-minute style instantly had everybody in the joint calling him Wild Child. Even today, Holmes recalls trying in vain to chase down Bachetti that night: "It sounded like he was twisting that motor 8,500 [RPMs], which was a lot back then. That thing was just screaming. But the track was heavy that night, and it worked for him." The following week, Ronnie ran third to Danny Johnson and Todd Burley in a 100-lapper, before pulling some big gear himself and zinging to a 30-lap win on May 28. A second, a third, and that victory ended up building him a nice launch pad for his title run.

He won again on July 16—a night we will hear more about in a moment—and on Aug. 20 came *this close* to taking a trophy that instead rode home with Jason Barney. "I remember that night," says Holmes, "because there was almost a fight later. I started in the back, and I had finally caught [Barney] as we got the white flag. Going into [turn] one he was up high, on the cushion, and I was way down low. Well, he saw me, so he turned off the cushion and shot straight across the track." The two cars thumped hard, and Jason Barney squirted away to score his only career feature win at Utica-Rome. Today, Holmes can put the whole

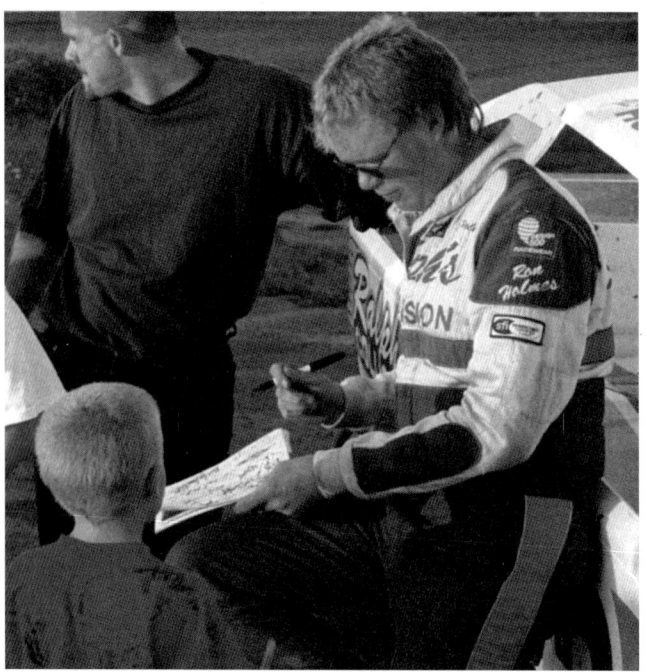

Keeping the fans happy: Ronnie Holmes, from nearby Oneida, doles out a few autographs. (Neff Family Collection)

Right: Danny Johnson was the man of the hour when the Super DIRT Series visited on a Thursday night in August. (Alex and Helen Bruce Photo)

episode down to one guy, Barney, hungry for his first win, and another guy, himself, eager to be rewarded for a great come-from-behind scramble. Back then, he was not so forgiving. "After the checkered flag I ran into his back bumper and flipped him off," Ronnie laughs. "And then we had a little discussion."

That year, again, announcer Shane Andrews interviewed the top-three finishers after each feature. It is revealing that the thing Shane mentions first about interviewing Holmes in those days is not the nights he won, but rather the times he nearly won.

"Ronnie hated to lose," Andrews recalls. "*Hated to lose.*"

Today, Holmes says it wasn't so much the losing as how he lost. Thanks to his normal high handicap, a byproduct of having done well so consistently, he was climbing a steep hill in those busy 30-lappers.

"I was always starting 16th or 18th," Ronnie says, "and I'd catch the leader, or leaders, right at the very end, like at the white flag. It gets frustrating to come that far and then have, like, one lap to do something."

Left: Wow! Ronnie Johnson (#4) and Alan Johnson aren't related, but here they're closer than brothers! (Post-Time Photo)

Bottom: John Barker's last Utica-Rome win came on a twin-feature night in July of 2000. (Post-Time Photo)

J.J. Michaels (#31, inside Gus Schmidt Jr.) looked for a time like he might win the track championship. (Post-Time Photo)

But it made for great action. "To watch Ronnie come through the field was amazing," Andrews says. "He had the nickname Hot Shoe, and he lived up to it."

Other names had their moments in bold print. Burley won in early June and mid-August; John Barker Jr. and J.J. Michaels split twin-20s on July 2; Mitch Gibbs and Dale Planck, big winners in past seasons, won on consecutive Sundays, Aug. 27 and Sept. 3. And the same season that marked the thrilling first feature victory by promising young Ronnie Johnson, on July 23, ended with a 100-lap score by his dad, Jack Johnson, on Sept. 22.

By the time of Jumpin' Jack's big victory, the points chase had already concluded. Its final weeks were hell on Hot Shoe Holmes.

"As I recall, I had a pretty good lead until the last few races, sitting comfortable," Ron says. "Then I had a couple bad weeks and everything changed, and J.J. had the points lead going into the last race. That had me worried. I was out of good motors, and J.J. was always fast."

Holmes trailed by six points, and thus needed to finish two spots ahead of Michaels to win the title. Come the pivotal feature, Ronnie went straight to work, jumping into an early lead. "But I could *not* get away from J.J.," he recalls. Indeed, they ran first and second from laps 9-18.

"I was driving absolutely as hard as I could, and so was he," says Holmes. "I mean, we were right on the edge of wrecking on every turn. Then, about halfway through the race, J.J. broke something—a torsion stop, maybe—and I still remember feeling like the whole world was just lifted off my shoulders. In fact, I actually took it easy after that." Holmes slipped to fourth, and yet finished the race "totally exhausted, mentally. It was brutal.

"But, you know, it's awesome to think about it now, the two of us racing that hard, side-by-side and nose-to-tail, without touching. J.J. was an awesome racer."

(This is not mere nice-guy talk a decade later. On the night in question, in a press release written by Doug Zupan, Holmes said, "I feel bad that J.J. had some bad luck. It would not have broken my heart to see him win the championship."

Reflecting now on 2000, Ronnie Holmes says, "We had a car that year that was just so comfortable, and so fast. John Baker was my crew chief, and we tried different things every week, just off-the-wall stuff, and it seemed like everything worked. We'd still run up front."

~

On Thursday night, Aug. 24, the throaty roar of big-block engines rang out for the first time since 1987, as the Super DIRT Series stopped in. After 100 sticky laps, Danny Johnson was standing in victory lane. Steve "Hurricane" Paine finished second ahead of Jack Johnson. Just missing the podium were Brett Hearn, fourth, and Alan Johnson in fifth.

Pretty good night for guys named Johnson, no?

~

At first glance, the DIRT Sportsman action in 2000 was absolutely one-sided compared to what went on with the 358-Modifieds. But *only* at first glance.

Jamie Christian completely overpowered the opposition, winning seven features, including the final two of the season. That was the second time Jamie had won twice consecutively, having managed the same trick on April 28 and May 4.

Ah, but a deeper examination of that season's Sportsman records paints a different picture. Among seven drivers winning one feature apiece was Kevin Crave, who maintained such a presence in the top five that by year's end not even the speedy Christian could catch him in the standings. It was Crave's first track championship. And fans were buzzing about young Willy Decker, third in the Sportsman tally, climbing that racing ladder.

Tom Denton and Jerry Holmes—yes, another of Ralph's boys—traded Pro Stock victories back and forth. Tom ended up with five to Jerry's four, and in the end the division's crown went to Denton. Frank Twing and the ever-competitive Bret Belden also stood in victory lane.

Dave Mannise still had the winning formula in the Pure Stocks, grabbing five features and another championship, his eighth.

And New Utica-Rome was experimenting with the scaled-down screamers known as Tobias Slingshots, miniature Modified look-alikes which ran on a small inner oval. Jackie Botindari topped the Senior Slingshots, while the Junior champ was A.J. Kingsley, son of track owners Eric and Gisele Kingsley.

~

Here's a neat memory: It's July 16, 2000, and the happiest guy in Vernon is named Holmes, but it isn't Ron and it isn't Jerry. Oh, both those guys are plenty pumped up, because earlier Ronnie won the 358-Modified main and now Jerry is pulling to a stop in victory lane, having taken the Pro Stock checkers. But the biggest smile in the joint belongs to *Ralph* Holmes, whose two racing sons have each won plenty, but never before on the same evening.

Ralph had been around Utica-Rome forever, cutting his racing teeth in 1963 in the old Overhead class in a hulking Oldsmobile previously owned and driven by Bernie Miller, who provided early guidance. Later, Ralph's first Modified coupe was constructed by another helpful pal, Sonney Seamon. He was among the Sunday-night regulars when heroes named Lazzaro, Flemke, Wimble, Evans, Cook, Stevens, and DeSarro were buzzing around Dick Waterman's bullring. "I knew all those guys forever," Ralph says. "We were all friends, and we all helped each other."

In the Pro Stocks, Tom Denton ended up leading both the win column and the points tally. (Post-Time Photo)

Oneida's racing Holmes clan: Proud papa Ralph (right) with his champion sons, Ronnie (left) and Jerry. (Don Edds Photo)

Like every journeyman racer, Ralph one day reached a crossroads, and for him the choice of which way to turn was not difficult. "I realized that my business had made all that racing possible over the years, and I decided it was time to pay more attention to the business, and to back off my own racing. That way, I could also start having some fun with the kids."

Ronnie and Jerry had raced go-karts and motocross, and gravitated toward stock cars. "I really thought I wouldn't get nervous watching them," Ralph says. "But there are certainly situations where it's *natural* to be nervous. Sometimes in the beginning, I felt like I was still out there myself.

"Seeing them both do well has made me feel really good. I mean, they've done far better than I did. Of course, they had better equipment, but they were very successful, both of them, and that made me pretty proud over the years."

That pride lives forever in the photos from July 16, 2000.

When you reminisce about all the families that have populated and popularized Utica-Rome—surnames like Kotary, Seamon, Henry, Johnson, Romano—just be sure you save room for this Holmes clan. Ronnie and Jerry were champion drivers; Ralph was a champion dad.

EYEWITNESS
1996–2000: DALE PLANCK

"It was like everything we did worked out right"

NOTE: Second-generation Modified racer Dale Planck is, without question, one of Utica-Rome Speedway's all-time greats. He is one of only three drivers—Richie Evans and Paul Jensen being the other two—to win four Modified championships at the track; Planck's titles came in 1994, '95, '97, and '99, and across that span of six seasons he parked in victory lane 35 times, far more than any other driver. By the close of the 2010 season, despite not having been a Utica-Rome regular for several years, he still sat atop the track's all-time Modified win list with 42, nine more than the legendary Evans. Indeed, few drivers have "owned" an era in the manner Planck owned much of the 1990s at Utica-Rome. In that same time frame, he earned three consecutive NASCAR Winston Series regional titles, 1994-96. A modest champion, Dale credits his success to the lessons he picked up from his late father, Denny Planck.

When I look back on what we accomplished in that period, sometimes I'm not sure how we did all that. In a pretty short time we won three NASCAR regional championships, and four track championships in six seasons at Utica-Rome, which was a really tough place with a lot of really good competition. Tommy Kinsella and Paul Jensen were always right there. Randy Glenski was really hot for a stretch. J.J. Michaels was on top of his game, and he was very consistent. Mike Romano was really fast. Mitch Gibbs won a lot of races. It was a very competitive period for Utica-Rome, that's for sure.

Being on top like we were is nice, but at the same time you're always wondering when somebody might come along and knock you down. It put a lot of pressure on me, week to week. The pressure was mostly something I kinda created myself, I'm sure. When you run that good for so long, all of a sudden it gets hard to take a sixth- or seventh-place finish, even though that's still a good run against that kind of competition.

Once he'd hit his stride, Dale Planck could run with the best. That's him leading Danny Johnson (#27) and Paul Jensen. (Don Edds Photo)

At the same time, there's outside pressure in that situation, too. Sometimes I felt like everybody was gunning for us, trying to get us down. It seemed like there was always a little bit of trouble through those years: teardowns, protests, things like that. But I've never been one to cheat; my dad never cheated when he raced, and he instilled in me the idea that if you've got to cheat to win, you're probably not working hard enough. I've always carried those words with me.

I didn't like having that sort of controversy around, but I guess maybe that's the price you pay if you're on top for any length of time, no matter where you're racing. We were so good for so long that some guys just assumed we had a big motor, or some super-secret thing that made us go fast. But, honestly, it was just a matter of us being on top of the tire program, the engine program, and the setups. A lot of it went back to me and my dad working hard in the shop, scratching our heads, coming up with our own setups.

When we won our first three Utica-Rome track championships in 1994, '95, and '97, each year we won more races than anybody. But when we won the fourth one in 1999, we didn't win the most races—we had two, and Mitch Gibbs and J.J. Michaels both had more—yet we were very steady. I was just as proud of that championship as I was of the other three, because consistency is something I've always strived for. Winning is awesome, for sure, but if I can run near the front against good competition and be in contention to win, week in and week out, I'm more than happy.

Looking back, I always had good sponsorships in that period, but in that '99 season a few things had changed, and I was pretty much doing it on my own. With that in mind, I couldn't put new tires on the car for every race, and do some of things I'd have liked to do. That had something to do with why we didn't win more, I'm sure. But we did have that consistency, which was the key.

Winning those NASCAR regional championships was a big deal for us. Especially the first one; that was incredible. See, when Utica-Rome and Fulton announced they were going NASCAR, that all sounded good, but I pretty much figured nobody from our tracks would ever be able to win a title like that. None of us was used to chasing points that way. So to go out that first year and put together the season we did, that was just unreal. The trip to Nashville for the Winston Racing Series awards banquet, going up on stage with a thousand people in the room, doing a speech, getting that huge trophy, all of that was really different for me, but it was great. And, of course, there was that check for $40,000, which was pretty great, too.

The neat thing was, all kinds of sponsorships and perks came out of those championships. We'd be in the NASCAR media guides and things like that, and in the newspapers and magazines. I'd be at the PRI trade show (in Columbus) and people from different parts of the country would know my name, and what I had done. So, yes, the prestige and the money was nice while we were winning those championships, but the support from different companies that resulted from those titles was a good thing, too.

I'm so glad that my dad got to see a lot of the success we had back then, because I wouldn't have done the things I ended up doing had it not been for him and his racing. As far back as I can remember, I was in the garage working on whatever I could, whether it was my own go-karts or my dad's stuff. I definitely learned from all that, and from going to all the tracks.

By the time I was about 14, I was *really* into it. When it was time to get ready to go racing, sometimes the guys who worked on the crew would be busy during the day at their regular jobs, but in the summer I'd be home from school. A lot of times, I would end up loading the ramp truck all by myself while my dad finished getting the car ready. I remember trying to figure out how to get all this stuff up onto that truck: a 200-pound air tank, a big-ass toolbox, all those tires ...

I remember one day asking my dad, "Hey, can you help me with this?"

He said, "What would you do if I wasn't here?"

Well, when he said that, it just made me determined to figure a way to do it on my own. I'd wedge a floor jack under the toolbox and get it up there a little at a time, and I'd find a way to get the air tank up on that truck, too. Whatever it took. Growing up that way, and the things he taught me, definitely taught me to become more resourceful, and that has paid off. I've always done my own setups, basically from the

New Utica-Rome's tenure as a NASCAR dirt track (note the Winston banner) was awfully good to young Mr. Planck. (Don Edds Photo)

A chip off the old block, Planck took the lessons he learned from his dad, Denny, and turned them into championships. (Don Edds Photo)

time I started and right to this day. I've had good help, and I'll always listen to people and their input, but I've tried hard to never have to rely on anybody but myself. That way, if I run bad, there is nobody to blame but me.

My dad passed away late in 1996. By that point, we had won two track championships at Utica-Rome, and we had won those three NASCAR titles back-to-back. Like I said, that NASCAR championship was something we never figured we could do even once, and here we were, winning three in a row. It was a major thing for me, and I know it was for my dad, too. Anyway, I had come home from the banquet in Nashville and we went through Christmas, and then he passed away. He had been extremely sick for the previous two years, suffering from cancer, but in that time he was at the shop almost every day and he was still able to come to the races. I think that's what kept him going, to be honest: just looking forward to being at the races. He was in a great amount of pain nearly all the time, but racing—whether he was at the shop or at the track—gave him a chance to get his mind off how bad he was feeling. While he was undergoing the treatments, he fell and broke his right arm; not long after that, he fell and broke his left arm. So here he was, with two broken arms on top of being as sick as he was, but when he was at the races and we were running good, it was like his suffering was gone for those few hours.

So in that sense, all that stuff—the wins and the championships—couldn't have come at a better time, because he was able to see us accomplish some of what we did. And we continued to do really well for a few years after that, like 1997 through '99, so maybe he was still helping us from above a little bit.

In racing, nothing ever stays the same for too long. It seems like the wins have come harder for me lately, so it's fun to reflect back on a time when it felt so much easier. Obviously, winning is never easy, and it definitely wasn't easy when we were winning those championships. But you'll have times in racing when it seems like you can't do anything wrong, and times when it seems like you can't do anything right. In that period, back from about 1994 to '99, it was like *everything* we did worked out right.

We rode a heck of a wave there for a while...

2001

Todd's Turn

Todd Burley is a guy any serious race fan would love to spend time with. Still on the sunny side of 40, he's in the thick of a career which even now finds him mixing it up with relative youngsters like Stewart Friesen and Matt Sheppard. And Burley is very much the modern driver, versed in chassis technology, articulate, able to explain in layman's terms what it's like to bullwhip a Modified around a fast track like Utica-Rome. Yet he is also happy to travel back down Memory Lane on a trip into his racing past, and maybe yours, too. As a kid in Spencerport, a Rochester suburb, he grew up immersed in that area's racing culture. He can tell you all about Mike Loescher and Lee Osborne, both of whom made spot appearances at Utica-Rome in the track's asphalt years before going on to other things: a Florida driving school and fabrication shop for Loescher, and a grand career hustling winged Sprint Cars around the United States for Osborne. And, of course, Burley can spin many a good yarn about the driver-turned-chassis builder who was the biggest Rochester hero of them all, Maynard Troyer.

Seven victories formed the basis of a track championship season for Spencerport racer Todd Burley. (Post-Time Photo)

Burley relied on what he called "great cars and a really solid motor program." The driver was pretty good, too! (Post-Time Photo)

But a word of warning: While a conversation with Burley can be fun, timing is everything.

"Todd is *intense*," says Shane Andrews, who in his years as Utica-Rome's announcer spoke with him on a weekly basis. "You go up to him early on a race day and he'll be jovial, he'll bust your chops, he'll joke around. But when it comes closer to race time, man, it's like somebody flips a switch. His whole attitude changes. He's focused. He has the blinders on."

~

In 2001, the intense Mr. Burley shook up things in Vernon much like his man Troyer had in 1973. That year, remember, Maynard—still very much an outsider—beat Jerry Cook to win a summertime 100-lapper, then edged out Bugsy Stevens for the overall win in the prestigious New Yorker 400.

Though he entered 2001 with three New Utica-Rome victories on his résumé, Burley still had a whiff of the invader to him. But he sure made himself at home; he won four DIRT 358-Modified features in the first half of the season, and in that same span placed second twice and third once. His fast start vaulted him into the points lead, and Burley did not let up down the stretch. He won seven times in all, more than double his closest competitor—Jack Johnson, with three wins—and as the season wound down, the track championship became a mere formality. "We had it wrapped up with, like, two weeks to go," Burley recalls. "I think we won by almost 100 points."

Actually, he's selling short that amazing '01 season: His margin was an incredible 154 points, over the surprising Ryan Baye. Burley's wins, all 30-lappers, came on May 20, June 10, July 8, right back again on July 15, Aug. 5, and another run of two straight on Aug. 19 and Aug. 26.

None of the wins came easy, given the usual handicapping procedure, but the July 8 feature was especially hard-fought. Even before halfway, it had boiled down to a two-man scrap: Burley, charging hard in second, and defending track champion Ron Holmes, up front. A month earlier, on June 10, Holmes had finished runner-up to Burley; this time, he had the lead and wanted to keep it. On lap 13, Burley appeared to have executed a pass, but a yellow flag flew, restoring Holmes's lead. On the restart both men entered turn one up high, but Burley glanced off the cushion, cut low, nosed ahead of Holmes, and then slipped right back to the high lane, effectively stalling his rival's momentum with a classic—if a tad overambitious—slide job.

Holmes was less than pleased. On the very next lap, the two cars made contact at the same end of the track. (Holmes temporarily lost second to the strong-running Baye, who soon dropped out of the battle when a driveshaft failed.) And the remaining laps sure didn't do much to cool down Hot Shoe Holmes; he crowded Burley's car toward the infield after the checkers, then skipped out on the customary post-race interview.

Burley, no shrinking violet, stood his ground. "I guess he does not like to get passed," he said of Holmes.

Holmes, quoted in the pits that night for the track's weekly post-race release, said, "That was definitely not a clean pass. [Burley] has been doing that to everyone. I had to hit the brakes when I shouldn't have had to. If I didn't, I would have been wrecked."

Nearly 10 years later, Holmes's opinion has softened … but not much.

"Todd's a hard racer, *really* hard, especially back then," Ronnie declared. "He was very aggressive with his slide jobs, I remember that. As the years went on, he figured things out a little more—the cars, the track—and he got better as a driver, too."

Clearly, Burley was already pretty darn good in '01. "We were really fast that year," he says. "We had great cars and a really solid motor program." He points out that in 2001, the track, still owned by Eric Kingsley, "was a little different than it is today. It was flatter, so you didn't carry as much corner speed. It was more stop-and-go, and we had a great combination of motor and car for that type of race track."

Here, Burley breaks into a big grin. "We were just so confident that year. I mean, we won those seven races, and we probably could've had two or three more if stuff hadn't happened."

~

The year's other 358-Modified winners were an interesting bunch. J.J. Michaels took the 40-lap opener—"You've got to love this place," he bubbled later—and a regular show on July 22. Mitch Gibbs, always tough, heated up as the weather did, winning on July 29 and Aug. 12. And John Ramsey, capable of surprising folks back to his first Vernon victory in 1990, took a 30-lapper on June 24.

And in the space of two weeks in September, two guys who defined the words "dark horse" barged into victory lane, paying that sacred ground the only visits of their Utica-Rome careers. On Sept. 2, Aaron Excell, 31 years of age and from East Hamilton, caught a nice break, starting outside the front row on a night when both he and his car were spot on. He led every lap, and the large holiday-weekend crowd loved it. Even the competitive Gibbs, who finished second, was thrilled for Excell. "He was just too much for me tonight," smiled Mitch, "and I am really happy for him."

And Ryan Baye, who'd had that heartbreaking mechanical failure back in July on the night of the Burley/Holmes dispute, capped his great year by winning a special open-competition 30-lapper on Sept. 9. He emerged victorious in a wild battle with veteran Andy Romano; on lap 23, knifing through lapped traffic, Baye got into the wall and handed Romano the lead. But Andy's engine immediately took sick, and Baye regained the top spot with five laps left. Romano held on for second.

"We got lucky tonight," said Baye, trophy in hand.

Maybe so, but it was persistence and a large dose of youthful enthusiasm, not luck, that carried Baye—barely into his 20s—to his strong runner-up finish in the points standings.

But, Todd Burley aside, three guys named Johnson made the biggest headlines in 2001. Brothers Danny and Alan copped the year's pair of 100-lappers, D.J. beating Pete Bicknell and Steve Paine on May 13, while Alan edged Brett Hearn, Bicknell, and Danny in a slugfest on Sept. 16.

And how about Jumpin' Jack Johnson? On June 17, steaming out of turn four with the white flag waving, Jack got a nose ahead of leader Steve Hulsizer and led the final lap. At a glance it was just a routine 30-lap weekly feature, but it happened to be win the 400th feature victory—yep, all documented—of Johnson's career. While acknowledging the milestone, Jack, who obviously sensed he had a good bit of winning left in him, had his priorities in order: "A heck of a race for the fans, wasn't it?" he remarked to Ron Moshier of the *Utica Observer-Dispatch*.

As pretty a sight as you'll see in racing: Jack Johnson giving his #12A a workout. Each of his three wins was dramatic. (Post-Time Photo)

Two Sundays later, on July 1, Jack was back and raring to get after it again, even at age 56. Twin 20-lappers were on the card, and Mr. Johnson started 14th in both of them. In the opener, he took the lead for keeps on lap 12, passing Hulsizer. In the nightcap, not dallying around this time, he swept around leader Burley on lap nine and drove away.

"Fourteen," he quipped, "must be our lucky number tonight."

~

For the second year in a row, the big-block Mods made a midweek Super

Left: In an August Super DIRT Series big-block show, Billy Decker led at the green and, in the end, held the checkers. (Ken Dippel Photo)

Bottom: Sportsman champion Tim Clemons won the season's first three features, then added four more. (Post-Time Photo)

Top: Jeff Pastorella, shown hustling his Camaro through turn one, grabbed seven feature wins and the Street Stock Crown. (Post-Time Photo)

Left: Bret Belden, who clearly had this Pro Stock gig figured out, took his third track title at Utica-Rome. (Post-Time Photo)

DIRT Series stop at New Utica-Rome. The 100-lapper on Aug. 23 was led flag-to-flag by Billy Decker, but it was anything but dull. Decker faced heavy pressure from first Tim Fuller, then Steve Paine, then Brett Hearn, and finally runner-up Tim McCreadie. Hearn finished third, Paine fourth.

And just a bit further back, Bobby Varin was in the eye of a few different storms, engaging in metal-to-metal contact with Paine, Danny Johnson, and Gary Tomkins. They banged as often under caution as under green, perhaps more, although Johnson and Varin ended up fifth and sixth.

~

Tim Clemons, who had a habit of winning pretty much anywhere he showed up, was back in the limelight at New Utica-Rome in 2001, earning seven victories on his way to the Sportsman track championship. It was to be the only title at the track for the popular driver from Gloversville, though in the early '90s he'd won three straight down the Thruway at Fonda Speedway. Tim opened the Vernon season by stealing the first three features, and made everyone else play catch-up. Five-time winner and local boy Willy Decker finished second in the standings, just ahead of Jamie Christian, who took two checkered flags.

In the Pro Stocks, West Edmeston's Bret Belden won the war—the track championship, in other words—although Jerry Holmes, Ralph's oldest boy, won the most battles, taking seven features. It was Bret's third title in the division.

Jeff Pastorella topped both the win column and the points tally in the Pure Stock class, stocking his trophy case with 11 feature awards and the championship prize. Dave Mannise, sticking to his vow to run only occasionally at New Utica-Rome, still managed four victories.

And eight drivers split up the 15 Slingshot features, with the championship falling to Denny Tilison.

Todd's Turn

Two guys who were there from the start, Rene "The Champ" Charland and photographer John Grady, ham it up a bit. (Utica-Rome Archive)

As part of the track's 40th anniversary, the family of the late Sonney Seamon was honored. That's Rita, Sonney's sweetheart, holding the plaque. (Post-Time Photo)

2002

New Management, New Champion, Sentimental Winners

Eric Kingsley and his staff did some terrific things at New Utica-Rome between 1998 and 2001. Just keeping the speedway alive in the uncertain spring of '98 took moxie. But it's important to note again that Kingsley never intended a second stint in ownership. So when rumors buzzed in 2001 that he was entertaining prospective buyers, few were surprised.

The picture cleared with an announcement that Kingsley had sold the track in a deal finalized on March 8, 2002. The buyer was Tom Cole, described as "a championship motorcycle racer from nearby Paris." Truth is, there was more to Cole than that. He was a co-owner and vice president of Gates-Cole Insurance, familiar to fans through its sponsorship of four-time Utica-Rome Modified champ Paul Jensen. He had also run a motorsports business, managing South Edmeston's Thunder Ridge Cycle Park in 1994. One

Utica-Rome's first season under the Cole family went well, with good fields and healthy crowds. A new era had dawned. (Post-Time Photo)

report described him as having "completely turned around" that facility.

Tom Cole and his father, Gene, had lunched with Kingsley a year earlier, discussing a possible purchase. "It looked like we had ourselves a deal," Gene Cole recalls. But, as is often the way in such matters, things unraveled. "But there were no hard feelings, or anything like that," says Gene. Talks resumed late in '01, carried through winter—Tom did some homework by attending the RPM Promoters' Workshops in Daytona Beach—and reached an agreeable resolution.

"I am extremely proud to be the new owner and promoter of Utica-Rome Speedway," said Cole, using the original name. "My goal is to make Utica-Rome one of the premier motorsports facilities in the Northeast."

And Eric Kingsley? Well, his contributions to Utica-Rome—at two crucial points in its stormy history—cannot be overstated. Nor can his long service to Fulton Speedway, where, through Bub Benway, he learned the ropes of track management. By 2002, the guy deserved a break.

"I've been doing this for 18 years," Kingsley told writer John Hill, "and it was just time." He did agree to lend advice and help to the new brass, particularly in the area of track preparation.

The transition was smooth, almost quiet. The track's weekly fare was unchanged: DIRT 358-Modifieds, Sportsman, Pro Stocks, and Pure Stocks. And much of Kingsley's staff—tower officials John Tiff Jr. and Jerry Brooks, pit steward Ray Turner, tech inspector Jon Button, PR man Doug Zupan, marketing rep Brenda Belden, and announcer Shane Andrews—remained on board.

That stability was a sign of things to come, for Utica-Rome was entering a period of constancy and progress. The Cole Era had begun.

~

Matt Sheppard, a 20-year-old out of Waterloo, blew into Utica-Rome that spring with a reputation as one of the coming kids in a DIRT 358-Modified. Within months, he had the respect of everyone in the place. Yes, he proved himself plenty quick, but more impressive was the calm, methodical way he went about his racing.

Oh, he also had the champion's trophy. No one that young had ever carried the big cup out of Utica-Rome, clear back to 1961 and the first champ, *The* Champ, Rene Charland. This was stunning stuff.

Today, Sheppard calls Utica-Rome "the kind of track where you need a well-balanced car." Not meaning to brag, he adds, "And you really need a good driver. The groove can change four, five times in one feature, so you've got to be ready to search out the best way around."

He was more than ready. In the May 5 opener, a 40-lapper, he trailed only winner Mitch Gibbs. Behind him were former track champ Ron Holmes, Jason Barney, and Sheppard's own car owner and mentor, Steve Paine. From there, Matt's run in the Nick's Cafe #28S was a study in consistency any veteran would have been proud of. In 15 points races, he had nine top-three finishes, two fourths and a fifth. He gapped the much more experienced Gibbs by 66 points.

Having helped save the speedway twice, Eric Kingsley turned over the keys to Utica-Rome in March of 2002. (Don Edds Photo)

Young phenom (and 2002 track champion) Matt Sheppard takes the low line in this tussle with popular J.J. Michaels. (Post-Time Photo)

Sheppard won just once, ironically on a night when he felt decidedly un-smooth. On Aug. 11, he caught leader Gibbs in traffic at the end of a 30-lapper. But he overcooked an inside pass, and slid into Mitch's car. By the time both drivers regained control, Sheppard had the lead. In victory lane he was subdued, particularly for a first-timer. "I really do not feel good about this win," said Matt. "I pushed up a little bit and got into the side of Mitch." Given the rest of his amazing season, it's easy to excuse that one bobble.

"For us, Utica-Rome was a new game, a new thing," Sheppard recalls. "But we ran up near the front every night."

In addition to the young champ and Gibbs (the latter won twice), 10 others captured Modified mains. Tops with three each were Todd Burley and Jack Johnson. Versatile Gordy Button topped a 50-lapper on Memorial Day weekend, with regular shows falling to Gus Schmidt Jr. (June 9), Steve Hulsizer (June 23) and Ted Lamb (Aug. 18).

The longest two features went to a couple of legends in the making: Danny Johnson beat Jumpin' Jack and Vic Coffey in a 100-lap Syracuse qualifier on Wednesday, June 19, and the 101-lap season finale on Sept. 20 saw Brett Hearn top Burley and Sheppard.

The remaining pair of winners deserves some sentimental reflection.

~

J.J. Michaels hadn't won at Utica-Rome since July 22, 2001. Back then he was aboard brother Lou's trusty '97 Troyer, and in the off-season they decided a new Troyer chassis was just the right upgrade. Trouble was, they found its four-link suspension a mystery. Their friend Rod Nacewicz says, "They went nowhere but backwards with that new car."

Coincidentally, Nacewicz—if the name seems familiar, Rod is a cousin to longtime Richie Evans crew chief Billy Nacewicz—had parked his own '97-vintage Mod, a TEO he'd fielded for Wayne Reutimann Jr. It now sat behind a friend's barn. Kidding around, Nacewicz told Louie they ought to drag his TEO out of the weeds and stick J.J. in it. Darned if Louie didn't think it was a fine idea. He sold his Modified, and hauled Rod's relic home.

"The car had a bird's nest in it, and three active beehives," Nacewicz laughs. "J.J. saw that thing and said, 'You've *got* to be kidding.'"

But Louie dabbed some paint here and there—still Reutimann blue and white—and powder-coated the frame. They borrowed an engine from Ronnie Egli, and on June 29 headed to Fulton, only to encounter fuel pump issues. The next night, J.J. arrived at Utica-Rome in no mood to race. But the first event on tap was a make-up feature from an earlier rainout, and J.J. was already qualified. Louie convinced him to give it a whirl.

"He started back in the pack," says Nacewicz, "and in 30 laps he got up to third [behind winner Jack Johnson and Sheppard]. J.J. had a habit of kissing the roof of his car after a really good run. Well, he got out, said, 'This ol' girl ain't bad,' and kissed the roof."

On a hunch, Nacewicz asked his wife Paula to buy a stuffed monkey. Come July 21, a year since J.J.'s last win, he showed it to his driver. "Tonight," Nacewicz declared, "we get the monkey off your back."

J.J. started the 30-lapper fourth and led early, but soon Sheppard, up from 14th, was on his tail. "What saved J.J.," says Nacewicz, "was that he *owned* turn two at Utica-Rome. He could pull anybody out of that corner. Whenever it looked like Matt had him, he'd get away out of turn two."

Michaels won by less than a car length. Mom Penny Michaels greeted him in victory lane, clutching that stuffed monkey. Over the P.A. system, announcer Andrews explained its significance. Then, says Nacewicz, "J.J. took that monkey and threw it into the infield. The crowd went nuts."

It was the only Utica-Rome victory for car owner Nacewicz. And, tragically, the final one for J.J. Michaels. In 2005, at just 45, he suffered a heart attack. Stents were installed, but his energy remained low. Doctors penciled in Nov. 10 for a possible coronary bypass, but tests determined that his weak heart made more surgery too risky. Instead he was placed on a waiting list for a transplant. It never came. On Nov. 14, 2005, J.J. Michaels died, leaving his wife, Kelly, and their one-year-old son, Tyler.

Michaels was an underdog hero. In addition to his 1998 NASCAR title (and 21 wins) at Utica-Rome, he was the '93 Outlaw circuit champion and the '94 Weedsport DIRT 358-Modified champion. Many still grieve his loss. Rod Nacewicz is consoled by his memories, and by a well-worn videotape of that Utica-Rome feature and victory lane ceremony from July 21, 2002. "I'll bet I watch that tape once a week," Rod says softly.

~

On Aug. 11, Jeff Kotary led every lap of the 358-Modified main. It was the first top-division win at Utica-Rome by a Kotary—one of the track's enduring tribes—since Dave Kotary won a pavement show in 1972.

Jeff is an interesting case. His dad, Adam "Fuzz" Kotary, was a nephew to the racing brothers—Cliff, Tom, and Robbie—who helped put Utica-Rome on the map. Jeff, born in 1970, grew up hearing of their ex-

Top: A photo that still stirs memories: The final Utica-Rome victory for J.J. Michaels, who died just three years later. (Post-Time Photo)

Right: Nostalgia nights quickly became a hallmark of the Cole regime. Here, Rene Charland steps ahead to take a bow. (Doug Zupan Photo)

ploits. Yet, incredibly, he never saw the track until he entered a 1985 Enduro race. He thrilled himself enough to put together a Pure Stock, then climbed the ladder to Pro Stocks, Sportsman cars, Modifieds.

Every rung brought more financial pressure; he says he wishes he'd raced with his famous forebears, when "the sport cost a lot less." But get him talking about that '02 victory, and all tensions dissolve.

"I was in such disbelief that I ran an extra lap, wide open, just to be sure," Jeff grins. "It wasn't until about a week down the road that it hit me: Hey, I won a race at Utica-Rome!"

As the track enters its second 50 years, Jeff is still at it, looking for that second Modified score. He says the latest generation of Kotarys is "mostly girls" with little interest in racing, so he might be the last of the clan to roar in Vernon. When he stops, so does a grand tradition.

~

Left: Jeff Kotary, yet another in a long line of that Rome racing clan, led the whole way in an August 30-lapper. (Doug Zupan Photo)

Bottom: Sportsman champ Jamie Christian aims his #55 to the low side of Jessica Zemken's #1. (Post-Time Photo)

Jamie Christian earned his second Sportsman title in '02, backing up the one he earned in '99. Jamie's opening-night victory was just one of five. Runner-up Tim Clemons matched Christian's win total, but could not match his average finishes.

Jason Rood did something rare, earning the Pro Stock championship without a feature win. Buddy Hencke was a seven-time winner, with Jim Normoyle and Bret Belden each taking three. Of note among the six single winners was popular Gerry Newman; her June 30 victory was the last of six in her Pro Stock/Street Stock career.

And Dave Mannise's Pure Stock mastery continued, though his '02 crown—his final one, it turned out—was the hardest earned of his nine. He and Chuck Cushman Jr. each won five times, with Mannise taking the title by the tiny margin of two points

2003

Planck

Dale Planck was a tough racer to pin down. Oh, when he first asserted his authority at Utica-Rome in the middle of the 1990s, he seemed fairly easy to figure out. He won 11 features on the way to his first track championship in 1994, eight on the way to his second in '95. In 1996 he lost the crown to Mitch Gibbs, but still topped the win column with seven. He won seven more the following year, when he copped his third championship. So given that four-year run of 33 victories in 80 starts—a magnificent slugging percentage—it was easy to peg Mr. Planck as a hammer-down gasser.

Then along came 1999, when he showed the Vernon crowd that he had more than one arrow in his quiver. If he couldn't win on brawn—speed—then he'd win on brains. Outpaced by both Gibbs and J.J. Michaels, and thus third on the victory list with "only" two, Planck won the title anyway by making full use of the opportunities left to him. He had 12 finishes of second or third, and the points just piled up. Arthur Ashe had a great line about how the keep-at-it persistence of fellow tennis icon John McEnroe would wear down opponents: "A nick here, a nick there, and pretty soon you're bleeding to death." That was Planck in 1999, nicking his rivals Sunday after Sunday.

And Planck became even more enigmatic in 2001-02, when what he nicked was most of his racing schedule; he raced only once at Utica Rome in '02, and that was in a one-shot ride. He was just past 30, a natural point for self-assessment, and admitted to reexamining his life. In his younger years he had raced professionally; now, with more responsibilities, he had taken on a full-time gig in the civilian world.

"It was race or eat," Planck told Ron Moshier of the *Utica Observer-Dispatch*. "I had to provide for my family and get a real job."

But the itch for competition remained. And when the chance came for Planck to return in 2003 with the new LYM Motorsports squad led by car owner Will Harriger, he jumped at it. The plan was to run Saturday nights at Fulton—operated since 1998 by Brewerton Speedway's Fink family—and Sunday evenings at Utica-Rome.

It took him no time at all to get back in the groove. On April 27, Planck opened the Utica-Rome season by beating Jack Johnson in the 40-lap DIRT 358-Modified main. "It's good to be back," he proclaimed.

It was his first Vernon triumph since Labor Day weekend of 2000. His next two times out he finished second, then won again. In the first four Sunday nights of his comeback, Dale's average finish was 1.5.

He was off to a championship start, and if you know anything about Planck, you know he reacts to a points fight the way a shark reacts to blood in the water. From the fifth week on, he finished second three times, third twice, fourth once, and fifth twice. It was enough to keep him in contention all year, and when the chase ended on Aug. 24 he was right there on top.

Planck told Moshier that returning to racing after his hiatus had felt "just like pushing the reset button." What everyone else saw was a great driver writing history. His two victories gave him a total of 42 at Utica-Rome, where he remains the track's all-time headline-division winner; Richie Evans is second with 33. And Planck's fifth championship moved him out of his previous three-way tie with Evans and Paul Jensen, securing his place as the most decorated champion in Utica-Rome's first 50 years.

"I learned a lot from stepping back for a year or two and reevaluating my life," Planck told Ron Moshier.

He stepped up his racing program after 2003, hitting the road more frequently, mostly on the DIRT circuit. But while his travels have meant he rarely gets to Utica-Rome anymore, those who saw him there have not forgotten the joy of watching Dale Planck in action.

"He's probably the best dirt-track racer I've watched there," recalls former announcer Shane Andrews. "He found something nobody else did. There wasn't much he couldn't do there."

~

Mitch Gibbs, the '96 track champion, came teasingly close to the 2003 title. The charger from North Norwich won twice, in 30-lappers on June 15 and Aug. 18, and the rest of his season was almost all good. Almost.

His nine top-five finishes and four other top-10s had him neck-and-neck with Planck into the Aug. 24 twin-20s that would decide everything. Then Gibbs flipped violently in the first feature, shaking him up a bit. No one ever accused Mitch of not being tough, so it was no surprise when he strapped into a backup car and took the green flag for the nightcap. Alas, the title had slipped away.

Ten other men won DIRT 358-Modified features in 2003. Todd Burley, getting better all the time, took three. Matt Sheppard, the defending track champ, won

Dale Planck had slowed his racing schedule a bit, but he hadn't slowed on the track. He was Utica-Rome's 2003 champion. (Post-Time Photo)

Top: Mitch Gibbs took a pair of DIRT 358-Modified wins, and very nearly took the track title, too. (Post-Time Photo)

Right: Top winner in a season packed with competitive cars was the increasingly smooth Todd Burley, who scored three times. (Post-Time Photo)

twice on his way to third in the points. And Brett Hearn, whose knack for winning big at Utica-Rome has been documented, copped a midweek 100-lapper (over Alan Johnson and Vic Coffey) on July 31 and the season-ending 100 (over Planck and Tim Fuller) on Sept. 14.

Solo victories went to Jim Rothwell, John Ramsey, Gus Schmidt Jr., and first-timers Pete Taylor and Dave Camara. And 2003 also saw the maiden Modified victory for Willy Decker, who was just warming up.

And it would be wrong not to give a special mention to Paul Jensen, who by 2003 had become an infrequent visitor to Utica-Rome, the track he ruled for a big chunk of the '90s. Jensen saddled up on Aug. 24 and won the opening half of that twin-20s program. It was Paul's 29th feature win at the track, which at the close of 2010 had him in a three-way tie for second with Burley and Tom Kinsella on the track's scroll of dirt winners.

~

It was a wild, wonderful season for the support divisions. There were first-time champions in the Sportsman and Pure Stock classes, Bill Shantel Jr. and Art Newman Jr., respectively, and a repeat king in the Pro Stocks in Jerry Holmes. And every division had its own little subplot, a story-behind-the-story jacking up the interest level.

First-time champs: Billy Shantel (left), smooth beyond his years, led the Sportsman ranks, with Art Newman Jr. (above) atop the Pure Stocks. (Post-Time Photos)

In the Sportsman ranks, Shantel, a young guy with a lot of laps under his belt, was as smooth as silk, and that's what earned him the title. Tim Clemons and Jamie Christian each had five wins to Billy's two, but the champ was always in the thick of things; aside from that pair of victories he had nine more top-five finishes.

But the big story of the Sportsman season was popular Jessica Zemken and her victory on June 29. Jessica was a teenaged second-generation driver from Canajoharie whose dad, Ray Zemken, won seven Sportsman features in 1992-93; he'd also been a multiple winner at Fonda. Jessica had made a few starts in '02 at Utica-Rome, raising eyebrows with a third-place finish in August. She was a cute blonde with a ready smile, and folks in the pits and the grandstands took notice.

But across the '03 season it became clear that she was hardly just a pretty-girl gimmick. True to her blue-collar racing roots, she displayed a roll-up-the-sleeves attitude between races, pitching in with things like tire changes and similar grunt work. On the track, she was getting the job done: third on opening night, fourth on June 8, and second on June 22 between winner Christian and third-place Clemons, the season's top winners.

When she beat Tim Sears and Paul Carey to the checkers on June 29, recalls announcer Andrews, "I thought the people were going to tear the fence down, they were so excited. I was waiting by the flagstand to go through the gate to do the interview, and it was tremendous. Here was this young lady who the fans absolutely loved, and to be in the middle of that was just fantastic."

Zemken ended up fourth in the season-long Sportsman tally, prompting much chatter about bigger things to come. She did not disappoint.

Like Planck in the top class, Jerry Holmes had briefly stepped away from racing, but it has never been easy to keep a Holmes away from Utica-Rome Speedway. And, to the dismay of his Pro Stock foes, Jerry sure hadn't rusted while he'd been gone. In 17 starts, he won six times, placed second four times, ran third three times, and finished fourth once. Bret Belden also had a fine season, notching two of his four feature wins in the final three weeks and closing to within 10 points of Holmes.

Pure Stock champion Art Newman Jr., a Rome resident whose dad had been part of the Richie Evans team clear back to the NASCAR coupe era, was another '03 example of good racing genes. A violent frontstretch flip in the summer derailed him briefly, but did not deter him; Art won twice, and finished in the top-five in nine of the division's 15 features.

But the big story in the Pure Stocks, in hindsight, was Dave Mannise. Though no one knew it at the time, his feature win on Aug. 18 was the last of Dave's in-

Top: Second-generation racer Jessica Zemken was really getting a handle on things, winning the Sportsman feature on June 29. (Post-Time Photo)

The incredible Pure Stock run of Dave Mannise closed in 2003, after 81 victories and nine championships. (Left: Don Edds Photo, Bottom: Post-Time Photo)

credible stint at Utica-Rome. In a stretch of 14 seasons spanning 1990-2003, he stacked up 81 wins in the division, an average of 5.785 per year. And that stat would look even more impressive if you knocked out the odd season—2003, for example—when he ran sparingly at the Vernon track.

He was Utica-Rome's Pure Stock champion nine times: 1990, '92, '94, '96-2000, and '02.

What Shane Andrews remembers most about Mannise is that the driver from Fulton understood the role his dominance had pushed him into. In other words, Dave Mannise *got* it.

"He was the villain," the announcer chuckles. "He won everything, so people would boo the living snot out of him. When he broke or crashed, they would cheer. But, you know, Dave would play that up; he was a very smart man that way. When they booed, he'd smile."

And if the grandstand-dwellers wanted to accuse him of out-spending or even out-*cheating* his Pure Stock rivals, well, Mannise had a subtle way of riling them up even further. "When he was interviewed," Andrews recalls, "he'd say, with this sinister laugh, 'How about this *motor*?'

"Yeah, Mannise was the ultimate black-hat guy."

The man sure won a lot of races, and made a lot of fans pay attention, in his years at Utica-Rome Speedway.

2004

Friesen Ignites; Jessica Delights

It was certainly a year of renewal at Utica-Rome. There were fresh faces in prominent places, including first-time track champions in all four weekly divisions. One of those champs, a boyish-looking DIRT 358-Modified driver with a familiar surname, would shake up the speedway's headline class like no newcomer had since Dale Planck's ascendancy in 1994. Another would hammer down the gender barrier in the process of copping the Sportsman title and continue her ascendancy toward becoming arguably the most accomplished female short-track racer in the Northeast.

And Gene Cole, while far from a new face at Utica-Rome—he had been around the place for years as a team sponsor, and was often beside his son, Tom, on race nights since

Young Stewart Friesen opened the season with four straight victories, later added three more, and cruised to the track championship. (Post-Time Photo)

Tom purchased the track in 2002—was taking a more active role in things. With an infectious enthusiasm for the sport and a knack for customer service springing from his 40-odd years in the insurance business, Gene Cole simplified the hectic business of operating a speedway with a bit of homespun wisdom: "I have a saying: 'It's all lemonade.' What I mean is, whether you're running an insurance agency or a race track, you're selling lemonade, you're trying to please the customer. So if you take care of the fans and the racers, you're doing your job."

It was still early in the Cole family's reign at Utica-Rome, but the customers—on both sides of the pit fence—were having a fine time. Not to mention one spectacular race season.

~

Stewart Friesen was not totally alien to Utica-Rome when he strolled into the pits on May 2, opening day. "I had been there in 2000, with a Sportsman car," he recalls. "I was 16 then, going racing with my mom and dad. We didn't finish that race—a fuel filter plugged up or something—but I liked the track right away. It was kinda tricky, but at the same time it was neat.

"It was one of the places I had been excited to go to, and once I was there I didn't want to leave. It just drew me in."

Well, maybe it was the family connection. The late Alex Friesen, who made such an impression in his single season operating Utica-Rome in 1996, was Stewart's uncle; Jamie Friesen, the young driver's dad, is Alex's brother. Whatever lay at the heart of it, there was a definite spark between the kid from Ontario and the half-mile oval on Route 5.

When he came back with a sharp DIRT 358-Modified fielded by Madsen Motorsports, young Stewart knew full well that he was stepping into a lion's den, and that he—as the newbie—would often end up prey. But right from that opener, he realized that something big was in his favor.

"They had just reconfigured the track, added tons of new clay, and changed the turns a little bit," Friesen remembers. "And I think that for the guys who had been doing really well there in the previous few years, their notes were now out to lunch."

The reshaped track forced every team, veterans and newcomers alike, into educated-guess mode. And it was Friesen's team whose guesses were closest to perfect. On opening day, jaws dropped when Friesen beat Mitch Gibbs and Todd Burley to the checkers. "That was a pretty emotional night," recalls then-announcer Shane Andrews. "Obviously, his family had had some involvement with that track, both with Alex and also with Stewart's grandfather, Stan. So to see him win there was special to a lot of people."

Of course, that special feeling also had to do with the unlikelihood of it all. What were the odds of a Utica-Rome rookie whipping so strong a field? And when in the world would something like that happen again?

Well, how about in the very next feature?

After a weekend off for rain, everyone gathered in Vernon on May 16, at which point the Friesen kid had the audacity to make it two in a row, this time beating John Ramsey and Willy Decker. Then came a third straight win, with Friesen topping Burley and Mark Flach. And on June 6, against impossible odds, Stewart Friesen made it four, this time over Gibbs and Brian Weaver, a Five Mile Point Speedway standout.

Looking back, Friesen thinks that in addition to the blank-slate nature of the reconfigured track, timing may have been in his favor. Traditionally, dirt tracks are full of natural moisture in the spring, owing to melting snows and the thawing of any deep frosts. After several weeks of sun and wind—and Utica-Rome gets plenty of both—they get drier, smoother, slicker, and tend to reward technical drivers, meaning those with patience and throttle control. Friesen, just a pup, was still far from a technical driver.

"The track was rough and heavy, and I was young and out of control," he laughs. "It just fit. We'd tear the body off the car, but still win the race."

That fourth win put him in very exclusive company. The record for consecutive top-division Utica-Rome victories belongs to legendary Ed Flemke, who took five straight on the pavement in 1964, including both 200-lap segments of that year's New Yorker 400. The only other two guys to win four straight are also iconic names: asphalt hero Richie Evans, who did it in '74, and Brett Hearn in his tremendous 1986 season.

It wasn't until June 20, on the fifth night of the season, that anyone else posed with the checkered flag after a 358-Modified feature at Utica-Rome. Todd Burley was the man of the hour, having pushed Friesen all the way back to ... *second*.

Another Sunday, another clenched fist, another checkered flag. Friesen had Utica-Rome wired in 2004. (Post-Time Photo)

That rocket-launch start made Friesen a championship favorite before the weather got warm. As June became July, he won twice more consecutively. "We had a big lead in the points halfway through the year," he says. "Then I started doing stupid things."

Actually, they were the kinds of things most guys his age would have been doing all year: making mistakes. "I rolled over one night, and stuff like that. I remember [Brian] Madsen asking me if I was trying to throw the championship away. He was like, 'Don't you *want* to win this?'"

That gentle talking-to seemed to work. In the last four points races, Friesen had two second-place finishes and a victory in the Aug. 22 closer. "We ended up winning by a pretty comfortable margin," Stewart says.

He had come in as the new kid. Now he was a champion.

After the regular season concluded, the track ran a Sept. 12 program headlined by a 40-lap feature. Friesen closed the season the way he'd opened it, by winning.

~

Friesen's eight victories and four rainouts left only eight trophies for his rivals, and it was quite a group that scrambled for them. Burley won twice, and Brian Weaver's victories on June 23 (a 50-lapper) and Aug. 23 were the only two he would ever notch at Utica-Rome. Bobby Varin also won twice, on July 25 and Aug. 15; Bobby had won often at Fonda, but those were the first of what would become many Utica-Rome triumphs.

The two single-win guys were at different points in their careers. Good guy Jamie Christian, a two-time Sportsman champ with 28 wins—still tops in the

Having graduated from the Sportsman ranks, Jamie Christian charged to a 358-Modified win in June. (Post-Time Photo)

Jessica Zemken's Sportsman championship was certainly no fluke. The lass took four feature wins, tops in the division. (Post-Time Photos)

record book in that class—accepted his first DIRT 358-Mod trophy on June 27, having beaten Varin and Dave Camara. And a late-August 108-lap special finished with superstar Alan Johnson leading a field of present and future studs: Pat Ward in second, then Varin, Pete Bicknell, and the newly-crowned prince of Utica-Rome, the Friesen lad.

~

The promise Jessica Zemken showed in 2003 blossomed in '04, and it didn't take long. She drove the family Sportsman to victory in the first three features of the year.

Now, occasionally every track produces a fluke winner. Sometimes that same driver will hit things just right and win again. But nobody flukes his—or her—way into three in a row, not in a DIRT Sportsman, and not at a joint universally acclaimed to be as difficult as Utica-Rome. So from the third race of that '04 season, there was a not-so-subtle shift in the way the area's racing junkies saw Zemken. Oh, the casual fans and the first-timers might still arch their eyebrows and grin about the teenaged blonde out the battling with the boys, but the diehards knew Jess was a racer. They knew.

That didn't mean the boys weren't going to joke about things occasionally. On the night of her third straight win, Mike Button finished third, and was thus interviewed post-race. "I asked Mike what he thought he had to do to beat Jessica?" recalls Shane Andrews, "His comment was, 'I guess I'm gonna have to start wearing a sports bra.'" The next week, Andrews was doing his usual afternoon pit crawl when he was beckoned by Bill Shantel Jr., the defending Sportsman champ. "Bill says, 'Hey, check this out.' He unzips his firesuit, and he's wearing a sports bra."

What makes the story memorable, of course, is how the rest of the evening went. "There's a hellacious race in the Sportsman feature," says Andrews. "Shantel is part of it, and so is Jessica. I remember the thing about the sports bra, and I tell the story [on the public-address system]. Wouldn't you know it, Shantel wins the race. In victory lane he's jumping up and down on the roof, and he unzips his suit and pulls it down. He's standing there wearing a sports bra. The place went nuts." Andrews remembers Jessica Zemken chuckling about the whole thing.

She won a fourth feature on July 11, and filled in the blanks nicely: two seconds, three thirds, two fourths, two fifths. That's 13 top-five finishes in 15 starts.

The Lady was a champ.

Button had a fine year himself, winning three times. Bridgewater's Paul Carey took a 25-lapper in June, and won again in August over the standard 20-lap distance. The longest feature, a 30-lap show on June 27, went to Eldon Payne. Other Sportsman winners were Steve Way, Scott Parliament, Bill Price and Kenny Stafford.

~

Pro Stock shoe Roy Fifield must have paid attention to Friesen and Zemken. He, too, dominated early, even

Roy Fifield won five straight features, and six overall, on his march to high honors in the Pro Stock class. (Post-Time Photo)

Friesen Ignites; Jessica Delights

Pure Stock champ Russ Marsden always seemed to have his act together. He could beat you with speed, or kill you with consistency. (Post-Time Photo)

bettering those two champions by racking up five straight victories. He added another in August. Jerry Holmes won three straight in mid-summer to follow one he'd earned in June, but the title went to Fifield.

Russ Marsden took a different approach to his Pure Stock championship. He watched Dave Pope win the season's first two races, then stole seven in a row. Russ ended up grabbing 10 of the division's 14 features. He would be a force across the next several seasons.

There were limited schedules for Four-Cylinder Super Stocks and IMCA Modifieds, and the champions were Chuck Powelczyk and George Cantanzano, respectively.

2005

Willy Boy Is Here

If some modern-day, motorsports-minded Norman Rockwell wanted to capture a slice of dirt-track Americana, he would have a wonderful time committing to canvas the story of Vernon's own Willy Decker, the 2005 champion in the 358-Modified division.

After all, what is more American than the kid who grows up close to the local speedway—"Right down the road from my house," says Willy, "just a couple miles away"—and grows up to be the track champion, the applause of his friends and neighbors ringing in his ears?

Decker's father had dabbled in drag racing "back in the day," as Willy puts it, racing at the old Utica-Rome strip and elsewhere in the area. But, curiously, no one in the family had much interest in the oval-track side of things, either before or after the track was converted from an asphalt bullring to a larger dirt track in 1979. But Willy ended up seeing a race there "when I was just a kid, eight, nine years old," and the sport got its hooks into him, and they set deep.

By the mid-'90s he had put together a Street Stock ride, and in 1995 he was one impressive young racer, finishing fifth in that division's standings on the strength of nine top-five finishes. Just one year later, in '96, he was the Street Stock champion, having won five features.

Hometowner Willy Decker had heard the engines roar at Utica-Rome since he was a kid. In 2005, his roared the loudest. (Post-Time Photo)

From there, Decker climbed the Utica-Rome ladder the same way all the old-time local heroes did. Just as Sonney Seamon, Richie Evans, Dick Fowler, and Dave Kotary rose through the ranks in the early '60s, starting in the Hobby classes and ending up as NASCAR Modified stars, Willy moved from the Street Stocks into the Sportsman, where in 1998 he dazzled with eight top-five finishes, three of them runner-up finishes. In 1999, he won the first two of what would be eight career Sportsman victories at the track, before he ended up in the 358-Modifieds in 2002; by the middle of the '03 season, he had won in that class, too.

Driving for Westmoreland's Tom Cullen, Decker was looking good wherever he competed. And whenever they rolled onto the track at Utica-Rome, the hometown fans were louder than the time before. And in 2005 he gave them plenty of reasons to get vocal, running in the thick of things all season long. He won two features, a regular 30-lapper on July 10 and half of the popular twin-20s program on Aug. 14, but what won Willy his championship was the unshakable way he hung around the front of the pack even on nights when the car was less than perfect. He finished second three times, third twice, fourth twice, and fifth three times. That gave him 12 top-fives in 20 starts, and he sprinkled in some top-10s as well.

Other guys were faster—and we'll get to them in a moment—but none could match Willy Decker's body of work across the full season. Given his relative lack of experience, the young man was spectacular.

That 2005 Utica-Rome championship, he admits, remains a career highlight. "I pretty much grew up here watching everybody race," says Willy. "So to actually get out and do it myself—and then to have success—has been pretty awesome."

Announcer Shane Andrews says, "The night he won the title, the place went crazy. I remember doing the victory lane interview. His crew dumped a 12-pack of beer over the top of both of us."

And why not? It had been an amazing year for Decker; he and the Cullen car also grabbed the Modified championship at the Can-Am Speedway, up in LaFargeville.

But there was nothing—*nothing*—like that feeling of succeeding at Utica-Rome, right down the road from his house, right down the road from the houses of those who knew him best.

"People relate to that," says Andrews. "The *local guy*. His dad had businesses in the area, his crew was from the area, and he was going up against all theses guys coming in from out of town: Todd Burley from Spencerport, Teddy Lamb from Cooperstown, Mitch Gibbs from Norwich. Willy was this local boy, raised right there in Vernon.

"And the hometown boy did good."

~

Say this for Gene Cole and for Dick Sweet, whom the Coles had hired as Utica-Rome's general manager heading into 2005: Neither of them has ever been indecisive.

You may have noted the absence of the acronym "DIRT" in this retelling of the '05 season. That's because Cole and Sweet, having their own ideas about the way things should run at their speedway—and also kicking around ideas about point funds and others incentives for their racers which might put them at odds with established DIRT programs—opted to withdraw from the sanctioning body Utica-Rome had been a part of since 1999.

"We just decided we wanted to be independent," says Gene Cole.

And that was that.

Bob Henry's #2 took the July 3 checkers, but had a suspect carburetor, elevating apparent runner-up Don Mattison's #10 to "co-winner" status. (Post-Time Photos))

Paul Carey was steady in the early weeks, then got jackrabbit fast. Four wins gave him the Sportsman crown. (Post-Time Photo)

~

It was quite a collection of talent that chased Willy Decker from one end of the season to the other. The top winners in the 358-Modified division were Bobby Varin—whose conquests included the longest event, the season-ending 75-lapper—and 2001 track champion Todd Burley. Each of them took four features. Like most of the fast guys, Burley has his thoughts on Utica-Rome, and his theories about what it takes to go fast there. "It's different on each end," says Todd. "Turn three is more sweeping [than turn one]. And the frontstretch is straight, where the backstretch is more of an arc. To be fast, the car has to be free, and yet still have enough drive to go forward. The tendency here is for the car to get real tight getting into [turn] three, so you want to free it up for that, but then you still need to be sure it has that forward bite." You don't argue with a record like Todd Burley's.

Joining Decker in the two-time winner's club were Dave Camara and Jamie Christian. Mitch Gibbs, Ted Lamb, Danny Johnson, and John Ramsey—in a 20-lapper—each visited victory lane once.

And, in one of the speedway's more bizarre occurrences, Don Mattison and Bob Henry were named "co-winners" of the 358-Modified feature on July 3, the result of a tech discrepancy—something to do with a carburetor, Dick Sweet recalls—that was iffy enough to elevate the guy who had finished second, Mattison, while at the same time not disqualifying the apparent winner, Henry. In the end, with management trying to do right by both competitors, each man got first-place money and first-place points, and each is credited with a Utica-Rome 358-Modified victory (ironically, the only one for both). So while they were able to smile about it, it no doubt gave something of a lifelong headache to meticulous track historian Doug Zupan, who, when digging through his 2005 statistics, probably catches himself wondering, just for an instant, why all those different drivers account for 20 individual victories when only 19 features were run?

~

Paul Carey won all four of his Sportsman features in the last two-thirds of the season, winning at mid-June, mid-July, and once each in August and September. Fortunately, he'd done enough running close to the front of the pack that by the time he got hot, he was able to capitalize on it and put himself in a solid position in the points. In the end, he nipped runner-up Bill Price by just seven points. Kenny Stafford and Steve Way each won three features, with Mike Button and Kyle Lewis scoring twice; for Lewis, these were his first Sportsman wins. Price, Jeremy Vunk, Brad Alger and Bill Shantel Jr. each earned a single victory. Jessica Zemken, star of the '04 campaign, was locked out of the win column but still finished fifth in the standings, and was already dabbling in the winged Sprint Cars she would soon attack wholeheartedly.

Jerry Holmes took another Pro Stock championship trophy, his third, home to Oneida. Eight times, Jerry's Sunday nights ended with congratulatory handshakes and backslaps, and photographers asking him to smile. He had 46 points on the second-place man, steady Bret Belden, when the counting was done. Belden and third-place points man Tom Denton each won twice, so it was a great year for former Pro Stock champs.

In the Pure Stocks, Russ Marsden was sure playing for keeps. On the way to his second straight track title, he won the season's first five features, finished fourth the next Sunday, then strung together five more victories. All told, he won 14 of the 18 features the division ran, and his points lead at season's end was a whopping 215.

Top: Pure Stock fixture Jim Thomas, beloved by all those who appreciate down-home, diehard racers. (Post-Time Photo)

Right: Oneida's Jerry Holmes had another stellar season, winning eight Pro Stock features and his third championship. (Post-Time Photo)

The IMCA Modifieds and the Super Stocks each ran full seasons, but that didn't change the championship pictures. George Cantanzano emerged again as the IMCA kingpin, with Chuck Powelczyk top dog one more time in the four-cylinder class.

~

Jim Thomas had enjoyed better years. He'd won nine Pure Stock features dating back to 1989, and had finished as high as second in the standings, but in 2005 he'd only managed three top-fives, with his best finish a third in July. When the engines stilled for the winter, he was eighth in points.

But to Shane Andrews, in his final year of announcing at Utica-Rome, the driver of the low-buck #140—whom Andrews regularly introduced to the crowds at the Junkyard Jet—represented the best of what weekly short-track racing was all about.

"I absolutely thought that guy was great," Andrews says. "He'd come into the track flat-towing his car, no trailer, behind a mini-bus. He had very little, but did a lot with it.

"You know, he'd get done with a heat race, and I'd see him come into the grandstand area, wearing his firesuit, carrying coffee he'd poured into one of those plastic cups that's the top of a Thermos. I'd see him down by the flagstand, smiling away, looking for his family. He'd go sit with them and watch some of the other races before he had to go back out and race again himself."

And hasn't rooting for Jim Thomas, or other guys like him, always been part of the fun of going to the speedway?

EYEWITNESS

2001–2005: GENE COLE

"You have to take care of your customers"

NOTE: *Gene Cole's racing roots far predate his family's 2002 purchase of the Utica-Rome Speedway. Born in Utica and raised in the Edmeston/New Berlin area, he was drawn to the stock car housed at the family garage and was soon "tearing apart old coupes." When he was 15, an uncle—the car's regular driver—did not turn up for a night's racing at Columbia Center, so Gene boldly designated himself the replacement. His driving career was interrupted by a stint in the military, after which Cole entered the insurance business as a salesman. When he bought an agency in Leonardsville, his career path was set; further acquisitions followed, and today Gates-Cole Insurance has ten regional offices. But Cole retained his zest for racing, sponsoring his pal Paul Jensen and attending races all over New York. Since taking over Utica-Rome, Cole has gained a reputation for catering to his fans and racers. In 2010, Jack Johnson, one of Utica-Rome's dirt legends, said, "Believe it or not, I don't know a lot about Gene Cole, and I've only talked to him a few times. But I know the guy loves racing, and it shows. He turned this place around."*

Looking back at my time as a fan and sponsor, I'm not sure that I ever consciously spent a night at the races surveying the scene as a potential promoter, but I would pay attention. I could *see* things. Some of those things stuck with me: rusty fences ready to fall down; bathrooms you didn't want to walk into, and that you knew your wife *would not* walk into. When we purchased Utica-Rome, improving those details was important.

We have made many improvements. I cannot say we ever had a timetable for most of them. Our philosophy was "Fix them as you find them." I'll give you an example: The first season owning the track, I watched several Modifieds hit the guardrail outside turns three and four; a few were wrecked very badly, others were bent up pretty good. Our plan was to eventually take the fence out, but that was all I needed to see. In a day's time, we had it out of there. We received imme-

When Gene Cole saw something he didn't like, he fixed it or nixed it. Case in point: the old guardrail in turns three and four was promptly removed in Cole's first season. (Post-Time Photos)

diate positive feedback from the competitors.

Some change did involve more pre-planning. Right away, one priority was nice, clean restrooms. Putting a bathroom attendant in both the ladies' and men's rooms was the best way to ensure the bathrooms remained clean the entire evening. And how many dirt tracks have you been to where you will find live flowers in the restrooms?

The parking area was another problem we addressed early on. Whenever there was a heavy rain, cars would get stuck in the mud. Since you have no control over the rain, you are left with fixing the parking lot. This meant improving drainage, adding fencing, and working the surface of the parking lot itself. These are little things, but important things. You have to take care of your customers, your fans.

Of course, you also have to take good care of the folks who compete at your track. I have been on that side of the fence too, as a driver and a sponsor. I think I know how those people want to be treated.

First, we established a good point fund. Joe Mirabito from Mirabito Fuel Group has been a large supporter of the point fund throughout the years, along with some help from Gates-Cole and our weekly 50/50 raffle. We paid out a $50,000 point fund. When it was announced it would be worth $8,000 to be the Utica-Rome champion, it shocked everyone. That was unheard of.

Next we addressed tires. They are a big expense for the racer. Our objective was to sell the tire to the driver at dealer cost. That proved to be a difficult task for all sorts of reasons, including the fact that it would undercut the other dealers. To make a long story short, we devised a system that allowed us to buy the tires at dealer cost, sell them at retail, and—this is a very big *and*—at the end of the season the difference between the dealer price and retail sale is given directly back to the driver in the form of a tire rebate check. Boy, that has added up. In different years, we have given back between $30,000 and $50,000 in tire rebates. That's money I could have put in my pocket as profit, but it is important to me that it go back to the racers. Fred Woodward from Lias Tire, who is the nicest man you will ever meet, has been a great help with this.

Making a deal with the man who sells the racing gas, whereby he could only charge a price that was so much over his cost, was also important to me. He might not make as much per gallon as another dealer at the next track, but he does a hell of a business here.

With all that being said, it is hard to keep everybody happy, no matter what you do. There are going to be some misunderstandings from time to time. A while back, I moved some fencing in the pits and created an area specifically to accommodate the giant haulers some teams are using today. I thought I was doing a nice thing. Well, a racer came in with a small, open trailer—a fellow I really like, by the way—and his team apparently felt they were being discriminated against because we were now asking them to park in a spot other than the one they were used to. One of his crew members even sent an angry letter. I made it a point to speak with the driver and explain that we only have space to fit so many big trailers, and we needed to make good use of that space. It wasn't something we did *against* one group, it was something we did *for* another group, but I suppose it is human nature that everyone sees things from their own perspective.

We simply try to treat fans, sponsors, and race teams decently. They are what make our track and our sport thrive.

One thing that is important for me to say: I have done none of this alone. You have to surround yourself with good people, and I have always been able to put the right people around me. That is the secret to everything I've ever done. When I opened my first insurance agency, I had one part-time employee, a local farm lady; now we have nearly 60 employees and 10 locations on the insurance side of business. I tell the employees who run each individual office to operate it as if it was their own. At the track, I've tried to think the same way, giving people room to work.

For several years, Dick Sweet was my general manager. He was just a great guy. Since Dick retired, Barb Clark has been director of operations. She is not only a really hard worker, but is also absolutely nuts about the history of this sport. Barb did such a good job selling the advertising signage in the infield that we actually had to create more sign space. That is a good problem to have! Also, our race director, John Tiff, is very dedicated, and is excellent at what he does.

Left: How long has Cole been around? Well, the coupes he drove were a bit less fancy than the Modifieds now running at his track! (Don Phoenix Photo, Jeff Ackerman Collection)

Bottom: "You've got to take care of your customers, your fans," says Gene Cole. Hence the picnic benches and spiffy concession stands. (Doug Zupan Photo)

And I have learned more about clay than I ever thought possible, through a guy named Randy Hirschey. He's an engineer who works with landfills. Several years ago I booked a lunch appointment hoping to pick his brain about dirt and clay, and it led to Randy becoming the consultant for our future clay projects. The joke I continue to make is that Randy ordered a hamburger, and that hamburger cost me $5,000. It was well worth it, because Randy definitely knows his clay. With his help, we were able to obtain very high quality clay: no sand, no stones, and no growth. Initially we put down between 800 and 900 loads of that new material. Annually, we need to add 100 to 150 loads to replace what is lost during the racing season. This is a big expense, but something that you have to do to maintain the quality of the track surface.

We have been successful here. Some years are better than others, and the reasons are not always in your control. In 2009 there were 26 scheduled events, and we were able to run 24 of them without weather issues. Good weather helps the bottom line a great deal.

I was not born a rich man, but I've worked hard and done OK. I had lot to lose when I bought the track, but I have been able to make things work. Today, even after all the money invested in improvements, I do not owe a dime on the place. So we will keep doing what we are doing to make our racing facility better.

Someone asked me if I wear a lot of hats on Sunday nights: Track owner, boss, maybe even an official if something big comes up. My answer: "Actually, I try to wear *none* of those hats on a race night." And I meant that. If a competitor comes up and complains about a call, I refer him back to the official who made that call. If the competitor tells me that official is a sonofabitch, I answer, "Well, that sonofabitch isn't gonna be overruled by me!" That's the way it has to be.

If I'm anything on Sunday night, maybe I'm the host, checking to make sure the sponsors in the VIP suite are pleased with everything, and keeping one eye on the grandstands, just trying to see if the fans are happy. Hell, there have been

Come race night, with the hard work done, "just let me be a fan," says Utica-Rome Speedway owner Gene Cole. (Otto Graham Photo)

times when I've seen someone walking around with a limp or on crutches, and I've given the person a ride to the restroom or concession stand. It's all about being nice to other human beings.

I do not want to be a boss on Sunday nights. The employees in charge do that. Just let me be a race fan.

2006

Hometown Hero, Take Two

Willy Decker was in quite a state, which was absolutely understandable. He had put in a hard 2006, and somehow he had managed to shape it into something good. As he stood in the pits in the afternoon of Sept. 10, he had won just a single Utica-Rome feature all season, back on June 11, but he had certainly knocked on the door all year long; he'd finished second five times, third once, fourth three times, and fifth three times. Now, all that consistency was on the verge of paying off. Heading into the final points night of the season, he was second in the 358-Modified points standings, but not far behind leader Bobby Varin. Willy understood that he was very much in contention for what could be, if everything went just right, his second straight 358-Modified championship at his home track.

And then the engine blew.

Willy Decker, every bit the modern-day local hero Sonney Seamon had been 35 years earlier, copped another track title. (Doug Zupan Photo)

Continuing his pattern of repeat visits to victory lane, Todd Burley won three times in 2006. (Doug Zupan Photo)

As Decker recalls, it happened in his heat race, and right here came one of those moments when being the local boy paid off, in a geographic sense. "We went home," he says, "and got our backup car."

This particular season's final points race was a bit non-traditional. The popular twin-20s program that had pretty much become a once-a-year fixture on the Utica-Rome calendar had been rained out on Aug. 27. The following week was a sponsored affair featuring the touring Empire Super Sprints, too busy a card to accommodate the double Mod features. So, not wanting fans to miss out on the exciting twin-20s, and unable to extend the season thanks to the normal autumn slate of special events that were fast approaching, Gene Cole, Dick Sweet, and the Utica-Rome brass bumped the standard weekly show set for Sept. 10, and penciled in those twins.

Double the fun for the fans, but double the stress on Willy Decker. Adding to his tension was the fact that, in the pre-race hustle just to get the backup prepped for battle, Decker either never had time to do—or had simple forgotten, the normal title-night math done by every racer in contention for a championship. He knew his primary rival was Bobby Varin, but that was about *all* he knew.

Laughing, Decker says, "I remember trying to figure out in my head, while we were racing, how many cars had to be between us, and all those kinds of variables, for me to win the championship."

He and the Tom Cullen car finished the first 20-lapper in fourth, one spot behind Varin, keeping things too tight for comfort. In the nightcap, Decker did his best to run his own race—and doing a fine job, eventually finishing second to Stewart Friesen—but couldn't help wondering what was going on with Varin, who, unbeknownst to Decker, had fallen out with an overheated engine.

"Finally, on a caution later in the race, I looked over and saw his car in the pits," says Decker. "That's when I knew we had the points wrapped up." He admits to feeling "a *lot* of relief, a lot of pressure gone."

And it was another uplifting occasion for fans of this hometown racer, this blue-collar guy who spent his weekdays working at Ferris Industries, headquartered in nearby Munnsville, where he assembled commercial mowing machines. Any fan can identify with a racer who says, as Willy Decker did recently, "I've got a full-time job, and then, with my racing, another full-time job afterwards." In an environment in which most top-level forms of short-track racing, dirt Modifieds included, have become the province of professionals, it is always good to see champions like Willy Decker.

"Willy always had talent, an immense amount of talent," says former track announcer Shane Andrews.

"Everybody knew that. And when he got into the right car and the right situation, like he had with Tommy Cullen, he proved it."

Incidentally, Utica-Rome was proving to be a nice place to be a track champion. The ability to pursue sponsors independently of any sanctioning body, in concert with a go-get-'em attitude on the part of the speedway management, had secured for the regulars some nice perks. Thirteen of the 17 race dates carried outside sponsorship of some sort. And Decker's 358-Modified title came with a point-fund check of $8,000, a very generous midwinter bonus, indeed. And Varin's runner-up prize of $6,000 was plenty more than many tracks in the Northeast paid their lead-division champions.

~

For the second year running, nobody won more than Bobby Varin. In 2005 he had shared that honor with Todd Burley, each of them having won four times, but the four features Varin grabbed in '06 were enough to put him alone atop the win column. Add these successes to the two mains he copped in 2004, and there emerges a picture of a guy who had very quietly figured out Utica-Rome as well as anybody had. Oh, other guys got bigger headlines—Stewart Friesen with his eight wins in '04, Decker with his two track championships—but if they were the home-run hitters, Varin was the batting champ. In fact, let's continue that baseball analogy: There's an old cliché that holds that if a man succeeds at any activity one-third of the time, he's doing well because, after all, that kind of hitting percentage in baseball gets a guy into the Hall of Fame. Well, Bobby Varin's 10 victories from 2004-06 gave him a batting average of .333.

Part of his success at Utica-Rome, Varin figures, was directly attributable to the fact that he was simply more active than most of his competition. Though always a Saturday-night regular at Fonda, he has also been an old-school, road-dog wanderer almost from his earliest Modified days in the late '80s. That gave him an open mind, an adjustable driving style, and, crucially, a growing bag full of tricks concerning chassis setups and tires, both important in the change-by-the-minute nature of dirt-track racing.

"In that period at Utica-Rome, I was one of the few guys there who was racing more than one night a week, and that helps so much," says Bobby. "For example, I think maybe we brought some of our knowledge about tires up there, and that's always an advantage."

A 30-lapper on May 28 was Varin's first score of the season, but he was most awesome in the summer heat, winning weekly features on July 23, July 30, and Aug. 6. He remembers losing momentum just after that streak thanks to a crash, but his Dover Brake team bounced back and, as mentioned, had him leading the points come that twin-20s finale.

The disappointment of that night is still in Varin's voice. Though he had finished third in the opening 20, there was trouble brewing. "We had a problem with the water pump, so of course the engine got hot," he recalls. "We didn't have a backup car, so we did everything we could in the time between races. We fixed the water pump, thinking we'd solved the problem, but we couldn't be sure because there were no hot laps or anything before the second feature.

"Probably three laps into that race I knew we had blown a head gasket, and it cost us the championship. Very unfortunate, but that's racing."

Bobby Varin won four times and gave Burley all he could handle in the battle for the 358-Modified championship. (Jay Fish Photo)

The guy who won the title, Decker, has high regard for the man he beat, saying of Varin, "He's a very aggressive driver, always on the wheel, every inch of every turn of every lap. When you race him, you get no rest; you give him an inch, and he'll take a mile. He's a thorn in your side."

Lest you think that last line is a put-down, Decker immediately translates: "Varin's one helluva driver. We've had issues at times, but he's a good guy to race with."

Todd Burley won 30-lappers in June, July, and September, making 2006 his seventh straight season as a multiple winner-event at Utica Rome.

Winning twice each in the 358-Mods were Stewart Friesen (at Utica-Rome at least semi-regularly in '06, having spent much of 2005 on the road) and A.J. Romano, who took a 75-lap Race of Champions Series event on Aug. 20 and then grabbed one of the final night's 20-lappers.

Left: A.J. Romano, out of another great Utica-Rome family, won two mains, including a 75-lap Race of Champions show. (Doug Zupan Photo)

Bottom: Back on a more regular basis in 2006 was Stewart Friesen, who twice proved he still knew how to get around the joint. (Doug Zupan Photo)

Popular victories went to Gus Schmidt (above) and Paul Kinney (right). If Paul looks extra happy, it's because it was his first win. (Doug Zupan Photos)

Ted Lamb topped the opening-night 30-lapper, and other weekly-show winners included Paul Kinney on June 18 (his only Utica-Rome victory) and, on successive weeks as June turned to July, Andy Bachetti and Gus Schmidt Jr.

And Alan Johnson, who could always be counted on to shine with big dough on the line, gassed it hard on May 14, winning the 68-lap Alex Friesen Memorial ROC feature over invaders Billy Decker and Tim Fuller.

~

The season had started off with an April 30 event featuring what were normally Utica-Rome's support divisions—Sportsman, Pro Stocks, Pure Stocks, and Super Stocks—plus the visiting Patriot Sprint Car tour and a regional Mini-Sprint Club. The marquee event was something called the Pumpkin Pie/Pepsi 100, a dentist's nightmare of a title which was in fact a long-distance Pro Stock feature with $3,000 to the winner. Jerry Holmes got the hefty prize and, presumably, the pie and the soda pop.

Then, to work off the sweets, Holmes went out and won eight more features, all across the normal 20-lap Pro Stock distance. Bret Belden saw the checkered flag wave for him four times, and winning twice each were Tom Denton and Jim Normoyle. Robert Langevin grabbed his only career victory on June 20, when he beat Belden to the wire.

Jerry Holmes won nine features, one of them a 100-lapper, and ruled the Pro Stock roost. (Doug Zupan Photo)

Mike Button, he of the racing Button clan—papa Jon and brother Gordy were, of course, also successful at Utica-Rome—captured his first Sportsman championship. Mike's title run was one of those stealthy numbers; he didn't win until the season's next-to-last Sunday, but by then he'd had nine other top-five finishes. In a year in which others blew hot and cold, Button's mechanized points production paid off. Steve Way led the win column with four, while defending champion Paul Carey, Billy Price, and Jeremy Vunk each scored twice. Solo victories went to Alan Barker, Kyle Lewis, Bill Shantel Jr., first-timers Danny Varin (Bobby's son) and Tim Nye, and Jessica Zemken, making limited starts but still on the hammer.

Russ Marsden once again left only table scraps for his Pure Stock rivals, grabbing the championship for the third consecutive time. Russ picked up 11 wins as he waltzed to the title, with Brandon Warner (twice), Chris Cunningham (twice), Ron Hawker and Curt Prevo winning the six races Marsden could not.

The IMCA Modifieds were again a regular feature, and eight different drivers elbowed their way into victory lane. Though Mike Smith got there most often, winning four times, the division champion was Jim Roberts, a three-timer. Kevin Buff won a pair of 15-lap main events to start the season off, while single victories in the IMCA class went to Dale Caswell, Rob Keller, Kevan Cook, Chris Thurston, and former track champ George Cantanzano.

2007

Two Great Names Return: The New Yorker and Friesen

Stewart Friesen was always a unique mix of the old and the new. He was just a kid, but his name was entwined with the rich history of stock car racing in the region. He was energetic, of his time, yet he carried a clear respect for tradition. So it was fitting that when the Utica-Rome brass dusted off a slice of the past by reviving the New Yorker event in the autumn of '07, Friesen ended up winning it. The race was at once something old and something new, as was this racer from Ontario.

Friesen had been away for much of 2005 and '06, rambling on the DIRT trail. He didn't exactly settle down in 2007, but he was back in action every Sunday night at Utica-

What a season it was for track champ Stewart Friesen, whose six feature wins included the New Yorker 200. (Post-Time Photo)

Rome, driving for Roger Heroux. And he didn't miss a beat, winning six features—capped by that New Yorker 200—and earning his second 358-Modified championship.

"We were able to really lay it down," Friesen recalls, appropriately blending modern language with the same easy, natural confidence in 2007 seen in Bill Wimble in 1967 or Kenny Tremont in 1987. The calendar may change, but racers are racers.

~

The New Yorker 200 was big news, drawing 64 cars on Saturday, Sept. 15. Whittling things down to the 28 feature cars was entertaining; seven wild heat races went to Pat Ward, Jeff Kotary, Jack Johnson, Todd Burley, Bobby Varin, A.J. Romano, and Mike Ricci. Then came four last-chance consis, won by Paul Kinney, Jim Davis, Ted Lamb, and Jamie Christian. Announcer Mike Mallett was talking himself hoarse describing the action.

But a great night became a wet one. Rain fell, and kept falling. Pulling the plug was a no-brainer; rescheduling the 200 was another matter. Sunday evening wouldn't work, because there was a special event at Fonda. The coming weekends were jammed with the year-end biggies, many of them offering points to drivers tied to various circuits, so getting everyone back to Utica-Rome in two weeks or a month would be difficult. Possible solutions were tossed about, and then someone suggested … *Sunday morning!*

A major race in the morning? Couldn't possibly work. *Could it?*

It could, and it did. The racers didn't have to make another round-trip to Vernon, and the only real hassle was that everyone had to throttle back on the partying in anticipation of the Sunday morning alarm bells. At just past 10:00 AM, flagman Matt Burdick, his arm no doubt still stiff from the previous night's workout, dropped the green on the New Yorker 200.

Burley had the early muscle, and at the halfway break he led a very strong Varin. Next came Friesen, Vic Coffey, Ricci, Alan Johnson, Willy Decker, Ward, Romano, and John Ramsey. In the second half, Burley and Varin resumed their war, with Friesen looking on

Though run on a rain date, the New Yorker kept its great "big show" feel. Here's the starting grid, ready to roll. (Joe Alexander Photo)

The image that lingers from 2007: Friesen on the gas, capping his banner year with an outstanding run in the New Yorker. (Jay Fish Photo)

from third. Just after Varin took the leap on lap 117, Friesen did a quick spin in turn one and lost a spot, but was fortunate enough to keep rolling and thus kept himself in contention.

As if atoning for his mistake, Friesen elevated his game. He tracked down and passed Coffey, Burley, and, on lap 142, leader Varin. From there, Friesen's lead was never challenged. Oh, the show was still a dandy, but the race was for second, which went to Varin, trailed by a late-surging Ronnie Johnson, Coffey, and Romano.

The old-style romp paid the new-style track champ a cool $10,000.

~

Friesen's campaign had success sprinkled from one end to the other. The track's schedule touched a portion of six different months, and he won a feature in each of them. Opening day, April 29, saw another weird post-race tech scene resulting in co-winners (shades of July '05). This time the drivers involved were Friesen, who took the checkers first—and whose carburetor was in dispute—and Dave Camara. Ultimately, both men were awarded first place money and points. Then Friesen won weekly 30-lappers on May 13, June 24, July 22, and Aug. 26, in addition to September's New Yorker score. On seven other Sundays he placed second, including three straight in July. In all, Stewart recorded 17 top-five finishes in 21 outings.

His car owner, Roger Heroux, was also responsible for preparing Utica-Rome's track surface. But every driver and eagle-eyed mechanic had the same chance

Willy Decker was again outstanding in '07. His five wins included a pair of 75-lap specials. (Jay Fish Photo)

to guess how Heroux's handiwork would be rearranged in the course of a feature—every dirt track being in a constant state of change—and Stewart Friesen mastered that better than anyone.

"We had brand-new cars, great motors, new tires all the time," he says. "We just had a great program that year."

~

Also enjoying a stellar season in the 358-Modifieds was two-time track champion Decker. Five times Willy went to victory lane, twice in 75-lap specials. After a Race of Champions Series 75 on May 13, he poked a bit of fun at runner-up Danny Johnson's nickname. "The Doctor was in the house," Willy proclaimed, "but Decker did the operating tonight." His other 75-lap score was a midweek affair on July 25.

Two Great Names Return: The New Yorker and Friesen

Jerry Holmes began the season with no solid plans. By year's end, he had secured his fifth Pro Stock crown. (Post-Time Photo)

For a second straight year, Mike Button, steadier than the rest, collected the Sportsman division championship. (Post-Time Photo)

For a fourth straight season, Russ Marsden was king of the hill in the Pure Stocks. He held the checkered flag eight times. (Post-Time Photo)

Friesen and Decker had won the last four track titles, igniting a nice little rivalry. Says Friesen, "Willy and I have been the bad guy and the good guy, depending on whose fans you were talking to. I know it's gotten heated in the grandstands, which is always pretty neat. People get passionate about it, which is cool to see."

But do they get along? "We tolerate each other," Stewart grins. "Willy has a parts business, so I buy tires from him and things like that. Yeah, we get along."

Pat Ward, tough and preparing to get tougher, won three features in '07, while Varin and Burley each took two. Dave Camara's shared victory on opening night was the last of his four career victories at Utica-Rome.

~

Mike Button had shown the Sportsman guys in 2006 that the way to win championships was not by going wild, but rather by minding one's own business. Too few of them paid attention, so Mike cheerfully accepted another title. Eleven drivers won features, led by Alan Barker and Brad Alger with three each; Button did not reach victory lane, but his 17 top-fives in 20 starts left everyone else gasping at points-tallying time.

And Russ Marsden completed a four-year run as Pure Stock king, winning eight features on the way to his title. Not since 2003 had someone not named Russ Marsden been the division's champion.

~

As 2007 dawned, Jerry Holmes had four Pro Stock titles—1997, 2003, '05, '06—and no plans for a fifth. He'd sold his car to a friend whose son planned to move up from the Pure Stocks, and hadn't built a replacement. It looked as if, by forfeit, someone else would be the Pro Stock champion.

Then something unexpected happened. The friend decided to give his boy more seat time in the Pure Stocks, and offered Holmes the ride. Since opening night had already come and gone, "I figured we didn't have a chance in the points," Jerry says. "So we decided we'd just go have fun. We didn't freshen the motor, or anything." It was an unfamiliar approach for Holmes, who had always been detail-oriented, but the result

Jim Normoyle, who won three times in the Pro Stocks, hustles his Monte Carlo around Utica-Rome. (Jay Fish Photo)

was very familiar. "We ended up winning a lot of races," he chuckles, "and the championship, too."

Some tough guys tried to stop him. Multiple winners included Chris Mackey (four), Jim Normoyle (three), and Bret Belden and Tom Denton (two each). A.J. Digsby, Chad Ray, and Louie Jackson each won once.

Jerry Holmes, like brother Ron, was a Utica-Rome lifer. He recalls sitting in the stands when their dad, Ralph, raced NASCAR coupes. When it came time for Jerry to take the wheel, he spent part of '96 driving for John Keegan in what were then called Street Stocks. A year later he had his own car, and his first title. In the years that followed, he dabbled briefly in Sportsman cars and took the occasional season off—most recently in 2004—but kept returning to the Pro Stocks, and to victory lane.

He won five times en route to his 2007 crown, tops in the division. "Every time you get a championship, it feels good," he says. "And if you won a lot of races that same year, it feels that much better." It's a feeling he got used to: Never in his five title seasons did any driver win more than Holmes, although in 1997 he had been tied.

Jerry modestly deflects credit. "Ray Hedger has helped me out so much," he says, calling out the fabricating whiz from the multi-generation Hedger racing tribe.

Though he hasn't run a race since the '07 season ended, Holmes has never retired, and says he may be back, depending on sponsorships. Still, if that never happens, he can look back on a stellar career. At the close of 2010 he led the all-time Pro Stock win list, and he has carried on the grand connection between the Holmes clan from Oneida and the oval in Vernon.

"Utica-Rome is close to home," he says, "so it's like everybody knows us."

Jerry has sure done his part to add to that perception. Starting in 2003, each time he won a feature he'd hand the trophy to some wide-eyed kid at the fence. He says, "I remember when I was little, seeing the driver standing there with the trophy. So I'll just pick out one kid and say, 'Here you go.' I've had so many parents thank me, and say they couldn't believe someone would do that. Well, I don't need another trophy. This way, you make a new fan, and that means more to me than any plaque."

Championship outlook, championship racer.

~

At season's end, Dick Sweet announced he was ending his three-year tenure as Utica-Rome's general manager. It was an amicable parting. At the awards banquet at the Turning Stone casino, Sweet was both roasted and toasted; after Doug Elkins (webmaster of the Doug's Dirt Diary site) led track employees in playfully poking fun at Sweet, the attendees gave Dick a standing ovation. Energetic Barb Clark, a fixture at area speedways for years, was assigned to the newly created post of director of operations.

Management's efforts to generate extra revenue for its racers continued to pay off. Race director John Tiff announced that the $25,000 point fund paid in '07 would be back in place in 2008, thanks chiefly to Gates-Cole Insurance and the Mirabito Fuel Group. And a unique tire-refund program channeling money back to racers in what amounted to re-

An aerial look at Utica-Rome, which by 2007 was established as one of the Northeast's most stable race tracks. (Photos by Fine)

bates—the brainstorm of track boss Gene Cole—would also return.

And in the odd-but-welcome category, Eric Kingsley, former owner of both the Utica-Rome and Fulton tracks, sold the rights to the Victoria 200 race name to Cole. Come July of '08, the Victoria—a Fulton mainstay since 1986—would roar in Vernon instead!

2008

Veteran's Day

Pat Ward, the veteran dirt-tracker out of King Ferry, New York, is so cool, so at ease, that you're almost tempted to poke him with a stick. That would be a mistake. The record shows that Ward, who has been winning races for better than 20 years, needs no outside stimulus to pick him up when it's time to go to work.

"Pat's funny," says Willy Decker, who has raced with Ward over hundreds of laps. "He's such a laid-back guy when you walk up and talk to him, but when he's in the car he's really aggressive."

In 2008, totally switched on, Ward kicked off a pair of Utica-Rome seasons in which nobody was in the same league when it came to gas-it-hard speed. In '08 alone, Ward won eight 358-Modified features, seven of them 30-lappers and the other in the annual twin-20s program.

When the dirt settled come autumn, Ward was hauling west on the New York Thruway, toward his home outside Genoa. The Utica-Rome champion's trophy rode with him.

~

After Stewart Friesen grabbed the opener on April 27, Ward copped his first Utica-Rome score on May 4. (The night is better remembered for a scary three-way wreck involving Jamie Christian, Mitch Gibbs, and Ted Lamb; Gibbs flipping car actually landed atop Lamb's. All three men were shaken up, with Lamb transported to the hospital for some observation.)

Pat won again on June 1, twice on June 29 (a make-up from an earlier rainout, then the scheduled event), July 6, Aug. 3, Aug. 17 (in a quick 20-lapper) and Aug. 31. Though he acknowledges how tough Utica-Rome is "because the track can be so different every week," he clearly had a handle on all its intricacies in 2008. Likewise, he had his opponents figured out; Friesen, Christian, and Decker were among those who played runner-up, and Ward showed Bobby Varin the way home on that final Sunday in August.

Ward and Varin knew each other dating back to the late '80s, when Varin was just climbing into Modifieds and Ward was hauling weekly to Fonda, where he first estab-

Pat Ward, the 2008 track champion. Champagne is the standard celebratory spray, but someone decided Silly String looked better on Pat. (Post-Time Photos)

lished himself as a winner. Utica-Rome is just one in the long list of tracks where the two have crossed paths. Both are fierce chargers, regular contenders for victory, yet there is a clear respect in Varin's tone when he discusses Ward.

"I've raced against Pat from the time I started," Bobby says. "He's a good, clean driver who always brings extra competition. But the one thing you can count on with Pat is, he's not going to bring too much [unwanted] excitement. You can race with him week after week after week, and not have a problem. There are other guys you get along with if you race 'em once a month, but if you race together every week it becomes a rivalry. That's never really happened with Pat and I. Yeah, we're rivals to some degree, because neither of us wants to lose to the other guy, but we run each other clean. We're also pretty good friends."

It's interesting to note the apparent contradiction in that description: the guy who drives hard but adds no extra hullabaloo. That's rare for a racer who drives as hard as everyone agrees Pat Ward does; normally, a hard-charger generates sparks on the track, and strong words off it. The difference may come down to an observation about Ward by Willy Decker, who notes, "Pat does this for a living. So however he does race-to-race, that's his paycheck." Unsaid was this: Crashing costs money.

Indeed, by 2008, Ward had come to embody the professional regional racer. He and his longtime ride in John Wight's gleaming red Gypsum Express #42p were a feared combination wherever they turned up, from a big-block DIRT show to those superheated Sunday-night 358-Modified brawls at Utica-Rome. Winning was something Mr. Ward had gotten used to.

Left: Danny Johnson (#27J) saved his tires in the Victoria 200, then made the winning pass on Pat Ward. (Jay Fish Photo)

Bottom: Focused and intense, Jack Johnson, puts some thought into his day's work at Utica-Rome. (Doug Elkins Photo)

Top: Few drivers can match the long-race stride of Bobby Varin, as demonstrated in the 2008 New Yorker 200. (Jay Fish Photo)

Just don't ask him to tell you much about it. Peacocking about his success just isn't Pat's style. "Yeah, we won eight features [in '08]," he says, shrugging. "That was really good."

~

Sure, there had been a few seasons in Utica-Rome's dirt-track era that lacked promotional razzle-dazzle: not a single long-distance show, no double-pointers, no midweek specials. At times that was understandable, because when a promoter is scratching for survival—as some were—he hesitates to get too optimistic with the dice. But in 2008, Gene Cole, pleased with his track's momentum, scheduled three races that couldn't be classified as anything less than special.

The first was on May 11, when Utica-Rome took its maiden crack at hosting the Victoria 200, so long a fixture at the Fulton Speedway. Cole had purchased the rights to the event from the Benway/Kingsley family, and invited the Race of Champions Dart Tour. Over 70 Modifieds appeared, and a great crowd filed through the front gate. It ended being a tire-management game, as long dirt-track events can be, and Danny Johnson played the game best. He tracked down Ward—who at one point led by nearly a straightaway—and at lap 160 Johnson took the lead. No one got close to Danny after that. In victory lane, he talked of having "saved our tires", while Ward lamented that he "should have been a little smarter" with his own rubber. (Which brings to mind what former announcer Shane Andrews says of Ward: "He's a class act, as graceful in defeat as he is in victory.") They were trailed by Billy Decker, Tim Fuller,

Top: Bobby Varin hustles the Dover Brake car past another competitor on his way to the New Yorker checkers. (Joe Alexander Photo)

Right: Brad Alger walked off with the Sportsman championship, collecting five wins along the way. (Post-Time Photo)

Willy Decker, Bobby Varin, Jimmy Phelps, Brett Hearn, Rick Laubach, and Matt Sheppard.

The second special was the "Richie Evans Remembered" affair on Aug. 13, a Wednesday-night 61-lapper honoring the track's great asphalt legend. Also part of the Andy Harpell's ROC series, this one was a flag-to-flag victory for Billy Decker, who topped Phelps, Alan Johnson, Willy Decker, and Brett Hearn. There were a couple of nice touches: The winner's take was $6,161.61, and the #61 flown by Evans for so many years was retired. Said Gene Cole, "Just like Babe Ruth is synonymous with the New York Yankees, Richie Evans is synonymous with Utica-Rome."

The third biggie was, of course, the Sept. 13 New Yorker 200. Bobby Varin, who in '07 had placed second in the autumn classic, was the dominant force in the 2008 edition. Except for stints of less than 20 laps on either side of the halfway break when Mitch Gibbs led, Varin had the hot hand. He did have a spirited dice with Gibbs and Ward when the second half went green—"I was on pins and needles," Varin admitted—but he also had a long stretch in which he was way out front, seemingly on cruise control.

"I get into a groove at that place in a long race," Varin says. "I get a good rhythm, a feel for what's going on. It's knowing you've got a lot of laps to run, and that you're racing the *track*, not your competitors.

"In a 30-lapper, you're racing your competition hard, trying to get through the field in a short time. There's been four or five guys there—Pat, Burley,

Friesen, Willy Decker, us—winning a lot of races over the time we're talking about, and when you get all those guys charging to the front in 30 laps, it's pretty intense. It's a whole different thing when you know you've got 100 laps to get it done, or 200."

His biggest test came on a restart at lap 160, when Ronnie Johnson, never the surrendering type, poked the nose of his #2RJ to the inside. But that only re-lit Varin's fire. At the checkers, he was up by seven seconds. Ronnie hung tough for second, followed by Gibbs, Ward and Phelps.

~

Brad Alger was the man to beat in the Sportsman division, and that applied whether you were racing him for points or checkered flags. Five times Alger stood in victory lane, three after standard 20-lappers plus a 40-lapper in July and a 50-lapper on New Yorker weekend. Mike Button, Casey Williams, and Steve Way each won twice, but Alger had their measure. His title was the first of his career at Utica-Rome.

Right: The Pure Stock championship fell to Chris Carr, whose consistency paid off in a big way. (Post-Time Photo)

Jim Normoyle, tight with the fabled Holmes clan, might have used some of Jerry's tips en route to the Pro Stock title. (Post-Time Photo)

Veteran's Day

The Pro Stock class served up a first-time champ who was fortunate enough to learn in a terrific classroom. Jim Normoyle worked alongside five-time champion Jerry Holmes at Ralph's Collision, the Oneida body shop owned by Jerry's dad, and naturally the two did their share of bench racing over the years. "I told him certain things," Jerry says with a laugh, "but I didn't tell him *everything*." And Jim certainly got the job done behind the wheel, winning four features on the way to his title. Bret Belden and Shawn Frost were three-time winners, with A.J. Digsby doubling up and six other drivers winning a feature apiece.

And in the Pure Stocks, Chris Carr broke Russ Marsden's four-year stranglehold on the champion's trophy. Marsden was still the man to beat on most Sundays, winning six times, but Carr—whose only two victories came consecutively in August—had 13 top-five finishes in 15 races. That gave Chris the crown.

~

It takes plenty of folks behind the scenes to put on a successful race program. That was true in Dick Waterman's pavement reign at Utica-Rome, when Ralph Ouderkirk was the NASCAR chief steward and John Tallini was waving the flags, and it was true under Gene Cole as the dirt track continued to flourish in 2008.

Barb Clark, Cole's new director of operations, seemed to be everywhere at once on a race night, operating with such a bubbly efficiency that one of the track's all-time driving heroes, the great Bill Wimble, took to calling her "Little Miss Dynamite." In addition to having worked at Utica-Rome for a decade in various capacities, Barb and her husband John had long been part of the regional stock car scene.

Elsewhere on the grounds, John Tiff Jr. had gained great respect as a race director, and was also handling public relations. Good guy Charlie Squires, a veteran of dozens of Northeast tracks whom everyone called "Tuna," was working as a pit steward. Mike Mallett and Jeff Barrett were manning the microphones. Doug Zupan and Jerry Brooks took care of scoring and handicapping. Connie Plows looked after a hundred things in the office. And on any given Sunday, there were a few dozen more faces doing important jobs few people noticed.

Energetic Barb Clark, Utica-Rome's new director of operations, addresses the crowd at a drivers' meeting. (Images by DC)

Those faces were downcast in August of '08, when Linda DeYulio died after a long illness. Ron DeYulio, Linda's husband, was—and is –Utica-Rome's longtime pace car driver, and Linda often rode shotgun. She was part of the extended family most ticket-buyers never get to know, but without whom Utica-Rome could not function.

2009

Laid-Back Pat, And Throttle Control

For 2009, there were interesting changes afoot at Utica-Rome. The purse for the headline division's weekly 30-lapper jumped to over $9,000, with two grand to the winner. And for the first time since 1987, big-block Modifieds would be a weekly staple, running alongside their 358 small-block cousins. The big-block rulebook would mirror DIRT's, while the 358-Mods now had the option of running dry-sump oil systems.

At a glance, the new rule didn't seem to change things much. Pat Ward was the 2009 track champ, just as he had been in '08, and won five features; and the guy who

Pat Ward, no doubt pondering another winning adjustment. Pat won five features on his way to another track championship. (Jay Fish Photo)

When the big blocks came in and good throttle control was critical to success, Pat Ward (42) and Bobby Varin ruled. (Images by DC)

went to victory lane the most was six-timer Bobby Varin, who had been among Utica-Rome's hottest hands for several seasons.

Ah, but the *way* they won suggested a great deal had changed. The extra horsepower and greater torque offered by the big-blocks transformed the art of hustling a Modified around Utica-Rome. Throttle control was key, and both Ward and Varin were virtuosos in that field. Bobby says, "Pat and I had extensive experience with big-blocks. I had driven them since 1989, and Pat even longer. It's not that there's an automatic advantage for the big-block; sometimes there is, sometimes there isn't. When the track is tacky, you can really get some speed out of a big-block. But when Utica-Rome gets slick it's like a skating rink, no traction at all, so all that power doesn't help you. I think some of the guys who'd run small-blocks for years couldn't get the hang of the extra power, the wheelspin you get with a big-block."

Varin won the season opener on April 19 and the final weekly show on Sept. 6. Both features covered the usual 30-lap distance. But his other four wins weren't usual at all: On June 28 in a "Thunder on the Thruway" event (in a car borrowed from son Danny) and again on July 22 (a midweek event honoring Bill Wimble), Varin emerged victorious in 50-lappers, and each time he won the very next weekly show.

But across the season, Ward's body of work was Vernon's best. All five of his wins came in regular Sunday-night programs: April 26, June 21, two straight on July 12 and 19, and Aug. 12. "We were fast," says Pat, "but we were also really consistent." He certainly was: In points-paying races, Ward finished second seven times, and had four finishes of fourth or fifth. If you're thinking 16 top-fives in 20 events sounds good enough

Bill Wimble, honored on July 22, greets Bobby Varin and car owner Dave Cruikshank in victory lane. (Otto Graham Photo)

to win a track championship and the accompanying $8,000 bonus, you're right.

Like Varin, Ward says understanding the big-block/small-block equation has been critical to his success; his team utilizes both. He points out that the track is more susceptible than most to getting slick due to its early start times. While a maintenance crew preparing a Saturday-night track can extend its tilling and watering into late afternoon, by which time the sun is sinking, the prep ends sooner at Utica-Rome because the racing starts earlier. "It's a Sunday," shrugs Pat, "and people need to get home because they've got to work Monday morning." Consequently, he says, "the sun just burns the place up. It'll dry out sometimes to where it gets slippery, and a small-block is definitely the way to go when it gets like that. But then, just when you think you absolutely *need* a small-block to run good here, we'll have a track that's heavy on the bottom and you'll need a big-block."

It's a complicated game, one Ward and Varin played best. "Hey, I had to learn to drive a big-block, too," says Varin. "I learned from the best: Jack Johnson, Bob McCreadie, guys who could soft-foot the throttle and win races. Now maybe these guys had to learn from Pat Ward and myself."

~

The two biggest races of the season had surprise endings. Both the Victoria 200 on May 10 and the New Yorker 200 on Sept. 13 fell to last-minute entries, guys best described as dark-horse picks despite their credentials.

For the Victoria 200, Gary Tomkins showed up with a second-hand, group-effort Modified. "Mike Payne bought the car, and Steve Roberts put the motor in it," he explained. "We thrashed and thrashed to get this car together." But there he was at the halfway mark, hounding Ward for the lead and—gadzooks!—passing him on lap 110. From that point, the Victoria 200 was all Tomkins. Oh, Gary's heart likely skipped a beat when Brett Hearn passed him in traffic and led laps 152-162—"I knew [Hearn] was there because the photographers were taking pictures"—but by the end Tomkins had waved *adios*. Hearn faded to third, behind runner-up Tim Fuller.

Lending credence to the Ward/Varin theory that Utica-Rome can be fickle, the victor declared, "I think the fact that I had a small-block made a big difference. I could bring the pace down a lot more than those guys [and] turn the car in the rubber better than they could." Tomkins, the 2004 Mr. DIRT champion out of Clifton Springs, banked $10,000.

Four months later, on a Saturday evening in September, another long-shot hauled ten grand out of Utica-Rome. That morning, Steve Paine was home in Waterloo, not even wanting to run the New Yorker 200. His team had been struggling. "I told the guys we shouldn't even come," he said.

Early in the feature, he was wishing he hadn't. After starting seventh, he quickly realized his chassis setup did not match the track surface. "Too tight," he later explained. "My car was dead slow." In no time at all, he lost touch with the top 10. But one groove after another wore out, and the track got slick. At lap 50, Paine had rebounded to fifth; by the halfway break, he was third. Realizing he was onto something, he bided his time in the second half, and shortly after three-quarters distance he trailed only Ward, who was on top for 91 laps. And when Ward suffered a flat left-rear tire on lap 162, Paine decided his two-hour drive to Vernon had been worthwhile.

The other two podium finishers were as pleased as Paine was, for different reasons. Runner-up Hearn lost an engine in his heat race, and qualified a backup car though the consi. From 22nd on the grid, he got close enough to Paine that they rubbed wheels with 11 laps to go. And Varin, third at the finish, overcame a minor crash in hot laps, a flat tire in his heat, a broken suspension in the opening 100 laps, and another flat on lap 126.

As of this book's publication, neither Gary Tomkins nor Steve Paine has won another Utica-Rome feature.

~

The only other multiple Modified winners were Stewart Friesen with three and Willy Decker and Todd Burley with two each. Decker was wheeling his own car, having parted company with Tom Cullen; that split would lead to more news down the road. And Mitch Gibbs had a 30-lap score in May, pushing his career Utica-Rome total to 22, eighth best all-time.

Two winners produced sentimental smiles and tears. Jack Johnson, 64 years young, copped a 30-lapper on May 31. The night before, he'd won a Fonda feature with a last-lap pass. That brilliant weekend brought forth this passage from *Utica Observer-Dispatch* writer Ron Moshier: "The older Jack Johnson gets, the more people want to know just how close he is to calling it quits. Turns out it's the question, not the driver, that's getting old."

When Jack's son Ronnie won half of a twin-20s program on August 16, it should have been cause for celebration. It was only the second time in history that a father/son combo had won Modified features in the same Utica-Rome season; yes, the Johnsons had also done it first, back in 2000. But instead a somber Ronnie dedicated the victory to his dad, whose fine spring became a horrible summer. Jumpin' Jack had gone to the hospital to get checked out after a Fonda tumble. Doctors X-rayed him, looking for broken ribs. They found cancer, too. Though the savage crash was certainly a godsend from a medical standpoint, it set in motion a long, rocky stretch for one of the Northeast's most popular racers.

Jack continued to attend races, unable to hide his pride in watching Ronnie follow in his footsteps. In 2010 he stood in the pits at Utica-Rome, where he had won 27 times, a stout total considering he'd seldom been a regular. Most of those came in his familiar #12A Modifieds, but he'd also won seven times between 2000-02 wheeling a DIRT 358-Modified. "I was driving for Brian Goewey," Jack recalled. "We ran here kinda hit-and-miss, never got serious about coming every week. No pressure."

He looked out at the dirt track and smiled. "I've had a lot of fun here. This place has been awesome to me over the years."

A lot of speedways were awesome to Jack Johnson. Honestly, though, that went both ways.

~

Jason Rood had known since 2002 what it felt like to be a Utica-Rome champion. That was the year he earned the Pro Stock title through sheer consistency, without a single victory. He sure changed his approach in '09, when he topped the Sportsman standings and also headed the win column with six feature wins. Jeff Leslie and Matt Janczuk made Rood sweat, winning five and three main events, respectively.

In the Pro Stocks, Tom Denton took his fourth championship, his first since 2000. Tom was razor-sharp all season, winning six features, twice as many as Shawn Frost, his nearest challenger.

Ron Hawker took the checkered flag first in 11 Pure Stock features, just over half of the 20 features run by the division. That stunning display of speed earned Ron his first track championship.

~

A 2009 footnote: Pat Ward's strength all season meant that to secure the Modified title, he needed only to start the final points event on Sept. 6. Good thing, because

Steve Paine, flanked by runner-up Brett Hearn (right) and third-place Bobby Varin after a great New Yorker 200. (Jay Fish Photo)

he fell out early with a blown engine. It was a rare misfortune for Ward, who across 2008 and '09 had won 13 Utica-Rome features.

"That's the way racing is sometimes," says Todd Burley, who back in '01 had won seven times on his way to the track title. "When you're on a roll, you're on a roll. I knew just how Pat was feeling. You're fast, and you're confident, and it feels like you can't do anything wrong."

Former track announcer Shane Andrews, having observed Ward for years, says, "Everybody has this idea that race drivers are bigger than life, that they have these brash personalities, this bravado that's as big as a mountain. Then you see Pat Ward, who's small in stature, quiet. But he's got the respect of all his competitors, and all the fans."

That seems to be enough for laid-back Pat.

Trying times: Jack Johnson (above), a winner in May, faced serious health issues; son Ronnie Johnson (left) also won, though his mind was often elsewhere. (J. Johnson, Post-Time Photo; R. Johnson, Jay Fish Photo)

2010

Stewart's Big Dance

Stewart Friesen's "breakout" season happened a long time before 2010. You can place it in 2004, the year he won eight features—four in a row—and his first Utica-Rome championship. And you can't discount what he pulled off in 2007: another track title and six more victories, including the New Yorker 200. But for all his success, Friesen never had a year quite like 2010. In his travels that season, he won 25 events; five came at Utica-Rome, where he earned his third crown, worth $8,000. He won another eight grand as champ of the "Thunder on the Thruway" mini-series, a joint effort between Utica-Rome's Gene Cole and Fonda Speedway boss Ric Lucia.

In fact, Friesen was fast wherever he went in 2010. He also won the track title at Five Mile Point Speedway; the Race of Champions Dirt Tour championship; and a $50,000 payday in the nation's biggest Modified show, the Super DIRT Week 300 at the New York State Fairgrounds.

Stewart's Utica-Rome season was stellar. He was part of a new squad formed by Westmoreland's Tom Cullen … Yes, the same Tom Cullen who had previously been involved with Friesen's rival, Willy Decker. "Back then, Tom and I *did not* get along," Friesen laughs. "We'd actually yell at each other going through tech."

Two of the era's dominant Modified racers: 2010 track champ Stewart Friesen inside, with Pat Ward up top. (Jay Fish Photo)

Friesen accepts the congratulations of Bobby Varin, who finished as runner-up in the Modified standings. (Images by DC)

When Decker and Cullen split, says Friesen, "Tom and I started talking, and it developed to where we put something big together."

What they put together was a team dedicated to Utica-Rome. Stewart was free to race wherever and whatever else he wanted, but on Sundays he'd be aboard Cullen's Westmoreland Golf Club #1.

"Tom just *lives* for Utica-Rome," says Friesen. "He's been going to that track his whole life. He and his guys would meet me in the shop on Sunday mornings, and their car was fresh even if I had raced three or four times already that week. By the time August came around, I think we had an edge on some of the guys. Their stuff was worn out, their *teams* were worn out, and we were in good shape."

Indeed. Friesen won on May 23, July 4, Aug. 1, Aug. 8, and Aug. 29. He had 16 top-five finishes in 19 Utica-Rome features, and at season's end led runner-up Bobby Varin by a comfortable 57 points.

Varin is full of praise for his younger rival. "Stewie and I have become pretty good friends," says Bobby. "And we have very similar driving styles. We're both

A threat anywhere he unloads, Billy Decker won a pair of "Thunder on the Thruway" 50-lappers. (Jay Fish Photo)

always gunning for it. I think we both run best when we've got a rabbit in front of us. But he's a lot of fun to race, and I always feel like if we beat him, we've accomplished something."

Beat him? For most of the guys he faced in 2010, it was a major feat just to get close to Stewart Friesen.

~

It was another wonderful season for special events, though not very kind to the Utica-Rome faithful. "Us track regulars, we used to have an advantage here," Todd Burley said at one point. "But that seems to have changed."

One popular theory was that the American Racer tires used at Utica-Rome for several years were now standard at enough tracks that the invaders were used to them. Or maybe it was something more basic, as vocalized by former track champ Willy Decker: "These guys who travel a lot, they're the best of the best. Sure, [the regulars] know this place, so we usually know what it's going to do. But these other guys adapt real well to any surface you give 'em because they've got so much experience."

Whatever it was, the outsiders really hauled away some dough. Just look at the four 50-lappers that made up Utica-Rome's half of the "Thunder on the Thruway" series: Each paid $5,000 to win, and that entire $20K went to non-regulars. Brett Hearn dominated on April

Tim McCreadie relaxed a bit with Stewart Friesen before the Victoria 200, then went to work and won it. (Jay Fish Photos)

5; Matt Sheppard, a Utica-Rome champ in 2002 but now an occasional visitor, ran away from Varin and Friesen on June 24 (a "Legends" night honoring former track owner Dick Waterman and NASCAR Modified icon Jerry Cook); and Billy Decker beat Ronnie Johnson on July 29, enjoying the experience so much that he came back on Sept. 10 to defeat Friesen and everybody else.

The only bright spot in the Thunder series for the regulars came when the points fund was paid at season's end: The top four exactly matched the Utica-Rome standings: Friesen, Varin, Ronnie Johnson, and Pat Ward.

And you couldn't get any more *outside* than the guy who stole the Victoria 200 on May 31. Oh, Tim McCreadie had done his share of Modified racing, but by now he was a full-fledged Late Model superstar, touring with the World of Outlaws and winning that group's title in 2006. But McCreadie has a nose for cash, so when the Victoria 200 snowed out on Mother's Day and was reset for Memorial Day, he found a ride in Vinnie Salerno's Modified. Getting there was a hassle, because McCreadie had a WoO commitment in West Virginia on Sunday night, but T-Mac made the trip worthwhile, banking $10,000 for the victory. All night, McCreadie was on the gas. As the first 100-lap segment wound down, he trailed only leader Varin, but Varin shredded a tire on lap 97. After the break, Timmy's only competition came from Ward, their

Top: Though he claimed to be pacing himself, Bobby Varin scored a dominating New Yorker 100 victory. (John Clifford Photo)

Pete Taylor (above) and Casey Williams (right) scored very popular Modified victories in 2010. (P. Taylor, Images by DC; C. Williams, Jay Fish Photo)

tussle made more dramatic by flashes of lightning from storms in the area. In the end, Ward could only stare at McCreadie's bumper as he took the checkers. Vic Coffey, strong-running Michael Storms, and Andy Bachetti rounded out the top five.

The natives were restless. Standing in the pits on Saturday, Sept. 11 for the New Yorker 100—note the shortened distance—Willy Decker said of the dominant invaders, in prizefighter parlance, "All you can do is keep your chin up, and keep swinging at 'em."

Bobby Varin has raced everywhere—he was the Fonda champ in this very season—but is every inch a Utica-Rome regular. He didn't hear Decker's comment, but he sure acted as if he had. Varin started his #00 from the pole and absolutely blew away the field, lapping up to eighth place.

"Bobby was in a league of his own," said runner-up Pat Ward. "I thought he might end up lapping *me* the way he was going."

Interestingly, Varin swears he was pacing himself. "Out front, I was able to keep the car straight, keep the tires under me, keep the wheelspin to a minimum. In those long races, you just calm down and keep looking for the best line. Really, you try to go as fast as you can without using up your equipment. It's so easy to push things too hard. You can overheat your tires, overheat your engine, or drive into the corner too hard and slide over the bank. There's all kinds of things you can do wrong."

Instead Varin did them right, and the locals could rejoice. The first-place purse was $10,000, to which Bobby added $2,500 in lap money. And the race continued his terrific string of finishes in the New Yorker: second in 2007, first in '08, and third in '09, all at 200 laps, and first in this 100-lapper. It was his 24th career victory at Utica-Rome, and he celebrated with car owner Dave Cruickshank, whose Dover Brake outfit had sponsored winning Modifieds since Buzzie Reutimann's coupe-era heyday. "Racing with Dave is a joy," says Varin. "He's a great guy to hang around with."

~

Ronnie Johnson had a stellar year, with three victories and 11 top-fives, and when he was on his game he could handle anybody in the joint. He made runners-up out of Friesen (on May 16 and June 20) and Ward (Sept. 5), and at Utica-Rome that's getting the job done. At season's end, R.J. nipped Ward for third spot in the standings.

"Ronnie was right there a *lot* [in 2010]," says Friesen. "If he got to the front, he was going to be tough."

In addition to those mentioned, three others captured points-paying races. Two were genuine underdogs. The other two were Burley and Ward. In the closing laps on July 11, Burley had Friesen throwing everything at him but the kitchen sink. A monster slide-job looked like it might do it for Friesen, but Burley gassed it hard and kept Friesen's car from clearing his own. It was a hard fight but a fair one, and Burley won it. One week later, on July 18, Ward's tough season brightened when he held off Friesen and popular Paul Jensen.

The first of the two upsets occurred on June 13, when Pete Taylor took an early lead and never surrendered it, even as Willy Decker, Ronnie Johnson, Jensen, and Burley tracked him down in the closing laps. It was Taylor's second career Utica-Rome score, his first since '03.

And on Aug. 29, Casey Williams exemplified coolness under pressure at the end of a 20-lapper, leading with Friesen on his tail. A pair of third-turn slide-jobs, one on the final lap, failed to rattle Casey, so fans saw a first-time winner beat the track champion. Good stuff!

~

It was cool that Bill Trexler Jr., who hit the 10-career-wins mark during the 2010 season, finally got himself a Utica-Rome Sportsman championship. Cool, too, that Tom Denton cruised to a fifth title in the Pro Stocks. And there's no way to not be happy whenever Chris Carr does something good, like winning his second Pure Stock crown, because Carr's yellow #50 is a rolling tribute to the late, great Sonney Seamon.

But the coolest thing seen all year long may have been the beaming face of Matt Janczuk after his Sportsman victory on Sept. 10. Just that morning, Matt had become the father of a bouncing baby girl.

~

The last word for 2010—and thus the last word on the track's first 50 years—goes to the guy who won the final race of that epoch.

"The atmosphere at Utica-Rome is really neat," says Bobby Varin. "At some tracks—Fonda, for exam-

Always a factor at Utica-Rome, Bill Trexler Jr. took a much-deserved championship in the Sportsman class. (Utica-Rome Archive)

Chris Carr, his paint job a tribute to Sonney Seamon, grabbed his second Pure Stock title. (Images by DC)

It was championship number five for Tom Denton, Pro Stock chauffeur extraordinaire. (Images by DC)

ple—the fans can be a rowdy group. They'll scream, they'll holler. Then you go up to a place like Utica-Rome, and even though they're serious fans, it feels almost like everybody's cheering for every driver. It's like a different mindset.

"Maybe it's because it's Sunday night, and everybody's getting ready to go back to work the next day, where on a Friday or a Saturday night they're going to go out, have a good time, and party it up. I guess by Sunday, everyone is back in their normal state of mind.

"All I know is, when you pull into that race track, you're just so comfortable."

Comfortable? That seems a strange word to associate with Bobby Varin … or Dale Planck … or Jack Johnson … or Richie Evans … or Lou Lazzaro … or Rene Charland … In other words, with any of the heroes who have made the Vernon track such a thrilling place since 1961.

But those who care passionately about the speedway—fans and racers alike—certainly understand. There is always comfort in coming home, after all, and for 50 years the Utica-Rome Speedway has been exactly that: a home to heroes, and to those who cheer them.

Here's to 50 more!

What a day! On Sept. 10, Matt Janczuk's wife delivered a daughter; that evening, Matt delivered a Sportsman victory. (Otto Graham Photo)

EYEWITNESS
2005–2010: STEWART FRIESEN

"These are really good times for Utica-Rome"

NOTE: Stewart Friesen was born into racing, the baby of a multi-generational clan of motorsports folks known best for their work in managing various speedways. Many would have bet on Stewart following in those promotional footsteps, but the kid was determined not to organize races, but to win them. He cut his driving teeth at the family's Ransomville Speedway, a situation fraught with the potential for political problems; the youngster resolved the issue by simply taking his show on the road. Ransomville's loss was the region's gain, because Stewart Friesen has become one of dirt-track Modified racing's brightest and most popular stars. In 2010 he had a dream season, winning his second Utica-Rome championship and capping the year with a huge Super DIRT Week Modified victory at Syracuse. Though clearly an exceptional driver, Stewart still has the Friesen family eye for business, giving him a rare split-screen perspective on short-track racing.

Images by DC

It's hard for me to say why we've done so well at Utica-Rome. Obviously, I've had great equipment. Right from when we started there in 2004 with the Madsens, we had that part of it covered. That was a good team, and they had good stuff. Then I got away from there a little bit, but I was able to come back in 2007 with Roger Heroux and basically pick up right where we'd left off. Again, a lot of that was because the equipment was really good. It was the same in 2010, with Tom Cullen's car.

I found Utica-Rome to be a really tricky place when I first went there, and, even though we've been successful there, it's still a really tricky place. It's a much more complicated track than it looks like it would be. There's a little bit of an uphill run, and there's a little bit of downhill, too. Turns one and two drive way differently from turns three and four. And, you know, the bottoms of the turns drive very differently from the tops, which is not the case at some tracks. Because of the layout and the

A champion in action: Stewart Friesen shows 'em how it's done. (Images by DC)

width of the track, the top groove at Utica-Rome is so sweeping and long, yet the bottom groove feels more like you're on a short quarter-mile track.

That difference makes the chassis setups you choose really critical. You might plan to run high or low, but your car has to work well enough everywhere, because you are never sure where you'll need to work well to pass people. We've tried quite a few things there that are different from what you might call our normal baseline setup—a lot of things with shocks, for example—and it is definitely a challenging track.

From a driving standpoint, it's the kind of place where it helps to know what you want to do on the next lap. Because it's so fast, you can lose a lot of speed if you break your rhythm, so you've got to anticipate a lot of your moves. Even when the track is slippery and slower, that extra bit of anticipation helps you catch a guy at just the right place, where you can get under his car and let your momentum carry you past him. You can pull off some pretty cool slide-job passes there, going from the bottom lane to the top. But, you know, when you start that move, you've better be sure where it's going to end up. You can't just drive it into the corner out of control. First of all, you've got to be absolutely sure you clear the other guy, or you'll wreck. Second, if you're carrying too much speed and you get to the top of the banking at the wrong spot, it's very easy to slide over the edge of the track and throw away all the work you've done up to that point. There's definitely a knack to going fast and passing at Utica-Rome.

From the beginning, I just seemed to fit the place, for whatever reason. We joke that it's because my Uncle Alex once owned the place and he's still there, pushing me around, haunting the place.

Because of my family's history—not just Uncle Alex, but going back to my grandfather—I grew up thinking first and foremost about the other side of racing, the promoting and officiating side. When I was young, my family was operating Ransomville Speedway. I was lucky enough to be in the tower whenever I wanted to, and to really see what went into running the races. Before I ever knew how to take a wheel off a car and put another one on, I knew how to score a race. I guess that was kind of backwards to the way a lot of drivers learn about the sport, because they start out interested in the actual racing and only learn about the other end when they have to.

But even with that involvement on the management side, I always knew I wanted to drive race cars. That was my passion. The business side of the sport was interesting, but to me the main thing was, "How can I start racing? How can we figure this out?" And once my dad and my uncle built a little go-kart track at Ransomville—I guess it was somewhere around 1992—I knew for sure that all I wanted to do was drive. I ran there on Thursday nights and Sunday afternoons, and from that point I pretty much wanted nothing to do with promoting or officiating. Instead of being in the tower on a race night, I wanted to be in the pits, looking at things, trying to figure out why the fast guys were fast.

When I first started racing, the family connection would come up sometimes in a negative way. I'd hear things about favoritism, and people wondering if I was getting away with stuff other guys didn't. I always thought it was the other way around; it seemed to me like I got harsher penalties than the next guy, and I couldn't get away with anything. I suppose the idea was, if someone in my family let it look as if I had gotten away with something, chaos would ensue. Over the years, I've been black-flagged, put to the tail, disqualified, you name it. Once I stopped competing at Ransomville on a regular basis—and I love that place, but I wouldn't want to race there every week because of all this—that kind of talk went away.

But, you know, it's not like I've ever forgotten about the business part of the sport. I can't ever really get away from it. I mean, whenever I'm off racing somewhere and I talk with my dad later, he'll ask, "How was the show? How was the crowd?" He taught me how to guess at crowd numbers by sectioning off the grandstand and counting that way, and sometimes I'll do that without even really thinking about it.

I'm sure that because of all that, I look at things a little differently than most other racers do. When an official makes a call, I'll try to think about everything that went into it before I decide whether they made the right call or the wrong call. And I guess that's not always a good thing, because if you think it over and come to the conclusion that you know the call was wrong, you feel like pulling your hair out even while you're out there in the car.

Friesen stops in for a chat with fellow Utica-Rome champion Todd Burley. (Doug Elkins Photo)

Stewart Friesen in his workshop. (Jay Fish Photo)

I think pretty often about the promotional side of things. I'm sure a lot of people in the grandstands and in the pits think every ticket sold at the gate is pure profit. They don't see the overhead that goes into a night of racing, they don't think about the taxes on the property, they don't consider all the other costs. These places are really expensive to run, and we've seen a lot of tracks go away over the years as a result. And there is so much more work involved than I'm sure most people realize. Even at a track like Utica-Rome Speedway, which you think of as having a big, built-in crowd, you've got to work hard to make it successful. And it's really scary at some other tracks, when you show up and the crowds are so small it feels as if there's nobody there. I always like going to places where you can see that the crowds are good, and the promoter has been able to put money into the place. It makes the whole night more enjoyable, and it also gives you confidence that the track is going to be around for a while.

What Gene Cole and his team have been able to do at Utica-Rome has been great. He's been a successful guy away from racing, with his insurance business, and I'm sure that has allowed him to devote a lot of resources toward his passion for racing. That has helped the speedway so much; they've been able to make a lot of improvements to the facility because he doesn't necessarily depend on the track for his income. That has definitely benefited the fans and the racers, and I'm sure it will for years to come.

It seems to me that these are really good times for Utica-Rome. Lately, it has been such a competitive place. To win a championship there, you're almost going to have to run in the top three every week, because if you don't, somebody else will. Somebody will get really hot—a Bobby Varin or a Pat Ward—and he's always going to be right up there unless he has a failure. And if you want to beat that guy, you'd better be good, week in and week out.

Somebody said to me that people tend to remember the guys who ran well at certain tracks when those tracks were going through good times, and if that's true—if they think of me in 20 years when they think about Utica-Rome Speedway—well, I'm glad about that. Right now, I'm thrilled to be a part of it.

It has always felt like home on a Sunday, a good place to go racing. And when you like a place and you have good results there, too, you want to keep going back.

2002-2010

Stable and Strong

2002: Mike Hulsizer (89) and Jack Johnson. (Post-Time Photo)

Track owner Gene Cole (right) with area icon Willie Wust. (Utica-Rome Archive)

Jim Normoyle, Pro Stock winner. (Doug Zupan Photo)

2006: A debut win for Paul Kinney. (Doug Zupan Photo)

Andy Bachetti, a 2006 Modified winner. (Doug Zupan Photo)

Track owners Gene and Gloria Cole. (Doug Elkins Photo)

Two-time Modified champion Pat Ward. (Jay Fish Photo)

Like father, like son: Jumpin' Jack (12a) and Ronnie Johnson. (Post-Time Photo)

Ronnie Johnson in the 2007 New Yorker. (Joe Alexander Photo)

Chris Carr, Pure Stocker extraordinaire. (Utica-Rome Archive)

Jim "Junkyard Jet" Thomas, perennial Pure Stock threat. (Utica-Rome Archive)

Local boy and two-time champ Willy Decker. (Doug Elkins Photo)

Danny Johnson, 2008 Victoria 200 king. (Images by DC)

2008: Willy Decker (1) battles Mitch Gibbs. (John Clifford Photo)

Gary Tomkins, 2009 Victoria 200 champ. (Images by DC)

Stable and Strong

Stewart Friesen, 2010. (Doug Elkins Photo)

Casey Williams continues a family tradition. (Doug Elkins Photo)

Jim Rothwell, a veteran hero. (Images by DC)

Legendary Bill Wimble with Utica-Rome's Barb Clark. (Dick Berggren Photo)

Old pals: Bill Wimble (left) and Dick Waterman, 2010. (Tom Loughlin Photo)

Tim McCreadie, interviewed by Mike Mallett. (Jay Fish Photo)

Todd Burley, champion. (Images by DC)

Three wide! Stewart Friesen (1), Mitch Gibbs (2), Danny Varin (18). (Images by DC)

Steve Paine, wide open. (Jay Fish Photo)

Stable and Strong

Billy Trexler, 2010 Sportsman champ. (Images by DC)

"T-Mac" wins the 2010 Victoria 200. (Jay Fish Photo)

2010: Billy Decker took two 50-lappers. (Otto Graham Photo)

Bret Belden: Husband, father, winner! (Utica-Rome Archive)

Young talent: Stewart Friesen leads Matt Sheppard. (John Clifford Photo)

Class: Stewart Friesen congratulates Mod winner Casey Williams, 2010. (Jay Fish Photo)

Bobby Varin, 2010 New Yorker 100 winner. (John Clifford Photo)

2010: Jack Johnson congratulates his winning son, Ronnie. (Images by DC)

Stable and Strong

Shawn Frost after a 2010 Pro Stock score. (Images by DC)

Another Pro Stock win for Tom Denton. (Images by DC)

"Programs! Get your programs!" (Images by DC)

Sail panels up! Ward and Friesen, 2010 Victoria 200. (Jay Fish Photo)

Utica-Rome Speedway Race Records and Statistics

Assistance in researching and compiling these records was provided by Doug Zupan, Mark Southcott, Brian Spaid, Andy Fusco, Tom Skibinski, Gary Spaid, Joseph Achzet, and Joe Patrick.

All-Time Modified Track Champions – 1961-2010

Year	Track Champion	Year	Track Champion
1961	Rene Charland	1987	Kenny Tremont Jr.
1962	Rene Charland	1988	SPEEDWAY WAS CLOSED
1963	Lou Lazzaro	1989	Paul Jensen
1964	Rene Charland	1990	Paul Jensen
1965	Pete Corey (M)/Tom Kotary (Sp)	1991	Tom Kinsella
1966	Ed Flemke (M)/Bill Wimble (Sp)	1992	Paul Jensen
1967	Bill Wimble (M)/Bernie Miller (Sp)	1993	Paul Jensen
1968	Sonney Seamon	1994	Dale Planck
1969	Jerry Cook	1995	Dale Planck
1970	Lou Lazzaro	1996	Mitch Gibbs
1971	Lou Lazzaro	1997	Dale Planck
1972	Richie Evans	1998	J.J. Michaels**/Roger Phelps
1973	Richie Evans	1999	Dale Planck
1974	Richie Evans	2000	Ron Holmes
1975	Sonney Seamon	2001	Todd Burley
1976	SPEEDWAY WAS CLOSED	2002	Matt Sheppard
1977	Geoff Bodine*/Sonney Seamon	2003	Dale Planck
1978	Richie Evans	2004	Stewart Friesen
1979	Bob Savoie (BB)/Donnie Wetmore (SB)	2005	Willy Decker
1980	Jon Button	2006	Willy Decker
1981	Dave Lape	2007	Stewart Friesen
1982	Jack Johnson	2008	Pat Ward
1983	SPEEDWAY WAS CLOSED	2009	Pat Ward
1984	SPEEDWAY WAS CLOSED	2010	Stewart Friesen
1985	Dave Lape		
1986	Brett Hearn		

*The track ran NEARA and open competition specials throughout the entire 1977 season. Bodine's track title is based on only three events: 7/31, 8/28 (100), and 9/04. Otherwise, it appears as if Sonney Seamon would have been the track champion.

**The first four weeks of the 1998 season were run under the New England Region of the NASCAR Racing Series. After a change in track management, NASCAR was dropped and the track was an independent. NASCAR Champions were for the first four races.

All-Time Modified Win List – 1961-2010
Includes all Modified events on asphalt and dirt run since track opened in 1961

Pos.	Driver	Wins	Winning Seasons	First Win	Last Win
1	Dale Planck	42	9	7/1/1992	5/25/2003
2	Richie Evans	33	8	9/19/1965	9/3/1978
3	Lou Lazzaro	32	11	9/9/1962	6/30/1979
4	Paul Jensen	29	11	7/16/1989	8/24/2003
	Tom Kinsella	29	7	6/10/1990	8/4/1996
	Todd Burley	29	10	7/29/1999	7/11/2010
7	Stewart Friesen	28	6	5/2/2004	8/29/2010
8	Jack Johnson	27	9	9/1/1979	5/31/2009
9	Ed Flemke	24	6	6/9/1963	9/6/1970
	Bobby Varin	24	7	7/25/2004	9/11/2010
11	Mitch Gibbs	22	10	6/2/1996	5/24/2009
12	Donnie Wetmore	21	7	8/3/1980	8/17/1997
	J.J. Michaels	21	9	6/11/1991	7/21/2002
14	Rene Charland	19	7	5/27/1962	7/14/1968
	Jerry Cook	19	9	8/11/1963	7/5/1974
16	Pat Ward	17	4	8/5/2007	7/18/2010
17	Willy Decker	16	6	5/29/2003	8/30/2009
18	Gordy Button Jr.	14	8	6/25/1989	5/26/2002
19	Bill Wimble	12	7	9/17/1961	7/30/1967
	Brett Hearn	12	5	5/9/1986	4/25/2010
21	Alan Johnson	11	6	4/23/1982	5/14/2006
22	Geoff Bodine	9	3	7/26/1974	7/2/1978
	Ted Lamb Jr.	9	7	7/23/1989	9/7/2008
24	Dave Lape	8	5	8/8/1971	8/29/1987
	Danny Johnson	8	7	7/23/1982	5/11/2008
	Roger Phelps	8	7	7/29/1990	7/12/1998
	Ron Holmes	8	4	7/30/1995	7/16/2000
28	Sonney Seamon	7	6	6/18/1967	6/19/1977
29	Dave Kotary	6	5	7/4/1965	8/13/1972
	Gus Schmidt Jr.	6	6	8/23/1998	9/2/2007
31	Ed Ortiz	5	2	9/24/1961	9/2/1962
	Tom Kotary	5	3	6/24/1962	7/11/1965
	Ernie Gahan	5	4	6/16/1963	8/13/1967
	Dick Fowler	5	4	7/7/1968	5/24/1974
	Doug Fuller	5	3	8/26/1990	6/8/1997
	Randy Glenski	5	1	5/23/1993	9/12/1993
	Ronnie Johnson	5	3	7/23/2000	9/5/2010
38	Lou Smith	4	2	5/31/1964	4/25/1965
	Don MacTavish	4	2	6/5/1966	9/23/1967
	Maynard Troyer	4	3	8/5/1973	8/6/1978
	Maynard Forrette	4	2	6/17/1973	8/11/1979
	Tom Wilson	4	2	7/4/1979	8/30/1981
	Mike Romano	4	3	7/30/1982	5/2/1999
	Kenny Tremont Jr.	4	1	6/12/1987	8/12/1987
	John Ramsey	4	4	7/29/1990	8/14/2005
	Jeff Walton	4	4	7/7/1991	8/16/1998
	Billy Decker	4	3	8/23/2001	9/10/2010
	Matt Sheppard	4	3	8/11/2002	6/24/2010
	Dave Camara	4	3	9/7/2003	4/29/2007
50	Ken Meahl	3	3	8/12/1962	8/30/1964
	Ken Shoemaker	3	1	5/26/1966	9/18/1966
	Bernie Miller	3	3	6/9/1968	7/28/1971
	Fred DeSarro	3	1	5/30/1971	8/15/1971
	Bugs Stevens	3	3	7/4/1971	9/2/1973
	Ed Peniazek	3	2	5/28/1972	6/3/1973
	Bob Savoie	3	1	8/4/1979	9/15/1979
	A.J. Romano	3	2	6/15/1986	9/10/2006
	Billy Pauch	3	3	9/16/1990	9/19/1993
	John Barker Jr.	3	3	8/6/1995	7/2/2000
	Steve Hulsizer	3	3	6/8/1997	6/23/2002
	Andy Bachetti	3	3	5/7/2000	6/17/2007
	Jamie Christian	3	2	6/27/2004	8/28/2005
63	Robbie Kotary	2	2	8/5/1962	5/31/1970
	Jim Luke	2	1	5/5/1963	8/25/1963
	Bob Zeigler	2	2	5/31/1964	6/20/1965
	Elton Hill	2	2	5/2/1965	7/10/1966
	Fran Kitchen	2	1	4/30/1967	7/16/1967
	Andy Romano	2	2	6/30/1968	6/28/1970
	Ray Sitterly	2	2	9/20/1970	5/23/1971
	Ron Newman	2	2	7/19/1970	7/18/1971
	Wally Warburton	2	1	6/2/1979	6/9/1979
	Chuck Kennison	2	1	8/3/1980	8/7/1980
	John Podolak	2	2	7/30/1982	9/3/1989
	Merv Treichler	2	1	8/6/1982	9/17/1982
	Jim Rothwell	2	2	8/2/1998	5/4/2003
	Pete Taylor	2	2	6/22/2003	6/13/2010
	Brian Weaver	2	1	6/23/2004	8/1/2004
78	Bill Rafter	1	1	9/10/1961	
	Cam Gagliardi	1	1	8/19/1962	
	Bill Torrisi	1	1	9/15/1963	
	Jerry Humiston	1	1	6/21/1964	
	Fred Harbach	1	1	9/5/1965	
	Gene Bergin	1	1	5/8/1966	
	George Pendergast	1	1	6/25/1967	
	Don Wayman	1	1	5/5/1968	
	Ken Platt	1	1	7/21/1968	
	Pete Corey	1	1	8/4/1968	
	Jerry Pennock Sr.	1	1	8/24/1969	
	John Kollar	1	1	5/24/1970	
	Bill Henry	1	1	7/26/1970	
	Bob Santos	1	1	6/4/1972	
	Denis Giroux	1	1	8/20/1972	
	Dick Clark	1	1	8/23/1974	
	Dave Nichols	1	1	7/24/1977	
	Chip Lanz	1	1	8/20/1978	
	Leroy Hurlbut	1	1	6/16/1979	
	Larry Dalmata	1	1	7/7/1979	
	Gary Iulg	1	1	8/17/1980	
	Art Kiser	1	1	5/17/1981	
	Freddie Brightbill	1	1	9/29/1985	
	Bob McCreadie	1	1	6/6/1986	
	Jack Cottrell	1	1	7/31/1987	
	Ray Dalmata	1	1	7/31/1987	
	Tim Dwyer	1	1	9/5/1987	
	Mike Arminio	1	1	7/2/1989	
	Jim Mahaney	1	1	7/8/1990	
	Bob Podolak	1	1	6/23/1991	
	Lou Michaels	1	1	8/11/1991	
	Pete Bicknell	1	1	4/26/1992	
	Dave Donath	1	1	7/19/1992	
	Billy Whittaker	1	1	7/4/1993	
	Mike VanDusen	1	1	9/15/1995	
	Bob Sitterly	1	1	7/28/1996	
	Jason Barney	1	1	8/20/2000	
	Aaron Excell	1	1	9/2/2001	
	Ryan Baye	1	1	9/9/2001	
	Jeff Kotary	1	1	8/11/2002	
	Don Mattison	1	1	7/3/2005	
	Bob Henry Jr.	1	1	7/3/2005	
	Paul Kinney	1	1	6/18/2006	
	Gary Tomkins	1	1	5/10/2009	
	Steve Paine	1	1	9/12/2009	
	Tim McCreadie	1	1	5/31/2010	
	Casey Williams	1	1	8/29/2010	

124 Drivers   747 Events   46 Seasons   9/10/1961 to 9/11/10

Opening Day Modified Feature Winners – 1961-2010

Year	Date	Laps	Winner
1961	10-Sep	30	Billy Rafter
1962	20-May	30	Ed Ortiz
1963	28-Apr	25	Tom Kotary
1964	26-Apr	30	Rene Charland
1965	25-Apr	30	Lou Smith
1966	1-May	30	Bill Wimble
1967	30-Apr	30	Fran Kitchen
1968	5-May	30	Don Wayman
1969	4-May	30	Jerry Cook
1970	3-May	100	Dick Fowler
1971	23-May	30	Jerry Cook
1972	21-May	30	Sonney Seamon
1973	6-May	100	Richie Evans
1974	24-May	30	Dick Fowler
1975	13-Jun	100	Sonney Seamon
1976	SPEEDWAY WAS CLOSED		
1977	12-Jun	50	Richie Evans
1978	21-May	50	Richie Evans
1979	30-May	60	Lou Lazzaro
1980	3-Aug	10	Chuck Kennison
1981	17-May	30	Art Kiser
1982	23-Apr	30	Alan Johnson
1983	SPEEDWAY WAS CLOSED		
1984	SPEEDWAY WAS CLOSED		
1985	16-Jul	100	Alan Johnson
1986	9-May	50	Brett Hearn
1987	26-Apr	100	Jack Johnson
1988	SPEEDWAY WAS CLOSED		
1989	11-Jun	25	Donnie Wetmore
1990	22-Apr	25	Ted Lamb Jr.
1991	14-Apr	40	Gordy Button Jr.
1992	26-Apr	40	Pete Bicknell
1993	2-May	40	Gordy Button Jr.
1994	24-Apr	40	Paul Jensen
1995	23-Apr	40	Dale Planck
1996	28-Apr	25	Dale Planck
1997	4-May	40	Dale Planck
1998	17-May	25	J.J. Michaels
1999	2-May	30	Mike Romano
2000	7-May	40	Andy Bachetti
2001	6-May	40	J.J. Michaels
2002	5-May	40	Mitch Gibbs
2003	27-Apr	40	Dale Planck
2004	2-May	30	Stewart Friesen
2005	1-May	30	Jamie Christian
2006	7-May	30	Ted Lamb Jr.
2007	29-Apr	46	Stewart Friesen
2008	27-Apr	30	Stewart Friesen
2009	19-Apr	30	Bobby Varin
2010	25-Apr	30	Brett Hearn

All-Time Asphalt Modified Feature Win List – 1961-1978

Pos.	Driver	Feature Wins	Winning Seasons	First Win	Last Win
1	Richie Evans	33	8	9/19/1965	9/3/1978
2	Lou Lazzaro	32	11	9/9/1962	8/6/1972
3	Ed Flemke	24	6	6/9/1963	9/6/1970
4	Rene Charland	19	7	9/17/1961	7/14/1960
	Jerry Cook	19	9	8/11/1963	7/5/1974
6	Bill Wimble	12	7	7/15/1962	7/30/1969
7	Geoff Bodine	9	3	7/26/1974	7/2/1978
8	Sonney Seamon	7	6	6/18/1967	6/19/1977
9	Dave Kotary	6	5	7/4/1965	8/13/1972
10	Ed Ortiz	5	2	9/24/1961	9/2/1962
	Tom Kotary	5	3	6/24/1962	7/11/1965
	Ernie Gahan	5	4	6/16/1963	8/13/1967
	Dick Fowler	5	4	7/7/1968	5/24/1974
14	Lou Smith	4	2	5/31/1964	4/25/1965
	Don MacTavish	4	2	6/5/1966	9/23/1967
	Maynard Troyer	4	3	8/5/1973	8/6/1978
17	Ken Meahl	3	3	8/12/1962	8/30/1964
	Ken Shoemaker	3	1	5/26/1966	9/18/1966
	Bernie Miller	3	3	6/9/1968	7/28/1971
	Fred DeSarro	3	1	5/30/1971	8/15/1971
	Bugs Stevens	3	3	7/4/1971	9/2/1973
	Ed Pieniazek	3	2	5/28/1972	6/3/1973
23	Robbie Kotary	2	2	8/5/1962	5/31/1970
	Jim Luke	2	1	5/5/1963	8/25/1963
	Bob Zeigler	2	2	5/31/1964	6/20/1965
	Elton Hill	2	2	5/2/1965	7/10/1966
	Fran Kitchen	2	1	4/30/1967	7/16/1967
	Andy Romano	2	2	6/30/1968	6/28/1970
	Ray Sitterly	2	2	9/20/1970	5/23/1971
	Ron Newman	2	2	7/19/1970	7/18/1971
	Dave Lape	2	2	8/8/1971	7/30/1972
32	Bill Rafter	1	1	9/10/1961	
	Cam Gagliardi	1	1	8/19/1962	
	Bill Torrisi	1	1	9/15/1963	
	Jerry Humiston	1	1	6/21/1964	
	Fred Harbach	1	1	9/5/1965	
	Gene Bergin	1	1	5/8/1966	
	George Pendergast	1	1	6/25/1967	
	Don Wayman	1	1	5/5/1968	
	Ken Platt	1	1	7/21/1968	
	Pete Corey	1	1	8/4/1968	
	Jerry Pennock Sr.	1	1	8/24/1969	
	John Kollar	1	1	5/24/1970	
	Bill Henry	1	1	7/26/1970	
	Bob Santos	1	1	6/4/1972	
	Denis Giroux	1	1	8/20/1972	
	Maynard Forrette	1	1	6/17/1973	
	Dick Clark	1	1	8/23/1974	
	Dave Nichols	1	1	7/24/1977	
	Chip Lanz	1	1	8/20/1978	

50 Drivers   248 Events   17 Seasons   9/10/1961 to 9/3/1978

All-Time Dirt Modified Win List

Pos.	Driver	Wins	Winning Seasons	First Win	Last Win
1	Dale Planck	42	9	7/1/1992	5/25/2003
2	Paul Jensen	29	11	7/16/1989	8/24/2003
	Tom Kinsella	29	7	6/10/1990	8/4/1996
	Todd Burley	29	10	7/29/1999	7/11/2010
5	Stewart Friesen	28	6	5/2/2004	8/29/2010
6	Jack Johnson	27	9	9/1/1979	5/31/2009
7	Bobby Varin	24	7	7/25/2004	9/11/2010
8	Mitch Gibbs	22	10	6/2/1996	5/24/2009
9	Donnie Wetmore	21	7	8/3/1980	8/17/1997
	J.J. Michaels	21	9	6/11/1991	7/21/2002
11	Pat Ward	17	4	8/5/2007	7/18/2010
12	Willy Decker	16	6	6/29/2003	8/30/2009
13	Gordy Button Jr.	14	8	6/25/1989	5/26/2002
14	Brett Hearn	12	5	5/9/1986	4/25/2010
15	Alan Johnson	11	6	4/23/1982	5/14/2006
16	Ted Lamb Jr.	9	7	7/23/1989	9/7/2008
17	Danny Johnson	8	7	7/23/1982	5/11/2008
	Roger Phelps	8	7	7/29/1990	7/12/1998
	Ron Holmes	8	4	7/30/1995	7/16/2000
20	Dave Lape	6	3	6/7/1981	8/29/1987
	Gus Schmidt Jr.	6	6	8/23/1998	9/2/2007
22	Doug Fuller	5	3	8/26/1990	6/8/1997
	Randy Glenski	5	1	5/23/1993	9/12/1993
	Ronnie Johnson	5	3	7/23/2000	9/5/2010
25	Tom Wilson	4	2	7/4/1979	8/30/1981
	Mike Romano	4	3	7/30/1982	5/2/1999
	Kenny Tremont, Jr.	4	1	6/12/1987	8/12/1987
	John Ramsey	4	4	7/29/1990	8/14/2005
	Jeff Walton	4	4	7/7/1991	8/16/1998
	Billy Decker	4	3	8/23/2001	9/10/2010
	Matt Sheppard	4	3	8/11/2002	6/24/2010
	Dave Camara	4	3	9/7/2003	4/29/2007
33	Maynard Forrette	3	1	7/14/1979	8/11/1979
	Bob Savoie	3	1	8/4/1979	9/15/1979
	A.J. Romano	3	2	6/15/1986	9/10/2006
	Billy Pauch	3	3	9/16/1990	9/19/1993
	John Barker, Jr.	3	3	8/6/1995	7/2/2000
	Steve Hulsizer	3	3	6/8/1997	6/23/2002
	Andy Bachetti	3	3	5/7/2000	6/17/2007
	Jamie Christian	3	2	6/27/2004	8/28/2005
41	Lou Lazzaro	2	1	5/30/1979	6/30/1979
	Wally Warburton	2	1	6/2/1979	6/9/1979
	Chuck Kennison	2	1	8/3/1980	8/7/1980
	John Podolak	2	2	7/30/1982	9/3/1989
	Merv Treichler	2	1	8/6/1982	9/17/1982
	Jim Rothwell	2	2	8/2/1998	5/4/2003
	Pete Taylor	2	2	6/22/2003	6/13/2010
	Brian Weaver	2	1	6/23/2004	8/1/2004
49	Leroy Hurlbut	1	1	6/16/1979	
	Larry Dalmata	1	1	7/7/1979	
	Gary Iulg	1	1	8/17/1980	
	Art Kiser	1	1	5/17/1981	
	Freddie Brightbill	1	1	8/28/1985	
	Bob McCreadie	1	1	6/6/1986	
	Jack Cottrell	1	1	7/31/1987	
	Ray Dalmata	1	1	7/31/1987	
	Tim Dwyer	1	1	9/5/1987	
	Mike Arminio	1	1	7/2/1989	
	Jim Mahaney	1	1	7/8/1990	
	Bob Podolak	1	1	6/23/1991	
	Lou Michaels	1	1	8/11/1991	
	Pete Bicknell	1	1	4/26/1992	
	Dave Donath	1	1	7/19/1992	
	Billy Whittaker	1	1	7/4/1993	
	Mike VanDusen	1	1	9/15/1995	
	Bob Sitterly	1	1	7/28/1996	
	Jason Barney	1	1	8/20/2000	
	Aaron Excell	1	1	9/2/2001	
	Ryan Baye	1	1	9/9/2001	
	Jeff Kotary	1	1	8/11/2002	
	Don Mattison	1	1	7/3/2005	
	Bob Henry, Jr.	1	1	7/3/2005	
	Paul Kinney	1	1	6/18/2006	
	Gary Tomkins	1	1	5/10/2009	
	Steve Paine	1	1	9/12/2009	
	Tim McCreadie	1	1	5/31/2010	
	Casey Williams	1	1	8/29/2010	

77 Drivers   501 Events   23 Seasons   5/30/1979 to 09/11/2010

Big Block Dirt Modified Feature Win List – 1979-2010

Pos.	Driver	Wins	Winning Seasons	First Win	Last Win	Driver	Wins	Winning Seasons	Date
1	Jack Johnson	20	6	9/1/1979	5/31/2009	John Podolak	1	1	7/30/1982
2	Bobby Varin	13	3	5/8/2005	9/11/2010	Mike Romano	1	1	7/30/1982
3	Alan Johnson	9	4	4/23/1982	5/14/2006	Freddie Brightbill	1	1	9/28/1985
4	Stewart Friesen	8	2	5/3/2009	8/29/2010	Bob McCreadie	1	1	6/6/1986
5	Brett Hearn	7	3	5/9/1986	4/25/2010	Jack Cottrell	1	1	7/31/1987
6	Dave Lape	6	3	6/7/1981	8/29/1987	Ray Dalmata	1	1	7/31/1987
	Pat Ward	6	2	4/26/2009	8/12/2009	Tim Dwyer	1	1	9/5/1987
8	Kenny Tremont Jr.	4	1	6/12/1987	8/12/1987	Gordy Button Jr.	1	1	9/25/1994
	Billy Decker	4	3	8/23/2001	9/10/2010	Dale Planck	1	1	5/11/1997
	Willy Decker	4	2	5/13/2007	6/7/2009	J.J. Michaels	1	1	7/19/1998
	Ronnie Johnson	4	2	8/16/2009	9/5/2010	Ron Holmes	1	1	7/26/1998
12	Maynard Forrette	3	1	7/14/1979	8/11/1979	Jim Rothwell	1	1	8/2/1998
	Bob Savoie	3	1	8/4/1979	9/15/1979	Ted Lamb Jr.	1	1	8/9/1998
	Tom Wilson	3	1	5/24/1981	8/30/1981	Jeff Walton	1	1	8/16/1998
	Danny Johnson	3	3	7/23/1982	5/11/2008	Gus Schmidt Jr.	1	1	8/23/1998
	Mitch Gibbs	3	2	8/30/1998	5/24/2009	John Barker Jr.	1	1	9/6/1998
	Todd Burley	3	2	6/14/2009	7/11/2010	A.J. Romano	1	1	8/20/2006
18	Lou Lazzaro	2	1	5/30/1979	6/30/1979	Gary Tomkins	1	1	5/10/2009
	Wally Warburton	2	1	6/2/1979	6/9/1979	Steve Paine	1	1	9/12/2009
	Merv Treichler	2	1	8/6/1982	9/17/1982	Tim McCreadie	1	1	5/31/2010
	Roger Phelps	2	1	7/5/1998	7/12/1998	Pete Taylor	1	1	6/13/2010
22	Leroy Hurlbut	1	1	6/16/1979		Matt Sheppard	1	1	6/24/2010
	Larry Dalmata	1	1	7/7/1979		Casey Williams	1	1	8/29/2010
	Art Kiser	1	1	5/17/1981					

47 Drivers   137 Events   17 Seasons   5/30/1979 to 09/11/2010

Late Model Track Champions – 1979-1982

Year	Track Champion
1979	Tom Williams
1980	Tom Williams
1981	Tom Williams
1982	Jim Rothwell (LM)/Paul Jensen (320)

Late Model Feature Win List – 1979-1982

Pos.	Driver	Wins	First Win	Last Win
1	Tommy Williams	21	6/2/1979	7/9/1982
2	Lonnie Riehlman	4	5/21/1982	8/20/1982
3	Bill Roese	3	7/21/1979	8/11/1979
4	Dick Schoonover	2	5/30/1979	7/7/1979
	Jim Rothwell	2	8/9/1981	4/30/1982
	Bob Podolak	2	6/11/1982	7/23/1982
	Paul Parker	2	7/30/1982	7/30/1982
	Paul Jensen	2	7/16/1982	8/6/1982
9	Jack Cottrell	1	7/4/1979	
	Paul Holic	1	8/2/1981	
	Randy Glenski	1	8/23/1981	
	George Hoffmier	1	4/23/1982	

12 Drivers   42 Events   5/30/1979 to 08/20/1982

Dirt Sportsman Track Champions – 1987- 2010

Year	Track Champion	Year	Track Champion	Year	Track Champion
1987	Alton Palmer	1998	Tony Buffa Jr.*/Jack Miller	2006	Mike Button
1992	Larry Bezner	1999	Jamie Christian	2007	Mike Button
1993	Larry Bezner	2000	Kevin Crave	2008	Brad Alger
1994	Jim Rothwell	2001	Tim Clemons	2009	Jason Rood
1995	Steve Hulsizer	2002	Jamie Christian	2010	Billy Trexler Jr.
1996	Steve Hulsizer	2003	Billy Shantel Jr.		
1997	Dan Yankowski	2004	Jessica Zemken		

*The first four weeks of the 1998 season were run under the New England Region of the NASCAR Racing Series. After a change in track management, NASCAR was dropped and the track was an independent. NASCAR Champions were for the first four races.

Sportsman Feature Win List – 1992-2010

Pos.	Driver	Wins	Winning Seasons	First Win	Last Win
1	Jamie Christian	28	8	8/6/1995	8/24/2003
2	Jim Rothwell	23	10	8/21/1988	5/23/2010
3	Tim Clemons	20	5	5/10/1992	8/3/2003
4	Steve Way	19	9	5/18/1997	6/13/2010
5	Steve Hulsizer	17	4	8/29/1993	7/21/1996
6	Ron Richardson	12	7	7/5/1992	6/13/1999
7	Mike Button	11	6	6/2/2002	7/12/2009
	Paul Carey	11	4	6/23/2004	6/10/2007
9	Jim Smith	10	5	5/17/1992	6/20/1999
	Billy Trexler Jr.	10	5	5/1/1994	8/29/2010
	Brad Alger	10	3	7/3/2005	9/14/2008
	Matt Janczuk	10	4	7/15/2007	9/10/2010
13	Larry Bezner	9	3	7/19/1992	7/24/1994
	Dan Yankowski	9	5	7/11/1993	7/11/1999
15	Willy Decker	8	3	6/6/1999	9/9/2001
	Jeff Leslie	8	2	5/17/2009	8/1/2010
17	Pete Campione	7	5	5/24/1992	6/15/1997
	Ray Zemken	7	2	6/21/1992	5/23/1993
	Jeremy Vunk	7	5	5/1/2005	8/30/2009
	Jason Rood	7	2	8/3/2008	9/6/2009
21	Billy Shantel Jr.	6	5	6/9/2002	8/6/2006
	Jessica Zemken	6	3	6/29/2003	4/30/2006
23	Ken Johnson	4	1	5/10/1992	9/6/1992
	Rick Miller	4	1	5/11/1997	8/17/1997
	Kevin Crave	4	3	6/27/1999	8/18/2002
	Billy Price	4	3	8/1/2004	7/30/2006
	Kenny Stafford	4	2	9/5/2004	8/14/2005
	Alan Barker	4	2	5/24/2006	8/26/2007
	Casey Williams	4	2	5/27/2007	9/7/2008
30	Geoff Plis	3	2	7/26/1992	6/12/1994
	Ron Holmes	3	1	6/13/1993	9/5/1993
	John Kinsella	3	3	7/9/1995	8/15/1999
	Tim Mayne	3	3	7/26/1998	8/4/2002
	Kyle Lewis	3	2	5/29/2005	7/9/2006
35	Stu Sheppard	2	1	5/15/1987	6/12/1987
	Alton Palmer	2	1	8/29/1987	9/5/1987
	Jimmy Phelps	2	2	6/23/1993	8/28/1994
	Bill Shantel Sr.	2	2	6/23/1996	7/5/1998
	Gus Schmidt Jr.	2	1	8/20/1996	8/25/1996
	Lance Lauffenberger	2	1	7/6/1997	8/3/1997
	Jack Miller	2	2	7/20/1997	7/18/1999
	Tony Buffa Jr.	2	1	5/24/1998	6/21/1998
	Daryl Hagen	2	1	8/4/2002	8/25/2002
	Danny Varin	2	2	7/23/2006	7/22/2007
	Tim Nye	2	2	9/10/2006	7/8/2007
	Chris Mackey	2	1	5/16/2010	7/18/2010
47	Guy Sheldon	1	1	4/26/1992	
	Jeff Kotary	1	1	4/30/1995	
	Greg Doust	1	1	6/4/1995	
	Bob Utter	1	1	8/13/1995	
	Joe Slawiak	1	1	8/27/1995	
	Jason Barney	1	1	4/28/1996	
	Alex Friesen	1	1	9/1/1996	
	Chris Schultz	1	1	8/29/1999	
	Mike Fusco	1	1	9/12/1999	
	Tony Ross	1	1	5/7/2000	
	Paul Kinney	1	1	7/16/2000	
	Jim Spano	1	1	8/24/2000	
	Steve Gray	1	1	8/27/2000	
	Shawn Donath	1	1	7/15/2001	
	Brian Murphy	1	1	9/2/2001	
	John Christian	1	1	5/26/2002	
	Butch Reiter	1	1	8/31/2003	
	Eldon Payne Jr.	1	1	6/27/2004	
	Scott Parliament	1	1	7/25/2004	
	David Towns	1	1	9/2/2007	
	Russ Hefti	1	1	8/24/2008	
	John Scarborough	1	1	5/31/2009	

68 Drivers   344 Events   19 Seasons   5/15/1987 to 9/10/2010

New Yorker Title Event History

Modifieds – Top 5 Feature Finishes

Event #	Date	Laps	Winner	2nd	3rd	4th	5th
21	9/11/2010	100	Bobby Varin	Pat Ward	Alan Johnson	Todd Burley	Billy Decker
20	9/12/2009	200	Steve Paine	Brett Hearn	Bobby Varin	Ronnie Johnson	Pat Ward
19	9/13/2008	200	Bobby Varin	Ronnie Johnson	Mitch Gibbs	Pat Ward	Jimmy Phelps
18	9/16/2007	200	Stewart Friesen	Bobby Varin	Ronnie Johnson	Vic Coffey	A.J. Romano
17	9/19/1993	100	Billy Pauch	Paul Jensen	Donnie Wetmore	Duane Howard	Randy Glenski
16	9/20/1992	50	Dale Planck	Donnie Wetmore	Pete Bicknell	Tom Kinsella	Randy Glenski
15	9/22/1991	50	Billy Pauch	Tom Kinsella	Paul Jensen	Billy Schinkel Jr.	Gordy Button Jr.
14	9/16/1990	50	Billy Pauch	Toby Tobias Jr.	Pete Bicknell	Roger Phelps	Donnie Wetmore
13	9/3/1978	200	Richie Evans	Jerry Cook	Chip Lanz	Ken Canestrari	Joel Thomas
12	8/30/1974	100	Geoff Bodine	Lou Lazzaro	Jerry Cook	Richie Evans	Ed Pieniazek
11	9/2/1973	Overall	Maynard Troyer	Bugs Stevens	Jerry Cook	Bernie Miller	Ed Pieniazek
		200	Bugs Stevens	Maynard Troyer			
		200	Maynard Troyer	Jerry Cook	Bugs Stevens		
10	9/5/1972	Overall	Richie Evans	Lou Lazzaro	Jerry Cook	Fred DeSarro	Ollie Silva
		200	Richie Evans	Ray Hendrick	Jerry Cook	Lou Lazzaro	
		200	Bugs Stevens	Bobby Santos	Richie Evans	Lou Lazzaro	Jerry Cook
9	9/5/1971	Overall	Richie Evans	Fred DeSarro	Jerry Cook	Billy Hensley	Lou Lazzaro
		200	Richie Evans	Fred DeSarro	Lou Lazzaro	Jerry Cook	Bernie Miller
		200	Richie Evans	Fred DeSarro	Jerry Cook		
8	9/6/1970	Overall	Ed Flemke	Robbie Kotary	Dick Fowler	Gene Mangino	Maynard Troyer
		200	Ed Flemke	Fred DeSarro	Dave Lape	Robbie Kotary	Rene Charland
		200	Lou Lazzaro	Ed Flemke	Robbie Kotary	Gerald Compton	Dick Fowler
7	9/1/1969	Overall	Lou Lazzaro	Jimmy Hensley	Bugs Stevens	Jerry Cook	
		200	Lou Lazzaro	Jimmy Hensley	Bugs Stevens	Fred DeSarro	Perk Brown
		200	Lou Lazzaro	Jerry Cook	Jimmy Hensley	Bugs Stevens	Perk Brown
6	9/1/1968	Overall	Lou Lazzaro				
		200	Lou Lazzaro	Ed Flemke	Bernie Miller	Sonney Seamon	Ron Narducci
		200	Lou Lazzaro	Sonney Seamon	Fred Harbach	Ron Narducci	Dick Fowler
5	9/3/1967	Overall	Jean Paul Cabana	Jerry Cook			
		200	Dave Kotary	Ed Flemke	Jean Paul Cabana	Lou Lazzaro	Jerry Cook
		200	Don MacTavish	Bugs Stevens	Bill Wimble	Jerry Cook	Jean Paul Cabana
4	9/11/1966	Overall	Bill Wimble				
		200	Bill Wimble	Ken Shoemaker	Rene Charland	Sonney Seamon	Jerry Cook
		200	Don MacTavish	Bill Wimble	Robbie Kotary	Ernie Gahan	Rene Charland
3	9/5/1965	Overall	Rene Charland	Bill Wimble			
		200	Bill Wimble	Rene Charland	Jerry Cook		
		200	Fred Harbach	Rene Charland	Jerry Humiston	Bill Wimble	Dick Dixon
2	9/6/1964	Overall	Ed Flemke	Rene Charland			
		200	Ed Flemke	Fred Harbach	Fats Caruso	Rene Charland	Lou Lazzaro
		200	Ed Flemke	Robbie Kotary	Rene Charland	Bill Wimble	Lou Lazzaro
1	9/1/1963	400	Lou Lazzaro	Bob Rossell	Ernie Gahan	Bill Wimble	Jean Paul Cabana

New Yorker Support Classes Event History

Sportsman New Yorker Top 5 Feature Finishes

Date	Laps	Winner	2nd	3rd	4th	5th
9/10/2010	30	Matt Janczuk	Billy Trexler Jr.	Chris Mackey	A.J. Filbeck	Claude Hutchings Jr.
9/11/2009	30	Rain				
9/14/2008	50	Brad Alger	Russ Hefti	Jason Rood	Mike Loney	A.J. Filbeck
9/14/2007	50	Brad Alger	Matt Janczuk	Mike Button	Michael Teachout	Greg Doust

Pro Stock New Yorker Top 5 Feature Finishes

Date	Laps	Winner	2nd	3rd	4th	5th
9/10/2010	25	Tom Denton	Bret Belden	Rocky Warner	Glenn Forward	Ed Ostrander
9/11/2009	25	Rain				
9/13/2008	25	Mark Effner	Bret Belden	Chris Mackey	Rob Seavy	Bill Knapp
9/16/2007	25	Louie Jackson	Jim Normoyle	Russ Marsden	Mark Effner	Rob Seavy

New Yorker Support Classes Event History Cont'd.

Pure Stock New Yorker Top 5 Feature Finishes

Date	Laps	Winner	2nd	3rd	4th	5th
9/10/2010	20	Ricky Breed	Chris Carr	Frank Hyatt	Ron Hawker	Rob Thieme
9/11/2009	20	Rain				
9/14/2008	30	Rich Green	Larry Bezner	Ricky Breed	Ron Wadforth	Nathan Peckham
9/14/2007	20	Dave Bruno	Dave Mannise	Russ Marsden	Ron Hawker	Chris Carr
9/19/1993	20	Steve Kotary	Dave Bruno			
9/20/1992	25	Rick Miller	Bill Kisselstein	Ricky Breed	Doug Cliff	Bob Melone
9/16/1990	15	Rick Miller	Norm Guinta	Bill Donovan	Carl Castelletti	Pete Campione

Asphalt Era Hobby/Support Division Champions – 1962-1978

Year	Driver
1962	Norm House (Late Model Hobby)
1963	Lou Smith/Bill Herrig (Overhead)
	Lucky Sutton (Flathead)
	Missing (Powder Puff)
1964	Sonney Seamon (Overhead)
	Lucky Sutton (Flathead)
1965	Buddy Thurston (Hobby)
	Dick Fowler (Figure 8)
1966	Kenny Platt (Hobby)
	Dick Delaney (Figure 8)
1967	Missing (Late Model)
	Missing (Figure 8)
1968	Norm Moyer (Late Model)
	Bob Engler (Charger)
1969	Don VanSlyke (Charger)
	Al Golley (Mini Stock)
1970	Buddy Thurston (Charger)

Year	Driver
1970	Jim Searles (Mini Stock)
1971	Buddy Thurston (Charger)
	Louie Lanza (Mini Stock)
1972	Buddy Thurston (Charger)
	Doug Rundell (Mini Stock)
1973	Chip Lanz (Charger)
	Jim Brown (Pure Stock)
	Hank Searles (Mini Stock)
1974	Chip Lanz (Charger)
	Cullen Hatfield (Pure Stock)
1975	Billy Seamon/Bob Engler (Street Stock)
	Jim Brown (Pure Stock)
1976	SPEEDWAY CLOSED
1977	Billy Seamon (Street Stock)
	Jeff Cobb (Pure Stock)
1978	Gene Kotary (Street Stock)
	Missing (Pure Stock)

Asphalt Era Charger/Street Stock Feature Win List – 1968 -1978

Pos.	Driver	Wins	Winning Seasons	First Win	Last Win
1	Buddy Thurston	22	7	5/4/1969	6/27/1975
2	George Caswell	13	5	9/20/1970	7/4/1975
	Chip Lanz	13	4	8/1/1971	9/6/1974
	Billy Seamon	13	3	5/16/1975	6/25/1978
5	Bob Engler	10	3	6/2/1968	8/27/1978
	Gene Kotary	10	3	8/1/1975	9/3/1978
7	Russ VanSlyke	8	4	6/14/1970	7/29/1973
8	Jake Eastman	6	5	6/1/1969	8/13/1978
9	Dave VanSlyke	5	3	6/8/1969	6/17/1973
	John Coleman	5	4	5/6/1973	7/2/1978
11	Hal Schreppell	4	2	7/7/1968	8/27/1969
	Bill Matzel	4	3	8/3/1969	8/15/1971
	Glen Cooper	4	2	8/9/1970	7/18/1971
14	Paul Pavelka	3	1	5/19/1968	9/8/1968
	Don Budlong	3	3	7/28/1968	6/28/1970
16	Steve Hawk	2	2	8/17/1969	5/31/1970
17	Glenn Forward	1	1	5/5/1968	
	Tom Engler	1	1	6/23/1968	
	Don VanSlyke	1	1	8/4/1968	
	Bob Larry	1	1	8/11/1968	
	Bill Trexler Sr.	1	1	7/19/1970	
	Kenny Burkert	1	1	7/26/1970	
	Lynn Morey	1	1	7/25/1975	

Missing: 1 Event from 1978 (9/10)
Missing: 2 Events from 1970 (5/3, 7/12)
Missing: 3 Events from 1969 (5/26, 8/25, 9/15)

32 Drivers   122 Events   10 Seasons   5/05/1968 to 9/03/1978

Amateur Track Champions – 1979-1982

Year	Track Champion
1979	Gerry Newman
1980	Did Not Compete
1981	Missing
1982	Gerry Newman

Pro Stock/Street Stock Track Champions – 1986-2010

Year	Track Champion	Year	Track Champion
1986	Nick Ryan	1999	Tom Denton
1987	Todd Hoffman	2000	Tom Denton
1989	Tom Sears Jr.	2001	Bret Belden
1990	Bret Belden	2002	Jason Rood
1991	Bret Belden	2003	Jerry Holmes
1992	Craig Pritchard	2004	Roy Fifield
1993	Rick Miller	2005	Jerry Holmes
1994	Wayne Archer	2006	Jerry Holmes
1995	Rick Miller	2007	Jerry Holmes
1996	Willy Decker	2008	Jim Normoyle
1997	Jerry Holmes	2009	Tom Denton
1998	Tom Denton*/Joe Palmer	2010	Tom Denton

*The first four weeks of the 1998 season were run under the New England Region of the NASCAR Racing Series. After a change in track management, NASCAR was dropped and the track was an independent. NASCAR Champions were for the first four races.

Pro Stock/Street Stock Feature Win List – 1985-2010

Pos.	Driver	Wins	Winning Seasons	First Win	Last Win
1	Jerry Holmes	56	11	6/9/1996	8/26/2007
2	Tom Denton	45	12	8/24/1997	9/10/2010
3	Bret Belden	33	14	10/1/1989	8/29/2010
4	Rick Miller	19	3	5/17/1992	9/24/1995
5	Steve Hulsizer	16	3	8/20/1989	9/1/1991
6	Jim Normoyle	15	7	6/23/2002	8/8/2010
7	Paul Carey	13	7	6/11/1989	6/16/1996
8	Joe Palmer	12	4	5/11/1997	7/13/2003
9	Dave Bruno	9	4	5/7/1995	8/11/2002
	Jason Rood	9	5	6/20/1999	6/5/2005
11	Joe Slawiak	8	2	6/20/1993	9/25/1994
	Buddy Hencke	8	2	5/26/2002	4/27/2003
	Shawn Frost	8	3	4/27/2008	6/13/2010
14	Todd Hoffman	7	2	7/15/1986	10/3/1987
	Mike Rolewicz	7	4	7/29/1990	7/10/1994
	Ron Holmes	7	2	5/19/1991	8/2/1992
17	Scott Moyer	6	4	7/16/1989	9/5/1999
	Rick Guernsey	6	2	5/23/1993	8/7/1994
	Wayne Archer	6	5	9/4/1994	8/1/1999
	Gerry Newman	6	5	7/9/1995	6/30/2002
	Roy Fifield	6	1	5/2/2004	8/15/2004
22	Tom Sears Jr.	5	2	6/25/1989	6/28/1992
	Herb DeVaul	5	4	5/26/1991	6/19/1994
	Willy Decker	5	1	6/2/1996	8/20/1996
	John Pietrowicz	5	2	6/17/2001	8/21/2005
26	Bobby Taylor	4	1	5/26/1986	8/31/1986
	Fred Tauss	4	2	10/9/1986	8/29/1987
	Bob Goutermout	4	1	6/3/1990	9/2/1990
	George Kiskiel	4	3	8/8/1993	8/9/1998
	Chad Ray	4	3	8/5/2001	5/13/2007
	Chris Mackey	4	1	5/20/2007	8/12/2007
32	Nick Ryan	3	1	6/15/1986	9/14/1986
	Tom Kinsella	3	1	6/18/1989	7/30/1989
	Bill Shantel Sr.	3	2	8/1/1993	7/17/1994
	Steve Kotary	3	1	4/28/1996	7/28/1996
	Bill Shantel Jr.	3	2	7/19/1998	6/27/1999
	Bill Knapp	3	3	7/6/2003	7/12/2009
	A.J. Digsby	3	3	5/6/2007	6/21/2009
	Mark Effner	3	2	5/25/2008	7/19/2009
	Rocky Warner	3	2	4/19/2009	4/25/2010
41	Tom Cannizzaro	2	2	7/28/1985	8/25/1999
	Bobby Knipe	2	2	7/27/1986	8/21/1988
	Bubba Tanner	2	1	7/22/1987	9/5/1987
	Jim Smith	2	2	9/3/1989	7/15/1990
	Craig Pritchard	2	1	7/21/1991	9/8/1991
	Ricky Breed	2	2	6/28/1992	8/22/1993
	Craig Henry	2	2	8/9/1992	5/22/1994
	Dick Sweet	2	1	6/6/1993	7/18/1993
	John Roese	2	2	6/18/1995	8/18/1996
	John Kiskiel	2	1	5/19/1996	6/23/1996
	Frank Twing	2	1	5/7/2000	7/2/2000
	Mark Hoffman	2	2	8/23/2001	9/1/2002
	Louie Jackson	2	2	9/14/2007	5/11/2008
	Rob Seavy	2	2	8/17/2008	4/26/2009
55	Scott Noel	1	1	6/2/1985	
	Dan DeLine	1	1	5/9/1986	
	Dave Werber	1	1	7/6/1986	
	Ed Kuck	1	1	8/3/1986	
	Kevin Blacken	1	1	8/13/1986	
	Tom Cohick	1	1	6/14/1992	
	John Kinsella	1	1	7/5/1992	
	Jeff Kotary	1	1	8/30/1992	
	Billy Abold Jr.	1	1	5/1/1994	
	Jim Becker	1	1	8/13/1995	
	Scott Ubner	1	1	8/20/1995	
	Don Newell Jr.	1	1	5/25/1997	
	Dave Moyer	1	1	7/15/2001	
	Denny Smith	1	1	6/23/2002	
	Dave Schulz	1	1	9/20/2002	
	Tom Kuck	1	1	9/14/2003	
	Bob Mills	1	1	7/11/2004	
	Eric Vanderhoof	1	1	5/15/2005	
	Robert Langevin	1	1	6/4/2006	
	Danny Ody	1	1	9/7/2008	
	Jeff Pastorella	1	1	7/5/2009	
	Glenn Forward	1	1	8/1/2010	

76 Drivers   422 Events   26 Seasons   6/02/1985 to 9/10/2010

Pure Stock Track Champions – 1987-2010

Year	Track Champion	Year	Track Champion	Year	Track Champion
1987	Steve Lockwood	1996	Dave Mannise	2004	Russ Marsden
1989	Mike Rolewicz	1997	Dave Mannise	2005	Russ Marsden
1990	Dave Mannise	1998	Dave Mannise	2006	Russ Marsden
1991	Jerry Sehn	1999	Dave Mannise	2007	Russ Marsden
1992	Dave Mannise	2000	Dave Mannise	2008	Chris Carr
1993	Steve Kotary	2001	Jeff Pastorella	2009	Ron Hawker
1994	Dave Mannise	2002	Dave Mannise	2010	Chris Carr

Pure Stock Feature Win List – 1988-2010

Pos.	Driver	Wins	Winning Seasons	First Win	Last Win
1	Dave Mannise	81	14	5/27/1990	9/7/2003
2	Russ Marsden	55	8	8/31/2003	9/10/2010
3	Jeff Pastorella	21	4	8/24/1997	9/9/2001
4	Ron Hawker	20	6	8/21/2005	7/11/2010
5	Jeff Thorp	16	4	6/2/1996	7/7/2002
6	Chuck Cushman Jr.	13	6	8/7/1994	7/31/2005
	Chris Carr	13	4	6/10/2007	8/1/2010
8	Rick Miller	12	2	7/23/1989	9/16/1990
9	Steve Kotary	11	1	5/16/1993	9/19/1993
10	Jim Thomas	9	7	6/25/1989	6/8/2003
	Norm Guinta	9	3	7/29/1990	7/26/1992
12	Chris Cunningham	8	4	8/1/2004	8/29/2010
13	Stan Clark	7	2	7/4/1993	9/14/1997
	Dave Pope	7	3	8/18/2002	5/16/2004
15	Mike Rolewicz	6	1	7/2/1989	10/1/1989
	Dave Bruno	6	2	6/12/1994	9/14/2007
17	Pete Campione	5	1	4/14/1991	8/11/1991
	Frank Hyatt	5	2	4/26/2009	6/13/2010
19	Wayne Archer	4	1	6/14/1992	9/13/1992
	Butch Reiter	4	3	7/18/1993	6/25/1995
	Steve Way	4	1	5/21/1995	9/10/1995
	Ed Kotary	4	1	6/11/1995	8/6/1995
23	Herb DeVaul	3	2	7/16/1989	4/29/1990
	Tom Cohick	3	1	5/5/1991	6/30/1991
	Todd Storace	3	1	5/19/1996	6/30/1996
	Chad Ray	3	2	6/20/1999	8/13/2000
	Herm Staats	3	2	6/27/1999	6/29/2003
	Art Newman Jr.	3	2	6/23/2002	8/18/2003
	Tim Janczuk	3	2	8/5/2007	8/24/2008
30	Ron Holmes	2	1	7/30/1989	9/3/1989
	Jerry Sehn	2	1	6/2/1991	6/9/1991
	Gene Mosher	2	1	5/22/1994	6/19/1994
	John Pietrowicz	2	2	7/2/1995	9/17/2000
	Rick Dote	2	2	7/14/1996	6/15/1997
	Lou Levea	2	2	8/25/1996	9/13/1998
	Waylan Wilczek	2	2	9/16/2001	9/2/2007
	Brandon Warner	2	1	5/14/2006	7/23/2006
	Curt Prevo	2	2	8/20/2006	7/1/2007
	Matt Ball	2	1	5/27/2007	6/24/2007
	Phil Norman	2	2	8/31/2008	7/19/2009
	Ricky Breed	2	1	8/8/2010	9/10/2010
42	Dan Rifenburgh	1	1	8/21/1988	
	Shawn Muldoon	1	1	6/18/1989	
	Dan Murphy	1	1	4/22/1990	
	Jerry Holmes	1	1	6/3/1990	
	Joe Palmer	1	1	7/29/1990	
	Jerry Salmonsen	1	1	5/19/1991	
	Joe Slawiak	1	1	7/7/1991	
	Scott Blumberg	1	1	8/16/1992	
	Mark Wallace	1	1	9/24/1995	
	Bob Bird	1	1	8/25/1996	
	Kelly Pope	1	1	6/29/1997	
	Jason Rood	1	1	8/3/1997	
	Doug Grimaldi	1	1	9/12/1999	
	Mark Effner	1	1	8/27/2000	
	George Schulze	1	1	8/5/2001	
	Ricky Trexler	1	1	5/18/2003	
	Dan Hoffman Sr.	1	1	6/19/2005	
	Ron Marsden	1	1	8/14/2005	
	Keith Stevenson	1	1	8/26/2007	
	Rich Green	1	1	9/14/2008	

61 Drivers   385 Events   23 Seasons   8/21/88 to 9/10/2010

All-Time Sprint Car Feature Winners – 1986-2010

Pos.	Driver	Wins	Seasons	First Win	Last Win
1	Gordy Button Jr.	4	3	5/25/1987	7/4/1999
	Dan Kaszubinski	4	4	9/1/2002	7/5/2009
	Chuck Hebing	4	3	4/30/2006	9/5/2010
4	Lance Yonge	3	3	8/2/1992	9/4/2005
	Justin Barger	3	2	7/6/2003	5/27/2007
	Steve Porier	3	3	5/28/2006	8/30/2008
	Jason Barney	3	2	5/25/2008	9/6/2009
	Jessica Zemken	3	2	5/24/2009	7/4/2010
9	Mike VanDusen	2	2	10/3/1987	8/31/1997
	Jeff Thomas	2	2	8/19/1990	5/24/1998
	Bobby Parrow	2	2	5/29/1994	9/1/1996
	Robbie Hart	2	2	7/9/1989	7/7/1996
	Doug Emery	2	2	9/17/2000	10/9/2002
	Jeff VanDusen	2	2	5/30/2004	9/3/2006
15	Dave Kelly	1	1	5/26/1986	
	Bill Peri	1	1	7/27/1986	
	George Sifo	1	1	6/11/1989	
	Mal Lane	1	1	8/20/1989	
	Bob Podolak	1	1	7/8/1990	
	Mike Woodring	1	1	5/26/1996	
	George Ely	1	1	5/25/1997	
	Lee Sanders	1	1	7/6/1997	
	Rich Wood	1	1	9/5/1999	
	George Suprick	1	1	5/28/2000	
	Mike Lauterborn	1	1	9/3/2000	
	Steve Dow	1	1	9/2/2001	
	Mike Lutz	1	1	5/25/2003	
	Mike Stelter	1	1	7/3/2005	
	Steve Lapine	1	1	7/23/2006	
	Matt Demitresek	1	1	7/22/2007	
	Dylan Swiernik	1	1	6/22/2008	
	Jamie Christian	1	1	5/16/2010	
	Matt Tanner	1	1	6/24/2010	
	Fred Rahmer	1	1	7/13/2010	

34 Drivers   59 Events   21 Seasons   5/26/86 to 9/05/2010

IMCA Modified Track Champions – 1998-2007

Year	Track Champion
1998	George Cantanzano
2004	George Cantanzano
2005	George Cantanzano
2006	Jim Roberts
2007	Jim Roberts

All-Time IMCA Modified Feature Winners – 1998-2008

Pos.	Driver	Wins	Winning Seasons	First Win	Last Win
1	George Cantanzano	19	5	6/8/2003	5/6/2007
2	Dale Caswell	8	4	7/25/2004	9/14/2008
	Jim Roberts	8	2	6/11/2006	9/14/2007
4	Sean Lias	7	4	7/26/1998	4/29/2007
5	Mike Smith	4	1	6/25/2006	8/20/2006
6	Kevin Buff	3	2	8/15/2004	5/14/2006
	Kevan Cook	3	2	8/13/2006	8/19/2007
	Aaron Jacobs	3	1	7/22/2007	8/26/2007
9	Cory Fachini	2	1	8/16/1998	8/23/1998
	Bill Anderson	2	1	5/1/2005	5/8/2005
11	Larry Bezner	1	1	8/2/1998	
	Randy Hall	1	1	8/9/1998	
	Don Alvord	1	1	8/30/1998	
	Rob Keller Jr.	1	1	7/16/2006	
	Chris Thurston	1	1	9/3/2006	

15 Drivers   64 Events   28 Seasons   7/26/1998 to 9/14/2008

Tobias Slingshot Track Champions – 2000-2001

Year	Track Champion
2000	Jackie Botindari (Senior)
	A.J. Kingsley (Junior)
2001	Denny Tilison

Tobias Slingshot Feature Wins – 2000-2001

Pos.	Driver	Wins	Winning Seasons	First Win	Last Win
1	J.J. Courcy	4	2	7/2/2000	6/10/2001
2	David Nimey	3	1	6/4/2000	8/27/2000
	Michael Teachout	3	1	7/1/2001	9/2/2001
4	Randy Marsh	2	1	6/17/2001	8/5/2001
	Dave Barrrows	2	1	7/24/2001	7/15/2001
	Denny Tilison	2	1	7/8/2001	8/19/2001
	Joe DeJohn	2	1	7/22/2001	8/26/2001
8	Todd Land	1	1	7/16/2000	
	Ryan Phelps	1	1	9/3/2000	
	A.J. Digsby	1	1	9/17/2000	
	Brian Thomas	1	1	5/20/2001	
	Mike Waterman	1	1	9/9/2001	

12 Drivers   23 Events   2 Seasons   6/04/2000 to 9/09/2001

Junior Slingshot Feature Wins – 2000

Pos.	Driver	Wins	First Win	Last Win
1	A.J. Kingsley	3	7/23/2000	8/27/2000
2	Larry Wight	2	7/16/2000	8/20/2000
3	Bryan Howland	1	6/4/2000	
	Weylyn Barrows	1	7/2/2000	
	Kyle Reuter	1	9/3/2000	

> 5 Drivers   8 Events 6/04/2000 to 9/03/2000

4-Cylinder Super Stock Track Champions – 2004-2005

Year	Track Champion
2004	Chuck Powelczyk
2005	Chuck Powelczyk

4-Cylinder Super Stock Feature Wins – 2004-2006

Pos.	Driver	Wins	Winning Seasons	First Win	Last Win
1	Chuck Powelczyk	10	2	6/6/2004	7/24/2005
2	Ken Carson	6	2	5/15/2005	4/30/2006
3	Jim Money	5	2	5/30/2004	8/21/2005
4	Joey Delacruz	3	1	5/8/2005	7/31/2005
5	Jack Hill	2	1	5/2/2004	5/16/2004
	Rich Murtaugh	2	1	7/10/2005	8/7/2005
7	Doug Farnsworth	1	1	9/4/2005	

> 7 Drivers   29 Events 3 Seasons 5/02/2004 to 4/30/2006

All-Time Super Late Model Win List – 2000-2010

Pos.	Driver	Wins	Winning Seasons	First Win	Last Win
1	Bob Close	1	1	8/17/2000	
	Ray Cook	1	1	7/30/2009	
	Scott Bloomquist	1	1	7/29/2010	

> 3 Drivers   3 Events 3 Seasons 8/17/2000 to 7/29/2010

Weekly Race Results – 1961-2010

1961

Track Champion: Rene Charland (NASCAR Sportsman)

NASCAR Sportsman Records – Weekly Results

Date	Laps	Winner	2nd	3rd	4th
6-Aug		Postponed			
13-Aug		Postponed			
20-Aug		Postponed			
27-Aug		Postponed			
3-Sep		Postponed			
10-Sep	30	Bill Rafter	Rene Charland	Lou Lazzaro	
17-Sep	30	Bill Wimble	Jeep Herbert	Jack Sleicher	
24-Sep	50	Ed Ortiz	Ernie Gahan	Pete Corey	Jeep Herbert

Total NASCAR Sportsman Wins

Driver	Wins
Bill Rafter	1
Bill Wimble	1
Ed Ortiz	1
3 Drivers	3 Events

NASCAR Sportsman Points

Pos.	Driver	Points
1	Rene Charland	134
2	Jack Sleicher	132
3	Lou Lazzaro	124
4	Bill Wimble	112
5	Chuck Mahoney	98

1962

Track Champions: Rene Charland (NASCAR Sportsman)
Norm House (Late Model Hobby)

NASCAR Sportsman Records – Weekly Results

Date	Laps	Winner	2nd	3rd	4th	5th
20-May	25	Ed Ortiz	Lou Lazzaro	Jeep Herbert	Pete Corey	
27-May	30	Rene Charland	Jeep Herbert	Ed Ortiz		
3-Jun	30	Rene Charland	Jeep Herbert	Ed Ortiz		
10-Jun	30	Rain				
17-Jun	35	Ed Ortiz	Ken Meahl	Bill Wimble	Rene Charland	
24-Jun	30	Tom Kotary	Ken Meahl	Rene Charland	Bill Wimble	
1-Jul	30	Tom Kotary	Cliff Kotary	Jeep Herbert	Ed Ortiz	
8-Jul	30	Ed Ortiz	Ken Meahl	Robbie Kotary		
15-Jul	30	Bill Wimble	Cam Gagliardi	Ed Ortiz		
22-Jul	25	Rene Charland	Bill Wimble	Lou Lazzaro		
29-Jul	25	Tom Kotary	Rene Charland	Bill Wimble	Al DeAngelo	
5-Aug	25	Robbie Kotary	Rene Charland	Ed Ortiz		
12-Aug	25	Ken Meahl	Jim Luke	Bill Wimble		
19-Aug	25	Cam Gagliardi	Rene Charland	Bill Wimble	Cliff Kotary	
26-Aug	25	Rene Charland	Lou Lazzaro	Jim Luke		
2-Sep	100	Ed Ortiz	Rene Charland	Lou Lazzaro	Jack Hart	Tom Kotary
9-Sep	150	Lou Lazzaro	Cam Gagliardi	Ed Ortiz	Jim Luke	Bill Wimble

Total NASCAR Sportsman Wins

Driver	Wins
Rene Charland	4
Ed Ortiz	4
Tom Kotary	3
Bill Wimble	1
Robbie Kotary	1
Ken Meahl	1
Cam Gagliardi	1
Lou Lazzaro	1
8 Drivers	16 Events

NASCAR Sportsman Points

Pos.	Driver	Points
1	Rene Charland	754
2	Ed Ortiz	694
3	Bill Wimble	662
4	Lou Lazzaro	614
5	Ken Meahl	528
6	Tom Kotary	
7	Jim Luke	
8	Cliff Kotary	
9	Rolly Staring	
10	Robbie Kotary	

1963

Track Champions: Lou Lazzaro (NASCAR Sportsman)
Lou Smith/Bill Herrig (Late Model Overhead)
William "Lucky" Sutton (Hobby Division)

NASCAR Sportsman Records – Weekly Results

Date	Laps	Winner	2nd	3rd	4th	5th
28-Apr	30	Tom Kotary	Robbie Kotary	Jim Luke	Rene Charland	Bill Wimble
5-May	25	Jim Luke	Ken Meahl	Bobby Cain	Rene Charland	Lou Lazzaro
12-May	25	Lou Lazzaro	Rene Charland	Jim Luke		
19-May	25	Rene Charland	Lou Lazzaro	Tom Kotary	Jim Luke	Jeep Herbert
26-May	30	Rene Charland	Cam Gagliardi	Ed Ortiz		
2-Jun	30	Rene Charland	Bill Wimble	Jerry Cook	Bob Zeigler	Ken Meahl
9-Jun	25	Ed Flemke	Bill Wimble	Lou Lazzaro	Lee Millington	Bob Zeigler
16-Jun	25	Ernie Gahan	Bob Zeigler	Jim Luke		
23-Jun	25	Rene Charland	Cam Gagliardi	Ken Meahl	Bill Wimble	
30-Jun	60	Ken Meahl	Cam Gagliardi	Lou Lazzaro	Ed Ortiz	Bill Wimble
7-Jul	25	Bill Wimble	Ed Ortiz	Jim Luke	Bob Zeigler	Rene Charland
14-Jul	25	Rene Charland	Gene Bergin	Ken Meahl		
21-Jul	25	Rain				
28-Jul	100	Ed Flemke	Rene Charland	Denny Zimmerman	Jean Paul Cabana	Guy Chartrand
4-Aug	25	Rain Delayed to 8/11				
11-Aug	25	Jerry Cook	Bill Wimble	Ken Meahl	Ernie Gahan	Bob Zeigler
	25	Bill Wimble	Rene Charland	Ed Ortiz	Bill Torrisi	Lou Lazzaro
25-Aug	30	Jim Luke	Ed Ortiz	Rene Charland	Bill Wimble	Bob Zeigler
1-Sep	400	Lou Lazzaro	Bob Rossell	Ernie Gahan	Bill Wimble	Jean Paul Cabana
8-Sep	25	Lou Lazzaro	Jerry Humiston	Rene Charland	Jerry Cook	Lou Smith
15-Sep	25	Bill Torrisi	Jim Luke	Lou Lazzaro	Jerry Humiston	Bob Zeigler
22-Sep	25	Ed Flemke	Gene Bergin	Jerry Humiston	Lou Smith	Jim Luke

Total NASCAR Sportsman Wins

Driver	Wins
Rene Charland	5
Lou Lazzaro	3
Ed Flemke	3
Bill Wimble	2
Jim Luke	2
Tom Kotary	1
Ernie Gahan	1
Ken Meahl	1
Jerry Cook	1
Bill Torrisi	1
10 Drivers	20 Events

NASCAR Sportsman Points

Pos.	Driver	Points
1	Lou Lazzaro	832
2	Rene Charland	794
3	Bill Wimble	778
4	Jim Luke	758
5	Bob Zeigler	690

1964

Track Champions: Rene Charland (NASCAR Sportsman)
Sonney Seamon (Overhead Division)
William Sutton (Hobby Flathead Division)

NASCAR Sportsman Records – Weekly Results

Date	Laps	Winner	2nd	3rd	4th	5th
26-Apr	30	Rene Charland	Jerry Cook	Jerry Humiston	Denny Zimmerman	Bill Wimble
3-May	30	Ed Flemke	Rene Charland	Ed Ortiz	Jerry Humiston	Jim Luke
10-May	30	Ernie Gahan	Ed Flemke	Bill Wimble	Rene Charland	Lou Lazzaro
17-May	30	Ed Flemke	Rene Charland	Jerry Humiston	Bill Wimble	Bob Zeigler
24-May	30	Rain Delayed To 5/31				
31-May	30	Bob Zeigler	Rene Charland	Lou Smith	Ed Ortiz	Lou Lazzaro
	30	Lou Smith	Ed Ortiz	Jim Luke	Lou Lazzaro	Rene Charland
7-Jun	100	Ed Flemke	Gene Bergin	Fred Harbach	Fats Caruso	Bill Slater
14-Jun	30	Ed Flemke	Rene Charland	Lou Lazzaro	Jerry Cook	Ed Ortiz
21-Jun	30	Jerry Humiston	Bob Zeigler	Jim Luke	Jerry Cook	Ed Flemke Sr.
28-Jun	30	Lou Smith	Bill Wimble	Jerry Cook	Ed Ortiz	Lou Lazzaro
5-Jul	30	Ed Flemke	Rene Charland	Tom Kotary	Elton Hill	Ed Ortiz
12-Jul	30	Ed Flemke	Rene Charland	Ernie Gahan	Jerry Cook	Ed Ortiz
19-Jul	30	Lou Lazzaro	Rene Charland	Jerry Humiston	Ed Flemke	Jerry Cook
26-Jul	30	Bill Wimble	Jim Luke	Fats Caruso	Jerry Cook	Ed Flemke
2-Aug	150	Rene Charland	Gene Bergin	Fred Harbach	Bill Slater	Dan Galullo
9-Aug	30	Lou Smith	Gene Bergin	Rene Charland	Jerry Humiston	Bob Zeigler
16-Aug	30	Rene Charland	Bill Wimble	Tom Bourget	Tom Kotary	Jerry Cook
23-Aug	30	OFF				
30-Aug	30	Ken Meahl	Jerry Humiston	Bob Zeigler	Ed Flemke	Lou Lazzaro
6-Sep	200	Ed Flemke	Fred Harbach	Fats Caruso	Rene Charland	Lou Lazzaro
	200	Ed Flemke	Robbie Kotary	Rene Charland	Bill Wimble	Lou Lazzaro
13-Sep	30	Ed Flemke	Lou Lazzaro	Rene Charland	Jerry Cook	Ken Meahl
20-Sep	30	Ed Flemke	Bob Zeigler	Tom Kotary	Rene Charland	Jerry Cook
27-Sep	30	Rain				
4-Oct	30	Ed Flemke	Elton Hill	Rene Charland	Jerry Cook	Tom Kotary

Total NASCAR Sportsman Wins

Driver	Wins
Ed Flemke	11
Lou Smith	3
Rene Charland	3
Ernie Gahan	1
Bob Zeigler	1
Jerry Humiston	1
Lou Lazzaro	1
Bill Wimble	1
Ken Meahl	1
9 Drivers	23 Events

NASCAR Sportsman Points

Pos.	Driver	Points
1	Rene Charland	920
2	Jerry Cook	866
3	Ed Flemke Sr.	786
4	Jerry Humiston	754
5	Jim Luke	754
6	Bill Wimble	618
7	Lou Lazzaro	614
8	Lou Smith	610
9	Tom Kotary	600
10	Bob Zeigler	578

1965

Track Champions: Pete Corey (NASCAR Modified)
Tom Kotary (NASCAR Sportsman)
Frank Mathalia (Hobby)
Dick Fowler (Figure 8)

NASCAR Modified/Sportsman Records – Weekly Results

Date	Laps	Winner	2nd	3rd	4th	5th
25-Apr	30	Lou Smith	Ken Meahl	Jerry Cook	Elton Hill	Rene Charland
2-May	30	Elton Hill	Ed Flemke	Fats Caruso		
9-May	30	Rene Charland	Frank Mathalia	Ken Meahl	Tom Kotary	Elton Hill
16-May	30	Rain				
23-May	30	Jerry Cook	Tom Kotary	Elton Hill		
30-May	30	Rene Charland	Jerry Cook	Ed Flemke		
6-Jun	100	Ed Flemke	Rene Charland	Elton Hill		
13-Jun	30	Ed Flemke	Don Moon	Bill Harmon		
20-Jun	30	Bob Zeigler	Ed Flemke	Rene Charland		
27-Jun	30	Jerry Cook	Ed Flemke	Don Moon		
4-Jul	30	Dave Kotary	Sonney Seamon	Bernie Miller		
11-Jul	30	Tom Kotary	Richie Evans	Dave Kotary		
18-Jul	30	Jerry Cook	Tom Kotary	Rene Charland	Fran Kitchen	Dick Fowler
25-Jul	30	Jerry Cook	Tom Kotary	Dave Kotary		
1-Aug	150	Jerry Cook	Dave Kotary	Tom Kotary		
8-Aug	30	Rain				
15-Aug	30	Rene Charland	Tom Kotary	Dave Kotary	Al Tomasi	Bill Havener
22-Aug	30	OFF				
29-Aug	30	Jerry Cook	Dave Kotary	Sonney Seamon		
5-Sep	200	Bill Wimble	Rene Charland	Jerry Cook		
5-Sep	200	Fred Harbach	Rene Charland	Jerry Humiston	Bill Wimble	Dick Dixon
12-Sep	30	Rene Charland	Tom Kotary	Jerry Cook		
19-Sep	30	Richie Evans	Sonney Seamon	Bernie Miller		

Total NASCAR Sportsman Wins

Driver	Wins
Jerry Cook	6
Rene Charland	4
Ed Flemke	2
Lou Smith	1
Elton Hill	1
Bob Zeigler	1
Dave Kotary	1
Tom Kotary	1
Bill Wimble	1
Fred Harbach	1
Richie Evans	1
11 Drivers	20 Events

NASCAR Sportsman Points

Pos.	Driver	Points
1	Tom Kotary	850
2	Jerry Cook	714
3	Rene Charland	712
4	Bernie Miller	610
5	Al Tomasi	564
6	Dick Fowler	492
7	Dave Kotary	470
8	Richie Evans	438
9	Bill Havener	412
10	Sonney Seamon	330

NASCAR Modified Points

Pos.	Driver	Points
1	Pete Corey	98
2	Charlie Trombley	50
3	Gil Hearne	48

1966

Track Champions: Ed Flemke (NASCAR Modified)
Bill Wimble (NASCAR Sportsman)
Kenny Platt (Hobby)
Dick Delaney (Figure 8)

NASCAR Modified/Sportsman Records – Weekly Results

Date	Laps	Winner	2nd	3rd	4th	5th
24-Apr	30	Rain				
1-May	30	Bill Wimble	Ernie Gahan	Frank Mathalia	Ed Flemke	Lou Toro
8-May	30	Gene Bergin	Lou Toro	Jerry Cook	Dave Kotary	Don MacTavish
15-May	30	Ed Flemke	Bill Wimble	Richie Evans	Frank Mathalia	Ernie Gahan
22-May	30	Jerry Cook	Lou Toro	Bill Wimble	Dave Kotary	Richie Evans
29-May	30	Ken Shoemaker	Ed Flemke	Gaston Desmarais	Frank Mathalia	Jerry Cook
5-Jun	100	Don MacTavish	Bill Wimble	Ed Flemke	Jerry Cook	Frank Mathalia
12-Jun	30	Ken Shoemaker	Richie Evans	Pete Hamilton	Ed Flemke	Bill Wimble
19-Jun	30	Jerry Cook	Ed Flemke	Irv Taylor	Ernie Gahan	Ken Shoemaker
26-Jun	30	Ernie Gahan	Ken Shoemaker	Rene Charland	Frank Mathalia	Pete Hamilton
3-Jul	100	Rene Charland	Ed Flemke	Frank Mathalia	Jerry Cook	Bill Wimble
10-Jul	30	Elton Hill	Ed Flemke	Bill Wimble	Rene Charland	Jerry Cook
17-Jul	30	Lou Lazzaro	Jerry Cook	Gaston Desmarais	Ed Flemke	Ernie Gahan
24-Jul	30	Ernie Gahan	Bill Wimble	Ed Flemke	Dave Kotary	Bernie Miller
31-Jul	30	Ed Flemke	Jerry Cook	Bill Wimble	Ken Shoemaker	Frank Mathalia
7-Aug	100	Bill Wimble	Rene Charland	Elton Hill	Jerry Cook	Ed Flemke
14-Aug	30	Rain				
21-Aug	30	OFF				
28-Aug	30	Bill Wimble	Rene Charland	Ed Flemke	Bernie Miller	Lou Lazzaro
4-Sep	200	Rain				
Twin 200s	200					
11-Sep	200	Bill Wimble	Ken Shoemaker	Rene Charland	Sonney Seamon	Jerry Cook
	200	Don MacTavish	Robbie Kotary	Bill Wimble	Ernie Gahan	Rene Charland
18-Sep	30	Ken Shoemaker	Lou Lazzaro	Jerry Cook	Sonney Seamon	Bill Wimble

Total NASCAR Sportsman Wins

Driver	Wins
Bill Wimble	4
Ken Shoemaker	3
Jerry Cook	2
Ernie Gahan	2
Ed Flemke	2
Don MacTavish	2
Gene Bergin	1
Rene Charland	1
Elton Hill	1
Lou Lazzaro	1
10 Drivers	19 Events

NASCAR Sportsman Points

Pos.	Driver	Points
1	Bill Wimble	872
2	Jerry Cook	846
3	Gaston Desmarais	766

NASCAR Modified Points

Pos.	Driver	Points
1	Ed Flemke	854
2	Frank Mathalia	806
3	Andy Romano	766

1967

Track Champions: Bill Wimble (NASCAR Modified)
Bernie Miller (NASCAR Sportsman)
Missing (Late Model)
Missing (Figure 8)

NASCAR Modified/Sportsman Records – Weekly Results

Date	Laps	Winner	2nd	3rd	4th	5th
30-Apr	30	Fran Kitchen	Ken Shoemaker	Bernie Miller	Ray Sitterly	Frank Mathalia
7-May	30	Snow				
14-May	30	Rain Delayed to 5/21				
21-May	30	Lou Lazzaro	Sonney Seamon	Kenny Shoemaker	Dave Lape	Robbie Kotary
	30	Rene Charland	Pete Corey	Jerry Cook	Ken Shoemaker	Don Wayman
28-May	30	Bill Wimble	Bruce Dostal	Dick Clark	Dave Lape	Rene Charland
4-Jun	100	Ed Flemke	Robby Kotary	Ken Shoemaker	Rene Charland	Bill Wimble
11-Jun	30	Ed Flemke	Ernie Gahan	Elton Hill	Bernie Miller	Dick Clark
18-Jun	30	Sonney Seamon	Ed Flemke	Lou Lazzaro	Ken Shoemaker	Andy Romano
25-Jun	30	George Pendergast	Richie Evans	Pete Corey	Bill Harmon	Rene Charland
2-Jul	100	Rain				
9-Jul	100	Ed Flemke	Bill Wimble	Rene Charland	Don MacTavish	Ernie Gahan
16-Jul	30	Fran Kitchen	Don Wayman	Dick Clark	Andy Romano	Jerry Cook
23-Jul	30	Rain				
30-Jul	30	Bill Wimble	Dave Lape	Richie Evans	Dick Clark	Rene Charland
6-Aug	100	Ed Flemke	Fred Harbach	Lou Lazzaro	Don MacTavish	Bill Wimble
13-Aug	30	Ernie Gahan	Lou Lazzaro	Jerry Cook	Bernie Miller	Rene Charland
20-Aug	OFF					
27-Aug	30	Rain				
3-Sep	200	Dave Kotary	Ed Flemke	Jean Paul Cabana	Lou Lazzaro	Jerry Cook
Twin 200s	200	Don MacTavish	Bugs Stevens	Bill Wimble	Jerry Cook	Jean Paul Cabana
10-Sep	30	Sonney Seamon	Dick Fowler	Bernie Miller	Jerry Cook	Dave Kotary
23-Sep	150	Don MacTavish	Jerry Cook	Bill Wimble	Sonney Seamon	Ken Shoemaker

Total NASCAR Modified Points

Driver	Wins
Ed Flemke	4
Fran Kitchen	2
Bill Wimble	2
Sonney Seamon	2
Don MacTavish	2
Lou Lazzaro	1
Rene Charland	1
George Pendergast	1
Ernie Gahan	1
Dave Kotary	1
10 Drivers	17 Events

NASCAR Sportsman Points

Pos.	Driver	Points
1	Bill Wimble	734
2	Lou Lazzaro	658
3	Andy Romano	596

NASCAR

Pos.	Driver	Points
1	Bernie Miller	764
2	Sonney Seamon	712
3	Jerry Cook	696

1968

Track Champions: Sonney Seamon (NASCAR Modified)
Bernie Miller (NASCAR Late Model)
Bob Engler (NASCAR Charger)

NASCAR Modified Records – Weekly Results

Date	Laps	Winner	2nd	3rd	4th	5th
5-May	30	Don Wayman	Dick Clark	Robbie Kotary	Jerry Cook	Sonney Seamon
12-May	30	Rain				
19-May	30	Rain Delayed to 5/26				
26-May	30	Lou Lazzaro	Sonney Seamon	Ken Platt	Dick Fowler	Dick Clark
	30	Richie Evans	Sonney Seamon	Andy Romano	Jerry Cook	Robbie Kotary
2-Jun	30	Lou Lazzaro	Paul Hamel	Jerry Cook	Dick Clark	Richie Evans
9-Jun	30	Bernie Miller	Jerry Cook	Richie Evans	Lou Lazzaro	Ed Flemke
16-Jun	30	Rain				
23-Jun	30	Dave Kotary	Bill Henry	Ken Shoemaker	Dave Gaul	Dick Clark
30-Jun	100	Andy Romano	Jerry Cook	Richie Evans	Dave Kotary	Ron Narducci
7-Jul	30	Dick Fowler	Robbie Kotary	Sonney Seamon	Dick Clark	Bernie Miller
14-Jul	30	Rene Charland	Lou Lazzaro	Sonney Seamon	Riche Evans	Ray Sitterly
21-Jul	30	Ken Platt	Al Tomasi	Lou Lazzaro	Maynard Forrette	Dick Clark
28-Jul	30	Richie Evans	Dave Lape	Sonney Seamon	Robbie Kotary	Rene Charland
4-Aug	30	Pete Corey	Jerry Cook	Bernie Miller	Sonney Seamon	Lou Lazzaro
11-Aug	50	Dave Kotary	Lou Lazzaro	Ed Pieniazek	Ron Narducci	Richie Evans
18-Aug	OFF					
25-Aug	30	Jerry Cook	Lou Lazzaro	Sonney Seamon	Bernie Miller	Dave Kotary
1-Sep	200	Lou Lazzaro	Ed Flemke	Bernie Miller	Sonney Seamon	Ron Narducci
Twin 200s	200	Lou Lazzaro	Sonney Seamon	Fred Harbach	Ron Narducci	Dick Fowler

Total NASCAR Modified Wins

Driver	Wins
Lou Lazzaro	4
Richie Evans	2
Dave Kotary	2
Don Wayman	1
Bernie Miller	1
Andy Romano	1
Dick Fowler	1
Rene Charland	1
Ken Platt	1
Pete Corey	1
Jerry Cook	1
11 Drivers	16 Events

NASCAR Modified Points

Pos.	Driver	Points
1	Sonney Seamon	680
2	Lou Lazzaro	676
3	Jerry Cook	634
4	Bernie Miller	634
5	Dick Clark	578

1969

Track Champions: Jerry Cook (NASCAR Modified)
Don VanSlyke (NASCAR Charger)
Al Golley (Mini Stock)

NASCAR Modified Records – Weekly Results

Date	Laps	Winner	2nd	3rd	4th	5th
4-May	30	Jerry Cook	Richie Evans	Lou Lazzaro	Dave Lape	Sonney Seamon
11-May	30	Snow				
18-May	30	Rain Delayed to 5/25				
25-May	30	Rain				
1-Jun	30	Lou Lazzaro	Jerry Cook	Bugs Stevens	Gaston Desmarais	Ed Pieniazek
	30	Bernie Miller	Ray Sitterly	Andy Romano	Sonney Seamon	Dick Fowler
8-Jun	30	Lou Lazzaro	Jerry Cook	Bugs Stevens	Ed Pieniazek	Sonney Seamon
15-Jun	30	Rain				
22-Jun	30	Jerry Cook	Dick Clark	Ken Platt	Dave Lape	Dick Fowler
29-Jun	100	Lou Lazzaro	Jerry Cook	Phil Spiak	Bernie Miller	Bob Santos
6-Jul	30	Delayed to 7/13, Power Issue				
13-Jul	30	Lou Lazzaro	Dave Lape	Jerry Cook	Dave Kotary	Bernie Miller
	30	Sonney Seamon	Dave Lape	Bob Santos	Jerry Cook	Dave Kotary
20-Jul	30	Jerry Cook	Sonney Seamon	Bob Santos	Dick Fowler	Andy Romano
27-Jul	30	Rain				
3-Aug	100	Lou Lazzaro	Bugs Stevens	Dick Clark	Jerry Cook	Ron Narducci
10-Aug	30	Rain				
17-Aug	30	Lou Lazzaro	Bernie Miller	Dick Fowler	Ken Platt	Jerry Cook
24-Aug	30	Jerry Pennock Sr.	Dave Lape	Dick Clark	Bernie Miller	Andy Romano
31-Aug	200	Lou Lazzaro	Jimmy Hensley	Bugs Stevens	Fred DeSarro	Perk Brown
	200	Lou Lazzaro	Jerry Cook	Jimmy Hensley	Bugs Stevens	Perk Brown
7-Sep	30	Rain				

Total NASCAR Modified Wins

Driver	Wins
Lou Lazzaro	8
Jerry Cook	3
Bernie Miller	1
Sonney Seamon	1
Jerry Pennock Sr.	1
5 Drivers	14 Events

NASCAR Modified Points

Pos.	Driver	Points
1	Jerry Cook	620
2	Lou Lazzaro	560
3	Dave Lape	528
4	Dick Fowler	484
5	Andy Romano	452

1970

Track Champions: Lou Lazzaro (NASCAR Modified)
Buddy Thurston (NASCAR Charger)
Jim Searles (Mini Stock)

NASCAR Modified Records – Weekly Results

Date	Laps	Winner	2nd	3rd	4th	5th
3-May	100	Dick Fowler	Ed Flemke	Jerry Cook	Dick Nephew	Lou Lazzaro
10-May	30	Rain Delayed to 5/24				
17-May	30	Rain				
24-May	30	John Kollar	Al Clark	Dave Lape	Andy Romano	Jerry Cook
	30	Rain Delayed to 5/31				
31-May	30	Robbie Kotary	Jerry Cook	Lou Lazzaro	Dick Fowler	Dave Lape
	30	Dave Kotary	Jerry Cook	Bill Henry	Dick Nephew	Dick Fowler
7-Jun	30	Jerry Cook	Ron Fazio	Dick Fowler	Bill Henry	Robbie Kotary
14-Jun	30	Lou Lazzaro	Jerry Cook	Dave Lape	Gene Mangino	Brian Ross
21-Jun	30	Rain				
28-Jun	30	Andy Romano	Gene Mangino	Robbie Kotary	Lou Lazzaro	Ron Fazio
5-Jul	100	Lou Lazzaro	Jerry Cook	Robbie Kotary	George Rettew	Andy Romano
12-Jul	30	Dick Fowler	Robbie Kotary	Lou Lazzaro	Steve Hall	Bill Henry
19-Jul	30	Ron Newman	Dick Fowler	John Kollar	Robbie Kotary	Rene Charland
26-Jul	30	Bill Henry	Dick Fowler	Ray Sitterly	Ron Newman	Bruce Dostal
2-Aug	30	Lou Lazzaro	Dave Lape	Ron Fazio	Lee Millington	Andy Romano
9-Aug	100	Ed Flemke	Fred DeSarro	Robbie Kotary	Jerry Cook	Bernie Miller
16-Aug	30	Rain				
23-Aug	30	Lou Lazzaro	Rene Charland	Robbie Kotary	Andy Romano	Bernie Miller
30-Aug	30	Rain Delayed to 9/13				
6-Sep	Overall	Ed Flemke	Robbie Kotary	Dick Fowler	Gene Mangino	Maynard Troyer
	200	Ed Flemke	Fred DeSarro	Dave Lape	Robbie Kotary	Rene Charland
	200	Lou Lazzaro	Ed Flemke	Robby Kotary	Gerald Compton	Dick Fowler
13-Sep	30	Rain				
20-Sep	30	Ray Sitterly	Lou Lazzaro	Dave Lape	Jerry Cook	Ron Newman

Total NASCAR Modified Wins

Driver	Wins
Lou Lazzaro	5
Dick Fowler	2
Ed Flemke	2
John Kollar	1
Robbie Kotary	1
Dave Kotary	1
Jerry Cook	1
Andy Romano	1
Ron Newman	1
Bill Henry	1
Ray Sitterly	1
11 Drivers	17 Events

NASCAR Modified Points

Pos.	Driver	Points
1	Lou Lazzaro	618
2	Jerry Cook	578
3	Dave Kotary	548
4	Dave Lape	538
5	Dick Fowler	476

1971

Track Champions: Lou Lazzaro (NASCAR Modified)
Buddy Thurston (NASCAR Charger)
Louie Lanza (Mini Stock)

NASCAR Modified Records – Weekly Results

Date	Laps	Winner	2nd	3rd	4th	5th
2-May	30	Rain				
9-May	30	Rain				
16-May	30	Rain Delayed to 5/23				
23-May	30	Jerry Cook	Robbie Kotary	Sonney Seamon	Lou Lazzaro	Dick Fowler
	30	Ray Sitterly	Ron Narducci	Dick Fowler	Fred DeSarro	Lou Lazzaro
30-May	30	Fred DeSarro	Dave Lape	Lou Lazzaro	Jerry Cook	Dick Fowler
6-Jun	30	Dick Fowler	Sonney Seamon	Lou Lazzaro	Robbie Kotary	Billy Nelson
13-Jun	30	Lou Lazzaro	Bernie Miller	Dick Clark	Robbie Kotary	Sonney Seamon
20-Jun	30	Lou Lazzaro	Robbie Kotary	Fred DeSarro	Sonney Seamon	Al Clark
27-Jun	30	Fred DeSarro	Ron Narducci	Dave Lape	Jerry Cook	Lou Lazzaro
4-Jul	100	Bugs Stevens	Bernie Miller	Fred DeSarro	Dave Lape	Jerry Cook
11-Jul	30	Lou Lazzaro	Fred DeSarro	Bernie Miller	Ralph Holmes	Dave Lape
18-Jul	30	Ron Newman	Dave Lape	Lou Lazzaro	Ray Sitterly	Bernie Miller
25-Jul	30	Bernie Miller	Ray Sitterly	Bugs Stevens	Dave Lape	Ralph Holmes
1-Aug	30	Jerry Cook	Fred DeSarro	Ralph Holmes	Dick Fowler	Ray Sitterly
8-Aug	30	Dave Lape	Ralph Holmes	Ray Sitterly	Dick Fowler	Jerry Cook
15-Aug	100	Fred DeSarro	Bugs Stevens	Lou Lazzaro	Jerry Cook	Sonney Seamon
22-Aug	30	Rain				
29-Aug	30	Jerry Cook	Bill Henry	Bugs Stevens	Ron Newman	Fred DeSarro
5-Sep	Overall	Richie Evans	Fred DeSarro	Jerry Cook	Billy Hensley	Lou Lazzaro
	200	Richie Evans	Fred DeSarro	Lou Lazzaro	Jerry Cook	Bernie Miller
	200	Richie Evans	Fred DeSarro	Jerry Cook		

Total NASCAR Modified Wins

Driver	Wins
Lou Lazzaro	3
Fred DeSarro	3
Jerry Cook	3
Richie Evans	2
Ray Sitterly	1
Dick Fowler	1
Bugs Stevens	1
Ron Newman	1
Bernie Miller	1
Dave Lape	1
10 Drivers	17 Events

NASCAR Modified Points

Pos.	Driver	Points
1	Lou Lazzaro	680
2	Jerry Cook	662
3	Dick Fowler	600
4	Ray Sitterly	590
5	Bernie Miller	570

1972

Track Champions: Richie Evans (NASCAR Modified)
Buddy Thurston (Street Stock)
Doug Rundell (Mini Stock)

NASCAR Modified Records – Weekly Results

Date	Laps	Winner	2nd	3rd	4th	5th
7-May	30	Rain				
14-May	30	Rain				
21-May	30	Sonney Seamon	Richie Evans	Bill Henry	Ralph Holmes	Bernie Miller
28-May	30	Ed Pieniazek	Al Clark	Mike Loescher	Lou Lazzaro	Jerry Cook
4-Jun	100	Bob Santos	Bernie Miller	Denis Giroux	Richie Evans	Jerry Cook
11-Jun	30	Lou Lazzaro	Richie Evans	Ralph Holmes	Ron Newman	Bernie Miller
18-Jun	30	Ed Pieniazek	Richie Evans	Bernie Miller	Jerry Cook	Ron Newman
25-Jun	30	Rain				
2-Jul	100	Richie Evans	Sonney Seamon	Denis Giroux	Jerry Cook	Mike Loescher
9-Jul	30	Richie Evans	Sonney Seamon	Ron Newman	Bernie Miller	Jerry Cook
16-Jul	30	Rain Delayed to 7/23				
23-Jul	30	Rain				
30-Jul	30	Dave Lape	Bernie Miller	Ron Newman	Ralph Holmes	Andy Romano
	30	Lou Lazzaro	Sonney Seamon	Jerry Cook	Richie Evans	Dave Lape
6-Aug	30	Lou Lazzaro	Richie Evans	Sonney Seamon	Jerry Cook	Ed Pieniazek
13-Aug	30	Dave Kotary	Richie Evans	Lou Lazzaro	Jerry Cook	Denis Giroux
20-Aug	30	Dennis Giroux	Dave Lape	Richie Evans	Sonney Seamon	Jerry Cook
27-Aug	30	Rain				
3-Sep	400	Rain				
10-Sep	Overall	Richie Evans	Lou Lazzaro	Jerry Cook	Fred DeSarro	Ollie Silva
	200	Richie Evans	Ray Hendrick	Jerry Cook	Lou Lazzaro	
	200	Bugs Stevens	Bobby Santos	Richie Evans	Lou Lazzaro	Jerry Cook

Total NASCAR Modified Wins

Driver	Wins
Lou Lazzaro	3
Richie Evans	3
Ed Pieniazek	2
Sonney Seamon	1
Bob Santos	1
Dave Lape	1
Dave Kotary	1
Dennis Giroux	1
Bugs Stevens	1
9 Drivers	14 Events

NASCAR Modified Points

Pos.	Driver	Points
1	Richie Evans	494
2	Sonney Seamon	444
3	Jerry Cook	422
4	Bernie Miller	398
5	Lou Lazzaro	396
6	Ralph Holmes	368
7	Andy Romano	364
8	Ron Newman	332
9	Ron Fazio	306
10	Dave Lape	302

1973

Track Champions: Richie Evans (NASCAR Modified)
Chip Lanz (NASCAR Street Stock)
Jim Brown (Pure Stock)
Hank Searles (Mini Stock)

NASCAR Modified Records – Weekly Results

Date	Laps	Winner	2nd	3rd	4th	5th
6-May	100	Richie Evans	Bernie Miller	Jerry Cook	Bugs Stevens	Andy Romano
13-May	30	Rain				
20-May	30	Rain				
27-May	30	Rain Delayed to 6/03				
3-Jun	30	Ed Pieniazek	Lou Lazzaro	Andy Romano		
	30	Richie Evans	Roger Griffith	Norm Moyer	Bernie Miller	Ray Sitterly
10-Jun	30	Jerry Cook	Richie Evans	Sonney Seamon	Maynard Forrette	Ed Pieniazek
17-Jun	30	Maynard Forrette	Richie Evans	Bernie Miller	Dick Fowler	Lou Lazzaro
24-Jun	30	Rain				
1-Jul	100	Rain				
8-Jul	100	Richie Evans	Bugs Stevens	Lou Lazzaro	Jerry Cook	Ed Pieniazek
15-Jul	30	Richie Evans	Sonney Seamon	Jerry Cook	Ed Pieniazek	Ray Sitterly
22-Jul	30	Richie Evans	Maynard Troyer	Andy Romano	Bernie Miller	Bugs Stevens
29-Jul	30	Richie Evans	Jerry Cook	Ed Pieniazek	Andy Romano	Bugs Stevens
5-Aug	100	Maynard Troyer	Jerry Cook	Richie Evans		
12-Aug	30	Sonney Seamon	Maynard Troyer	Richie Evans	Jerry Cook	Andy Romano
19-Aug	30	Richie Evans	Sonney Seamon	Maynard Troyer	Bill Henry	Bugs Stevens
26-Aug	35	Richie Evans	Maynard Forrette	Jerry Cook	Bugs Stevens	Bernie Miller
2-Sep	Overall	Maynard Troyer	Bugs Stevens	Jerry Cook	Bernie Miller	Ed Pieniazek
	200	Bugs Stevens	Maynard Troyer			
	200	Maynard Troyer	Jerry Cook	Bugs Stevens		

Total NASCAR Modified Wins

Driver	Wins
Richie Evans	8
Maynard Troyer	2
Ed Pieniazek	1
Jerry Cook	1
Maynard Forrette	1
Sonney Seamon	1
Bugs Stevens	1
7 Drivers	15 Events

NASCAR Modified Points

Pos.	Driver	Points
1	Richie Evans	494
2	Sonney Seamon	444
3	Jerry Cook	422
4	Bernie Miller	398
5	Lou Lazzaro	376
6	Ralph Holmes	368
7	Andy Romano	364
8	Ron Newman	332
9	Ron Fazio	306
10	Dave Lape	302

1974

Track Champions: Richie Evans (NASCAR Modified)
Chip Lanz (NASCAR Charger)
Cullen Hatfield (Pure Stock)

NASCAR Modified Records – Weekly Results

Date	Laps	Winner	2nd	3rd	4th	5th
3-May	100	Rain				
10-May	100	Rain				
17-May	100	Rain				
24-May	30	Dick Fowler	Jerry Cook	Andy Romano	Richie Evans	Bill Henry
31-May	30	Rain				
7-Jun	30	Richie Evans	Rene Charland	Ed Pieniazek	Jerry Cook	Sonney Seamon
14-Jun	100	Richie Evans	Geoff Bodine	Jerry Cook	Sonney Seamon	Dick Fowler
21-Jun	30	Rain				
28-Jun	30	Rain				
5-Jul	100	Jerry Cook	Richie Evans	Bernie Miller	Maynard Forrette	Geoff Bodine
12-Jul	30	Richie Evans	Jerry Cook	Sonney Seamon	Geoff Bodine	Roger Griffith
19-Jul	30	Rain				
26-Jul	30	Geoff Bodine	Richie Evans	Sonney Seamon	Jerry Cook	Maynard Forrette
2-Aug	100	Geoff Bodine	Richie Evans	Sonney Seamon	Bernie Miller	Ken Canestrari
9-Aug	30	Geoff Bodine	Bernie Miller	Jerry Cook	Richie Evans	Sonney Seamon
16-Aug	OFF					
23-Aug	30	Dick Clark	Lou Lazzaro	Richie Evans	Sonney Seamon	Rene Charland
30-Aug	New Yorker 100	Geoff Bodine	Lou Lazzaro	Jerry Cook	Richie Evans	Ed Pieniazek

Total NASCAR Modified Wins

Driver	Wins
Geoff Bodine	4
Richie Evans	3
Dick Fowler	1
Jerry Cook	1
Dick Clark	1
5 Drivers	10 Events

NASCAR Modified Points

Pos.	Driver	Points
1	Richie Evans	490
2	Jerry Cook	440
3	Sonney Seamon	436
4	Geoff Bodine	376
5	Bernie Miller	364
6	Rene Charland	282
7	Bill Henry	274
8	Dick Fowler	264
9	Bill Matzel	260
10	Ken Canestrari	236

1975

Track Champions: Sonney Seamon (Modified)
Billy Seamon/Bob Engler (Street Stock)
Jim Brown (Pure Stock)

Modified Records – Weekly Results

Date	Laps	Winner	2nd	3rd	4th	5th
6-Jun	100	Rain				
13-Jun	100	Sonney Seamon	Lou Lazzaro	Dick Fowler	Jerry Cook	Roger Griffith

Total Modified Wins

Driver	Wins
Sonney Seamon	1
1 Driver	1 Event

1976
Track was closed

1977

Track Champions: Geoff Bodine (NASCAR Modified)
Billy Seamon (Street Stock)
Jeff Cobb (Pure Stock)

Modified Records – Weekly Results

Date	Laps	Winner	2nd	3rd	4th	5th
12-Jun	50	Richie Evans	Sonney Seamon	Dave Nichols	Mike Loescher	Roger Griffith
19-Jun	50	Sonney Seamon	Dave Nichols	Maynard Troyer	Dave Kotary	Roger Griffith
26-Jun	50	Sonney Seamon	Dave Nichols	George Kent	Maynard Troyer	Dave Lee
3-Jul	100	Richie Evans	Sonney Seamon	Jerry Cook	Roger Griffith	Randy Hedger
10-Jul	50	Maynard Troyer	Mike Loescher	Bernie Miller	Roger Griffith	Dave Kotary
17-Jul	50	Richie Evans	Jerry Cook	Sonney Seamon	Guy Robinson	Dave Nichols
24-Jul	50	Dave Nichols	Jerry Cook	Sonney Seamon	Guy Robinson	Randy Hedger
31-Jul	100	Geoff Bodine	Richie Evans	Mike Loescher	Jerry Cook	Roger Griffith
7-Aug	50	Rain				
14-Aug	100	Rain				
21-Aug	50	Rain Delayed to 8/28				
28-Aug	50	Richie Evans	Sonney Seamon	Dave Kotary		
	100	Geoff Bodine	Richie Evans	Sonney Seamon	Bernie Miller	Chip Lanz
4-Sep	100	Richie Evans	Geoff Bodine	Jerry Cook	Sonney Seamon	John Rosati
11-Sep	50	Rain				

Total NASCAR Modified Wins

Driver	Wins
Richie Evans	5
Sonney Seamon	2
Geoff Bodine	2
Maynard Troyer	1
Dave Nichols	1
5 Drivers	11 Events

Note: The track ran NEARA and open competition specials throughout the entire season. Bodine's track title is based on only three events: 7/31, 8/28 (100 Laps), and 9/04. Otherwise, it appears as if Sonney Seamon would have been the track champion.

1978

Track Champions: Richie Evans (NASCAR Modified)*
Gene Kotary (Street Stock)

NASCAR Modified Records – Weekly Results

Date	Laps	Winner	2nd	3rd	4th	5th
14-May	100	Rain				
21-May	50	Richie Evans	Chip Lanz	Roger Griffith	Dick Clark	Dave Kotary
28-May	100	Geoff Bodine	Jerry Cook	Richie Evans	Wayne Anderson	Dave Kotary
4-Jun	100	Richie Evans	Roger Griffith	Dick Clark	Wayne Anderson	Bob Book
11-Jun	50	Richie Evans	Jerry Cook	Chip Lanz	Randy Hedger	Dick Clark
18-Jun	50	Rain				
25-Jun	50	Geoff Bodine	Jerry Cook	Chip Lanz	Wayne Anderson	Dick Clark
2-Jul	100	Geoff Bodine	Richie Evans	Jerry Cook	Dave Kotary	Chip Lanz
9-Jul	50	Richie Evans	Jerry Cook	Tom McCann	Dave Kotary	Dick Clark
23-Jul	50	Richie Evans	Jerry Cook	Geoff Bodine	Dick Clark	Bernie Miller
30-Jul	50	Richie Evans	Jerry Cook	Chip Lanz	Bernie Miller	Dave Kotary
6-Aug	100	Maynard Troyer	Richie Evans	Jerry Cook	Dick Clark	Bernie Miller
13-Aug	50	Richie Evans	Jerry Cook	Bernie Miller	Dick Clark	
20-Aug	50	Chip Lanz	Dick Clark	Randy Hedger	Gordie Smith	Bernie Miller
27-Aug	50	Richie Evans	Jerry Cook	Chuck Frisbie	Dick Clark	Bernie Miller
3-Sep	New Yorker 200	Richie Evans	Jerry Cook	Chip Lanz	Ken Canestrari	Joel Thomas

Total NASCAR Modified Wins

Driver	Wins
Richie Evans	9
Geoff Bodine	3
Maynard Troyer	1
Chip Lanz	1
4 Drivers	14 Events

NASCAR Modified Points*

Pos.	Driver	Points
1	Richie Evans	160
2	Jerry Cook	156
3	Chip Lanz	108
4	Dick Clark	106
5	Dave Kotary	104
6	Geoff Bodine	94
7	Roger Griffith	78
8	Randy Hedger	60
9	Wayne Anderson	60
10	Jim Paternoster	46

**The first seven races were run under NASCAR sanction. The remaining events were run as an independent.

1979

Track Champions: Bob Savoie (Modified)
Donnie Wetmore (Small Block Modified)
Tom Williams (Late Model)
Gerry Newman (Amateur)

Open Competition Modified Records – Weekly Results

Date	Laps	Winner	2nd	3rd	4th	5th
30-May	60	Lou Lazzaro	Andy Romano	Bob Savoie	Mike Romano	Ron Miller
2-Jun	35	Wally Warburton	Jim Johnson	Bob Savoie	Fred Brooks	Butch Simmons
9-Jun	35	Wally Warburton	Jim Winks	Leroy Hurlbut	Duane Decker	John Barker Jr.
16-Jun	35	Leroy Hurlbut	Larry Dalmata	Rene Charland	Rick Gray	Jim Johnson
23-Jun	35	Rain				
30-Jun	50	Lou Lazzaro	Maynard Forrette	Bob Savoie	Leroy Hurlbut	Ted Luft
4-Jul	50	Tommy Wilson				
7-Jul	35	Larry Dalmata	Tommy Wilson	Leroy Hurlbut	Bud Hinman	Wally Warburton
14-Jul	35	Maynard Forrette	Wally Warburton	Bob Savoie	Lou Lazzaro	John Barker Jr.
21-Jul	35	Maynard Forrette	Bud Hinman	Rick Gray	Chuck Kennison	Ned Kinney
28-Jul	35	Rain				
4-Aug	35	Bob Savoie	Wally Warburton	Bud Hinman	Donnie Wetmore	Rick Gray
11-Aug	30	Maynard Forrette	Bud Hinman	Tommy Wilson		
18-Aug	35	Rain				
25-Aug	35	Cancelled due to poor track conditions				
1-Sep	35	Jack Johnson	Mike Romano	Bob Savoie	Leroy Hurlbut	Wally Warburton
8-Sep	25	Bob Savoie	Larry Dalmata	John Barker Jr.	Donnie Wetmore	Ed San Soucie
15-Sep	25	Bob Savoie	Larry Dalmata	Ed San Soucie	Donnie Wetmore	John Kollar

Total Modified Wins

Driver	Wins
Maynard Forrette	3
Bob Savoie	3
Wally Warburton	2
Lou Lazzaro	2
Leroy Hurlbut	1
Tom Wilson	1
Larry Dalmata	1
Jack Johnson	1
8 Drivers	14 Events

Modified Points

Pos.	Driver	Points
1	Bob Savoie	656
2	Bud Hinman	476
3	Rick Gray	474
4	Fred Brooks	462
5	Butch Simons	444
6	Chuck Kennison	404
7	Ned Kinney	388
8	Wally Warburton	380
9	Mike Noto	328
10	Leroy Hurlbut	316

1980

Track Champions: Jon Button (Small Block Modified)
Tom Williams (Late Model)

Small Block Modified Records – Weekly Results

Date	Laps	Winner	2nd	3rd
3-Jul	25	Cancelled		
6-Jul	25	Cancelled		
10-Jul	25	Cancelled		
13-Jul	25	Cancelled		
17-Jul	25	Cancelled		
20-Jul	25	Cancelled		
24-Jul	25	Cancelled		
27-Jul	25	Cancelled		
31-Jul	25	Cancelled		
3-Aug	10	Chuck Kennison	F. August	Donnie Wetmore
	15	Donnie Wetmore	Lonny Riehlman	Chuck Kennison
7-Aug	25	Chuck Kennison		
10-Aug	25	Donnie Wetmore		
14-Aug	25	Rain		
17-Aug	25	Gary Iulg	Duane Decker	Donnie Wetmore
21-Aug	25	Cancelled		

Total Modified Wins

Driver	Wins
Chuck Kennison	2
Donnie Wetmore	2
Gary Iulg	1
3 Drivers	5 Events

1981

Track Champion: Dave Lape (DIRT Modified)

DIRT Modified Records – Weekly Results

Date	Laps	Winner	2nd	3rd	4th	5th
17-May	30	Art Kiser	Andy Romano	Ken Hanson	Rick Gray	Larry Dalmata
24-May	30	Tommy Wilson	Jack Johnson	Lou Lazzaro	Andy Romano	Mark Livingston
31-May	30	Jack Johnson	Tom Corellis	Dave Lape	Tommy Wilson	Art Kiser
7-Jun	30	Dave Lape	Tommy Wilson	Ken Hansen	John Dahm	Bud Hinman
14-Jun	30	Dave Lape	Jack Johnson	Mike Romano	Andy Romano	Ken Hansen
21-Jun	30	Rain				
28-Jun	30	Jack Johnson	Mike Romano	Tommy Wilson	Lou Lazzaro	Art Kiser
5-Jul	100	Dave Lape	Jack Johnson	Mike Romano	Art Kiser	Bud Hinman
12-Jul	50	Jack Johnson	Tommy Wilson	Dave Lape	Mike Romano	Ray Dalmata
19-Jul	30	Rain delayed to 8/02				
26-Jul	30	Rain				
2-Aug	30	Jack Johnson	Dave Lape	Tommy Wilson	Bud Hinman	Mike Romano
	30	Dave Lape	Tommy Wilson	Mike Romano	Tom Corellis	Andy Romano
9-Aug	50	Tommy Wilson	Jack Johnson	Dave Lape	Andy Romano	Ray Dalmata
16-Aug	30	Rain				
23-Aug	30	Jack Johnson	Dave Lape	George Sifo	Tommy Wilson	Bud Hinman
30-Aug	30	Tommy Wilson	C.D. Coville	Dave Lape	Andy Romano	Greg Borek
6-Sep	50	Jack Johnson	Tommy Wilson	Jack Emerson	George Sifo	Ray Dalmata

Total DIRT Modified Wins

Driver	Wins
Jack Johnson	6
Dave Lape	4
Tommy Wilson	3
Art Kiser	1
4 Drivers	14 Events

DIRT Modified Points

Pos.	Driver	Points
1	Dave Lape	397
2	Tom Wilson	389
3	Jack Johnson	356
4	Bud Hinman	299
5	Mike Romano	278
6	Rich Gray	274
7	Andy Romano	254
8	George Sifo	239
9	Lou Lazzaro	205
10	Art Kiser	178

1982

Track Champions: Jack Johnson (DIRT Modified)
Paul Jensen (DIRT 320-Modified)

DIRT Modified Records – Weekly Results

Date	Laps	Winner	2nd	3rd	4th	5th
23-Apr	30	Alan Johnson	Randy Glenski	Gary Iulg	Gene Bik	Andy Romano
30-Apr	30	Jack Johnson	Randy Glenski	Alan Johnson	Jeff Kappesser	Tommy Wilson
7-May	30	Alan Johnson	Jack Johnson	Greg Borek	Randy Glenski	Jeff Kappesser
14-May	30	Alan Johnson	Jeff Kappesser	Tommy Wilson	Andy Romano	Greg Borek
21-May	30	Jack Johnson	Tommy Wilson	Randy Glenski	Andy Romano	Bob Sitterly
28-May	50	Rain				
4-Jun	30	Jack Johnson	Randy Glenski	John Podolak	Greg Borek	Mike Romano
11-Jun	30	Alan Johnson	Jack Johnson	Mike Romano	John Birosh	John Podolak
18-Jun	30	Jack Johnson	Alan Johnson	John Podolak	Gene Bik	Mark Terry
25-Jun	30	Rain				
2-Jul	50	Alan Johnson	Jack Johnson	John Podolak	Jeff Kappesser	Gene Bik
9-Jul	30	Alan Johnson	Jack Johnson	Tommy Wilson	Jeff Kappesser	Randy Glenksi
16-Jul	30	Jack Johnson	Randy Glenski	Tommy Wilson	Mike Colsten	Jeff Kappesser
23-Jul	30	Danny Johnson	Jack Johnson	Randy Glenski	Merv Treichler	Alan Johnson
30-Jul	20	John Podolak	Jeff Kappesser	Danny Johnson	Mike Romano	Tommy Wilson
	20	Mike Romano	Jack Johnson	Randy Glenski	Danny Johnson	John Podolak
6-Aug	30	Merv Treichler	Harry Behrent	John Podolak	Mike Romano	Danny Johnson
13-Aug	30	Jack Johnson	Alan Johnson	Mike Romano	Jeff Kappesser	Randy Glenski
17-Aug	82	Jack Johnson	Jimmy Horton	Danny Johnson	C.D. Coville	Dave Lape
20-Aug	30	Jack Johnson	Merv Treichler	Mike Romano	John Podolak	Jeff Kappasser
28-Aug	Twin 20s	Rain				
3-Sep	Twin 40s	Rain				
17-Sep	100	Merv Treichler	Jack Johnson	Danny Johnson	John Podolak	Mark Fleury

Total DIRT Modified Wins

Driver	Wins
Jack Johnson	8
Alan Johnson	6
Merv Treichler	2
Danny Johnson	1
John Podolak	1
Mike Romano	1
6 Drivers	19 Events

DIRT Modified Points

Pos.	Driver	Points
1	Jack Johnson	718
2	Alan Johnson	604
3	Randy Glenski	547
4	Jeff Kappesser	473
5	Mike Romano	465
6	John Podolak	436
7	Tommy Wilson	407
8	Ben Novak	394
9	Walt Koperda	364
10	John Leonard	360

1983 – 1984
Track was closed

1985

Track Champion: Dave Lape (DIRT Modified)

DIRT Modified Records – Weekly Results

Date	Laps	Winner	2nd	3rd	4th	5th
25-Jun	100	Rain delayed to 7/16				
16-Jul	100	Alan Johnson	Jack Johnson	Jimmy Horton	Joe Plazek	Will Cagle
	85	Dave Lape	Bob McCreadie	Alan Johnson	John Birosh	Jimmy Horton
14-Aug	100	Jack Johnson	Dave Lape	Brett Hearn	C.D. Coville	Richie Burgess
29-Sep	200	Freddie Brightbill	John Hewitt	Dave Lape	Ray Dalmata	Chuck Akulis

Total DIRT Modified Wins

Driver	Wins
Alan Johnson	1
Dave Lape	1
Jack Johnson	1
Freddie Brightbill	1
4 Drivers	4 Events

DIRT Modified Points

Pos.	Driver	Points
1	Dave Lape	270
2	Jack Johnson	247
3	Jimmy Horton	228
4	Ray Dalmata	222
5	Alan Johnson	196
6	Danny Johnson	194
7	C.D. Coville	184
8	Richie Burgess	175
9	Will Cagle	170
10	Phil Carlone	168

1986

Track Champion: Brett Hearn (DIRT Modified)
Brett Hearn (DIRT 320-Modified)

DIRT Modified Records – Weekly Results

Date	Laps	Winner	2nd	3rd	4th	5th
9-May	50	Brett Hearn	C.D. Coville	Dave Lape	Randy Glenski	John Birosh
6-Jun	40	Bob McCreadie	Brett Hearn	Dave Lape	Richie Burgess	Tommy Wilson
24-Jun	100	Rain				
15-Jul	86	Brett Hearn	Danny Johnson	Charlie Rudolph	Bob McCreadie	Doug Hoffman
1-Aug	50	Rain				
3-Aug	50	Brett Hearn	Steve Paine	Alan Johnson	Ray Dalmata	Dave Lape
13-Aug	100	Brett Hearn	Bob McCreadie	Alan Johnson	Jimmy Horton	Charlie Rudolph
22-Aug	100	Brett Hearn	Alan Johnson	John Birosh	Ray Dalmata	Dave Lape
28-Sep	200	Rain, Rescheduled to 4/26/87 & shortened to 100 laps				

Total DIRT Modified Wins

Driver	Wins
Brett Hearn	5
Bob McCreadie	1
2 Drivers	6 Events

DIRT Modified Points

Pos.	Driver	Points
1	Brett Hearn	470
2	Dave Lape	374
3	Bob McCreadie	332
4	Mike VanDusen	244
5	Alan Johnson	243
6	Jim Rajczi	234
7	Tommy Wilson	226
8	Lou Lazzaro	216
9	Ray Dalmata	200
10	John Birosh	194

DIRT 320-Modified Records – Weekly Results

Date	Laps	Winner	2nd	3rd	4th	5th
15-Jun	30	A.J. Romano	Roger Horvath	Steve Behrent	Mitch Gibbs	Rich Ricci Jr.
27-Jul	50	Brett Hearn	Mike Ricci	Maynard Forrette	Richie Tobias Jr.	A.J. Romano
24-Aug	50	Cancelled, moved to 10/9 - 86 Laps				
12-Sep	86	Rain				
9-Oct	86	Brett Hearn	Alan Johnson	Billy Schinkel Jr.	John Moravec	Billy Decker

1987

Track Champion: Kenny Tremont Jr. (DIRT Modified)

DIRT Modified Records – Weekly Results

Date	Laps	Winner	2nd	3rd	4th	5th
26-Apr	100	Jack Johnson	Kenny Tremont Jr.	Kenny Brightbill	Dave Lape	Alan Johnson
15-May	50	Jack Johnson	Alan Johnson	Chuck Akulis	Dave Lape	Ray Dalmata
12-Jun	25	Kenny Tremont Jr.	Brett Hearn	Jack Johnson	Maynard Forrette	Bob McCreadie
	25	Jack Johnson	Kenny Tremont Jr.	Billy Decker	Brett Hearn	Dave Lape
16-Jun	100	Alan Johnson	Dave Lape	Doug Hoffman	Danny Johnson	Billy Decker
14-Jul	87	Rain				
22-Jul	87	Kenny Tremont Jr.	Mike Romano	Jimmy Horton	Chuck Akulis	Dave Lape
31-Jul	20	Kenny Tremont Jr.	Bob McCreadie	Dave Lape	Tommy Wilson	Billy Decker
	20	Jack Cottrell	Pat Ward	Bob McCreadie	Kenny Tremont Jr.	Chuck Akulis
	20	Ray Dalmata	Jack Johnson	Kenny Tremont Jr.	Bob McCreadie	Billy Decker
12-Aug	61	Kenny Tremont Jr.	Dave Lape	Alan Johnson	Danny Johnson	Jack Johnson
29-Aug	30	Dave Lape	C.D. Coville	Mike Romano	Ray Dalmata	Pat Ward
5-Sep	30	Tim Dwyer	Dave Lape	Tommy Wilson	Jack Cottrell	Ray Dalmata

Total DIRT Modified Wins

Driver	Wins
Kenny Tremont, Jr.	4
Jack Johnson	3
Alan Johnson	1
Jack Cottrell	1
Ray Dalmata	1
Dave Lape	1
Tim Dwyer	1
7 Drivers	12 Events

DIRT Modified Points

Pos.	Driver	Points
1	Kenny Tremont Jr.	720
2	Dave Lape	651
3	Jack Johnson	634
4	Chuck Akulis	620
5	Ray Dalmata	596
6	Billy Decker	560
7	Alan Johnson	518
8	Pat Ward	508
9	Bob McCreadie	494
10	Tommy Wilson	481

1988
Track was closed

1989

Track Champions: Paul Jensen (Outlaw Modified)
Tom Sears Jr. (Street Stock)
Mike Rolewicz (Pure Stock)

Outlaw Modified Records – Weekly Results

Date	Laps	Winner	2nd	3rd	4th	5th
11-Jun	25	Donnie Wetmore	Mike Arminio	Gordy Button Jr.	Dale Planck	Bob Savoie
18-Jun	25	Donnie Wetmore	John Podolak	Mike Arminio	Mike Romano	John Phelps
25-Jun	25	Gordy Button Jr.	Ted Lamb Jr.	Paul Jensen	Doug Fuller	Mike Arminio
2-Jul	25	Mike Arminio	Paul Jensen	Jimmy Chester	Gordy Button Jr.	Larry Radney
9-Jul	25	Donnie Wetmore	Gordy Button Jr.	Mike Arminio	Paul Jensen	John Podolak
16-Jul	25	Paul Jensen	Donnie Wetmore	John Phelps	John Podolak	Ted Lamb Jr.
23-Jul	25	Ted Lamb Jr.	Gordy Button Jr.	Mike Arminio	John Podolak	Donnie Wetmore
30-Jul	25	Donnie Wetmore	Ron House	Doug Fuller	John Ramsey	Skip Cadwell
6-Aug	25	Rain				
13-Aug	25	Gordy Button Jr.	Paul Jensen	Ron House	Ted Lamb Jr.	John Podolak
20-Aug	25	Paul Jensen	Jim Mahaney	Gordy Button Jr.	John Podolak	Doug Fuller
27-Aug	25	Paul Jensen	Ted Lamb Jr.	John Podolak	Doug Fuller	Jim Mahaney
3-Sep	25	John Podolak	Ted Lamb Jr.	Gordy Button Jr.	Doug Fuller	Bob Podolak
10-Sep	25	Rain				
17-Sep	50	Rain				
1-Oct	30	Paul Jensen	Donnie Wetmore	Doug Fuller	Jim Mahaney	Don Dietz Jr.
15-Oct	40	Paul Jensen	Ted Lamb Jr.	Gordy Button Jr.	Jim Mahaney	Doug Fuller

Total Small Block Modified Wins

Driver	Wins
Paul Jensen	5
Donnie Wetmore	4
Gordy Button Jr.	2
Mike Arminio	1
Ted Lamb Jr.	1
John Podolak	1
6 Drivers	14 Events

Final Small Block Modified Point Standings – Missing

1990

Track Champion: Paul Jensen (Outlaw Small Block Modified)

Outlaw Small Block Modified Records – Weekly Results

Date	Laps	Winner	2nd	3rd	4th	5th
22-Apr	25	Ted Lamb, Jr.	Doug Fuller	Gordy Button Jr.	Paul Jensen	Tom Kinsella
29-Apr	25	Gordy Button Jr.	Paul Jensen	Ted Lamb Jr.	Tom Kinsella	Bob Podolak
6-May	25	Paul Jensen	Donnie Wetmore	Jim Mahaney	Ted Lamb Jr.	Doug Fuller
13-May	25	Rain				
20-May	25	Rain				
27-May	40	Paul Jensen	Ted Lamb Jr.	Doug Fuller	Donnie Wetmore	Will Smith
3-Jun	25	Ted Lamb Jr.	Gordy Button Jr.	Paul Jensen	Ron House	Jeff Walton
10-Jun	25	Tom Kinsella	Donnie Wetmore	Paul Jensen	Roger Phelps	Jim Mahaney
17-Jun	25	Gordy Button Jr.	Doug Fuller	Larry Radney	Donnie Wetmore	Roger Phelps
24-Jun	25	Donnie Wetmore	Ted Lamb Jr.	Larry Radney	Gordy Button Jr.	Ron House
1-Jul	40	Rain Delayed to 7/08				
8-Jul	40	Jim Mahaney	Doug Fuller	Paul Jensen	Roger Phelps	Tom Kinsella
	25	Ted Lamb Jr.	Donnie Wetmore	Jim Mahaney	Paul Jensen	John Podolak
15-Jul	25	Gordy Button Jr.	Nick Ryan	Paul Jensen	John Ramsey	Rich Tobias Jr.
22-Jul	25	Gordy Button Jr.	Donnie Wetmore	Ted Lamb Jr.	John Ramsey	Doug Fuller
29-Jul	15	Roger Phelps	Paul Jensen	Jeff Walton	Ted Lamb Jr.	Gordy Button Jr.
	15	John Ramsey	Paul Jensen	Doug Fuller	Larry Radney	John Podolak
5-Aug	25	Rain				
12-Aug	25	Donnie Wetmore	Paul Jensen	Tom Kinsella	Ted Lamb Jr.	Jeff Walton
19-Aug	25	Donnie Wetmore	Gordy Button Jr.	Dale Planck	Larry Radney	Roger Phelps
26-Aug	25	Doug Fuller	Roger Phelps	Paul Jensen	Donnie Wetmore	Jeff Walton
2-Sep	25	Paul Jensen	Jim Mahaney	Mike Ricci	Ted Lamb Jr.	Roger Phelps
9-Sep	25	Rain				
16-Sep	50	Billy Pauch	Rich Tobias Jr.	Pete Bicknell	Roger Phelps	Donnie Wetmore

Total Outlaw Small Block Modified Wins

Driver	Wins
Gordy Button Jr.	4
Ted Lamb Jr.	3
Donnie Wetmore	3
Paul Jensen	3
Tom Kinsella	1
Jim Mahaney	1
Roger Phelps	1
John Ramsey	1
Doug Fuller	1
Billy Pauch	1
10 Drivers	19 Events

Outlaw Small Block Modified Points

Pos.	Driver	Points
1	Paul Jensen	824
2	Doug Fuller	742
3	Donnie Wetmore	740
4	Ted Lamb Jr.	718
5	Roger Phelps	698
6	Gordy Button Jr.	582
7	Tom Kinsella	564
8	Tom Juhl Sr.	488
9	John Ramsey	470
10	Larry Radney	446

1991

Track Champion: Tom Kinsella (Outlaw Small Block Modified)

Outlaw Small Block Modified Records – Weekly Results

Date	Laps	Winner	2nd	3rd	4th	5th
14-Apr	40	Gordy Button Jr.	Roger Phelps	Bob Podolak	Dave Donath	Mike Jacobs
21-Apr	25	Rain				
28-Apr	25	Donnie Wetmore	Lou Michaels	Tom Kinsella	Doug Fuller	Paul Jensen
5-May	25	Donnie Wetmore	J.J. Michaels	Gordy Button Jr.	Paul Jensen	Lou Michaels
12-May	40	Tom Kinsella	Alan Johnson	Tom Juhl Jr.	J.J. Michaels	Lou Michaels
19-May	25	Donnie Wetmore	Nick Ryan	Roger Phelps	Lou Michaels	Doug Fuller
26-May	25	Donnie Wetmore	J.J. Michaels	Roger Phelps	Roger Laureno	Doug Fuller
2-Jun	25	Roger Phelps	Paul Jensen	Lou Michaels	J.J. Michaels	Doug Fuller
9-Jun	25	Donnie Wetmore	Jeff Walton	J.J. Michaels	Tom Kinsella	Mike Root
16-Jun	25	J.J. Michaels	Tom Kinsella	Paul Jensen	John Ramsey	Gordy Button Jr.
23-Jun	25	Bob Podolak	Paul Jensen	Tom Kinsella	Tom Juhl Jr.	Jeff Walton
30-Jun	25	Paul Jensen	Tom Kinsella	Donnie Wetmore	Roger Phelps	Gordy Button Jr.
7-Jul	25	Jeff Walton	Roger Phelps	Doug Fuller	Bob Podolak	Paul Jensen
14-Jul	25	Rain				
21-Jul	20	Donnie Wetmore	Paul Jensen	J.J. Michaels	Doug Fuller	Lou Michaels
	20	Tom Kinsella	Paul Jensen	Donnie Wetmore	Doug Fuller	Jeff Walton
28-Jul	25	Tom Kinsella	Doug Fuller	Jeff Walton	Bob Podolak	Paul Jensen
4-Aug	25	Postponed at lap 7 – RAIN. Delayed to 8/18				
11-Aug	25	Lou Michaels	Paul Jensen	Jeff Walton	Tom Kinsella	Donnie Wetmore
18-Aug	25	Tom Kinsella (PPD feature)	Donnie Wetmore	Doug Fuller	Paul Jensen	J.J. Michaels
	25	J.J. Michaels	Tom Kinsella	Tom Juhl Jr.	Paul Jensen	Roger Phelps
21-Aug	25	Rain Delayed to 8/28				
25-Aug	25	Paul Jensen	Donnie Wetmore	Doug Fuller	Jeff Walton	Tom Kinsella
28-Aug	35	Donnie Wetmore	Tom Kinsella	Doug Worthing	Jim Mahaney	Doug Fuller
1-Sep	25	Donnie Wetmore	Tom Kinsella	Doug Fuller	Paul Jensen	Dave Donath
8-Sep	25	Tom Kinsella	Pete Bicknell	Paul Jensen	Nick Ryan	Roger Phelps
15-Sep	25	Rain				
22-Sep	50	Billy Pauch	Tom Kinsella	Paul Jensen	Billy Schinkel	Gordy Button Jr.

Total Outlaw Small Block Modified Wins

Driver	Wins
Donnie Wetmore	8
Tom Kinsella	5
J.J. Michaels	2
Paul Jensen	2
Gordy Button Jr.	1
Roger Phelps	1
Bob Podolak	1
Jeff Walton	1
Lou Michaels	1
Billy Pauch	1
10 Drivers	23 Events

Outlaw Small Block Modified Points

Pos.	Driver	Points
1	Tom Kinsella	1004
2	Donnie Wetmore	974
3	Paul Jensen	972
4	Doug Fuller	848
5	J.J. Michaels	824
6	Lou Michaels	718
7	Tom Juhl Jr.	664
8	Roger Phelps	650
9	Jeff Walton	612
10	Gordy Button Jr.	576

1992

Track Champion: Paul Jensen (Outlaw Modified)

Outlaw Small Block Modified Records – Weekly Results

Date	Laps	Winner	2nd	3rd	4th	5th
5-Apr	40	Rain				
12-Apr	40	Rain				
26-Apr	40	Pete Bicknell	Jeff Walton	Billy Whittaker	Nick Ryan	Gordy Button Jr.
3-May	25	Rain Delayed to 5/10				
10-May	25	Tom Kinsella	Donnie Wetmore	Paul Jensen	J.J Michaels	Roger Phelps
	25	Tom Kinsella	Doug Fuller	Roger Phelps	Ron House	Tom Juhl Jr.
17-May	25	Tom Kinsella	Paul Jensen	Bob Podolak	Donnie Wetmore	Tom Juhl Jr.
24-May	25	Paul Jensen	Roger Phelps	Gordy Button Jr.	Bob Podolak	J.J. Michaels
31-May	25	Rain				
7-Jun	25	Rain				
14-Jun	25	Roger Phelps	Paul Jensen	Tom Kinsella	Gordy Button Jr.	Donnie Wetmore
21-Jun	25	Rain Delayed to 6/28				
24-Jun	40	Rain Delayed to 7/1				
28-Jun	25	J.J. Michaels	Donnie Wetmore	Lou Michaels	John Ramsey	Doug Fuller
	25	Tom Kinsella	Lou Michaels	Donnie Wetmore	Paul Jensen	Bret Belden
1-Jul	40	Dale Planck	Paul Jensen	Roger Phelps	Gordy Button Jr.	Doug Fuller
5-Jul	25	Tom Kinsella	Gordy Button Jr.	Paul Jensen	Roger Phelps	J.J. Michaels
12-Jul	25	Rain				
19-Jul	15	Dave Donath	Donnie Wetmore	Gordy Button Jr.	John Barker Jr.	Paul Jensen
	15	Tom Kinsella	Paul Jensen	Lou Michaels	Roger Phelps	Doug Fuller
26-Jul	25	Donnie Wetmore	Paul Jensen	Gordy Button Jr.	John Barker Jr.	Roger Phelps
2-Aug	25	Paul Jensen	Tom Kinsella	Lou Michaels	John Barker Jr.	John Cunningham
9-Aug	25	Tom Kinsella	Roger Phelps	Donnie Wetmore	Paul Jensen	J.J. Michaels
16-Aug	25	Paul Jensen	Roger Phelps	Gordy Button Jr.	Donnie Wetmore	Tom Kinsella
19-Aug	40	Tom Kinsella	Paul Jensen	Dale Planck	Donnie Wetmore	John Barker Jr.
23-Aug	25	J.J. Michaels	Lou Michaels	Paul Jensen	Dave Donath	Roger Phelps
30-Aug	25	Tom Kinsella	Paul Jensen	Gordy Button Jr.	J.J. Michaels	Roger Phelps
6-Sep	25	Paul Jensen	Donnie Wetmore	Gordy Button Jr.	Lou Michaels	Jeff Walton
13-Sep	25	Paul Jensen	Gordy Button Jr.	Donnie Wetmore	Tom Kinsella	Shawn Donath
20-Sep	50	Dale Planck	Donnie Wetmore	Pete Bicknell	Tom Kinsella	Randy Glenski
26-Sep	25	Gordy Button Jr.	Donnie Wetmore	Tom Kinsella	Paul Jensen	Jeff Walton

Total Outlaw Small Block Modified Wins

Driver	Wins
Tom Kinsella	9
Paul Jensen	5
J.J. Michaels	2
Dale Planck	2
Pete Bicknell	1
Roger Phelps	1
Dave Donath	1
Donnie Wetmore	1
Gordy Button Jr.	1
10 Drivers	23 Events

Outlaw Small Block Modified Points

Pos.	Driver	Points
1	Paul Jensen	1002
2	Tom Kinsella	968
3	Roger Phelps	888
4	Donnie Wetmore	832
5	Doug Fuller	772
6	J.J. Michaels	702
7	Louie Michaels	676
8	Gordy Button Jr.	658
9	Tom Juhl Jr.	596
10	John Barker Jr.	596

1993

Track Champion: Paul Jensen (Outlaw Modified)

Outlaw Small Block Modified Records – Weekly Results

Date	Laps	Winner	2nd	3rrd	4th	5th
2-May	40	Gordy Button Jr.	Doug Fuller	Paul Jensen	Bob Savoie	Billy Whittaker
	25	Gordy Button Jr.	John Barker Jr.	Paul Jensen	Bob Savoie	Donnie Wetmore
9-May	25	Doug Fuller	Lou Michaels	Tom Kinsella	J.J. Michaels	Bob Savoie
16-May	25	Tom Kinsella	John Ramsey	J.J. Michaels	Dale Planck	Randy Glenski
23-May	25	Randy Glenski	Roger Phelps	Paul Jensen	J.J. Michaels	Gordy Button Jr.
30-May	25	Tom Kinsella	Gordy Button Jr.	J.J. Michaels	Jeff Walton	Doug Fuller
6-Jun	25	Tom Kinsella	Ted Lamb Jr.	Roger Phelps	J.J. Michaels	Donnie Wetmore
13-Jun	25	Doug Fuller	Dale Planck	Tom Kinsella	Paul Jensen	Roger Phelps
20-Jun	25	Dale Planck	Donnie Wetmore	Jeff Walton	Roger Phelps	Paul Jensen
23-Jun	50	Randy Glenski	Dale Planck	Roger Phelps	J.J. Michaels	Doug Fuller
27-Jun	25	Paul Jensen	Randy Glenski	Gordy Button Jr.	Jeff Walton	Dale Planck
4-Jul	20	Billy Whittaker	J.J. Michaels	John Barker Jr.	Dale Planck	John Ramsey
	20	Dale Planck	Lou Michaels	J.J. Michaels	Roger Phelps	Jeff Walton
11-Jul	25	Doug Fuller	Tom Kinsella	Jeff Walton	Dale Planck	Roger Phelps
18-Jul	25	Paul Jensen	John Ramsey	Dale Planck	Lou Michaels	Doug Fuller
25-Jul	25	Tom Kinsella	Billy Whittaker	Doug Fuller	John Barker Jr.	Dale Planck
1-Aug	25	Tom Kinsella	J.J. Michaels	Lou Michaels	Paul Jensen	John Barker Jr.
8-Aug	25	Randy Glenski	Paul Jensen	Donnie Wetmore	Dale Planck	Billy Whittaker
15-Aug	25	Paul Jensen	J.J. Michaels	Roger Phelps	Doug Fuller	Bob Sitterly
22-Aug	25	Roger Phelps	Tom Kinsella	Randy Glenski	Doug Fuller	Paul Jensen
29-Aug	25	Randy Glenski	Dale Planck	J.J. Michaels	Gordy Button Jr.	Tom Kinsella
5-Sep	25	Gordy Button Jr.	Donnie Wetmore	Randy Glenski	Paul Jensen	Dale Planck
12-Sep	20	Randy Glenski	J.J. Michaels	Paul Jensen	Bob Podolak	Crash Nash
19-Sep	100	Billy Pauch	Paul Jensen	Donnie Wetmore	Duane Howard	Randy Glenski

Total Outlaw Small Block Modified Wins

Driver	Wins
Tom Kinsella	5
Randy Glenski	5
Gordy Button Jr. Jr.	3
Doug Fuller	3
Paul Jensen	3
Dale Planck	2
Billy Whittaker	1
Roger Phelps	1
Billy Pauch	1
9 Drivers	24 Events

Outlaw Small Block Modified Points

Pos.	Driver	Points
1	Paul Jensen	948
2	Doug Fuller	908
3	J.J. Michaels	882
4	Dale Planck	842
5	Billy Whittaker	800
6	Roger Phelps	776
7	Gordy Button Jr.	766
8	John Barker Jr.	710
9	Randy Glenski	656
10	Tom Kinsella	646

1994

Track Champion: Dale Planck (NASCAR Outlaw Modified)

NASCAR Outlaw Modified Records – Weekly Results

Date	Laps	Winner	2nd	3rd	4th	5th
24-Apr	40	Paul Jensen	Roger Phelps	Tom Kinsella	Randy Glenski	John Barker Jr.
1-May	25	Dale Planck	Bob Sitterly	Tom Kinsella	John Barker Jr.	Ted Lamb Jr.
8-May	25	Rain				
15-May	25	Rain				
22-May	25	Dale Planck	Randy Glenski	Roger Phelps	Donnie Wetmore	Ted Lamb, Jr.
29-May	25	Tom Kinsella	Ron Holmes	Dale Planck	Roger Phelps	Billy Whittaker
5-Jun	25	Rain				
12-Jun	25	Dale Planck	Paul Jensen	Billy Whittaker	Bob Sitterly	John Barker Jr.
19-Jun	25	Dale Planck	Donnie Wetmore	Tom Kinsella	Billy Whittaker	Roger Phelps
26-Jun	25	PPD until 7/3 (T-Storm)				
3-Jul	25	Roger Phelps	Tom Kinsella	Gordy Button Jr.	Dale Planck	Dave House
	25	Tom Kinsella	Ron Holmes	Paul Jensen	Gordy Button Jr.	John Barker Jr.
10-Jul	25	Dale Planck	Roger Phelps	Billy Whittaker	Gordy Button Jr.	John Barker Jr.
17-Jul	25	Dale Planck	Roger Phelps	Paul Jensen	Ron Holmes	Randy Glenski
24-Jul	25	Dale Planck	Tom Kinsella	Bob Sitterly	Paul Jensen	Randy Glenski
31-Jul	25	Paul Jensen	Tom Kinsella	Dale Planck	John Barker Jr.	Ron Holmes
7-Aug	25	Dale Planck	Bob Sitterly	Tom Kinsella	Bob Podolak	John Barker Jr.
14-Aug	25	Rain				
21-Aug	25	Rain				
28-Aug	20	Paul Jensen	Tom Kinsella	Ted Lamb Jr.	Dale Planck	Ron Holmes
	20	PPD until 9/4				
1-Sep	25	Dale Planck	Paul Jensen	Tom Kinsella	Gordy Button Jr.	Billy Whittaker
4-Sep	20	Dale Planck	Tom Kinsella	Andy Romano	John Barker Jr.	Ted Lamb Jr.
	25	Dale Planck	Paul Jensen	Tom Kinsella	Billy Whittaker	Andy Romano
11-Sep	25	Paul Jensen	Gordy Button Jr.	Tom Kinsella	Bob Podolak	Roger Phelps
25-Sep	25	Gordy Button Jr. (OC)	Dale Planck	Paul Jensen	Roger Phelps	Ron Holmes

Total Outlaw Modified Wins

Driver	Wins
Dale Planck	11
Paul Jensen	4
Tom Kinsella	2
Roger Phelps	1
Gordy Button Jr.	1
5 Drivers	19 Events

Outlaw Modified Points

Pos.	Driver	Points
1	Dale Planck	988
2	Tom Kinsella	822
3	Roger Phelps	748
4	John Barker Jr.	718
5	Paul Jensen	684
6	Billy Whittaker	630
	Ron Holmes	630
8	Donnie Wetmore	510
9	Bob Sitterly	504
10	Joel Thomas	434

1995

Track Champion: Dale Planck (NASCAR Outlaw Small Block Modified)

NASCAR Outlaw Small Block Modified Records – Weekly Results

Date	Laps	Winner	2nd	3rd	4th	5th
23-Apr	40	Dale Planck	Tom Kinsella	Ron Holmes	Mike Romano	Gordy Button Jr.
30-Apr	25	Dale Planck	Paul Jensen	John Barker Jr.	Gordy Button Jr.	Roger Phelps
7-May	25	Tom Kinsella	Dale Planck	Roger Phelps	Donnie Wetmore	Gordy Button Jr.
14-May	25	Rain				
21-May	25	Jeff Walton	Paul Jensen	Dale Planck	Tom Kinsella	Donnie Wetmore
28-May	25	Rain				
4-Jun	25	Gordy Button Jr.	Dale Planck	Ron Holmes	John Ramsey	Paul Jensen
11-Jun	25	Paul Jensen	Jeff Walton	Ron Holmes	Dale Planck	Gordy Button Jr.
18-Jun	25	Tom Kinsella	Dale Planck	Bob Sitterly	John Ramsey	Jeff Walton
25-Jun	25	Donnie Wetmore	Gordy Button Jr.	Dale Planck	Jeff Walton	Tom Kinsella
2-Jul	25	Dale Planck	John Ramsey	Tom Kinsella	Ron Holmes	Jeff Walton
9-Jul	25	Dale Planck	Tom Kinsella	Mike Romano	Roger Phelps	Gordy Button Jr.
16-Jul	25	Rain				
23-Jul	25	Rain				
30-Jul	25	Ron Holmes	John Barker Jr.	Dale Planck	Jeff Walton	Bob Sitterly
6-Aug	20	Dale Planck	Gordy Button Jr.	Mike Romano	Roger Phelps	Ron Holmes
	20	John Barker Jr.	Jeff Walton	Donnie Wetmore	Tom Kinsella	Gordy Button Jr.
13-Aug	25	Paul Jensen	Tom Kinsella	Mike Romano	John Barker Jr.	Gordy Button Jr.
20-Aug	20	Tom Kinsella	Dale Planck	Jeff Walton	Paul Jensen	Gordy Button Jr.
	20	Dale Planck	Jeff Walton	Dave House	Bob Sitterly	Donnie Wetmore
27-Aug	25	Tom Kinsella	Donnie Wetmore	Mike Romano	Ron Holmes	John Barker Jr.
31-Aug	25	Rain				
3-Sep	25	Tom Kinsella	Ron Holmes	Dale Planck	Paul Jensen	Mike Romano
7-Sep	25	Rain				
10-Sep	20	Dale Planck	Tom Kinsella	John Barker Jr.	Ron Holmes	Mike VanDusen
	20	Dale Planck	Paul Jensen	Gordy Button Jr.	Mitch Gibbs	Tom Kinsella
15-Sep	35	Mike VanDusen	Tom Kinsella	Dale Planck	Paul Jensen	Mike Romano

Total NASCAR Outlaw Small Block Modified Wins

Driver	Wins
Dale Planck	8
Tom Kinsella	5
Paul Jensen	2
Jeff Walton	1
Gordy Button Jr.	1
Donnie Wetmore	1
Ron Holmes	1
John Barker Jr.	1
Mike VanDusen	1
9 Drivers	21 Events

NASCAR Outlaw Modified Points

Pos.	Driver	Points
1	Dale Planck	916
2	Tom Kinsella	878
3	Ron Holmes	788
4	Jeff Walton	760
5	Gordy Button	744
6	Donnie Wetmore	726
7	Paul Jensen	716
8	John Barker Jr.	708
9	Roger Phelps	574
10	John Ramsey	552

1996

Track Champion: Mitch Gibbs (NASCAR 358-Modified)

NASCAR 358-Modified Records – Weekly Results

Date	Laps	Winner	2nd	3rd	4th	5th
28-Apr	25	Dale Planck	Tom Kinsella	Jeff Walton	Danny Johnson	Mitch Gibbs
5-May	25	Mike Romano	Tom Kinsella	Dale Planck	Mitch Gibbs	J.J. Michaels
12-May	25	Rain				
19-May	25	Dale Planck	Jeff Walton	Mitch Gibbs	Danny Johnson	Tom Kinsella
26-May	25	Ron Holmes	Dale Planck	Mitch Gibbs	John Barker Jr.	Mike Romano
2-Jun	25	Mitch Gibbs	Tom Kinsella	John Barker Jr.	Paul Jensen	Mike VanDusen
9-Jun	20	Dale Planck	Paul Jensen	Mitch Gibbs	Tom Kinsella	John Barker Jr.
	20	Tom Kinsella	Mike VanDusen	Ron Holmes	Mitch Gibbs	Jeff Walton
16-Jun	25	Mike Romano	Dale Planck	Ron Holmes	J.J. Michaels	Tom Kinsella
23-Jun	25	Mitch Gibbs	Mike Romano	Jeff Walton	Mike VanDusen	Tom Kinsella
30-Jun	25	Mitch Gibbs	Paul Jensen	Roger Phelps	J.J. Michaels	Ron Holmes
7-Jul		OFF				
14-Jul	25	Dale Planck	Tom Kinsella	Jeff Walton	Mitch Gibbs	John Barker Jr.
21-Jul	25	Paul Jensen	Danny Johnson	Tom Kinsella	Mitch Gibbs	Jeff Walton
28-Jul	20	Bob Sitterly	Shawn Donath	Jeff Walton	Ron Holmes	Danny Johnson
	20	Paul Jensen	J.J. Michaels	John Barker Jr.	Dale Planck	Shawn Donath
4-Aug	25	Tom Kinsella	Mitch Gibbs	John Barker Jr.	Paul Jensen	Roger Phelps
11-Aug	25	Dale Planck	Tom Kinsella	J.J. Michaels	Danny Johnson	Mitch Gibbs
18-Aug	25	Dale Planck	Paul Jensen	Tom Kinsella	Mitch Gibbs	J.J. Michaels
20-Aug	25	Dale Planck	Jeff Walton	John Barker Jr.	J.J. Michaels	Ron Holmes
25-Aug	25	Mitch Gibbs	Ron Holmes	John Barker Jr.	Jeff Walton	Dale Planck
1-Sep	25	J.J. Michaels	Paul Jensen	Ron Holmes	Andy Romano	Roger Phelps
8-Sep	25	Rain				
15-Sep	50	Rain				

Total NASCAR 358-Modified Wins

Driver	Wins
Dale Planck	7
Mitch Gibbs	4
Mike Romano	2
Tom Kinsella	2
Paul Jensen	2
Ron Holmes	1
Bob Sitterly	1
J.J. Michaels	1
8 Drivers	20 Events

NASCAR 358-Modified Points

Pos.	Driver	Points
1	Mitch Gibbs	846
2	Dale Planck	805
3	John Barker Jr.	762
4	Ron Holmes	747
5	Paul Jensen	740
6	Tom Kinsella	736
7	J.J. Michaels	701
8	Jeff Walton	682
9	Roger Phelps	568
10	Bob Sitterly	549

1997

Track Champion: Dale Planck (NASCAR 358-Modified)

NASCAR 358-Modified Records – Weekly Results

Date	Laps	Winner	2nd	3rd	4th	5th
4-May	40	Dale Planck	Mitch Gibbs	Ron Holmes	John Barker Jr.	Jeff Walton
11-May	40	Dale Planck (OC)	Kenny Brightbill	Brett Hearn	Tim Fuller	Billy Decker
18-May	25	J.J. Michaels	Joe Slawiak	Ted Lamb Jr.	Ron Holmes	Dale Planck
25-May	25	Dale Planck	Ron Holmes	Tom Kinsella	Dave House	Paul Jensen
1-Jun	25	Rain				
8-Jun	20	Doug Fuller	Roger Phelps	Joel Thomas	Mike Hulsizer	Dave House
	20	Steve Hulsizer	J.J. Michaels	Dale Planck	Ron Holmes	Bob Sitterly
15-Jun	25	Dale Planck	Ted Lamb, Jr.	Pete Taylor	J.J. Michaels	Jeff Walton
22-Jun	25	Mitch Gibbs	Ron Holmes	Dale Planck	Donnie Wetmore	Jeff Walton
29-Jun	25	Donnie Wetmore	Dale Planck	J.J. Michaels	Joe Slawiak	Steve Hulsizer
6-Jul	25	J.J. Michaels	Ron Holmes	Paul Jensen	Ted Lamb, Jr.	John Barker Jr.
13-Jul	25	Dale Planck	Jeff Walton	Ron Holmes	J.J. Michaels	Paul Jensen
20-Jul	25	J.J. Michaels	Steve Hulsizer	Bob Sitterly	Ron Holmes	Mitch Gibbs
27-Jul	25	J.J. Michaels	Ron Holmes	Mitch Gibbs	Dale Planck	Donnie Wetmore
3-Aug	25	Jeff Walton	Mitch Gibbs	J.J. Michaels	Ted Lamb Jr.	Dale Planck
10-Aug	25	Dale Planck	J.J. Michaels	Mitch Gibbs	Dave House	John Barker Jr.
17-Aug	20	Donnie Wetmore	Ron Holmes	Dale Planck	Steve Hulsizer	Paul Jensen
	20	J.J. Michaels	Dave House	Donnie Wetmore	Ron Holmes	Doug Fuller
24-Aug	25	Paul Jensen	Ted Lamb Jr.	Jeff Walton	Dale Planck	John Barker Jr.
31-Aug	25	Roger Phelps	Jeff Walton	Ron Holmes	Gus Schmidt	Joe Slawiak
7-Sep	25	Rain				
14-Sep	25	Dale Planck	J.J. Michaels	Paul Jensen	Ron Holmes	Dave House

Total NASCAR 358-Modified Wins

Driver	Wins
Dale Planck	7
J.J. Michaels	5
Donnie Wetmore	2
Doug Fuller	1
Steve Hulsizer	1
Mitch Gibbs	1
Jeff Walton	1
Paul Jensen	1
Roger Phelps	1
9 Drivers	20 Events

NASCAR 358-Modified Points

Pos.	Driver	Points
1	Dale Planck	858
2	J.J. Michaels	801
3	Ron Holmes	782
4	John Barker Jr.	630
5	Jeff Walton	623
6	Bob Sitterly	620
7	Roger Phelps	593
8	Paul Jensen	591
9	Doug Fuller	575
10	Dave House	542

1998

Track Champions: Roger Phelps (Open Competition Modified)
J.J. Michaels (NASCAR Modified)*

*The first four weeks of the season were run under the New England Region of the NASCAR Winston Racing Series. After a change in track management, NASCAR was dropped and the track was run as an independent. NASCAR Track Champions for NUR in 1998 only included the first four races.

NASCAR/Open Competition Modified Records – Weekly Results

Date	Laps	Winner	2nd	3rd	4th	5th
17-May	25	J.J. Michaels *	Billy Wilcox	Ron Holmes	John Barker Jr.	Bob Sitterly
24-May	25	J.J. Michaels *	Ron Holmes	John Barker Jr.	Dave House	Steve Hulsizer
31-May	25	Rain				
6-Jun	25	Ron Holmes *	Paul Jensen	J.J. Michaels	Jeremy Smith	Dave House
14-Jun	25	Rain				
21-Jun	25	Paul Jensen *	Ron Holmes	J.J. Michaels	Jim Rothwell	Roger Phelps
28-Jun		CLOSED				
5-Jul	25	Roger Phelps	Ron Holmes	Mitch Gibbs	Steve Hulsizer	Dave House
12-Jul	25	Roger Phelps	Mitch Gibbs	Steve Hulsizer	J.J. Michaels	Dave House
19-Jul	25	J.J. Michaels	Roger Phelps	Paul Jensen	Doug Fuller	Mitch Gibbs
26-Jul	25	Ron Holmes	Gus Schmidt Jr.	Paul Jensen	J.J. Michaels	Ted Lamb Jr.
2-Aug	25	Jim Rothwell	J.J. Michaels	John Barker Jr.	Mitch Gibbs	Jeremy Smith
9-Aug	25	Ted Lamb Jr.	John Barker Jr.	J.J. Michaels	Mike Hulsizer	Mitch Gibbs
16-Aug	25	Jeff Walton	Ron Holmes	Roger Phelps	Dave House	Mitch Gibbs
23-Aug	25	Gus Schmidt Jr.	Ron Holmes	Roger Phelps	Doug Fuller	Jim Rothwell
30-Aug	25	Mitch Gibbs	Paul Jensen	Dave House	J.J. Michaels	Ron Holmes
6-Sep	25	John Barker Jr.	Roger Phelps	Dave House	Paul Jensen	Doug Fuller
13-Sep	35	Mitch Gibbs	Ron Holmes	Jim Rothwell	Doug Fuller	Roger Phelps

Total Modified Wins

Driver	Wins
J.J. Michaels	3
Ron Holmes	2
Roger Phelps	2
Mitch Gibbs	2
John Barker Jr.	1
Jeff Walton	1
Gus Schmidt Jr.	1
Jim Rothwell	1
Ted Lamb Jr.	1
Paul Jensen	1
10 Drivers	15 Events

NASCAR Modified Points
*First 4 Events of the Season

Pos.	Driver	Points
1	J.J. Michaels	192
2	Ron Holmes	192
3	John Barker Jr.	166
4	Paul Jensen	150
5	Roger Phelps	132
6	Billy Wilcox	128
7	Bob Sitterly	124
8	Dave House	122
9	Doug Fuller	118
10	Lance Lauffenberger	104

Open Competition Modified Points
Remainder of the Season after NASCAR

Pos.	Driver	Points
1	Roger Phelps	392
2	Dave House	390
3	Mitch Gibbs	374
4	J.J. Michaels	348
5	Paul Jensen	334
6	Doug Fuller	324
7	John Barker Jr.	320
8	Ron Holmes	314
9	Jeremy Smith	296
10	Jim Rothwell	290

1999

Track Champion: Dale Planck (DIRT 358-Modified)

DIRT 358-Modified Records – Weekly Results

Date	Laps	Winner	2nd	3rd	4th	5th
2-May	30	Mike Romano	Dale Planck	Jim Rothwell	John Barker Jr.	A.J. Romano
9-May	50	Rain delayed to 7/29				
16-May	30	Mitch Gibbs	Dale Planck	J.J. Michaels	John Barker Jr.	Mike Romano
23-May	30	J.J. Michaels	Mike Romano	Dale Planck	Dave House	Mitch Gibbs
30-May	30	Dale Planck	Todd Burley	Mitch Gibbs	Mike Romano	Jeff Walton
6-Jun	30	J.J. Michaels	Ron Holmes	Dale Planck	Steve Hulsizer	Mitch Gibbs
13-Jun	30	Ron Holmes	Mitch Gibbs	Roger Phelps	Ted Lamb Jr.	Dale Planck
20-Jun	30	Mitch Gibbs	Jeff Walton	Dale Planck	Mike Hulsizer	Todd Burley
27-Jun	30	Mitch Gibbs	J.J. Michaels	Ron Holmes	Jeff Walton	John Barker Jr.
4-Jul	30	Steve Hulsizer	Dale Planck	Todd Burley	Gus Schmidt Jr.	Jeff Walton
11-Jul	30	Ron Holmes	Mitch Gibbs	J.J. Michaels	Jerry Higbie Jr.	Roger Phelps
18-Jul	30	Mitch Gibbs	Ron Holmes	Dale Planck	Todd Burley	J.J. Michaels
29-Jul	50	Todd Burley	Dale Planck	J.J. Michaels	Bobby Varin	John Barker Jr.
1-Aug	30	Gus Schmidt Jr.	Dale Planck	Ron Holmes	Jeff Walton	John Barker Jr.
8-Aug	30	Rain				
15-Aug	30	J.J. Michaels	Ted Lamb Jr.	Dale Planck	Ron Holmes	Mitch Gibbs
22-Aug	30	Mitch Gibbs	Dale Planck	Gus Schmidt Jr.	J.J. Michaels	Jeff Walton
25-Aug	99	Danny Johnson	Steve Paine	J.J. Michaels	Ron Holmes	Pete Bicknell
29-Aug	30	Dale Planck	J.J. Michaels	Ron Holmes	Roger Phelps	John Barker Jr.
5-Sep	30	J.J. Michaels	Mitch Gibbs	Jeff Walton	Jim Rothwell	John Barker Jr.
12-Sep	30	Mitch Gibbs	Dale Planck	Jim Rothwell	Jason Barney	John Barker Jr.
24-Sep	100	Brett Hearn	Steve Paine	Danny Johnson	Andy Bachetti	Tim Fuller

Total DIRT 358-Modified Wins

Driver	Wins
Mitch Gibbs	6
J.J. Michaels	4
Dale Planck	2
Ron Holmes	2
Mike Romano	1
Steve Hulsizer	1
Todd Burley	1
Gus Schmidt Jr.	1
Danny Johnson	1
Brett Hearn	1
10 Drivers	20 Events

DIRT 358-Modified Points

Pos.	Driver	Points
1	Dale Planck	909
2	Mitch Gibbs	863
3	Ron Holmes	755
4	J.J. Michaels	744
5	Jim Rothwell	736
6	John Barker Jr.	721
7	Jeff Walton	718
8	Roger Phelps	679
9	Gus Schmidt Jr.	623
10	Mike Hulsizer	538

2000

Track Champion: Ron Holmes (DIRT 358-Modified)

DIRT 358-Modified Records – Weekly Results

Date	Laps	Winner	2nd	3rd	4th	5th
7-May	40	Andy Bachetti	Ron Holmes	Pete Bicknell	Ronnie Johnson	Tim Clemons
14-May	100	Danny Johnson	Todd Burley	Ron Holmes	Pat Ward	Tim Clemons
21-May	30	Rain				
28-May	30	Ron Holmes	Todd Burley	Mitch Gibbs	J.J. Michaels	Pete Bicknell
4-Jun	30	Todd Burley	Dale Planck	J.J. Michaels	Gus Schmidt Jr.	Steve Hulsizer
11-Jun	30	Rain				
18-Jun	30	Rain				
25-Jun	30	Rain				
2-Jul	20	John Barker Jr.	Steve Hulsizer	Jim Rothwell	Dale Planck	J.J. Michaels
	20	J.J. Michaels	Mitch Gibbs	Gus Schmidt Jr.	Dale Planck	Billy Wilcox
9-Jul	30	Rain				
16-Jul	30	Ron Holmes	Andy Bachetti	Tim Clemons	J.J. Michaels	Dale Planck
23-Jul	30	Ronnie Johnson	Roger Phelps	Ron Holmes	Tim Clemons	Ted Lamb Jr.
30-Jul	30	Rain				
6-Aug	30	Rain				
13-Aug	30	Todd Burley	Billy Wilcox	Tim Clemons	J.J. Michaels	Mark Schoonover
20-Aug	30	Jason Barney	Ron Holmes	Todd Burley	J.J. Michaels	Mitch Gibbs
27-Aug	30	Mitch Gibbs	Dale Planck	Jack Johnson	J.J. Michaels	John Barker Jr.
3-Sep	30	Dale Planck	Jack Johnson	Mitch Gibbs	Ron Holmes	Ted Lamb Jr.
22-Sep	100	Jack Johnson	Brett Hearn	Dale Planck	Todd Burley	J.J. Michaels

DIRT Big Block Modified Results

Date	Laps	Winner	2nd	3rd	4th	5th
24-Aug	100	Danny Johnson	Steve Paine	Jack Johnson	Brett Hearn	Alan Johnson

Total DIRT 358-Modified Wins

Driver	Wins
Ron Holmes	2
Todd Burley	2
Andy Bachetti	1
Danny Johnson	1
John Barker Jr.	1
J.J. Michaels	1
Ronnie Johnson	1
Jason Barney	1
Mitch Gibbs	1
Dale Planck	1
Jack Johnson	1
11 Drivers	13 Events

DIRT 358-Modified Points

Pos.	Driver	Points
1	Ron Holmes	519
2	Dale Planck	501
3	J.J. Michaels	496
4	Billy Wilcox	483
5	Tim Clemons	474
6	Roger Phelps	467
7	Gus Schmidt Jr.	439
8	Ronnie Johnson	418
	John Barker Jr.	418
10	Todd Burley	380

2001

Track Champion: Todd Burley (DIRT 358-Modified)

DIRT 358-Modified Records – Weekly Results

Date	Laps	Winner	2nd	3rd	4th	5th
6-May	40	J.J. Michaels	Ron Holmes	Todd Burley	Ryan Baye	Roger Phelps
13-May	100	Danny Johnson	Pete Bicknell	Steve Paine	Tim Fuller	Brett Hearn
20-May	30	Todd Burley	Jack Johnson	Gus Schmidt Jr.	Jason Barney	Paul Jensen
27-May	30	Rain				
3-Jun	30	Rain				
10-Jun	30	Todd Burley	Ron Holmes	Jack Johnson	Roger Phelps	Steve Hulsizer
17-Jun	30	Jack Johnson	Todd Burley	Steve Hulsizer	Mitch Gibbs	Jason Barney
24-Jun	30	John Ramsey	Jason Barney	Ron Holmes	Jack Johnson	Paul Jensen
1-Jul	20	Jack Johnson	Steve Hulsizer	Wayne Reutimann Jr.	Mitch Gibbs	Ryan Baye
	20	Jack Johnson	Todd Burley	Gus Schmidt Jr.	John Barker Jr.	Ryan Baye
8-Jul	30	Todd Burley	Ron Holmes	Paul Jensen	Gus Schmidt Jr.	Steve Hulsizer
15-Jul	30	Todd Burley	John Ramsey	Alan Johnson	J.J. Michaels	Paul Jensen
22-Jul	30	J.J. Michaels	Jack Johnson	Mitch Gibbs	Todd Burley	Ryan Baye
29-Jul	30	Mitch Gibbs	Todd Burley	Gus Schmidt Jr.	Jack Johnson	Jason Barney
5-Aug	30	Todd Burley	Steve Hulsizer	J.J. Michaels	Ryan Baye	Jason Barney
12-Aug	30	Mitch Gibbs	Todd Burley	Ryan Baye	Roger Phelps	John Ramsey
19-Aug	30	Todd Burley	Gus Schmidt Jr.	Jack Johnson	Mitch Gibbs	John Barker Jr.
26-Aug	30	Todd Burley	Aaron Excell	Ryan Baye	Jack Johnson	Ted Lamb Jr.
2-Sep	30	Aaron Excell	Mitch Gibbs	Roger Phelps	Ron Holmes	Gus Schmidt Jr.
9-Sep	30	Ryan Baye	Andy Romano	Jim Mahaney	Pete Taylor	Joel Thomas
16-Sep	100	Alan Johnson	Brett Hearn	Pete Bicknell	Danny Johnson	Jack Johnson

DIRT Big Block Modified Results

Date	Laps	Winner	2nd	3rd	4th	5th
23-Aug	100	Billy Decker	Tim McCreadie	Brett Hearn	Steve Paine	Danny Johnson

Total DIRT 358-Modified Wins

Driver	Wins
Todd Burley	7
Jack Johnson	3
J.J. Michaels	2
Mitch Gibbs	2
Danny Johnson	1
John Ramsey	1
Aaron Excell	1
Ryan Baye	1
Alan Johnson	1
9 Drivers	19 Events

DIRT 358-Modified Points

Pos.	Driver	Points
1	Todd Burley	814
2	Ryan Baye	660
3	Jason Barney	654
4	Gus Schmidt Jr.	632
5	J.J. Michaels	619
6	Jack Johnson	594
7	John Ramsey	584
8	Mitch Gibbs	539
9	Steve Hulsizer	536
10	Paul Jensen	517

2002

Track Champion: Matt Sheppard (DIRT 358-Modified)

DIRT 358-Modified Records – Weekly Results

Date	Laps	Winner	2nd	3rd	4th	5th
5-May	40	Mitch Gibbs	Matt Sheppard	Ron Holmes	Jason Barney	Steve Paine
12-May	30	Rain				
19-May	30	Rain				
26-May	50	Gordy Button Jr.	Ryan Baye	Ron Holmes	Matt Sheppard	Steve Hulsizer
2-Jun	30	Todd Burley	Ryan Baye	Jack Johnson	Matt Sheppard	Jim Rothwell
9-Jun	30	Gus Schmidt Jr.	Tony Ross	Gordy Button Jr.	Mike Hulsizer	Jim Rothwell
16-Jun	30	Postponed to June 30				
19-Jun	100	Danny Johnson	Jack Johnson	Vic Coffey	Jeff Trombley	Mitch Gibbs
23-Jun	30	Steve Hulsizer	Mitch Gibbs	Matt Sheppard	John Ramsey	Mark Flach Jr.
30-Jun	30	Jack Johnson	Matt Sheppard	J.J. Michaels	Gordy Button Jr.	Steve Hulsizer
	30	Todd Burley	Matt Sheppard	Ryan Baye	Gordy Button Jr.	Jeff Kotary
7-Jul	30	Jack Johnson	Jason Barney	Billy Wilcox	Ryan Baye	John Ramsey
14-Jul	30	Mitch Gibbs	Gus Schmidt Jr.	Matt Sheppard	Gordy Button Jr.	Jim Rothwell
21-Jul	30	J.J. Michaels	Matt Sheppard	Gordy Button Jr.	Ryan Baye	Mitch Gibbs
28-Jul	30	Postponed to August 11				
4-Aug	30	Jack Johnson	Gus Schmidt Jr.	Ryan Baye	J.J. Michaels	Jason Barney
11-Aug	30	Matt Sheppard	Mitch Gibbs	J.J. Michaels	Aaron Excell	Ryan Baye
	30	Jeff Kotary	Matt Sheppard	Jason Barney	Gus Schmidt Jr.	Ryan Baye
18-Aug	30	Ted Lamb Jr.	Mitch Gibbs	Jim Rothwell	Jason Barney	Matt Sheppard
25-Aug	30	Todd Burley	Gordy Button Jr.	Matt Sheppard	Ron Holmes	Jeff Kotary
20-Sep	101	Brett Hearn	Todd Burley	Matt Sheppard	Alan Johnson	Pat Ward

DIRT Big Block Modified Results

Date	Laps	Winner	2nd	3rd	4th	5th
22-Aug	100	Rain				

Total DIRT 358-Modified Wins

Driver	Wins
Jack Johnson	3
Todd Burley	3
Mitch Gibbs	2
Brett Hearn	1
Danny Johnson	1
Gordy Button Jr.	1
Gus Schmidt Jr.	1
Jeff Kotary	1
J.J. Michaels	1
Matt Sheppard	1
Steve Hulsizer	1
Ted Lamb Jr.	1
12 Drivers	17 Events

DIRT 358-Modified Points

Pos.	Driver	Points
1	Matt Sheppard	783
2	Mitch Gibbs	717
3	Ryan Baye	677
4	Gordy Button Jr.	677
5	Jason Barney	649
6	Jeff Kotary	574
7	Jim Rothwell	568
8	Gus Schmidt Jr.	568
9	Paul Kinney	524
10	John Ramsey	513

2003

Track Champion: Dale Planck (DIRT 358-Modified)

DIRT 358-Modified Records – Weekly Results

Date	Laps	Winner	2nd	3rd	4th	5th
27-Apr	40	Dale Planck	Jack Johnson	John Ramsey	Todd Burley	Pete Taylor
4-May	30	Jim Rothwell	Dale Planck	Willy Decker	Todd Burley	Mitch Gibbs
11-May	100	Rained Out				
18-May	30	Matt Sheppard	Dale Planck	Gus Schmidt Jr.	Willy Decker	Paul Kinney
25-May	30	Dale Planck	J.J. Michaels	Ryan Baye	Paul Kinney	Willy Decker
1-Jun	30	Rain				
8-Jun	30	Todd Burley	Mitch Gibbs	Willy Decker	John Ramsey	Ted Lamb Jr.
15-Jun	30	Mitch Gibbs	Dale Planck	Jim Rothwell	J.J. Michaels	Todd Burley
19-Jun	100	Rain Cancelled				
22-Jun	30	Pete Taylor	Todd Burley	Matt Sheppard	Chuck Hebing	Dale Planck
29-Jun	30	Willy Decker	Matt Sheppard	Dale Planck	Mitch Gibbs	Ted Lamb Jr.
6-Jul	30	Todd Burley	Dale Planck	Pete Bicknell	Matt Sheppard	Paul Jensen
13-Jul	30	Gus Schmidt Jr.	Mitch Gibbs	Todd Burley	Matt Sheppard	Dale Planck
20-Jul	30	Matt Sheppard	Mitch Gibbs	Dale Planck	Todd Burley	Willy Decker
27-Jul	30	Rain				
3-Aug	30	Rain Delayed to 8/17				
10-Aug	30	Rain				
17-Aug	30	Mitch Gibbs	John Ramsey	Ted Lamb Jr.	Matt Sheppard	Gus Schmidt Jr.
	30	Todd Burley	Matt Sheppard	Mitch Gibbs	Gus Schmidt Jr.	Paul Kinney
24-Aug	20	Paul Jensen	Paul Kinney	Aaron Excell	Dale Planck	John Ramsey
	20	John Ramsey	Dale Planck	Jim Rothwell	Mike Ward	Mitch Gibbs
31-Aug	OFF					
7-Sep	40	Dave Camara	Mitch Gibbs	Paul Jensen	Ted Lamb Jr.	John Bellinger
14-Sep	100	Brett Hearn	Dale Planck	Tim Fuller	Alan Johnson	Matt Sheppard

DIRT Big Block Modified Results

Date	Laps	Winner	2nd	3rd	4th	5th
31-Jul	100	Brett Hearn	Alan Johnson	Vic Coffey	Matt Sheppard	Gary Tomkins

Total DIRT 358-Modified Wins

Driver	Wins
Todd Burley	3
Dale Planck	2
Mitch Gibbs	2
Matt Sheppard	2
Brett Hearn	2
Jim Rothwell	1
Pete Taylor	1
Willy Decker	1
Gus Schmidt Jr.	1
Paul Jensen	1
John Ramsey	1
Dave Camara	1
12 Drivers	18 Events

DIRT 358-Modified Points

Pos.	Driver	Points
1	Dale Planck	740
2	Mitch Gibbs	732
3	Matt Sheppard	698
4	Todd Burley	663
5	Willy Decker	619
6	Mark Flach	580
7	John Ramsey	566
8	Paul Kinney	553
9	Jeff Kotary	546
10	Dave Rauscher	542

2004

Track Champion: Stewart Friesen (DIRT 358-Modified)

DIRT 358-Modified Records – Weekly Results

Date	Laps	Winner	2nd	3rd	4th	5th
25-Apr	30	Rain				
2-May	22	Stewart Friesen	Mitch Gibbs	Todd Burley	Willy Decker	Mark Flach Jr.
9-May	30	Rain				
16-May	30	Stewart Friesen	John Ramsey	Willy Decker	Dave Camara	Brian Weaver
23-May	30	Rain				
30-May	30	Stewart Friesen	Todd Burley	Mark Flach Jr.	Dave Camara	Gus Schmidt Jr.
6-Jun	30	Stewart Friesen	Mitch Gibbs	Brian Weaver	Mark Flach Jr.	Dave Camara
13-Jun	30	Rain				
20-Jun	30	Todd Burley	Stewart Friesen	Brian Weaver	Bobby Varin	Paul Jensen
23-Jun	50	Brian Weaver	Willy Decker	Mark Flach Jr.	John Ramsey	Bobby Varin
27-Jun	30	Jamie Christian	Bobby Varin	Dave Camara	Willy Decker	Brian Weaver
4-Jul	30	Stewart Friesen	Todd Burley	Mitch Gibbs	Dave Camara	Bobby Varin
11-Jul	30	Stewart Friesen	Todd Burley	Dave Camara	Bobby Varin	Mitch Gibbs
18-Jul	30	Rain				
25-Jul	30	Bobby Varin	Mitch Gibbs	Mark Flach Jr.	Dave Camara	Paul Jensen
1-Aug	30	Brian Weaver	Stewart Friesen	Mitch Gibbs	Mark Flach Jr.	Dave Camara
8-Aug	30	Todd Burley	Dave Camara	Willy Decker	Mitch Gibbs	Paul Jensen
15-Aug	30	Bobby Varin	Stewart Friesen	Dave Camara	Mitch Gibbs	Brian Weaver
22-Aug	30	Stewart Friesen	Dave Camara	Bobby Varin	Willy Decker	Todd Burley
26-Aug	108	Alan Johnson	Pat Ward	Bobby Varin	Pete Bicknell	Stewart Friesen
29-Aug	30	Rain				
5-Sep	OFF					
12-Sep	40	Stewart Friesen	Bobby Varin	Todd Burley	Mitch Gibbs	Jamie Christian

Total DIRT 358-Modified Wins

Driver	Wins
Stewart Friesen	8
Todd Burley	2
Brian Weaver	2
Bobby Varin	2
Jamie Christian	1
Alan Johnson	1
6 Winners	16 Events

DIRT 358-Modified Points

Pos.	Driver	Points
1	Stewart Friesen	806
2	Dave Camara	749
3	Mitch Gibbs	702
4	Todd Burley	684
5	Brian Weaver	682
6	Mark Flach Jr.	672
7	Bobby Varin	670
8	Jamie Christian	642
9	Willy Decker	641
10	Gus Schmidt Jr.	632

2005

Track Champion: Willy Decker (358-Modified)

358-Modified Records – Weekly Results

Date	Laps	Winner	2nd	3rd	4th	5th
1-May	30	Jamie Christian	Dave Camara	Todd Burley	Paul Kinney	Gus Schmidt Jr.
8-May	66 1/2	Bobby Varin	Willy Decker	Jason Barney	Ronnie Johnson	Mitch Gibbs
15-May	30	Dave Camara	Mitch Gibbs	Willy Decker	Todd Burley	Ron Holmes
22-May	30	Rain				
29-May	30	Todd Burley	Mitch Gibbs	Bobby Varin	Dave Camara	Willy Decker
5-Jun	30	Dave Camara	Mitch Gibbs	Ted Lamb Jr.	Dave Rauscher	Brian Weaver
12-Jun	30	Rain				
19-Jun	30	Bobby Varin	Mitch Gibbs	Willy Decker	Dave Camara	Jamie Christian
26-Jun	30	Todd Burley	Willy Decker	Mitch Gibbs	Brian Weaver	John Ramsey
3-Jul	30	Don Mattison/Bob Henry Jr. *	Mitch Gibbs	John Ramsey	Ted Lamb Jr.	Bobby Varin
10-Jul	30	Willy Decker	Todd Burley	Ted Lamb Jr.	Bobby Varin	Jack Johnson
17-Jul	30	Todd Burley	Paul Kinney	Mitch Gibbs	Gus Schmidt Jr.	Jack Johnson
24-Jul	30	Bobby Varin	Todd Burley	Brian Weaver	Mark Flach Jr.	Danny Johnson
31-Jul	30	Mitch Gibbs	Brian Weaver	Ted Lamb Jr.	Jamie Christian	Bobby Varin
7-Aug	30	Todd Burley	Bobby Varin	Jamie Christian	Willy Decker	Ted Lamb Jr.
14-Aug	20	John Ramsey	Willy Decker	Danny Johnson	Don Mattison	Bobby Varin
14-Aug	20	Willy Decker	Danny Johnson	John Ramsey	Todd Burley	Mitch Gibbs
21-Aug	30	Ted Lamb Jr.	Brian Weaver	Paul Kinney	Bobby Varin	Willy Decker
28-Aug	30	Jamie Christian	Todd Burley	Paul Kinney	Jack Johnson	Danny Johnson
4-Sep	30	Danny Johnson	Ted Lamb Jr.	Todd Burley	Willy Decker	Bobby Varin
11-Sep	75	Bobby Varin	Ted Lamb Jr.	Chad Phelps	Jack Johnson	Willy Decker

*Don Mattison & Bob Henry Jr. both declared winners due to tech miscue.

Total 358-Modified Wins

Driver	Wins
Todd Burley	4
Bobby Varin	4
Willy Decker	2
Dave Camara	2
Jamie Christian	2
Mitch Gibbs	1
Don Mattison	1
Bob Henry Jr.	1
John Ramsey	1
Ted Lamb Jr.	1
11 Drivers	19 Events

358-Modified Points

Pos.	Driver	Points
1	Willy Decker	925
2	Todd Burley	860
3	Mitch Gibbs	821
4	Bobby Varin	792
5	Ted Lamb Jr.	770
6	Gus Schmidt Jr.	767
7	Paul Kinney	756
8	Jamie Christian	727
9	John Ramsey	718
10	Don Mattison	657

2006

Track Champion: Willy Decker (358-Modified)

358-Modified Records – Weekly Results

Date	Laps	Winner	2nd	3rd	4th	5th
7-May	30	Ted Lamb Jr.	Bobby Varin	Todd Burley	Willy Decker	Brian Weaver
14-May	68	Alan Johnson	Billy Decker	Tim Fuller	Bobby Varin	Stewart Friesen
21-May	30	Rain				
28-May	30	Bobby Varin	Willy Decker	Todd Burley	Ted Lamb Jr.	Bob Henry Jr.
4-Jun	30	Todd Burley	Mitch Gibbs	Ted Lamb Jr.	Bobby Varin	Willy Decker
11-Jun	30	Willy Decker	Paul Kinney	Ted Lamb Jr.	John Ramsey	Mitch Gibbs
18-Jun	30	Paul Kinney	Bobby Varin	Ted Lamb Jr.	Willy Decker	Dave Rauscher
25-Jun	30	Andy Bachetti	Willy Decker	Todd Burley	Bob Henry Jr.	Mitch Gibbs
2-Jul	30	Rain				
9-Jul	30	Gus Schmidt Jr.	Willy Decker	Mitch Gibbs	Ted Lamb Jr.	Jamie Christian
16-Jul	30	Todd Burley	Andy Bachetti	Bobby Varin	Stewart Friesen	Jack Johnson
23-Jul	30	Bobby Varin	Brian Murphy	Stewart Friesen	Mitch Gibbs	Willy Decker
30-Jul	30	Bobby Varin	Todd Burley	Paul Kinney	Jamie Christian	Mark Flach Jr.
6-Aug	30	Bobby Varin	Stewart Friesen	A.J. Romano	Ted Lamb Jr.	Willy Decker
13-Aug	30	Stewart Friesen	Todd Burley	Mitch Gibbs	Jamie Christian	Ted Lamb Jr.
20-Aug	75	A.J. Romano	Jerry Higbie	Willy Decker	Mitch Gibbs	Jeff Trombley
27-Aug	Twin 20s	Rain Postponed to 9/10				
3-Sep	30	Todd Burley	Willy Decker	Stewart Friesen	Bobby Varin	Ted Lamb Jr.
10-Sep	20	A.J. Romano	Mitch Gibbs	Bobby Varin	Willy Decker	Ted Lamb Jr.
	20	Stewart Friesen	Willy Decker	Ted Lamb Jr.	Paul Kinney	Todd Burley

Total 358-Modified Wins

Driver	Wins
Bobby Varin	4
Todd Burley	3
Stewart Friesen	2
A.J. Romano	2
Alan Johnson	1
Ted Lamb Jr.	1
Andy Bachetti	1
Paul Kinney	1
Gus Schmidt Jr.	1
Willy Decker	1
10 Drivers	17 Events

358-Modified Points

Pos.	Name	Points
1	Willy Decker	828
2	Bobby Varin	808
3	Ted Lamb Jr.	801
4	Todd Burley	786
5	Jamie Christian	701
6	Paul Kinney	695
7	Mitch Gibbs	671
8	Gus Schmidt Jr.	612
9	David Orr	565
10	John Ramsey	554

2007

Track Champion: Stewart Friesen (358-Modified)

358-Modified Records – Weekly Results

Date	Laps	Winner	2nd	3rd	4th	5th
29-Apr	46	Dave Camara/Stewart Friesen*	Pat Ward	Mitch Gibbs	Alan Johnson	A.J. Romano
6-May	30	Todd Burley	Bobby Varin	Pat Ward	Andy Bachetti	Jack Johnson
13-May	75	Willy Decker	Danny Johnson	Bobby Varin	Vic Coffey	Ronnie Johnson
20-May	30	Stewart Friesen	Bobby Varin	Alan Johnson	A.J. Romano	Willy Decker
27-May	30	Bobby Varin	Todd Burley	John Ramsey	Stewart Friesen	Gus Schmidt Jr.
3-Jun	30	Rain				
10-Jun	30	Willy Decker	Stewart Friesen	Bill Shantel Jr.	Ryan Phelps	Bobby Varin
17-Jun	30	Andy Bachetti	Todd Burley	Willy Decker	Stewart Friesen	Gus Schmidt Jr.
24-Jun	30	Stewart Friesen	Pat Ward	Willy Decker	Andy Bachetti	Ted Lamb Jr.
1-Jul	30	Willy Decker	Stewart Friesen	Andy Bachetti	Pat Ward	Bobby Varin
8-Jul	30	Pat Ward	Stewart Friesen	Todd Burley	Willy Decker	A.J. Romano
15-Jul	30	Willy Decker	Stewart Friesen	Bill Shantel Jr.	John Ramsey	Pat Ward
22-Jul	30	Stewart Friesen	Todd Burley	Pat Ward	Bill Shantel Jr.	Ryan Phelps
25-Jul	75	Willy Decker	Pat Ward	Stewart Friesen	Ted Lamb Jr.	Brett Hearn
29-Jul	30	Bobby Varin	Stewart Friesen	Pat Ward	Ted Lamb Jr.	Willy Decker
5-Aug	30	Pat Ward	Ted Lamb Jr.	Willy Decker	Stewart Friesen	Todd Burley
12-Aug	30	Todd Burley	Stewart Friesen	Pat Ward	Willy Decker	Bobby Varin
19-Aug	20	Pat Ward	Willy Decker	Stewart Friesen	John Ramsey	Ted Lamb Jr.
	20	Willy Decker	Ted Lamb Jr.	Pat Ward	John Ramsey	Paul Kinney
26-Aug	30	Stewart Friesen	Todd Burley	A.J. Romano	Ted Lamb Jr.	Willy Decker
2-Sep	30	Gus Schmidt Jr.	Stewart Friesen	Pat Ward	Bobby Varin	Todd Burley
9-Sep	30	Rain				
15-Sep	200	Rain Delayed to 9/16				
16-Sep	200	Stewart Friesen	Bobby Varin	Ronnie Johnson	Vic Coffey	A.J. Romano

*Dave Camara & Stewart Friesen both declared winners due to tech miscue.

Total 358-Modified Wins

Driver	Wins
Stewart Friesen	6
Willy Decker	6
Pat Ward	3
Todd Burley	2
Bobby Varin	2
Dave Camara	1
Andy Bachetti	1
Gus Schmidt Jr.	1
8 Drivers	21 Events

358-Modified Points

Pos.	Name	Points
1	Stewart Friesen	1071
2	Willy Decker	1006
3	Pat Ward	1006
4	Ted Lamb Jr.	910
5	Todd Burley	901
6	Gus Schmidt Jr.	812
7	Bobby Varin	802
8	Bill Shantel Jr	782
9	John Ramsey	771
10	A.J. Romano	757

2008

Track Champion: Pat Ward (358-Modified)

358-Modified Records – Weekly Results

Date	Laps	Winner	2nd	3rd	4th	5th
27-Apr	30	Stewart Friesen	Willy Decker	Mitch Gibbs	Paul Kinney	Jim Davis
4-May	30	Pat Ward	Stewart Friesen	A.J. Romano	Bobby Varin	Willy Decker
11-May	200	Danny Johnson	Pat Ward	Billy Decker	Tim Fuller	Willy Decker
18-May	30	Rain				
25-May	30	Stewart Friesen	Paul Kinney	Pat Ward	Andy Bachetti	Bobby Varin
1-Jun	30	Pat Ward	Jamie Christian	Mitch Gibbs	Willy Decker	Bobby Varin
8-Jun	30	Willy Decker	Pat Ward	Stewart Friesen	Paul Jensen	Paul Kinney
15-Jun	30	Rain Delayed to 6/29				
22-Jun	30	Willy Decker	Pat Ward	Mitch Gibbs	Bob Henry Jr.	Stewart Friesen
29-Jun	30	Pat Ward	Mitch Gibbs	Willy Decker	Bobby Varin	John Ramsey
	30	Pat Ward	Mitch Gibbs	Bobby Varin	Stewart Friesen	Alan Barker
6-Jul	30	Pat Ward	Jim Davis	Mitch Gibbs	Ted Lamb Jr.	Jamie Christian
13-Jul	30	Rain				
20-Jul	30	Rain				
27-Jul	30	Stewart Friesen	Pat Ward	Ronnie Johnson	Willy Decker	Bob Henry Jr.
3-Aug	30	Pat Ward	Stewart Friesen	Mitch Gibbs	Bobby Varin	Gus Schmidt Jr.
10-Aug	30	Rain				
13-Aug	61	Billy Decker	Jimmy Phelps	Alan Johnson	Willy Decker	Brett Hearn
17-Aug	20	Willy Decker	Pat Ward	Jim Davis	Gus Schmidt Jr.	Bobby Varin
	20	Pat Ward	Willy Decker	Mitch Gibbs	Jim Davis	Bobby Varin
24-Aug	30	Stewart Friesen	Bobby Varin	Paul Kinney	Jim Davis	Mitch Gibbs
31-Aug	30	Pat Ward	Bobby Varin	Ted Lamb Jr.	Paul Kinney	Danny Varin
7-Sep	30	Ted Lamb Jr.	Ronnie Johnson	Jim Davis	Jamie Christian	Bobby Varin
14-Sep	200	Bobby Varin	Ronnie Johnson	Mitch Gibbs	Pat Ward	Jimmy Phelps

Total 358-Modified Wins

Driver	Wins
Pat Ward	8
Stewart Friesen	4
Willy Decker	3
Danny Johnson	1
Billy Decker	1
Ted Lamb Jr.	1
Bobby Varin	1
7 Drivers	19 Events

358-Modified Points

Pos.	Name	Points
1	Pat Ward	936
2	Willy Decker	834
3	Bobby Varin	803
4	Stewart Friesen	790
5	Mitch Gibbs	784
6	Paul Kinney	724
7	Jamie Christian	684
8	Jim Davis	670
9	Ted Lamb Jr.	628
10	Paul Jensen	616

2009

Track Champion: Pat Ward (Big Block Modified)

Big Block Modified Records – Weekly Results

Date	Laps	Winner	2nd	3rd	4th	5th
19-Apr	30	Bobby Varin	Mitch Gibbs	Todd Burley	Pat Ward	Ted Lamb Jr.
26-Apr	30	Pat Ward	Paul Kinney	Jack Johnson	Todd Burley	Ronnie Johnson
3-May	30	Stewart Friesen	Paul Kinney	Willy Decker	Mitch Gibbs	Pat Ward
10-May	200	Gary Tomkins	Tim Fuller	Brett Hearn	Stewart Friesen	Pat Ward
17-May	30	Stewart Friesen	Jamie Christian	Brian Weaver	Ronnie Johnson	Pat Ward
24-May	30	Mitch Gibbs	Ronnie Johnson	Stewart Friesen	Bobby Varin	Willy Decker
31-May	30	Jack Johnson	Pat Ward	Ronnie Johnson	Stewart Friesen	Casey Williams
7-Jun	30	Willy Decker	Todd Burley	Stewart Friesen	Bobby Varin	Ronnie Johnson
14-Jun	30	Todd Burley	Pat Ward	Stewart Friesen	Bobby Varin	Willy Decker
21-Jun	30	Pat Ward	Ronnie Johnson	Stewart Friesen	Willy Decker	Bobby Varin
28-Jun	50	Bobby Varin	Pat Ward	Ronnie Johnson	Mitch Gibbs	Todd Burley
5-Jul	30	Bobby Varin	Paul Kinney	Mitch Gibbs	Todd Burley	Stewart Friesen
12-Jul	30	Pat Ward	Paul Kinney	Ronnie Johnson	Willy Decker	Stewart Friesen
19-Jul	30	Pat Ward	Stewart Friesen	Casey Williams	Ronnie Johnson	Bobby Varin
22-Jul	50	Bobby Varin	Pat Ward	Stewart Friesen	Brett Hearn	Willy Decker
26-Jul	30	Bobby Varin	Pat Ward	Stewart Friesen	Willy Decker	Ronnie Johnson
2-Aug	30	Rain				
9-Aug	30	Todd Burley	Pat Ward	Bobby Varin	Paul Kinney	Danny Varin
12-Aug	30	Pat Ward	Bobby Varin	Ronnie Johnson	Ted Lamb Jr.	Willy Decker
16-Aug	20	Stewart Friesen	Danny Varin	Paul Kinney	Brian Weaver	Pat Ward
	20	Ronnie Johnson	Pat Ward	Bobby Varin	Stewart Friesen	Paul Jensen
23-Aug	30	Rain				
30-Aug	30	Willy Decker	Pat Ward	Brian Weaver	John Ramsey	Bobby Varin
6-Sep	30	Bobby Varin	Ronnie Johnson	Todd Burley	Willy Decker	Ted Lamb Jr.
13-Sep	200	Steve Paine	Brett Hearn	Bobby Varin	Ronnie Johnson	Pat Ward

Total Big Block Modified Wins

Driver	Wins
Bobby Varin	6
Pat Ward	5
Stewart Friesen	3
Willy Decker	2
Todd Burley	2
Gary Tomkins	1
Mitch Gibbs	1
Jack Johnson	1
Ronnie Johnson	1
Steve Paine	1
10 Drivers	23 Events

Big Block Modified Points

Pos.	Name	Points
1	Pat Ward	1043
2	Stewart Friesen	1001
3	Bobby Varin	991
4	Willy Decker	922
5	Ronnie Johnson	918
6	Todd Burley	916
7	Paul Kinney	817
8	Jamie Christian	767
9	Danny Varin	761
10	Brian Weaver	724

2010

Track Champion: Stewart Friesen (Big Block Modified)

Big Block Modified Records – Weekly Results

Date	Laps	Winner	2nd	3rd	4th	5th
25-Apr	50	Brett Hearn	Tim Fuller	Jimmy Phelps	Bobby Varin	Pat Ward
2-May	30	Bobby Varin	Stewart Friesen	Todd Burley	Alan Barker	Larry Wight
9-May	200	Snow Delayed to 5/31				
16-May	30	Ronnie Johnson	Stewart Friesen	Bobby Varin	Jason Rood	Casey Williams
23-May	30	Stewart Friesen	Bobby Varin	Mitch Gibbs	Todd Burley	Casey Williams
30-May	30	Bobby Varin	Stewart Friesen	Pat Ward	John Ramsey	Bob Henry Jr.
31-May	200	Tim McCreadie	Pat Ward	Vic Coffey	Michael Storms	Andy Bachetti
6-Jun	30	Rain				
13-Jun	30	Pete Taylor	Willy Decker	Ronnie Johnson	Paul Jensen	Todd Burley
20-Jun	30	Ronnie Johnson	Stewart Friesen	Brad Alger	Bobby Varin	Todd Burley
24-Jun	50	Matt Sheppard	Bobby Varin	Stewart Friesen	Jimmy Phelps	Ronnie Johnson
27-Jun	30	Bobby Varin	Alan Barker	Ronnie Johnson	Todd Burley	Ted Lamb Jr.
4-Jul	30	Stewart Friesen	Pat Ward	Paul Jensen	Brad Alger	Paul Kinney
11-Jul	30	Todd Burley	Stewart Friesen	Willy Decker	Casey Williams	Ronnie Johnson
18-Jul	30	Pat Ward	Stewart Friesen	Paul Jensen	Ronnie Johnson	Paul Kinney
25-Jul	30	Bobby Varin	Pat Ward	Danny Varin	Stewart Friesen	Brian Weaver
29-Jul	50	Billy Decker	Ronnie Johnson	Stewart Friesen	Jimmy Phelps	Paul Kinney
1-Aug	30	Stewart Friesen	Pat Ward	Ronnie Johnson	Bobby Varin	Casey Williams
8-Aug	30	Stewart Friesen	Willy Decker	Pat Ward	Ronnie Johnson	Bobby Varin
15-Aug	30	Rain				
22-Aug	30	Rain				
29-Aug	20	Casey Williams	Stewart Friesen	Todd Burley	Pat Ward	Danny Varin
	20	Stewart Friesen	Willy Decker	Pat Ward	Bobby Varin	Danny Varin
5-Sep	30	Ronnie Johnson	Pat Ward	Stewart Friesen	Todd Burley	Bobby Varin
10-Sep	50	Billy Decker	Stewart Friesen	Vic Coffey	Pat Ward	Todd Burley
11-Sep	100	Bobby Varin	Pat Ward	Alan Johnson	Todd Burley	Billy Decker

Total Big Block Modified Wins

Driver	Wins
Bobby Varin	5
Stewart Friesen	5
Ronnie Johnson	3
Billy Decker	2
Brett Hearn	1
Tim McCreadie	1
Pete Taylor	1
Matt Sheppard	1
Todd Burley	1
Pat Ward	1
Casey Williams	1
11 Drivers	22 Events

Big Block Modified Points

Pos.	Name	Points
1	Stewart Friesen	1013
2	Bobby Varin	956
3	Ronnie Johnson	929
4	Pat Ward	927
5	Willy Decker	815
6	Todd Burley	804
7	Danny Varin	740
8	Casey Williams	733
9	Brad Alger	704
10	Paul Kinney	696

Index

Adams, Bobby, 118
Afton Speedway, Afton, NY, 221, 234, 246
Airborne Park, Plattsburgh, NY, 33, 65, 67, 83, 99, 145, 146, 147 and throughout
Akulis, Chuck, 227
Albany-Saratoga Speedway, Malta, NY, 17, 23, 33, 39, 41, 42, 46, 54 and throughout
Alger, Brad, 283, 298, 304, 305
All Star Circuit of Champions, 131
Allison, Bobby, 157, 160
American Racing Drivers Club (ARDC), 15, 131, 132, 133
American-Canadian Tour (ACT), 220
Anderson, Wayne, 109
Andrews, Shane, 246, 249, 258, 164, 266, 272, 273, 276 and throughout
Angell, Vern, 113, 232
Archer, Wayne, 202, 210
Area Auto Racing News (AARN), 176
Arfons, Art, 122-124
Arminio, Mike, 180
Armstrong, Dick, 83, 105, 108
Austin, Lou, 74
Bachetti, Andy, 248, 293, 314, 322
Baker, Clifford W., 106, 128, 138, 140, 176
Baker, John, 251
Baldwin, Dorothy, 88
Barger, Justin, 131
Barker, Alan, 294, 298
Barker Jr., John, 212, 212, 225, 240-242, 245, 249 and throughout
Barney, Jason, 131, 248, 249, 264
"Baron Daemon", 133, 134
Barrett, Jeff, 306
Barry, Art, 80, 82
Baye, Ryan, 258, 259
Bear, Jerry, 101
Bechy, Jim, 48, 132, 157-162, 166, 167, 171, 172 and throughout
Behrent, Steve, 170
Belden, Ashley, 185
Belden, Brenda, 185, 264
Belden, Bret, 185, 195, 196, 251, 261, 268, 273, 283 and throughout
Bellinger, Ed, 177

Benway, Millard "Bub", 89, 103, 105, 177-179, 184, 185, 188-190 and throughout
Benway, Ray, 177
Benway, Victoria, 177, 184
Berggren, Dick, 156
Bergin, Gene, 18, 26, 43
Bezner, Larry, 200, 202, 206, 210
Bianco, Peter "Junior", 16, 19, 25, 41, 81, 91
Bicknell, Pete, 185, 192, 200, 201, 278
Birosh, John, 154, 160, 168, 223
Blacken, Kevin, 171
Blanchard, Doc, 67, 115
Bloomquist, Scott, 132
Bodine, Brett, 109
Bodine, Eli, 91
Bodine, Geoff, 82, 87, 90, 91, 95, 105, 106, 108-109 and throughout
Boehler, Len, 62, 76, 77, 100, 159
Boggie, Tom, 96
Bonneville Salt Flats, Bonneville, UT, 123
Boonville Herald, 142
Boratyn, Lucy, 133
Bosley, Len, 49, 116
Botindari, Jackie, 251
Bowman Gray Stadium, Winston-Salem, NC, 100
Boyd, Lenny, 132
Boyd, Lew, 41
Brando, Lou, 24, 36, 39, 122
Brenn Jr., Ken, 226
Brewerton Speedway, Brewerton, NY, 30, 67, 70, 178, 189, 192, 193, 195 and throughout
Brightbill, Fred, 160, 161, 227
Brightbill, Ken, 175, 226, 230, 235, 236
Brookfield Speedway, Brookfield, NY, 67, 195, 204
Brooks, Fred, 140
Brooks, Jerry, 246, 264, 306
Brown, Bill, 131
Brown, Jim, 87, 95, 98, 106
Brown, Perk, 59, 60
Bruno, Dave, 213
Buff, Kevin, 294
Buffa, Tony, 242
Burdick, Chip, 245

Burdick, Matt, 296
Burgess, Jack, 31, 88, 242
Burgess, Rich, 160, 226
Burley, Todd, 245, 247, 248, 250, 257-259, 265, 270-71 and throughout
Burlingame, John, 13
Burrows, Bonnie, 175
Burrows, Brenda, 175
Burrows, Fred, 152, 157, 159, 164, 166, 173, 175, 176 and throughout
Burt, Dave, 161
Burth, Mike, 98
Busch, Kyle, 192
Button, Gordy, 128, 131, 179, 180, 182, 189, 193, 194 and throughout
Button, Jon, 127, 128, 144, 264, 294
Button, Mike, 128, 279, 283, 294, 298, 305
Byron, Red, 142
Cabana, Jean-Paul, 18, 49
Cagle, Will, 160, 169, 209
Camara, Dave, 271, 278, 283, 297, 298
Camino, Jim, 11
Campione, Pete, 200, 206, 213
Can-Am Speedway, LaFargeville, NY, 151
Canandaigua Speedway, Canandaigua, NY, 177
Canestrari, Ken, 112
Cantanzano, George, 242, 280, 284, 294
Caraway Speedway, Asheboro, NC, 100
Carey, Paul, 196, 272, 279, 283, 294
Carr, Chris, 305, 306, 315, 323
Carrington, Dave, 144
Carucci, Vic, 91, 110
Caruso, Mario "Fats", 18, 24, 26, 33
Castronovo, Phil, 124,125
Caswell, Dale, 294
Caswell, George, 83, 87, 94, 95, 98
Catamount Stadium, Milton, VT, 99
Charland, Rene, 1-4, 6, 9-14, 17, 19, 22, 24-27 and throughout
Charlotte Speedway - Dirt Track, Concord, NC, 142
Chartrand, Jean-Guy, 18, 120
Chemung Speedrome, Chemung, NY, 91, 103
Childress, Richard, 192, 220
Christian, Jamie, 213, 245, 251, 261, 267, 268, 277, 283 and throughout

Cicconi, Lou, 132
Civic Stadium, Buffalo, NY, 7, 8
Clark, Al, 67, 80
Clark, Barb, 238, 287, 299, 306, 324
Clark, Dick, 48, 91, 92, 109, 111, 118
Clark, John, 238, 306
Clark, Stan, 206, 238, 242
Cleary, Leo, 83
Clement, John, 13, 15
Clemons, Tim, 200, 245, 260, 261, 268, 272
Coffey, Vic, 271, 296, 297, 314
Cole, Gene, 39, 148, 198, 204, 205, 215, 223, 264 and throughout
Cole, Gloria, 204, 322
Cole, Joe, 212
Cole, Tom, 263, 264, 275, 276
Coleman, John, 87, 94, 95, 98
Colwell, George, 101
Compani, Ralph, 150, 151, 153, 156, 157, 163, 165, 166, 176 and throughout
Compani, Ron, 150-154, 156, 157, 163-166, 176 and throughout
Compton, Gerald, 64
Conley, Tico, 154
Connelly, Bob, 193, 195, 240, 241
Connelly, Cathy, 194
Conte, Ralph, 127
Cook, Jerry, 19, 20, 24, 3-33, 36, 42, 43, 48 and throughout
Cook, Kevan, 294
Cook, Ray, 132
Cook, Sue, 100, 101
Corazzo, Billy, 83
Corey, Pete, 9, 48, 54, 55, 80, 118
Cottrell, Jack, 140, 174
Coville, C.D., 152, 160, 164, 170, 226
Cozze, Frank, 194
Crave, Kevin, 245, 251
Cruickshank, David, 308, 314
Cullen, Tom, 282, 290, 291, 309, 311, 312
Cunningham, Chris, 294
Curley, Tom, 156, 220, 223
Cushman Jr., Chuck, 268
Dalmata, Larry, 139, 150
Dalmata, Ray, 150, 152, 160, 164, 174
Danbury Fair Racearena, Danbury, CT, 28
Danish, Steve, 58
Darlington Raceway, Darlington, SC, 142
Davis, Jim, 296
Davis, John, 101
Davis, Randy, 152

Daytona International Speedway, Daytona Beach, FL, 8, 35-37, 44, 57, 58, 60
Decker, Billy, 260, 261, 293, 312, 313, 326
Decker, Deek, 225
Decker, Willy, 168, 222, 223, 245, 251, 261, 271, 276 and throughout
DeCotis, Mark, 108
Delaney, Dick, 44, 132
DeLine, Dan, 171
Denton, Tom, 230, 242, 246, 251, 293, 299, 315
DeSalvo, Pete, 127
DeSarro, Fred, 37, 64, 65, 74, 76-78, 80, 83-84 and throughout
Devil's Bowl Speedway, West Haven, VT, 145, 146, 147
DeVore, Lyle, 220, 234
DeWitt, Gene, 84, 85
DeYulio, Linda, 306
DeYulio, Ron, 306
Digsby, A.J., 299, 306
DiOrio, Louis, 138
Dixon, Dick, 21, 28, 32
Dodge, Herb, 220
Dog Track Speedway, Moyoc, NC, 17
Donath, Dave, 200
Donnelly, Glenn, 150, 151, 153, 158, 164, 165, 176, 177 and throughout
Dostal, Bruce, 67, 119
Douglas, Tom, 159
Doust, Greg, 213
Dow, Steve, 131
Drake, Lloyd, 152
Drivers Independent Race Tracks (DIRT), 151, 153, 158, 160, 165, 173, 176, 177 and throughout
Duncan, Sue, 133
Dwyer, Tim, 174
Earnhardt, Dale, 192
Eastern Bandits, 9, 13, 22, 24
Eastern Limited Sprints (ELS), 131
Eastern Motorsports Press Assoc. (EMPA), 169
Eastman, Pepper, 204
Egli, Ronnie, 265
Eilenburg, Carl, 176
Elkins, Doug, 299
Ely, George, 131
Emery, Doug, 131
Empire Super Sprints (ESS), 131, 179, 290
Enders, Kevin, 224
Engler, Bob, 55, 98, 106, 111, 143
ESTA Dragstrip, Cicero, NY, 122, 126, 127

Evans, Richie, 14, 15, 16, 28, 33, 34, 37, 44, 48 and throughout
Evans Jr., Richie, 191
Evans, Tara, 191
Excell, Aaron, 259
Fachini, Cory, 242
Fazio, Ron, 48, 119
Fidanza, Jennifer, 220, 234
Fifield, Roy, 279
Five Mile Point Speedway, Kirkwood, NY, 195, 311
Flach, Mark, 276
Flemington Speedway, Flemington, NJ, 214
Flemke, Ed, 9, 13, 22, 24-28, 31, 33, 36-37 and throughout
Fonda Speedway, Fonda, NY, 9, 13, 16, 17, 31, 32, 42, 46 and throughout
Foote, Red, 9
Forbes, Richie, 127
Forbes, Roger, 127
Fornoro, Nokie, 132
Forrette, Maynard "Cyclone", 86, 87, 117, 140, 163, 170, 245
Fort Dix Speedway, Plumstead Twp., NJ, 9, 13
Forward, Glenn, 48
Fowler, Dick, 28, 33, 53, 56, 64, 65, 74, 75 and throughout
Foy, Joe, 220, 233
France Sr., Bill, 36, 41
Fray, Lou, 61
Friesen, Alex, 214, 223, 224, 230, 232-234, 240, 276
Friesen, Jamie, 276, 319
Friesen, Stan, 214, 233, 234, 240, 276, 318
Friesen, Stewart, 168, 218, 257, 275-278, 290-292, 295-297 and throughout
Frisbie, Chuck, 111
Frost, Shawn, 306, 328
Fuller, Doug, 179, 182, 183, 189, 192, 204, 205, 235 and throughout
Fuller, Tim, 261, 293, 309
Fulton Speedway, Fulton, NY, 60, 64, 89, 103, 177-180, 184, 188-189 and throughout
Fusco, Andy, 105, 166
Gage Jr., Jim, 150
Gagliardi, Cam, 14, 19
Gahan, Ernie, 9, 18, 19, 24, 26, 31, 36, 39-41, 43 and throughout
Gapp, Wayne, 121
Garlits, Don, 122, 126, 128
Gater Racing News, 64, 134, 168, 198, 242
Gerow, Frederick, 138

Gibbs, Mitch, 219, 220, 221, 230, 235-236, 241, 245, and throughout
Giroux, Denis, 81-83, 112, 120
Glen Ridge Motorsports Park, Fultonville, NY, 145, 148
Glenski, Randy, 152, 154, 195, 200, 203-205, 228 and throughout
Goewey, Brian, 309
Golley, Al, 61, 68
Gordon, Jeff, 169
Goutermout, Bob, 185
Grady, John, 1, 4, 6, 41, 42, 87, 262
Graham, Otto, 14
Gray, Rick, 140
Griffith, Roger, 86, 96, 104, 105, 108
Guernsey, Rick, 210
Hall, Moe, 127
Hall, Rich, 98
Hallquist, Roy, 21, 28
Hamilton, Pete, 44-47, 48, 85, 115, 175, 213
Hanson, Ken, 151
Harbach, Fred, 18, 24, 33, 56, 117
Hardacre, Garth, 123
Harman, Billy, 32, 48
Harpell, Andy, 214, 304
Harriger, Will, 269
Hart, Robbie, 131
Hartshorn, George, 161
Hawker, Ron, 294, 310
Hayes, Seymour, 150
Hearn, Brett, 160, 167-172, 179, 230, 235, 236, 245 and throughout
Hebing, Chuck, 131
Hedger, Hugh, 92
Hedger, Randy, 105, 110
Hedger, Ray, 299
Hedger, Ron, 61, 92
Hencke, Buddy, 268
Hendrick, Ray, 37, 69, 71, 72, 83
Hennessy, Joan, 133
Henry, Bill, 53, 66, 67, 74, 96, 119, 120
Henry, Bob, 282, 283
Henry, Craig, 152, 174, 196
Henry, Scott, 68
Hensley, Jimmy, 59, 60, 71, 72, 74
Herb, Dave, 183,184
Herbert, Howard "Jeep", 9, 48, 60
Heroux, Roger, 234, 240, 241, 246, 296, 297, 317
Herrig, Willie, 20, 21
Hertline, Bob, 127
Hewitt, John, 160, 161
Heydenreich, Johnny, 132
Hill, Elton, 24, 33, 43, 50

Hill, John, 233, 234, 240
Hillin, Bobby, 227
Hinman, Buddy, 140
Hirschey, Randy, 288
Hirschman, Tony, 208
Hmiel, Gordy, 127
Hmiel, Steve, 101
Hoag, Dutch, 84, 177, 242
Hoffman, Doug, 214
Hoffman, Todd, 171, 174, 175
Hoffmier, George, 155
Holic, Paul, 152
Hollebrand, Pete, 58, 88, 102
Hollinger, Claude, 88
Hollis, David W., 183-184
Holmes, Jerry, 174, 183, 184, 223, 238, 251, 252, 262 and throughout
Holmes, Ralph, 28, 48, 74, 75, 80, 96, 128, 118 and throughout
Holmes, Ron, 196, 206, 212, 229, 234-235, 237-238 and throughout
Horton, Jimmy, 160, 230
Horvath, Roger, 170
House, Norm, 14
Howard, Duane, 205
Hulsizer, Mike, 321
Hulsizer, Steve, 185, 195, 196, 206, 210, 213, 222, 223 and throughout
Humiston, Jerry, 26, 27, 32
Humphrey, Dave, 61, 132
Hurlbut, Leroy, 139
Hutter, Ron, 121, 213
Ingersoll, Bernie, 9, 24, 35-39, 122
Ingersoll, Marge, 35
Islip Speedway, Islip, NY, 13, 17, 33, 40
Iulg, Gary, 143, 155
Ivo, Tommy, 122-124
Jackson, Louie, 299
Jamieson, Dave, 98
Janczuk, Matt, 310, 315, 316
Jensen, Eric, 182
Jensen, Paul, 62, 155, 178, 179, 182, 183, 189, 192-194 and throughout
Jensen, Stella, 182
Johnson, Alan, 154, 155, 159, 160, 170, 174, 175, 178 and throughout
Johnson, Danny, 154, 160, 170, 171, 232, 245, 248 and throughout
Johnson, Jack, 140, 150, 151, 157, 159, 160, 164, 166 and throughout
Johnson, Ken, 200
Johnson, Ron, 249, 250, 297, 305, 309, 310, 313-315 and throughout
Jones, Joe, 14, 15
Jones, Wilbur, 33, 34

Jordan, Charlotte, 183
Judkins, Bob, 47
Juhl Jr., Tom, 194
Kappesser, Jeff, 154
Kaszubinski, Dan, 131
Kay, Johnny, 132
Keegan, John, 299
Keller, Rob, 294
Kelly, Jim, 220
Kennedy, John F., 14
Kennison, Chuck, 143
Kent, George, 87, 104-105, 112, 177
Kerfien, Chuck, 242
King, Jim, 212, 246
Kingsley, A.J., 251
Kingsley, Eric, 178, 189, 190, 193, 197, 198, 207-209 and throughout
Kingsley, Gisele, 178, 214, 251
Kinney, Paul, 293, 296, 322
Kinsella, John, 213
Kinsella, Tom, 180, 182, 189, 191-194, 198-200, 203, 212 and throughout
Kiser, Art, 151, 164
Kiskiel, John, 152
Kitchen, Fran, 47, 48
Knipe, Bobby, 171, 176
Kollar, John, 66, 67
Koszela, Sonny, 76, 77
Kotary, Adam "Fuzz", 266
Kotary, Albert, 30
Kotary, Betty, 49, 83
Kotary, Charles, 142, 143
Kotary, Cliff, 14, 28, 29, 106, 142, 162, 266
Kotary, Dave, 21, 28, 29, 30, 31, 32, 49, 53 and throughout
Kotary, Ed, 213
Kotary, Gene, 97, 98, 106. 111
Kotary, Jeff, 213, 266, 267, 296
Kotary, Robbie, 14, 19, 21, 24, 30, 43, 64, 65 and throughout
Kotary, Steve, 206, 223
Kotary, Tom, 14, 17, 21, 24, 29, 30, 34, 83, 107 and throughout
Kuck, Ed, 171
LaFrance, Marcel, 227
Lamb Jr., Ted, 179, 180, 182, 183, 189, 190, 234, 241 and throughout
Lamberton, Gary, 234
Lancaster Speedway, Lancaster, NY, 8, 13, 64, 82, 86, 89, 103, 214 and throughout
Lane, Mal, 131
Langevin, Robert, 293

Langhorne Speedway, Langhorne, PA, 54, 155
Lanz, Barney, 110
Lanz, Chip, 83, 87, 93, 94, 95, 108, 110
Lanza, Lou, 68, 77
Lape, Dave, 50, 54, 61, 64, 67, 75-77, 82-83 and throughout
Lape, Jackie, 165
LaShure, Curt, 17
Laubach, Rick, 304
Lauterborn, Mike, 131
Lazzaro, Lou, 4, 6, 12, 16-19, 24-28, 31, 32 and throughout
Lebanon Valley Speedway, West Lebanon, NY, 54
LeRicheux, Chuck, 24, 36, 39, 55, 122
Lesik, Joe, 1-4, 5, 6, 11, 15, 17, 21 and throughout
Lesik, John, 1, 23
Lesik, Stanley, 1, 3, 23
Leslie, Jeff, 310
Lewis, Kyle, 283, 294
Lockwood, Steve, 174
Loescher, Mike, 80, 15, 105, 257
LoPiccolo, Steve, 103, 105-107, 138, 176, 177, 207
Loughridge, Paul, 132, 161
Lucia, Ric, 311
Luke, Jim, 17, 19
Lutz, Mike, 131
Lyons, Marty, 161
Mackey, Chris, 299
MacTavish, Don, 40, 41, 43, 47, 49-50, 52, 54, 57-58 and throughout
Madsen, Brian, 277
Mahaney, Jim, 179, 182, 229
Mahoney, Chuck, 4, 11, 12, 14, 141-144, 150, 176
Mahoning Valley Speedway, Lehighton, PA, 214
Mallett, Mike, 296, 306
Malone, Jack, 18
Mann, Johnny, 132
Mannise, Dave, 186, 202, 206, 210, 213, 214, 223, and throughout
Manny, Andre, 18
Mantz, Johnny, 142
Marcello, Donny, 65
Marsden, Dave, 280
Marsden, Russ, 280, 283, 294, 298, 306
Martinsville Speedway, Martinsville, VA, 17, 74, 76, 82, 83, 100, 110, 161 and throughout
Mathalia, Frank, 28, 32, 43, 44, 47, 13
Mattison, Don, 282, 283

Maugeri, Vinnie, 69
Maurer, Randy "Buster", 83, 86
Maurer, Woody, 134
McClelland, Darrell, 33, 43, 50
McCreadie, Bob, 160, 168-170, 176, 308
McCreadie, Tim, 261, 313-315, 325, 326
McCredy, Dave, 8, 32, 40, 46
McDowell, John, 101
Meahl, Ken, 14, 15, 19, 27, 32
Merrittville Speedway, Ontario, Canada, 8, 13
Michaels, A.J., 193
Michaels, J.J., 193, 194, 198-200, 204, 216, 223, 230 and throughout
Michaels, Johnny, 177, 193
Michaels, Kelly, 193, 266
Michaels, Lou, 193, 194, 198, 199, 265
Michaels, Penny, 266
Michaels, Tyler, 266
Midstate Speedway (Morris Fairgrounds), Morris, NY, 96, 195
Miller, Bernie, 28, 34, 46, 47, 52-54, 56, 61, 73-74 and throughout
Miller, Jack, 213, 242
Miller, Rick, 186, 202, 206, 213, 214, 223, 238
Miller, Ron, 139
Millington, Lee, 113
Mirabito, Joe, 286
Monadnock Speedway, Winchester, NH, 111
Monroe County Fairgrounds, Rochester, NY, 8, 9, 59
Moon, Don, 33
Morey, Lynn, 98
Morgan, Rod, 152
Moshier, Ron, 175, 176, 182, 183, 187-190, 214, 220 and throughout
Moyer, Norm, 55
Moyer, Scott, 185, 196
Muldowney, Shirley, 122-124, 126, 128
Murphy, Jack, 177
Nacewicz, Billy, 96, 265
Nacewicz, Paula, 265
Nacewicz, Rod, 265, 266
Nagle, Bonnie, 97
Nagle, Dave, 97, 109
Narducci, Ron, 56
National Hot Rod Assoc. (NHRA), 122
Naum, Jack, 177
Nazareth Raceway, Nazareth, PA, 169
Nelson, Bill, 135
Nephew, Dick, 9, 10
New Egypt Speedway, New Egypt, NJ, 99
Newberry, Bob, 127

Newman, Gerry, 139, 140, 152, 155, 228, 268
Newman, Ron, 48, 66, 67, 76, 80, 119
Newman Jr., Art, 271, 272, 273
Nichols, Dave, 104, 105
Nimey, Junior, 12
Noel, Scott, 161
Normoyle, Jim, 293, 299, 305, 306, 321
North American Mud Bog Assoc., 132
Northeast Auto Racing Assoc. (NEARA), 103-105, 138, 177, 208
Northeast Midget Association (NEMA), 132
Norwood Arena, Norwood, MA, 18, 24, 40, 146
NY State Stock Car Assoc. (NYSSCA), 35, 61, 81, 174, 237
Nye, Tim, 294
O'Brien, Dick, 134
Old Dominion Speedway, Manassas, VA, 9, 14
Oneida Daily Dispatch, 18, 138, 143, 151
O'Neil, Don, 48
Orange County Fair Speedway, Middletown, NY, 169, 170
Ortiz, Ed, 9, 12-15, 24, 26, 30, 58, 75 and throughout
Osborne, Lee, 177, 257
Oswego Speedway, Oswego, NY, 36, 134, 136, 177, 193, 198, 214
Otto, Ed, 36
Ouderkirk, Ralph, 6, 11, 22, 58, 306
Owens, Cotton, 142
Paine, Steve, 170, 245, 251, 261, 264, 278, 309, 310 and throughout
Palmer, Alton, 174
Palmer, Joe, 238, 242
Park, Steve, 208
Parker, Paul, 155
Parliament, Scott, 279
Parrow, Bobby, 131
Parts Peddler, 224
Pastorella, Jeff, 261
Patrick, Norm, 134
Patriot Sprint Tour, 293
Pauch, Billy, 182, 184, 185, 194, 195, 205, 206, 214 and throughout
Payne, Bill, 86
Payne, Eldon, 279
Payne, Mike, 309
Pendergast, George, 48
Penn Can Speedway, Susquehanna, PA, 195
Penn National Speedway, Grantville, PA, 156

Pennock, Jerry, 61
PerforMax Motor News, 220, 221
Petty, Lee, 142
Petty, Richard, 17
Phelps, Jimmy, 206, 210, 304
Phelps, Roger, 179, 182, 183, 185, 193, 198, 200, 204 and throughout
Pieniazek, Ed, 80, 81, 87, 91
Plainville Stadium, Plainville, CT, 42
Planck, Dale, 179, 197, 199-201, 204, 207-210, 212-213 and throughout
Planck, Denny, 209, 256
Planck, Leslie, 199
Platt, Ken, 28, 44, 53
Platt, Sonny, 152
Plazek, Joe, 160
Plis, Geoff, 200, 210
Plows, Connie, 306
Pocono Raceway, Long Pond, PA, 128, 130
Podolak, Bob, 131, 155, 178, 179, 193
Podolak, John, 155, 180
Poffenberger, Ken, 125,126
Poirier, Steve, 131
Pope, Dave, 280
Powelczyk, Chuck, 280, 284
Prevo, Curt, 294
Price, Bill, 279, 283
Price, Mike, 134
Pritchard, Craig, 196, 202
Puchyr, Ted, 9, 31, 43
Putman, Dick, 154, 165
Race of Champions, 54, 86, 91, 92, 97, 214, 292, 296 and throughout
Racing Promotion Monthly, 214
Radford, Paul, 120
Rafter, Bill, 6, 7, 8, 113, 177
Rahmer, Fred, 131
Ramsey, John, 182, 212, 259, 271, 276, 283, 296
Ransomville Speedway, Ransomville, NY, 13, 214, 223, 233, 317, 318
Ray, Chad, 299
Ray, Mike, 191
Razey, Dave, 161
Reading Fairgrounds Speedway, Reading, PA, 156, 175
Reiter, Butch, 206
Rettew, George, 65
Reutimann, Buzzie, 314
Reutimann Jr., Wayne, 265
Rexford, Bill, 142
Reynolds, Dean, 176
Ricci, Mike, 170, 296
Rice, Kevin, 213, 242

Richards, C.J., 106
Richardson, Ron, 200, 206, 213, 245
Riehlman, Lonnie, 155
Riffenburgh, Dan, 176
Riverside Park Speedway, Agawam, MA, 1, 18, 21, 26, 27, 33, 42, 61
Roberts, Glenn "Fireball", 142
Roberts, Jim, 294
Roberts, Steve, 309
Roese, Bill, 140
Rolewicz, Mike, 180, 185, 196
Rolling Wheels Raceway Park, Elbridge, NY, 106, 209
Romano, A.J., 145, 148, 170, 245, 292, 296, 297
Romano, Andy, 48, 58, 65-67, 87, 131, 139, 145-148 and throughout
Romano, Joe, 145
Romano, Mike, 139, 140, 145, 148, 150, 151, 155, 164 and throughout
Rome Sentinel, 162
Romit, Tony, 15, 132
Rood, Jason, 268, 310
Rood, Lonnie, 227
Rosati, John, 105
Rose, Jerry, 91
Rosner, Fred, 1, 2, 6, 9, 13, 14, 19, 25, 32 and throughout
Rossell, Bob, 18
Rothwell, Jim, 155, 176, 200, 206, 210, 213, 238, 242 and throughout
Roush, Jack, 121
Rudolph, Charlie, 170, 171, 225
Ruffing, Ed, 150
Ruggiero, Reggie, 208
Rundell, Doug, 83
Russell, Bill, 127
Ryan, Nick, 160, 171
Salerno, Vinnie, 313
Sanders, Lee, 131
Santos, Bob, 74, 81, 82, 84, 159
Savoie, Bob, 140
Schinkel Jr., Billy, 170, 194
Schmidt Jr., Gus, 242, 245, 250, 265, 271, 293
Schneibel, Randy, 97
Schoonover, Dick, 138, 140, 195
Schremmer, Herm, 127
Schumacher, Don, 123
Seamon, Billy, 98, 106, 111
Seamon, Clayton "Sonney", 14, 16, 28, 34, 43, 51, 52, 54, 56 and throughout
Seamon, Diane, 68
Seamon, Paul, 112
Seamon, Rita, 68, 96, 97, 108, 112, 262

Seamon, Wayne, 96
Sears, Tim, 272
Sears Jr., Tom, 180
Sehn, Jerry, 196
Shampine, Jim, 177
Shangri-La Speedway, Owego, NY, 67, 97, 98, 99, 103, 112
Shantel Jr., Bill, 229, 271, 272, 279, 283, 294
Sheldon, Guy, 200
Sheppard, Matt, 257, 264-266, 304, 313
Sheppard, Stu, 174
Shoemaker, Ken, 32, 42, 44, 47, 54, 75, 112, 117 and throughout
Short Track Organization for Racing and Marketing (STORM), 223, 234
Sifo, George, 131
Silva, Ollie, 84
Simons, Bob, 140
Simpson, Dick "Suitcase", 98
Sitterly, Bob, 223, 229
Sitterly, Ray, 47, 66, 67, 74, 75
Skibinski, Jerry, 171
Slater, Bill, 18, 26, 114
Slawiak, Joe, 210, 213
Sleicher, Jack, 6, 7, 8
Smales, Cal, 96
Smith, Carl, 226
Smith, Dianne, 226
Smith, Gordie, 111
Smith, Jim, 185, 200, 206, 210, 245
Smith, Lou, 20, 21, 27, 31, 32, 115
Smith, Mike, 294
Smith, Will, 195
Snow, Gene, 122, 125, 126
South Boston Speedway, South Boston, VA, 59
Southside Speedway, Richmond, VA, 9
SPEED-TV, 246
Spencer Speedway, Williamson, NY, 64, 86, 103
Spiak, Phil, 56, 116
Spraker, Jake, 145, 148
Squires, Charlie, 306
Stafford, Kenny, 279, 283
Stafford Motor Speedway, Stafford Springs, CT, 54, 83, 99, 146
Stanley, Richard, 138
Stefanik, Mike, 208
Stelter, Mike, 131
Stevens, Bugsy, 37, 49, 52, 59, 62, 64, 67, 69 and throughout
Stevens, Wanda, 133
Stewart, Tony, 131
Stock Car Racing, 220

Index 391

Stockham, Corky, 224
Stockwell, Chick, 28
Stoppiello, Ralph, 158
Storms, Michael, 314
Stratton, Paul, 138
Stygar, John, 25
Suprick, George, 131
Sutton, William "Lucky", 20, 28
Sweet, Dick, 195, 234, 246, 282, 283, 287, 290, 299 and throughout
Syracuse Fairgrounds Speedway, Syracuse, NY, 30, 155, 311, 317
Syracuse Herald-Journal, 134
Syracuse Post-Standard, 223, 224, 233, 236, 237, 240
Talerico, Mike, 103, 105, 107, 138, 176, 177, 207
Tallini, John, 61, 68, 74, 96, 107, 232, 306
Tanner, Bubba, 174
Tattersall Jr., Harvey, 21, 39
Tauss, Fred, 171, 174
Taylor, Bobby, 171
Taylor, Pete, 271, 314, 315
Thomas, Herb, 142
Thomas, Jeff, 131
Thomas, Jim, 284, 323
Thomas, Joel, 112, 117
Thompson, Mickey, 123
Thompson Speedway, Thompson, CT, 40, 76, 100, 105, 108, 130, 161
Thorp, Jeff, 242
Thunder Mountain Speedway, Center Lisle, NY, 221
Thunder Ridge Cycle Park, South Edmeston, NY, 263
Thunder Road Speedway, Barre, VT, 156
Thurston, Buddy, 28, 33, 34, 48, 55, 67, 68, 77, 83 and throughout
Thurston, Chris, 294
Tiff Jr., John, 264, 287, 299, 306
Tilison, Denny, 261
Tobias, Richie, 185
Tobias, Ronnie, 184
Tomkins, Gary, 261, 309, 323
Torrisi, Bill, 19
Treichler, Merv, 155
Tremont Jr., Ken, 174-176, 227, 296
Tremont Sr., Ken, 174
Trenton Speedway, Trenton, NJ, 86, 92
Trexler Jr., Bill, 210, 315, 326
Trinkhaus, Frank, 32, 157, 187
Tropeano, Pete, 125
Troyer, Maynard, 65, 67, 86-88, 91, 95, 104-105, and throughout
Tubbs, Terry, 95, 98

Turner, Curtis, 142
Turner, Ray, 264
Twing, Frank, 251
United Racing Club (URC), 131
United Stock Car Racing Club, 39
Utica Daily Press, 16, 110, 153, 156, 159, 161
Utica Observer Dispatch, 2, 12, 16, 17, 21, 106, 107, 132 and throughout
Utter, Bob, 213
Vandewalker, Ernie, 14
VanDusen, Jeff, 131
VanDusen, Mike, 131, 212, 241
VanSlyke, Dave, 83, 87, 115, 132
VanSlyke, Don, 61, 118
VanSlyke, Russ, 83, 87
Varin, Bobby, 277, 278, 283, 289-292, 296, 297, 301-304 and throughout
Varin, Danny, 294, 308, 325
Ventura, Ralph, 138
Vernon Downs Racetrack, Vernon, NY, 142
Vicari, Lindy, 156
Victoria Speedway, Duanesburg, NY, 9, 13, 16
Vollertsen, Jim, 103
Vunk, Jeremy, 283, 294
Walrath, Earl, 200
Walsh, Ron, 125
Walton, Jeff, 193, 194, 212, 231, 234, 235, 242, 244 and throughout
Warburton, Wally, 139, 140
Ward, Pat, 168, 218, 296, 301-304, 307, 308, 311, 313 and throughout
Warner, Brandon, 294
Warren, Bentley, 177
Waterford Speedbowl, Waterford, CT, 18
Waterloo Speedway, Waterloo, NY, 8
Waterman, Dorothy, 35, 128, 136, 138
Waterman, Richard, 2, 3, 23-25, 30, 35-39, 46, 52, 55 and throughout
Waters, Pete, 134
Way, Steve, 213, 279, 283, 305
Wayman, Don, 48, 53, 208
Weaver, Brian, 276, 277
Weedsport Speedway, Weedsport, NY, 106, 150, 153, 154, 163-166, 169
Weidner, Nolan, 237
Werber, Dave, 171
Westmore, Ethel Searing, 237
Wetmore, Bridget, 237
Wetmore, Donnie, 143, 178-180, 182-185, 189, 192, 193, 195 and throughout
Wetmore Jr., Donnie, 237

Wetmore, Marcia, 178-180, 189, 198, 207, 220, 224, 234, 235, 237 and throughout
Wetmore, Stanley, 237
Whitbeck, Bob, 54
Whittaker, Billy, 204
Wight, John, 302
Wilcox, Billy, 240
Williams, Casey, 305, 314, 315, 324, 327
Williams, Tommy, 140, 143, 152, 153, 156, 246
Williamson, Clarence "Speedy", 14, 15, 113
Wilson, Tommy, 139, 150, 151, 152, 157, 164, 166
Wimble, Bill, 6, 8, 9, 10, 14, 17-19, 24, 27 and throughout
Wimble, Nancy, 88
Winks, Jimmy, 139, 177
Winston Racing Series, 207, 208, 209, 212
Wood, Charlene, 127
Wood, Rich, 131
Woodring, Mike, 131
Woodward, Fred, 286
World of Outlaws, 313
Wright, Cliff, 43, 146
Yankowski, Dan, 206, 213, 237, 238
Yonge, Lance, 131
Yunick, Smokey, 215
Zabele, Jim, 98
Zanardi, Pete, 15, 78
Zautner, Bobby, 43
Zautner, Donnie, 43
Zeigler, Bob, 26
Zemaitis, John, 214, 219, 233, 234, 240, 241
Zemken, Jessica, 131, 200, 232, 272, 273, 278, 279, 283 and throughout
Zemken, Ray, 200, 202, 206, 224, 272
Zimmerman, Dennis, 9, 22, 100, 114
Zupan, Doug, 16, 143, 232, 250, 264, 283, 306